AN INTRODUCTION TO
ECONOMIC ANALYSIS
AND POLICY

AN INTRODUCTION TO ECONOMIC ANALYSIS AND POLICY

BY

J. E. MEADE

Formerly Fellow of Hertford College, Oxford

AMERICAN EDITION EDITED BY

C. J. HITCH

Fellow of the Queen's College, Oxford

WITH AN INTRODUCTION BY

A. H. HANSEN

Professor of Political Economy, Harvard University

New York

OXFORD UNIVERSITY PRESS

1938

INTRODUCTION

BY ALVIN H. HANSEN

*Professor of Political Economy in the School of Business
Administration, Harvard University*

SOME years ago when American 'institutionalists' were particularly vocal, it was commonly argued that the apparatus of theoretical economics was applicable (if at all) only to a simon-pure *laisser-faire* system. It was then postulated that the existing economic order had developed institutions so far removed from the abstractions of the pure theorist that all conclusions drawn from the intricate logical constructions had utterly no validity. The logic chopping of quibbling economists had, it was argued, become as meaningless as the metaphysical exercises of the medieval scholastics. Instead, so ran the argument, one ought to 'look and see' what was actually going on, to accumulate facts and measure secular and cyclical changes in significant economic data. One ought, moreover, it was said, to observe and describe the development of institutions and to note the changes and modifications in the structure and behavior of the economic organism. Theory had no place in the 'realistic' study of economic life.

But the more one observed and described, the more the desire grew to understand *why* the economic machinery acted as it did, and especially to understand why it so often acted perversely. Indeed, the grubbing for facts stimulated theory. The apparatus of analysis became even more complicated. New theoretical tools were devised. A leading illustration is the development of the theory of monopolistic competition.

It is by now fairly evident that the theoretical apparatus which professional economists have gradually constructed during the last two centuries is indispensible, not only for an *under-*

standing of why an economy, whether free or controlled, operates to produce certain results, but also as a means of testing the
validity and workability of alternative policies. And not infre-
quently in the history of economic science the conflict over
appropriate policy has served to sharpen the tools of economic
analysis.

Mr. Meade's book is rightly called *An Introduction to Economic
Analysis and Policy*. The task of subjecting economic policy in a
rapidly changing world to the scrutiny and guidance of economic
analysis is a difficult but necessary one. This book has the great
merit of expounding the analytical apparatus of present-day
economic theory in a manner that makes it relevant to the many
pressing problems for the solution of which practical men,
whether government officials, business men, or labor leaders,
have a right to expect light and guidance. Boldly and courage-
ously, Mr. Meade arrives at definite conclusions with respect to
policy many of which are certainly highly debatable. For the
enlightened reader and student, however, it is the mastery of the
tools of analysis and the perception that these tools are relevant
to policy formation that is really important.

Too frequently American university and college students
come through their studies in economics with a jumbled mass of
facts, but with little comprehension of their meaning and of the
validity, workability, and economic consequences of proposed
lines of action. To achieve a workable knowledge of economic
theory is no easy task, but it is certainly not too much to expect
that university and college trained people shall be willing to pay
the necessary price to acquire this equipment. The publication
of an American edition of Mr. Meade's book should help to
hasten the coming of the day when we shall no longer be a nation
of 'economic illiterates.'

AUTHOR'S PREFACE

IN recent years there have been important developments in economic theory—notably in the analysis of money and unemployment by Mr. Keynes, and in the theory of imperfect competition by such writers as Mrs. Robinson and Professor E.Chamberlin. Many of these new ideas are not yet available to any but the trained economic theorist; for new scientific work must always at first be stated in technical terms. It is the primary object of this book to expound the whole corpus of economic theory without taking any knowledge of technical terms for granted and with full use of the more recent developments. I have not shirked any point in which economic analysis is relevant for the determination of economic policy; and for this reason this book is not always easy to read. But I have tried to write in such a way that any one with patience and the power of clear reasoning can understand it.

In this book I have discussed economic theory with direct reference to the economic problems of the modern world. As a teacher of the subject I have often found that men who come to economics to find an answer to the pressing problems of the moment cannot see that the formal analysis of the text-book has anything to do with the real world. Such formal analysis is, however, essential for a full understanding of practical problems, and the rigid text-book analysis must be mastered; but in this book I have attempted to supplement that training by combining it with the direct discussion of economic problems. This method has made it necessary to advocate a particular economic policy.

There is nothing original in this work, which is a transcription of the work of many authors; and it is impossible for me to enumerate fully the writers to whom I am indebted. Nearly every economic author whom I have read has directly or indirectly affected this book. But there are certain authors whom I must

mention specifically, and I hope that I will be excused if I have
failed to acknowledge direct indebtedness to others. Mr. J.M.
Keynes's *Treatise on Money* and *General Theory of Employment,
Interest and Money* have inspired the whole of Part I of this
book, which has also been directly influenced by the work of
Mr. R.F.Kahn; and certain passages in Chapters VI and VIII of
Part I have been recast after reading Mr. R.F.Harrod's *Trade
Cycle*. Part II has been constructed on the foundations of Mrs.
Robinson's *Economics of Imperfect Competition*, Professor Cham-
berlin's *The Theory of Monopolistic Competition*, Professor
Pigou's *Economics of Welfare*, and articles by Mr. R.F.Harrod
and other authors; while pp. 166–9 are a transcription of an
argument in Mr. R.F.Kahn's article in the *Economic Journal*, for
March 1935, entitled 'Some Notes on Ideal Output.' Chapter
VIII of Part II has gained much from articles of Mr. M.Dobb,
Mr. H.D.Dickinson, and Mr. A.P.Lerner in the *Economic Jour-
nal* and the *Review of Economic Studies*. Part III owes much to
Dr. Hugh Dalton's *The Inequality of Incomes* and Mr. Wedg-
wood's *The Economics of Inheritance*, while Chapter IV of this
Part is largely based on the works on Public Finance of Dr.
Hugh Dalton, Professor Pigou, Sir Josiah Stamp, and others. In
Part IV I have made use of Professor A.M.Carr-Saunder's *World
Population* and the work of Mr. Kuczynski, to whom we are in-
debted for the measurement of the trend of population by means
of the 'net reproduction rate.' Part V is based upon many works
on the theory of money, as well as upon text-books on interna-
tional trade, such as Professor Taussig's *Theory of International
Trade* and Mr. R.F.Harrod's *International Economics*.

Mrs. Robinson has read the whole of the manuscript of Parts I
to IV, and I am very grateful for the many material improvements suggested by so able a professional economist. Dr. N.J.
Abercrombie has nobly played the part of the intelligent ama-
teur, and his detailed criticisms have greatly improved the exposition. My sister has done the same for Part I and suggested
the insertion of an important section. I have been greatly helped

by my wife in revising the book. I wish to express my great gratitude to Mr. C.J.Hitch for undertaking the preparation of a special edition of this book for the American reader. In addition to the changes to which he refers above, he has prepared the graphs and the Appendix on the Graphs, and has in many cases suggested improvements in the argument of the text. In particular parts of Chapter VI of Part II and of Chapters IV and V of Part V, and the arguments on pp. 77–81 and 276–82 have been recast for this edition in the light of his criticisms. The rewriting of pp. 77–81 has been helped by suggestions made to me by Mr. D.H.Robertson and that of pp. 276–82 by suggestions of Mr. R.F.Harrod.

Mr. J.M.Cassels of Harvard University has given much help in the preparation of this edition, and Mr. J.K.Galbraith of Harvard has made many valuable suggestions. Mr. B.D.White of Oxford has kindly read the proofs and compiled the index. To all of these I would express my sincere gratitude.

J.E.M.

Geneva
  January 1938

NOTE TO THE AMERICAN EDITION

THE problems discussed by Mr. Meade and his analysis of them seem to me to be at least as appropriate to America as to England. In preparing the American edition, therefore, I have not changed the organization of the book or the general tenor of the argument. I have made some changes on theoretical points with the approval and co-operation of the author, substituted descriptions of the relevant American economic and financial institutions for the English, and modified the examples, spelling, and punctuation where this seemed desirable from the point of view of making the book more intelligible and useful to American readers.

C.J.H.

New York
  April 1938

TABLE OF CONTENTS

List of Tables   xv

List of Graphs   xvii

Introduction   xix

Part I

UNEMPLOYMENT

I. Can the Economic System Work?   3

II. The Rate of Interest and Expenditure on Additional Capital Goods   15

III. The Function of the Banks   22

IV. The Control of Banking Policy   35

V. The Planning of Public Works   43

VI. Direct Control of Expenditure on Consumption   55

VII. Wages and Unemployment   68

VIII. The Proper Criterion of Policy   82

IX. Other Methods of Reducing Unemployment   91

Part II

COMPETITION AND MONOPOLY

I. The Meaning of Perfect Competition   101

II. The Advantages of Perfect Competition   117

III. The Disadvantages of Perfect Competition   125

IV. Imperfect Competition between Sellers   132

V. Imperfect Competition between Purchasers   151

VI. The Disadvantages of Monopolistic Conditions   159

VII. The Control of Monopoly   181

VIII. Public Management and Planning of Industry   204

Part III

THE DISTRIBUTION OF INCOME

I. How Should Income Be Distributed?   220

II. Inequalities of Income from Work   227

III. Inequalities of Income from Property   236

IV. Equality by Taxation   246

V. Redistribution or Public Ownership of Property   265

PART IV

THE SUPPLY OF THE PRIMARY FACTORS OF PRODUCTION

I. Land, Labor, and Capital 272

II. The Optimum Supply of Labor 276

III. The Optimum Supply of Capital 296

IV. Simultaneous Variations in the Supply of Labor and Capital 303

PART V

INTERNATIONAL PROBLEMS

I. The Balance of Payments 307

II. The Gold Standard 321

III. Free Exchange Rates 344

IV. International Trade 356

V. Free Trade and Protection 368

VI. International Movements of Labor and Capital 384

VII. International Economic Co-operation 391

VIII. The Economic Causes of War 402

Suggestions for Further Reading   409

Appendix on the Graphs   411

Index   425

LIST OF TABLES

I. A Combined Balance Sheet of the Member Banks   25

II. A Balance Sheet of the Federal Reserve Banks   26

III. The Average and the Marginal Product of Labor   72

IV. The Ratio between the Marginal Products of Two Factors Differs in Two Industries   120

V. The Ratio between the Marginal Products of Two Factors is the Same in Two Industries   121

VI. The Yield of Investment in Education   230

VII. A Proportionate Income Tax   251

VIII. A Progressive Income Tax   252

IX. The Optimum Population   286

X. The Net Reproduction Rate   291

XI. The Items in America's Balance of Payments   308

XII. Illustration of Main Items in Balance of Payments   311

XIII. Alternative Method of Illustrating the Balance of Payments   312

XIV. The Ratio between the Marginal Costs of Two Commodities Differs in Two Countries   362

XV. The Ratio between the Marginal Costs of Two
     Commodities is the Same in Two Countries   363

CHART I
(*at end of book*)

1. The Cost Conditions of a Single Firm

2 (A). The Demand for the Output of a Single Firm
        Perfect Competition

2 (B). The Demand for the Output of a Single Firm
        Imperfect Competition

3. The Effect of a Maximum Legal Selling-price on the
    Demand Shown in Table 2 (B)

4. The Demand for the Output of a Commodity, Showing
    its Total Value to Consumers

5. The Effect of a Maximum Legal Selling-price on the
    Demand Shown in Table 4

CHART II
(*at end of book*)

6 (A). The Demand for Labor by a Single Firm
        Perfect Competition in the Sale of the Product

6 (B). The Demand for Labor by a Single Firm
        Imperfect Competition in the Sale of the Product

7 (A). The Supply of Labor to a Single Firm.
        Perfect Competition in the Hire of Labor

7 (B). The Supply of Labor to a Single Firm. Imperfect
        Competition in the Hire of Labor

8. The Effect of a Maximum Legal Commodity Price on
   the Demand for Labor Shown in Table 6 (B)

9. The Effect of a Minimum Legal Wage-rate on the
   Supply of Labor Shown in Table 7 (B)

LIST OF GRAPHS

I. Cost and Demand Conditions in a Firm:
   Perfect Competition   142

II. Cost and Demand Conditions in a Firm:
    Imperfect Competition   143

III. The Demand for Labor in a Firm: Perfect
     Competition in Sale of Product and Hire of Labor   156

IV. The Demand for Labor in a Firm: Imperfect
    Competition in Sale of Product and
    Perfect Competition in Hire of Labor   156

V. The Demand for Labor in a Firm:
   Perfect Competition in Sale of Product and
   Imperfect Competition in Hire of Labor   157

VI. The Demand for Labor in a Firm: Imperfect
    Competition in Sale of Product and Hire of Labor   157

VII. The Effect of a Maximum Legal Price on the
     Output of a Firm Selling in an Imperfect Market   198

VIII. The Optimum Population   287

INTRODUCTION

BEFORE any economic system can provide the highest possible standard of living for the greatest possible number of people, four conditions must be fulfilled.

1. No economic resources which are willing to work must stand idle. This problem—the problem of unemployment or of 'poverty in the midst of plenty'—is discussed in Part I.

2. The available economic resources must be set to work to produce in the greatest possible quantities those products which consumers most desire; this condition will remain unfulfilled, so long as it is possible by producing less of one thing to produce more of another which consumers desire more urgently. This is the problem of competition and monopoly, which is the subject of Part II.

3. The income of the community must be distributed among individuals in such a way that the greatest possible satisfaction is obtained from the limited national income. The distribution of income is the subject of Part III.

4. Welfare will not be the highest possible unless a proper balance between work and leisure is maintained, and unless the total population and the total stock of capital are available in the most appropriate amounts. Part IV discusses this problem of the 'optimum' supply of the factors of production—labor and capital.

If these four conditions are fulfilled, economic welfare will be the highest which it is possible with a given knowledge of industrial technique to obtain from a given supply of natural resources. Parts I to IV are based on the assumption of a self-contained economic system. But in the real world no economy is isolated in this way; for each government must consider the effect of its economic policy upon economic relations with other countries. Part V is therefore devoted to international economic problems.

This discussion gives rise to no further fundamental economic problem, but shows merely the international aspects of the four fundamental questions discussed in Parts I to IV.

Some of these problems are more urgent and some are more easily solved than others. The most glaring economic absurdity at present is the existence of unemployed resources in a world in which there are many needs still to be satisfied. For this reason the policy discussed in Part I—together with its international aspects in Part V—is the most pressing and the nearest to 'practical politics.' Fortunately, as we shall see, the solution of this problem needs least governmental interference. This problem should certainly be solved before all others; for, as long as there are unemployed resources it is possible to produce a larger real income and so to improve every one's standards without causing anyone to be worse off. The solution of this problem—unlike the problem of redistributing income—requires no change of heart and offends no vested interests; it requires simply a clearer understanding, and if the argument of Chapter VIII of Part V is correct, its solution should strengthen the economic foundations of world peace. The problem of Part IV, with the exception of the question of the best balance between work and leisure discussed on pp. 276 to 282, is the most far removed from 'practical politics'; for it involves controlling the size of the population.

Opinions are likely to differ as to whether the problem of Part II or that of Part III should take precedence in any practical economic programme. On the one hand, the redistribution of income involves in its clearest form the problem of 'vested interests,' since it is impossible to redistribute income without making some persons worse off than before; whereas the solution of the problems raised in Part II will increase the total national income available for distribution, and is therefore theoretically compatible with a rise in every one's standards. On the other hand, as we shall argue in Chapter IV of Part III, income can be safely redistributed by a simple extension of the existing taxing function of government; whereas the problem of Part II cannot be successfully met without a large measure of government control over industry.

It is not suggested that a definite order of preference can be laid down in any practical economic policy for the solution of the different problems discussed in this book. Different readers will lay the emphasis on different problems; and—as we shall show more than once in the course of this book—there are many reforms which will aid the solution of more than one problem at the same time. But no sound economic policy can tackle every problem at once; and it is, I think, at least certain that the problem of unemployment should immediately receive the greatest emphasis. Beyond this, these introductory remarks may enable the reader to preserve a better balance in his judgment as he moves through the details of the following pages.

In the text two methods of illustrating the argument have been employed—arithmetic examples and graphs. These methods are in most respects alternative; they are different ways of presenting the same information. *Readers who are not mathematically minded may ignore the graphs without missing any of the argument*, and for their convenience sections of the text which apply to the graphs have been indented and placed within brackets. Readers who prefer the graphical presentation, on the other hand, should find these sections and the graphs accompanying them an aid in understanding the argument. They are advised to read the Appendix on the Graphs at the end of the book before studying the graphs in the text.

AN INTRODUCTION TO
ECONOMIC ANALYSIS
AND POLICY

Part I
UNEMPLOYMENT

I

CAN THE ECONOMIC SYSTEM WORK ?

THE problem to be discussed in this first Part is the existence of unused economic resources while members of the community still have unsatisfied needs; in other words, we shall attempt to solve the problem of 'poverty in the midst of potential plenty.' Up to Part V we shall assume that this country forms an economic world of its own, cut off from every outside contact. It would of course be impossible in the real economic world to devise a satisfactory policy for the cure of unemployment without reference to foreign trade and the foreign exchanges. But problems must be discussed one at a time, however much in the real world the solution of any one affects the solution of every other; and in Part V it will be shown that a suitable international economic policy can be adopted to fit in with the internal policies suggested in this Part.

The problem which we shall discuss in this Part is more restricted than the complete problem of unemployment. We might distinguish three different sorts of unemployment which are common in the modern world. There will, in the first place, be some unemployment even in the best organized society at the best of times because some industries or firms will be expanding and others contracting. It takes time for men to learn new jobs, to move to new districts, or to hear of existing vacancies when they have lost a job. This unemployment is usually called 'normal.' Something will be said of the means of reducing it in Part II, Chapter VII. The second type, which is called 'structural' or 'special,' differs from normal unemployment chiefly in degree. It is the result of catastrophic contractions in particular industries and areas caused, for example, by the loss of export markets in a war. This type of unemployment can be reduced to some

extent by the same sort of measures appropriate to the treatment
of normal unemployment, but special measures for the rehabilita-
tion of the specific industries or areas concerned are also likely to
be necessary. The third type of unemployment, which is usually
called 'cyclical,' and accounts for the major part of unemployment when it is most severe,[1] is caused by the demand for labor
contracting not in one but in almost all occupations at the same
time. People are unemployed not because they are slow to move
to another job, but because there are no jobs. It is the cure of
this type of unemployment which is the subject of this Part.

We can start by dismissing the theory that there is some fundamental flaw in the existing monetary or pricing system. It is perfectly true—and must never be forgotten until the problem is
solved—that modern communities are not at the present time
successfully insuring that their unemployed resources shall be
set to work to make those things which are still needed. But the
problem of unemployment is capable of solution without any
revolutionary change in our economic system.

The question comes down to this: is it possible, without intro-
ducing socialism or a complete change in our monetary system,
to distribute among consumers enough money to buy at prices
covering their cost of production all the goods and services which
we would be able to produce if our resources were fully utilized?
It is sometimes held that the existing economic system can never
distribute purchasing power sufficient to cover the costs of the
output which is produced for sale; but this view is fallacious. Let
us take an illustration. The cost of producing consumption
goods [2] can be reduced to—

1. The London *Economist* estimates that in England at the bottom of the depression in 1932 a little more than a third of the unemployment existing
   was 'cyclical,' and a little less than a third 'normal' and 'special' respectively. By 1937 the 'cyclical' unemployment had almost disappeared, but
   'normal' and 'special' unemployment were of about the same magnitude
   as in 1932. Reliable statistics on which such estimates could be based are
   lacking in America, but the importance of cyclical unemployment, relatively to the others, is undoubtedly much greater than in England.
2. By consumption goods we mean commodities, such as boots, clothes,
   food, etc., which are sold directly to consumers for the immediate satis-

 (i) the wages of labor employed in their production;
(ii) the interest to be paid on the capital borrowed by the manufacturers;
(iii) the rent or royalties which the manufacturer must pay to the owners of the land or other property used in the production of consumption goods;
(iv) the cost to the manufacturers of purchasing from other manufacturers or farmers the raw materials necessary to make the finished commodities;
 (v) a payment which must be allowed for repairing and replacing the machinery and plant which wears out during the process of production of the commodities; and
(vi) a profit to the manufacturers sufficient to induce them to carry on with their production.

It is easier to discuss this matter by taking a simple numerical example. Let us suppose that each of these six items of cost is $100 a year; then in order to sell the annual output of consumption goods at prices which cover their cost of production the manufacturers must receive a total amount of $600 for the sale of their output. In order to produce this output costing $600 they pay $100 to labor during the year, $100 as interest on capital, $100 as rent of land, $100 for raw materials, $100 for the upkeep of their plant, and $100 they regard as income sufficient to repay them for the trouble they have taken. The first three items of cost, namely the $300 paid out in wages, interest, and rent during the year, are clearly available to be spent in this year by the public on the purchase of $300's worth of the product. But what of the other $300? Are the payments for raw materials, for upkeep of plant, and for a profit for the manufacturers of consumption goods, available to be spent on this year's output?

There is no inherent reason why they should not be so avail-

faction of human needs; and by capital goods we mean commodities such as machines, bricks, raw materials, etc., which cannot directly satisfy human needs, but which are used to aid in the production of consumption goods.

able. The $200 spent on raw materials and on the repair and upkeep of machinery have been received by the manufacturers of raw materials or of machinery. They in turn will have paid part of the $200 as wages to labor, part as interest on the capital, and part as rent for the land which they are using to produce raw materials and machines; part of the $200 the manufacturers of raw materials will have kept as the necessary profit for themselves. All these sums have therefore been distributed by manufacturers of raw materials and machines in the form of wages, interest, rent, or profit and are available to be spent on consumption goods. If, however, the manufacturers of raw materials and machines have themselves to spend something—e.g. $10—on raw materials and machines for the upkeep of their plant, they will have distributed in wages, interest, rent, and profit only $190 out of the $200 that they received. But in this case some other manufacturers of raw materials and machines will have received $10 from those who are producing raw materials and machines for the manufacturers of consumption goods, and this second set of manufacturers will in turn have received $10, which they in turn will have distributed. If this second set of manufacturers has some raw material cost to meet out of the $10 received for the sale of their product, then they in turn will have spent this on the product of a third set of manufacturers. Thus in the end the whole sum will have been distributed in wages, interest, rent, or profit, all available to be spent on consumption goods.

The first five elements in the cost of producing consumption goods—i.e. the $500 paid by the manufacturers of consumption goods in the course of the year in wages, interest, rent, cost of raw materials, and cost of upkeep of machinery and plant—have all therefore directly or indirectly been distributed to consumers as income available for expenditure on consumption goods. It is sometimes objected that, although this is true, yet the whole of this income cannot be available in the hands of consumers to purchase this year's output of consumption goods. For, it is argued, only part of this income will have been distributed to consumers *this* year so as to form an income with which *this* year's output of consumption goods can be bought; the remaining part of this income will have been distributed to consumers *last* year and will already have been spent on *last* year's output of consumption goods. The $300 paid out this year by the manufacturers of consumption goods directly in wages, interest, and rent will be available as the income of consumers to be spent on this year's output. But the $200 spent this year on raw materials and the replacement of machinery will be spent on the purchase of raw materials and machines which were made last year; and the wages, interest, and rent which were paid for the manufacture of these raw materials and machines will have been distributed last year as income and therefore will already have been spent on last year's output of consumption goods. Thus, the argument concludes, of the $500 of cost with which we are at the moment concerned, only that part—in our example $300—which is directly distributed as wages, rent, and interest will be available this year to buy this year's output of consumption goods: that part—in our example $200—which is spent on raw materials and the replacement of machines will already have been distributed and spent on consumption goods. Therefore the amount distributed in income this year to buy this year's output is necessarily less than the cost of producing this year's output, and unemployment is bound to result.[1]

We may admit that this year $300 is distributed directly by the manufacturers of consumption goods in wages, interest, and rent, and that $200 is spent on raw materials and machines which were produced last year. We may admit also that the income from the production of these raw materials and machines was distributed and spent last year. But it is false to conclude that only $300 can be available this year to purchase this year's output of consumption goods. For *next* year an output of consumption goods will be produced, and the manufacturers of con-

---

1. This, as I understand it, is the essential point in the analysis of Major C.H.Douglas.

sumption goods will have to purchase raw materials and to repair and replace their machinery next year to produce next year's output. Moreover, the producers of raw materials and machines will realize this and will produce raw materials and machines this year in order to sell them next year to the manufacturers of consumption goods. If the producers of raw materials and machines expect to receive from the manufacturers of consumption goods as much next year as was received this year, no trouble need arise. The manufacturers of raw materials and machines will be distributing $200 in wages, interest, and rent to produce raw materials and machines to be sold next year to the manufacturers of consumption goods, and this $200 is available as income this year for expenditure on this year's output of consumption goods. Thus $500 is available as income for expenditure on this year's output of consumption goods.

We have found no inherent flaw in the economic system as far as the first five elements of cost enumerated on p. 5 are concerned. All these costs *may* at least be balanced by an equal income available to be spent on the finished product. But we have supposed that the consumption goods cost $600 to produce; and so far we have allowed for a distribution of only $500 purchasing power to consumers to buy these goods. The remaining element of cost is the manufacturers' profit. The actual amount of profit is a residual item depending upon the difference between the manufacturers' receipts and their other costs. In our example the manufacturers must receive a profit of $100 if they are to carry on production at the existing level. Will they receive this necessary profit of $100? There is no inherent reason why they should not. If the manufacturers themselves spend $100 on consumption goods, the total amount spent on consumption goods will be $600 and this will just cover the cost of producing them, including $100 profit for the manufacturers. On the other hand there is no inherent reason why the manufacturers should be receiving just $100, rather than more or less. If they are themselves spending $150 on consumption goods, the total amount spent on consumption goods will be $650; and if $650 are spent on consumption goods, manufacturers will in fact be receiving a profit of $150. If, on the other hand, manufacturers are spending only $50 on consumption goods, only $550 in all will be spent on consumption goods, so that they will in fact be receiving a profit of only $50.

We may conclude that it is quite possible for the economic system to distribute sufficient purchasing power, but that at any one time it may be distributing more or less purchasing power than is necessary to buy up the output of finished goods at their cost—the cost including that profit to manufacturers without which they will not continue their production. In the former case manufacturers will be making profits larger than is necessary to induce them to carry on the existing production, and in the latter case they will be receiving less than is necessary. In the former case they will have some incentive to plan for a larger production and they will attempt to employ more labor and to hire more capital for this purpose, so that output will be increased and more resources will be employed. In the latter case manufacturers will be induced to restrict the scale of their production since they are not receiving enough to induce them to continue at the present scale, and this will throw labor and capital out of employment. If they are just covering their costs and just receiving a sufficient profit to induce them to continue at the present scale they will make no attempt to produce more or less.

We have still to decide what it is that determines whether the distribution of purchasing power is sufficient or not to cover costs of production, since we have only shown so far that sufficient purchasing power *may* be distributed. In order to develop this part of our discussion it is convenient to examine the argument of those who hold that if any persons save part of their income it is bound to be impossible to sell the whole of the output of consumption goods at their costs; for, it is argued, if people spend on consumption goods less than the whole of their income, i.e. less than the total cost of producing consumption goods, the price of consumption goods must fall below their cost of production.

Let us expound this argument by continuing the numerical example used above. Let us suppose that an amount of consumption goods is produced in a particular year the total costs of which are $600, and that $600 is distributed directly or indirectly in wages, rents, interests, and profit, and is available to be spent on these consumption goods. The argument which we have to consider is that, if those receiving this income of $600 decide to spend only part of it—say $400—on consumption goods, and to save the remaining $200, then only $400 will be spent on goods which cost $600 to produce. In these circumstances it would appear that the total amount spent on consumption goods cannot cover the cost of producing them, even though sufficient purchasing power is being distributed as income to cover their costs.

But there is still no reason why the economic system should not be made to function successfully. For if people are saving $200 of their incomes it should be possible for manufacturers to borrow the $200 to spend on capital goods in order to develop their concerns. If this is being done, then there is no reason why consumption goods should be sold at prices below their cost of production. For if $200 is borrowed this year and spent by manufacturers on additional capital goods [1] to develop their capital equipment, those persons who manufacture these additional capital goods will receive $200 in the course of the year as wages, rent, interest, or profit, and they can spend this sum on consumption goods. Again we must conclude that there is no inherent reason why expenditure on consumption goods should fall below the total cost of producing them, even if consumers save

1. By the annual expenditure on additional capital goods is meant that part of the annual amount spent in purchasing machines, factories, raw materials, etc., which is not required simply to replace and maintain the machines, factories, raw materials, etc., which are worn out in the course of the year's production. In other words, it means the amount spent in the year on increasing the community's stock of capital goods.

part of their income. The system will work so long as sufficient is borrowed for expenditure on additional capital goods.

If the foregoing argument is correct we have shown that the present economic system *may* distribute sufficient purchasing power to cover the total cost of producing consumption goods even if people save part of their income. But we have not attempted to prove that it must always do so; indeed, in face of the recent depression such a contention would be nonsense. It is quite possible that consumption goods costing $600 are produced this year and that the manufacturers of these goods are receiving only $500 for their sale. Then the total amount distributed directly or indirectly in income in respect of the production of these goods will only be $500. There is nothing impossible or, indeed, improbable about such a situation in which the producers of consumption goods will not be covering their total costs.

The argument and example of the last pages help to show how it can be insured that sufficient is spent on consumption goods to cover the total costs of their production. The producers of consumption goods may themselves spend on consumption goods less than is sufficient to cover their costs. But this deficiency of expenditure can be made up, if a sufficient amount is borrowed and spent on additional capital goods. For if the producers of capital goods have large enough incomes, their expenditure on consumption goods will make good the deficiency. Thus suppose that there is an output of consumption goods costing $600 and that the producers of these goods, because they wish to save part of their income, will only spend $400 themselves on the purchase of consumption goods. Then, in order that $600 in all should be spent on consumption goods, a further $200 must be spent on them by other people. In other words, the producers of additional capital goods must be receiving a sufficient income to cause them to spend $200 on consumption goods. If the producers of additional capital goods wish themselves to save one-third of their income and to spend only two-thirds of it on consumption goods, then in order that $200 should be spent by them on consumption goods they must be receiving $300 for the sale of additional capital goods. If, instead of $300, only $270 were being spent on additional capital goods, then the producers of additional capital goods would be receiving only $270, of which they would be saving one-third or $90 and spending two-thirds or $180 on consumption goods. In this case the total expenditure on consumption goods, costing $600 to produce, would only be $580, of which $400 represents expenditure by the producers of consumption goods and $180 expenditure by the producers of additional capital goods.

This analysis enables us to conclude that there are only two fundamental ways in which the total expenditure on consumption goods can be made to increase: either more must be spent on additional capital goods; or else, without any diminution in the amount spent on additional capital goods and so without any diminution in the incomes of the producers of these goods, income receivers must spend a larger proportion of their income on consumption goods. Let us take as an illustration the numerical example which we have already given. Suppose that consumption goods costing $600 are being produced, and that $270 is being spent on additional capital goods, and suppose further that the producers of consumption goods are spending $400 and the producers of additional capital goods are spending $180 on consumption goods. Then the total expenditure on consumption goods is $580. There are two ways in which this expenditure on consumption goods may be increased by $20. In the first place, expenditure on additional capital goods might be increased. If producers of these goods continued to spend two-thirds of their income an increase in capital expenditure from $270 to $300 would induce them to spend $200 instead of $180 on consumption. In the second place, people might be induced to spend a larger proportion of their incomes. If the amount spent on additional capital goods remained unchanged at $270, and the producers of consumption goods were to spend $410 instead of $400 and the producers of additional capital goods $190 instead of $180 on consumption goods, then the total expenditure on consumption goods would be increased from $580 to $600 and this would be sufficient to cover the cost of producing these goods.

In order that the problem of cyclical unemployment may be solved it is necessary that the total amount spent on the community's output of consumption goods or of additional capital goods should be great enough to induce the manufacturers of these goods to extend their output until they have absorbed all those resources of the community which are cyclically unemployed; i.e., all those whose unemployment is due to the *general* unprofitability of industry rather than to the difficulty of moving resources from one job to another. If, therefore, unemployment of this sort exists, it is necessary to do one of three things.

(a) More money may be spent on additional capital goods. This will directly increase the money demand for additional capital goods, will raise their price in relation to their cost of production, and will induce the manufacturers of these goods to employ more men to increase their output. But as we have just shown, it will do more than this. It will increase the total incomes of those producing these goods, and if it is not accompanied by a rise in the proportion of income saved it will also cause expenditure on consumption goods to rise. This in turn will raise the price of consumption goods in relation to their costs and will induce the manufacturers of consumption goods also to employ more men to increase their output. Chapters II to V of this Part are devoted to a discussion of the ways in which expenditure on additional capital goods can be increased.

(b) People may be induced to spend a larger amount on consumption goods without there being any corresponding reduction in the amount spent on additional capital goods. Measures designed to bring this about are discussed in Chapter VI of this Part.

(c) It is equally clear that a reduction in the cost of production per unit of output of consumption goods or of additional capital goods will increase the profit of manufacturers and induce them to employ more men to increase their output, provided that such a reduction in costs of production is not accompanied by a similar reduction in the total amount spent on consumption goods and on additional capital goods. The possibility of measures of this kind is discussed in Chapter VII of this Part.

II

THE RATE OF INTEREST AND EXPENDITURE ON
ADDITIONAL CAPITAL GOODS

WE concluded in the last chapter that an increase in the amount spent on additional capital goods would indirectly increase the demand for consumption goods. In this chapter it will be shown that a fall in the rate of interest will increase the total amount spent on additional capital goods, so that if it is possible to lower the rate of interest it will be possible thereby to increase the demand for every type of commodity. Expenditure on capital development may be divided into three groups. In the first place, manufacturers may spend money on new machinery or plant to extend their existing equipment or to set up a new firm. Secondly, Federal, state, and municipal governments may spend money on the development of the capital equipment necessary for the provision of such communal services as prisons, hospitals, schools, or roads. Thirdly, individuals may spend money on new capital goods, such as houses, which will serve their needs directly in the future.

Let us suppose that a manufacturer has to decide whether it is profitable for him to borrow money in order to put in a new machine to develop his business. In addition to the price of the machine he will have to consider two things before coming to a decision:

(i) what difference it would make to the profitability of his business if he had the new machine, and

(ii) at what rate of interest he can borrow the money to install the new machine.

(i) If he had the new machine he could produce more, and could therefore expect to receive a larger amount of money from his sales. Let us suppose that if he had the new machine he could so increase his output that he would receive $50 more each year from the sale of his product. At the same time he will have to spend more on raw materials, on wages, and on repair and depreciation of the new machine each year. Suppose that these additional costs will amount to $45 a year. Then he will make a net additional profit of $5 a year. If the machine costs $100 to purchase and install, he will make a rate of profit on the cost of the machine of 5 per cent per annum.

(ii) On the other hand, he will have either to borrow the money to buy the machine or else buy it with his own money which he could otherwise have lent at a certain rate of interest. If the rate of interest at which money can be borrowed and lent is 6 per cent per annum it will clearly be unprofitable for him to install the machine. But if the rate of interest is 4 per cent per annum, it will pay him to install the machine, since he can make a profit of 5 per cent per annum on $100 borrowed at 4 per cent per annum. We now come to a conclusion of fundamental importance: *A fall in the rate of interest at which money can be borrowed, or a rise in the rate of profit which can be expected on any capital development, will cause an increase in the amount of additional machinery and plant which a manufacturer will find it profitable to install.*

In the real world, of course, computations of the profitability of a new machine cannot be made with the accuracy and certainty which we have assumed in the above example. But this does not seriously affect the validity of the argument. At a given rate of interest there will always be some capital extensions which business men, taking the uncertainty of the future into account, will think just not worth making. At a lower rate of interest they would become, in the opinion of these same business men, just worth making. And this is likely to be the case whatever the rate of interest. In any firm there are probably at any one time a number of different ways in which it would be possible for the manufacturer to extend his plant. Some extensions may be reckoned to earn a high rate of profit; others may be reckoned to earn a slightly lower rate of profit, and so on. For this reason, as the rate of interest falls, more extensions will become profitable and more money will be spent on capital development. In this connection it is important to realize that a business, even if it is doing so badly that it is not employing all the capital equipment which it already possesses, may find it profitable to invest in new capital equipment if the rate of interest is sufficiently low. Such a business will not, of course, find it profitable to invest in machinery of the kind which it already possesses; but with a low rate of interest it may find it profitable to invest in machinery of an entirely new type. For instance, in a depressed coal mine much equipment may be lying idle, but it may be possible to invest in mechanical coal-cutters which the mine does not already possess. If the owners of the mine expect to make 3 per cent on an investment in this type of machinery it will pay them to do so as soon as the rate of interest falls below 3 per cent even though it may not pay them to use fully the other types of equipment which they already possess.

A similar argument will apply when considering whether to set up a new company or a new firm. The promoters of a new company must first compare the rate of profit to be expected upon the new company's capital with the rate of interest at which money can be lent or borrowed; and as the rate of interest falls there will be a larger and larger number of industries in which it becomes profitable to spend money on new capital goods for the formation of new business units.

The second type of expenditure on capital goods is also dependent upon the rate of interest. In the modern world governments must necessarily undertake a large amount of expenditure on capital development which cannot be left to private enterprise. Roads, schools, prisons, battleships, street-lighting, drainage, and water supply are instances of such expenditure. In some cases it is impossible to assess the rate of profit which can be made on the investment. It is, for example, not easy to say what rate of profit a state expects on the erection of a new prison or lunatic asylum. In other cases for purposes of social policy the actual rate of profit which could be earned on the investment is deliberately neglected, although it is capable of being reckoned. A new school, if it were run simply as a profit-making institution, could earn a definite rate of profit, but, for reasons at the moment irrelevant, this consideration is not taken into account. Nevertheless, the amount which governments spend on such capital development is very largely affected by the rate of interest at which money can be borrowed; for a fall in the rate of interest will reduce the future tax burden which is necessary to meet the interest on the money borrowed for any particular scheme of development.

As an example of the third type of expenditure on capital development, namely expenditure on capital goods which provide direct services to individuals, we may take expenditure on private houses. Here again the rate of interest will be very important in deciding the amount of expenditure undertaken, whether the building of the house is undertaken by a governmental authority, by a development builder, or by the individual householder himself. Suppose that it costs $1,000 to build a one-room house, $2,000 to build a two-room house, $3,000 to build a three-room house, and so on. (It is not pretended that these figures are realistic; they are chosen merely to provide a simple illustration of the principle involved.) If an individual can borrow money from a building society at 10 per cent per annum or if he himself can lend money at 10 per cent, then each room will cost him $100 a year in interest, since he must borrow $1,000 at 10 per cent or refrain from lending $1,000 at 10 per cent for each room in his new house. If, however, the rate of interest is only 5 per cent, then he must pay in interest to the building society or give up in interest on his savings only $50 a year for each room. Thus the lower the rate of interest the greater will be the number of people who can afford to build themselves houses and the larger will be the size of the houses which are built.

The effect is the same if the house is built by a governmental authority, or by a development builder who intends to sell or rent it at a profit. If either decides to build a three-room house costing $3,000 it must borrow $3,000 or refrain from lending $3,000 of its own money. If the rate of interest is 10 per cent the annual interest charge will be $300 a year, and for the construction of the house to be financially worth while it must be rented at a price which will cover this sum. But if the rate of interest were only 5 per cent it would be worth while building the same house so long as it could be rented at a price which would cover $150 per year in interest charges. Thus the lower the rate of interest, the lower will be the prices at which new houses can profitably be rented. But the lower the rents of houses, the more houses people will wish to hire and the larger will be the houses which they can afford, so that a fall in the rate of interest is bound to increase the total amount spent on house construction. This argument is not, of course, seriously modified if the government subsidizes the cost of houses. For if a given subsidy is paid, it will cover part of the cost and so part of the rent of the house. But it still remains true that, the lower the rate of interest, the lower will be the rent at which the subsidized house can be let to cover that part of the cost of its construction which is not already met by the subsidy.

We have thus shown that a fall in the rate of interest may increase expenditure on capital development of several kinds. But the effect of changes in the rate of interest on the total expenditure on goods is cumulative, so that this form of control is more effective than is apparent at first sight. If there is a reduction in the rate of interest at which money can be borrowed, then more money will be spent on capital development. But this will not only increase the demand for additional capital goods; it will also increase the incomes of the producers of these goods. These producers may save part of their increased incomes, but part they will spend on consumption goods. And even this is not the end of the story. The producers of consumption goods will be receiving greater incomes; and, though they may save part of their increased incomes, they will in turn spend part of the increase in their incomes on consumption goods. Thus a secondary increase in the demand for consumption goods will take place, which will again increase the incomes of those producing consumption goods, part of which may be spent on consumption goods, causing a tertiary increase in the demand for such goods. In this way the demand for consumption goods will increase cumulatively by a series of ever-diminishing increases in demand, leading to increased incomes and increased expenditure. Such increases in expenditure on consumption goods will have a further effect upon the demand for additional capital goods; for the increased expenditure on consumption goods will raise the price at which such goods can be sold and so will raise the profit which can be made on the use of capital for the production of consumption goods. The result of this will be a further increase in the amount which it is profitable for the producers of consumption goods to spend on capital development, and the circle of increasing expenditure and profits will be started again.

These cumulative effects make any means of controlling investment a very important instrument for controlling the total demand for commodities and thereby total employment. It is the conclusion of this chapter that the rate of interest is a means of controlling investment; that a fall in the rate of interest will always tend to increase the demand for capital goods and consumption goods. The importance of this conclusion, while great, must not be exaggerated. There are other factors beside the rate of interest which affect expenditure on additional capital goods, and in some circumstances their joint influence may be so strong as to counteract any conceivable change in the interest rate. Furthermore, decisions to undertake new investment take time to put into effect, and the beneficial results of low interest rates may therefore appear too slowly to suit persons impatient to cure a pressing social evil. Nevertheless, if the rate of interest can be lowered whenever there is cyclical unemployment we shall have found one way, always effective partially and if given time, in which total expenditure on capital development and on consumption goods can be adjusted to maintain full employment. In the next chapter we show that the rate of interest can be lowered by appropriate banking policy.

III

THE FUNCTION OF THE BANKS

WE may best show how the banks can control the rate of interest by discussing the Federal Reserve system. Other banking systems differ from the Federal Reserve system in their conventions and legal restrictions, but the essential features are much the same everywhere. In the United States the situation is complicated by the fact that numerous commercial banks are outside the Federal Reserve system; but this complication, while it limits the effectiveness of the control exercised by the Federal Reserve Banks, does not affect the principles on which regulation is based.

We shall see later that it is largely through their control of the amount of money that the banks control the rate of interest, and it is necessary, therefore, to see how the Federal Reserve system can control the amount of money in existence. To do this we must first examine the balance sheet of a commercial bank. A bank's balance sheet, like the balance sheet of any other concern, is bound to balance; that is to say, it is drawn up in such a way that the items on the assets side of the account are exactly equal to the items on the liabilities side. The liabilities of an ordinary commercial bank are composed of—

(i) Capital. This is the money which has been borrowed for the formation of the bank and which the bank therefore owes to the stockholders.

(ii) Surplus. This is the profit made by the bank but not yet distributed in dividends. This item again is a liability, because the bank owes this money to the owners of the bank's capital. It is this item which must be adjusted to make the bank's balance sheet balance. If an asset of the bank deteriorates in value, the surplus is written down by an equivalent amount.

(iii) Deposits. These consist of (a) demand deposits, which may be checked against, or withdrawn on demand; and (b) time deposits, which the banks are obliged to pay only after a certain number of days notice has been given. Both represent money deposited by the public, and owed by the banks to the public. Together they constitute much the most important item on the liabilities side both in size and in its effect on the economic system.

The assets of the bank can be divided into three main heads, which require a number of subdivisions.[1]

(i) Cash. The bank will hold a certain amount of cash in order to meet the requirements of any of its depositors who wish to change the money they have deposited with it into cash. The bank counts as cash all notes and coin in its vaults.

(ii) Reserve with Federal Reserve Bank. Each bank which is a member of the Federal Reserve system is required to keep on deposit with the Federal Reserve Bank in its district a certain proportion—which may vary from 7 to 26 per cent—of its demand deposits, and a certain smaller proportion—3 to 6 per cent—of its time deposits. These two items, cash and deposits with the Federal Reserve Bank, are normally adequate to enable the bank to cash any amount of its deposit liabilities that may be required at any one moment, and still retain a large margin of safety—although if all depositors wished to cash all their deposits at the same time, as occasionally happens during periods of panic, only a fraction could be accommodated.

1. In order to simplify the balance sheet certain minor items have been omitted. The bank's own buildings constitute part of its assets. Interbank deposits and checks in process of collection result in a 'Due from banks' item on the assets side of the sheet and a 'Due to banks' item on the liabilities side.

(iii) Loans and Investments. The rest of the money lent to the bank—i.e. that amount of its capital, its surplus, and its deposit liabilities which it does not keep at hand in cash or on deposit with a Federal Reserve Bank—the bank will lend to others to earn interest. These loans and investments may take many forms. Some may be made for very short periods to other financial institutions. Some will represent advances to the government by the purchase of government securities; these may take the form either of Treasury Bills, which are promises by the government to pay a certain sum of money in a few months' time, or of long-term government bonds, which are promises to pay a certain amount of interest every year, together with the promise to pay back the sum borrowed after a definite term of years. Other loans by the bank may take the form of bills 'discounted for' or bought from merchants, these being promises on the part of the merchants to pay certain sums in a few months' time. Others may consist of investments by the bank in industry or real estate. Finally, the bank will have 'advanced' certain sums to producers to enable them to carry on their business, and to individuals to enable them to buy motor cars, houses, or securities, and for miscellaneous purposes.

What has been said is true not only of one commercial bank but of all banks. We may therefore draw up a combined balance sheet of all the commercial banks which are members of the Federal Reserve system. Such a combined balance sheet (with hypothetical round figures) is shown in Table I. It will be observed that the banks are represented as keeping a reserve on deposit with the Federal Reserve Banks amounting to 10 per cent of their demand deposits and 3 per cent of their time deposits. Ten per cent is the average reserve which banks are required to maintain against demand deposits, and 3 per cent the reserve against time deposits, when requirements are a minimum.

Table I

A Combined Balance Sheet of the Member Banks of the Federal Reserve System

Liabilities			Assets	
		(In millions of dollars)		
(a) Capital stock		3,500	(d) Reserve with the Federal Reserve Bank	2,800
(b) Surplus		1,500	(e) Cash	2,000
(c) Deposits			(f) Loans and discounts	14,000
Demand	25,000		(g) Investments	21,200
Time	10,000			
		35,000		
		$40,000		$40,000

To complete our simplified picture of the banking system it is necessary to discuss the Federal Reserve Banks. The Federal Reserve Banks regulate the issue of Federal Reserve notes, which comprise the most important part of the nation's currency; they are the government's bankers in the sense that the government keeps its deposit accounts with the Federal Reserve Banks; and, finally, as we have already seen, they hold the balances which the member banks have deposited with them as their required legal reserve, and which we have represented in (d) of Table I as being $2,800 millions.

The balance sheet of a Reserve Bank is similar in many ways to the balance sheet of a commercial bank. On the liabilities side there is an item representing capital and surplus, another representing deposits, and, in addition, an item representing Federal Reserve notes in circulation, which are subject to redemption by the Reserve Banks on demand. On the assets side the principal items are gold certificates, representing gold deposited by the Reserve Bank with the U.S. Treasury, cash in vaults, bills bought and discounted, and U.S. Government securities. As in the case of the member banks the balance sheets of the Reserve Banks can be combined, and such a combined balance sheet, again with round hypothetical figures, is illustrated in Table II.[1]

1. As in the case of the member banks' balance sheet minor items have been omitted. For an explanation of the complete statement the student is referred to an article in the *Federal Reserve Bulletin* for July 1935.

TABLE II

A Combined Balance Sheet of the Federal Reserve Banks

Liabilities   Assets

(In millions of dollars)

(a) Capital and surplus	300	(e) Gold certificates	5,600
(b) Federal Reserve notes in circulation	4,000	(f) Cash	250
		(g) Bills discounted	100
(c) Member bank deposits	2,800	(h) Bills bought	50
(d) Government deposits	1,400	(i) U.S.Gov't securities	2,500
	8,500		8,500

The Federal Reserve Banks' function as a note issuing authority is relatively simple. Federal Reserve notes are printed as member banks require them; they must be backed by gold certificates to the extent of at least 40 per cent, and for the balance by government bonds or commercial paper. When a member bank needs additional currency it 'cashes' its deposit with a Federal Reserve Bank just as an individual would with a commercial bank.

But the principal form of money is no longer currency; a far greater volume of transactions is now financed by means of checks drawn against deposits in commercial banks, and we are now in a position to see how the Federal Reserve Banks can control the amount of this type of money in existence. If they wish to increase the volume of deposits they will purchase securities (usually government bonds) from the public on the stock exchange. Let us suppose that the Banks purchase $10 millions worth of securities; they will pay for these by means of a check which the sellers will deposit with their commercial banks, and which these banks, in turn, will collect from the Federal Reserve Banks. As a result of these transactions the Federal Reserve Banks will find their securities, on the assets side, up by $10 millions, and their deposits by member banks, on the liabilities side, also up by $10 millions. The member banks, similarly, will find their reserves with the Federal Reserve Banks and their own deposit liabilities up by $10 millions. But the reserves which the banks are required to maintain have now become excessive. If, as has normally been the case, they have been required to keep reserves to the extent of about 10 per cent of their demand deposits, in this new situation they will be holding a larger proportion than 10 per cent.

In order to reduce their reserve ratio to 10 per cent again the member banks will themselves attempt to lend more or will invest their spare cash in securities. As they do so their assets and their deposit liabilities will be increased; for they will pay for the new securities—or will make the new sums which they lend available to the borrowers—by adding these sums to the deposits of those who are selling securities to them or borrowing from them. So long as people do not wish to cash any of these new deposits but only to make check payments, the member banks will not lose any of their extra reserves. In these circumstances they will go on lending more or buying more securities until the increase in their deposit liabilities is $100 millions, or ten times the increase of $10 million in their cash assets. In other words, they will buy securities or make new advances to the sum of $90 millions.[1]

Precisely the same result can be achieved by means of varying the legal reserve which member banks are required to maintain. Until 1935 the reserves had been fixed by law at 3 per cent for time deposits and 7, 10, and 13 per cent, depending upon the location of the bank, for demand deposits. By the Banking Act of that year, however, the Reserve Banks were given the power to vary these requirements between the former level and twice that level. The effect of lowering average reserve requirements from 15 per cent, say, to 10 per cent would clearly be to free a third of the member banks' reserves against demand deposits, which

1. We have simplified the discussion by ignoring time deposits; i.e., of deposits not subject to check. In the normal case a part of the increase in total deposits for which the Reserve Banks are responsible will be kept in the form of time deposits; and to the extent that this is done the expansion in demand deposits will be less, and the expansion in total deposits (i.e., demand and time together) will be greater, than we indicate. It is a disputed point whether time deposits, which are roughly a third of the total deposits of member banks, should be counted as 'money.'

could then be used to expand these deposits by 10 times the amount of the freed reserves.

By either of these methods then—the purchase of securities or the lowering of member bank reserve requirements—the Federal Reserve Banks can induce the member banks to make additional loans and investments and thereby increase the total volume of bank deposits—the most important form of money—in existence. But this is only true with three important provisos. In the first place the member banks may nullify the action of the Reserve Banks by allowing their reserve ratios to rise above the legal minimum. If the Reserve Banks have purchased $10 millions of securities, as in our example, when the average reserve ratio is 10 per cent, the member banks may simply increase their margin of safety by holding 'excess reserves' in preference to lending the $90 millions required to keep their reserve ratio constant. In normal times this proviso is not important, since the holding of excess reserves involves the banks in financial loss. In times of crisis or depression, however, banks may feel that the legal reserve is an inadequate protection against possible 'runs,' or that there are no earning assets which may be purchased with safety, and excess reserves, as a result, become an important item.

In the second place, the attempt of the Federal Reserve Banks to increase the quantity of money may be defeated by the member banks or the money market reducing their borrowing from the Federal Reserve Banks. The member banks have the right to 'rediscount' certain types of 'eligible' notes and bills with the Federal Reserve Banks; and the Federal Reserve Banks have the right to buy commercial bills, as they do by fixing an 'acceptance rate' and taking whatever bills banks or acceptance dealers offer for sale at that rate. Bills rediscounted are shown as (g) in Table II, bills bought as (h). One or both items have at most times been considerable, and the normal effect of the Reserve Banks' buying securities, in the first instance, is a reduction in their amount. As the Reserve Banks increase credit by the purchase of securities the member banks use their new resources to retire their indebtedness to the Reserve Banks; or the money market, to which the new funds tend to come, finds that it needs to sell fewer bills to the Reserve Banks. The increase in item (i) of the Reserve Banks' assets is thus counteracted, wholly or in part, by a reduction in items (g) and (h), so that the new reserves available to the member banks to serve as a basis for the expansion of their deposits is equal not to the increase in (i) but to that increase *minus* the decreases in (g) and (h). If the Reserve Banks continue to buy securities they can eventually increase member bank reserves, because items (g) and (h) would in time be reduced by such a process to something like zero; but small purchases not only may but are likely to be offset in whole or in part by a reduction in these assets over the amount of which the Reserve Banks exercise inadequate control.

In the third place the public may offset the effect of the Reserve Banks' action if it cashes part of its deposits with the member banks. If the public decides to cash $10 millions of its deposits the member banks must secure this amount of Federal Reserve notes [1] from the Reserve Banks, thus reducing their reserves. Items (c) and (d) of Table I would each be down by $10 millions. This in itself will reduce the reserve ratio of the member banks and will force them, unless they previously possessed excess reserves or unless they borrow additional ones by 'rediscounting' bills with the Reserve Banks, to reduce their deposit liabilities by selling securities or demanding the repayment of loans. The Federal Reserve Banks cannot prevent people from cashing their deposits with the member banks, but it has the technical power to offset any action of this kind. For so long as there are no limits to the amount of securities which the Reserve Banks can purchase they can increase the reserves of the member banks by more than the amount of cash withdrawn by the public.

1. It is assumed for simplicity that Federal Reserve notes are the only type of currency. In fact they comprise about 70 per cent of the total, and the argument would need to be modified in detail only if the other types were considered.

In fact there is a limitation to the amount of securities which the Federal Reserve Banks can purchase by the requirement that they maintain a reserve of gold certificates or lawful money amounting to at least 35 per cent of their deposit liabilities and 40 per cent of Federal Reserve notes. At the present time the gold reserve is so large that the limitation is not an effective one, but it might become so at some future time. A further limitation, which caused trouble during the last depression, resulted from the requirement that only certain types of notes and commercial bills should be used as the security behind that part of the Federal Reserve notes not backed by gold. This was modified by the Banking Act of 1933 to permit government bonds to be used as well, and as long as this is permitted this further limitation is ineffective.

We may conclude that if the Federal Reserve Banks are to have full control of the amount of money in all circumstances they must be assured of four things. In the first place, they should be certain that the member banks will not considerably increase their reserve ratio above the legal minimum; otherwise a purchase or sale of securities by the Reserve Banks or a change in the legal minimum may be offset by action of the member banks. In the second place, the Federal Reserve Banks should have complete control over the quantities of all categories of their assets; in particular, of the bills which they rediscount for member banks or buy on the market. In the third place they should be free from any legal restriction on their purchases of securities or their issue of Federal Reserve notes. Finally, of course, they should have control not of part but of all the money in the system; which would mean that all banks should be members of the Federal Reserve system, and that the Federal Reserve note should be the only form of currency. These four conditions could probably be fulfilled with relatively little fundamental change in the present banking system. In the next chapter we shall revert to the question of the reforms which are necessary to give the Reserve Banks full control over the amount of money. At the moment we shall assume that they have this control, and shall proceed to show how it can be exercised in order to raise or lower the rate of interest.

We have already seen that if the Reserve Banks wish to increase the amount of money they will buy securities and that in consequence of this the member banks will purchase securities or extend their advances to industry to prevent their reserve ratio from rising. This purchase of securities by the Federal Reserve Banks and by the member banks will cause the rate of interest to fall. The increased demand for securities on the stock exchange will raise their price, for the banks can only induce people to sell securities by offering a higher price for them, and a rise in the price of fixed interest securities is equivalent to a fall in the rate of interest at which money can be lent or borrowed. This can most easily be seen in the case of a security which pays a perpetual income with no promise of redemption. Suppose that the annual interest income paid is $3, and the nominal value of the security $100. If the market value fell from this figure to $50 it would be possible to obtain an income of $3 a year by investing just $50; in other words the rate of interest would be 6 per cent. If the price rose to $200, on the other hand, one would have to pay that amount to earn $3 a year; the rate of interest would have fallen to $1\frac{1}{2}$ per cent. If there is a promise of redemption the general rule that the higher the price of the security the lower is the rate of interest will still hold good, although the relationship between the two will be less simple.

The purchase of government securities by the banks with newly created money will, as we have shown, directly raise the price of these securities and so lower the rate of interest yielded by them. But such action will indirectly lower the rate of interest on other forms of securities. Suppose that the yield on government securities is 5 per cent and the yield on industrial securities is 6 per cent. If the banks now purchase government securities with new money, and drive up their price so that the yield on them falls to 4 per cent this will indirectly raise the price of and lower the yield on industrial securities. The people who have sold the government securities to the banks for new money will probably not wish to hold all this money idle in the form of deposits with the banks, where they obtain a relatively low rate of interest. They will seek to purchase securities with the money and may be tempted to purchase industrial securities which still yield 6 per cent in place of the government securities, on which the yield is now only 4 per cent. This purchase of industrial securities will raise their price and so lower the rate of interest yielded by them. But now the people who have sold industrial securities will be holding the new money, and they in turn will not wish to hold it idle but will purchase other industrial securities, the price of which has not yet risen and the yield on which is still relatively high. Thus by a series of repercussions the price of all securities will rise in harmony with the price of government securities, and the rate of interest on industrial securities, i.e., the rate of interest at which industrialists can borrow by the issue of new securities, will fall.

The commercial banks can increase their deposits not only by buying securities but also by lending more in direct advances to industry; and in order to induce people to borrow more they must offer to lend at lower rates or on less adequate security. So in this case again an increase in the amount of money will have the effect of lowering the rate of interest, though it will be the rate of interest on advances to industry and not on government securities which is directly affected. A considerable increase in this type of direct borrowing from the banks is not very probable in the first instance. For industrialists borrow from the banks mainly to finance their holding of stocks of finished goods, of raw materials, and of goods in process of manufacture rather than for extensions of their machinery or plant. The amount of such stocks held by industrialists is probably little affected by the rate of interest at which they can borrow money from the banks for this purpose, but is mainly dependent upon the demand for their products. The interest paid by industries on the money which they have borrowed to purchase stocks is usually only a small proportion of their costs of production, and a fall in the rate of interest on such loans will have little direct effect upon the amount which they will borrow. When, therefore, the banks increase the amount of money, they will have to rely in the first instance mainly on the purchase of securities. But when this action has caused the rate of interest on long-term industrial securities to fall, it will stimulate expenditure on capital development and will increase the demand for capital goods and for consumption goods in the way described in the last chapter. When this happens, manufacturers will have an incentive to produce more and will therefore wish to borrow more from the banks to hold larger stocks. Thus, indirectly, an increase in the amount of money, brought about in the first place by a purchase of securities by the banks, will after a time enable the banks to lend more in direct advances to industry.

A fall in market rates of interest is also likely to stimulate directly expenditure on consumption goods, and this will reënforce the favorable effects of the policy on employment. People will tend to spend a larger proportion of their incomes on consumption after a fall in the rate of interest for two reasons: (i) a high rate of interest probably encourages people to save, and a lower rate would therefore make spending relatively more attractive; and (ii) a *fall* in the rate of interest, as opposed to a *low* rate of interest, increases the value of securities, and it is notorious that many people look upon an appreciation of the value of securities which they hold as a windfall profit which they are entitled to spend on houses, motor cars, radios, and general consumption. The effect of a low rate of interest in stimulating consumption is probably not important in the normal case, but the effect of the appreciation of the value of securities may be considerable, and it is likely to be the first effect of a policy of monetary expansion to make itself felt in the economic system.

If the argument of the preceding chapters is correct the primary object of the Reserve Banks in times of general unemployment should be to purchase securities and to reduce reserve requirements in order to reduce the rate of interest and so to stimulate capital and consumption expenditure.[1] A very great deal can be done not only by the actual policy adopted by the Reserve Bank but by public explanation of the object of this policy. The rate of interest on securities always approximates to the rate which people expect to rule in the future. If they expect the rate of interest on securities to be 5 per cent in the future, it will be difficult to lower the rate much below this figure even if the banks purchase very large amounts of securities; for as soon as the price of securities rises so that the yield on them is appreciably below 5 per cent, people will sell securities in large amounts to the banks. They will then hold idle deposits of money in the expectation that yields will rise and security prices fall again in the near future, so that the securities can be bought back again at a profit. The authorities of the Federal Reserve system could, to a large extent, meet difficulties of this kind by making their intentions clear. Suppose, for example, that a slump had started: they might state publicly and in unambiguous language that they were determined to reduce yields on securities rapidly from a 5 per cent to a 3 per cent basis; that they would almost certainly not allow yields to rise above 3 per cent in the near future, and would reduce them still further if such action proved necessary to absorb labor; that they had the power to reduce interest rates by increasing the supply of money; that they would increase the supply of money, however great the increase might have to be, in order to achieve their object; and that this was practically the sole object of their policy. Such a declaration would cause investors to adjust their expectations about interest rates much more easily, and would therefore diminish the extent to which the Banks would have to purchase securities to lower interest rates by a certain amount.

1. It must be remembered that in fact the policy of the Reserve Banks will vitally affect economic and financial relations with other countries. In Part V we shall conclude that even when these effects are considered the primary object of their policy should be that stated here.

IV

THE CONTROL OF BANKING POLICY

WE have concluded that the banks should increase the amount of
money and lower interest rates when there is general unemployment. In this chapter we shall discuss the degree of control which
the state must exercise over the banks to insure that this policy
is carried out. In particular we must decide whether it is necessary to nationalize the Federal Reserve and commercial banks.
There are three arguments which can be advanced in favor of
the nationalization of the banks; these arguments must be clearly
distinguished, for only one of them is relevant to our present
problem.

The first argument is that it is wasteful and inefficient to have
numerous small commercial banks with competing offices in each
locality. It is argued that if the banks were nationalized and all
the banking business in each locality were concentrated in one
establishment, the business of banking could be carried out at
a smaller cost, since a smaller number of buildings, clerks, etc.,
would be needed to carry out the same total amount of business.
This argument applies to many other forms of business. It is
equally arguable that there are too many separate stores in a
given locality, or too many separate concerns producing electric
appliances for these appliances to be produced as efficiently as
possible. These arguments may be valid, but they have no direct
connection with the adoption of a banking policy designed to
prevent unemployment. Such arguments will be examined in
Part II, where they are relevant.

Secondly, it is argued that the banks make unduly large profits and should therefore be owned by the state, to whom such income should belong. That argument would apply chiefly to the
commercial banks, since the Federal Reserve Banks under exist-

ing law are forbidden to pay more than 6 per cent on their stock. It may be a valid argument, but it applies with equal force to the national ownership of the capital invested in any profitable industry. It will be examined in Part III, in which the distribution of income is discussed. The argument has no direct connection with the question whether the banks can be made to carry out the policy already suggested for the prevention of unemployment.

Thirdly, it is argued that unless the banks are nationalized it will be impossible to insure that they adopt the policy of expansion which is necessary to prevent unemployment. It is this argument with which we are now concerned.

It is, of course, essential that in times of unemployment the Federal Reserve Banks should adopt the appropriate policy for increasing the amount of money and lowering interest rates. This requires, in the first place, that there must be a ruling body capable of adopting a unified co-ordinated policy and of enforcing it upon the several Reserve Banks. It is not clear that this condition is fulfilled under existing law, which divides responsibility for control among several different authorities. The rates at which the Banks discount bills are jointly determined by the Reserve Banks and the Board of Governors. Policy regarding purchases and sales of securities is in the hands of an Open Market Committee, on which both the Reserve Banks and the Board of Governors are represented. Reserve requirements for member banks are fixed by the Board of Governors. In addition the Treasury, with its Exchange Stabilization Fund and its inactive gold account, is in a position to control the gold reserves of the Federal Reserve Banks, and therefore within limits its credit policy. This division of responsibility is clearly undesirable from our point of view, but it is probably less serious than it seems. The Board of Governors would doubtless, in most cases, be able to enforce its will upon the other policy-making authorities, and this would be the case, *a fortiori*, if it were acting in agreement with the Treasury. Furthermore, it seems probable that under its present constitution the system would adopt any policy upon which the ad-

ministration insisted; or that, if it refused, steps could be taken
to insure that it did so. As a first essential point we must assume
that either the Reserve Banks are able and willing to adopt the
appropriate monetary policy or that the administration is in a
position to insist upon the adoption of this policy. And it must
not be forgotten that in order to mitigate unemployment by
banking policy this is all that matters; who controls or owns the
Reserve Banks and who receives the profits are for this purpose
irrelevant.

We are left with the more difficult question whether the Reserve Banks, assuming that they are right-minded and acting in
unison, can enforce their monetary policy upon the other financial institutions in the country. There are five possible difficulties
which they may encounter. They may be prevented from carrying out their policy—

(a) because of its effects upon the foreign exchanges and their
    gold reserves;
(b) because a substantial proportion of the commercial banks
    and of the note issue lies outside their control;
(c) by the action of the member banks;
(d) by the action of the money market;
(e) by the fact that their policy might make it impossible for the
    member banks to cover their costs.

The first difficulty cannot be discussed here, because it is impossible to deal with the effects of internal monetary policy upon
the rate of exchange and upon the amount of gold exported without a full discussion of international economic problems. An attempt to meet this point will be made in Part V of this book.

The second difficulty is one to which we referred in the previous chapter (pp. 22 and 29–30). The existence of State banks outside the Federal Reserve system is an anomaly of federal government, and one for which it is difficult to discover a rational ex-
cuse. In fact, however, some 85 per cent of commercial bank deposits are in banks within the system, and the limitation upon

control resulting from the existence of the other 15 per cent is probably not serious. The variety of currency issues for which the Federal Reserve Banks are not responsible is also an historical anomaly, but again one which is not of great practical importance. Seventy per cent of currency notes are Federal Reserve notes, and the other 30 per cent are in relatively fixed supply.

The third difficulty is that the banks which are members of the system are in a position to defeat the policy of the Reserve Banks in at least two ways. They may, as we saw in Chapter III (p. 28) allow their cash reserves to increase above the minimum, and thus offset a purchase of securities or a lowering of reserve requirements by the Reserve Banks. It would not be necessary to nationalize the member banks for this reason provided that it could be insured that they would not permit their reserves to vary greatly from the minimum. This might be done by agreement, or by punitive taxation which would be imposed when excess reserves exceeded a certain maximum. The difficulty is that in times of crisis the banks believe that the minimum reserve is not adequate for safety; and a scheme for enforcing maximum reserves would therefore have to be coupled with a genuine scheme for insuring bank deposits. Secondly, the commercial banks may, within limits, defeat the policy of the Reserve Banks by making use of their privilege to borrow from the Reserve Banks by rediscounting notes and bills, and to retire their borrowing at will. The Reserve Banks could control this tendency by resolutely raising their discount rates to such a height that banks would borrow only in emergencies and at financial loss to themselves. Actually they have not followed this practice, but have relied chiefly upon the desire of member banks to keep out of debt to the Federal Reserve and upon eligibility requirements for the bills rediscounted—neither of which has proved very effective.

The fourth difficulty is very similar. As a rule the Reserve Banks have purchased any eligible bills offered them at their acceptance rate by banks or acceptance dealers, which has meant that this important category of their assets was not completely under their control. As in the case of the use of the rediscounting privilege by the member banks an adequate remedy exists in the form of the acceptance rate. By resolutely raising this rate to any height necessary to make sales to the Federal Reserve unprofitable the Reserve Banks could insure that bills would be sold to them only in an emergency and for a short period. But again, they have not followed this practice, chiefly because they have attempted to make the commercial bill a safe and cheap method for business to secure circulating capital; and the result has been that whenever funds have become scarce on the money market the Reserve Banks have had to buy large quantities of bills. If the funds were scarce as a result of a restrictive policy adopted by the Federal Reserve, this purchase of bills would, in part, offset the effects of that policy.

The final difficulty which might stand in the way of the adoption of the proper monetary policy by the Reserve Banks is the possibility that it would make the member banks unable to cover their costs. The banks are bound to incur considerable running expenses, and can only meet these expenses by the difference between the yield which they earn on their assets and the interest which they pay on money deposited with them. If interest rates are reduced to a very low figure it might become impossible for the banks to meet these expenses. Moreover, if the banks are properly pursuing the policy of buying government securities during a slump, even if their price is already high, they may be involved in some capital loss due to these transactions. For, as we shall argue in Chapter VIII of this Part, the banks should sell government securities and raise interest rates if the demand for labor increases too much; and the banks may therefore be obliged to sell at a low price, when the rate of interest is high, government securities which they have bought at a high price.

These difficulties are to some extent illusory. For, in the first place, if the banks purchase a large volume of securities, the fall in their income due to low yields on securities will be counterbalanced by the fact that they are earning this yield on a larger number of securities; and their expenses will certainly not increase in proportion to the increase in their holding of securities. In the second place, when the banks start to purchase securities in order to lower interest rates, they may at first purchase securities at a relatively low price; it is only during the later stages of such a policy of monetary expansion that they will probably be obliged to purchase securities which already stand at a high price. And when the banks start to sell securities to prevent a boom, they may at first sell securities at a relatively high price and only in the later stages, if the boom proceeds, will they be obliged to sell securities at an abnormally low price. It is therefore by no means certain that they will, on the whole, be involved in any net capital losses due to these transactions.

If the banks are involved in serious difficulties of this kind, they might be permitted by agreement among themselves to counterbalance these losses by reducing the rate of interest which they pay on their deposit liabilities, or by levying bank charges on all money deposited with them. Such action may cause people to buy securities with their deposits instead of keeping money deposited with the banks, and this will help in raising the price of securities and lowering interest rates. This policy can only lead to any difficulty if it causes people to hold many more notes and this tendency, as we saw in the previous chapter, could be offset within wide limits by the Reserve Banks. If the banks cannot meet their expenses by these means, it would be better for the Reserve Banks or the government to subsidize their costs on approved principles rather than to abandon the desired financial policy. Such an eventuality is probably remote.

In short, the banking policy suggested in the previous chapter can be carried out provided that the following conditions are fulfilled. The Reserve Banks should control the major portion of commercial banks (preferably all) and the note issue. They must be able to prevent the member banks accumulating large excess reserves. They must be able to prevent, except in an emergency and temporarily, the member banks and the money market from bringing bills to be rediscounted or purchased. And finally, in the remote contingency that this policy makes it impossible for the member banks to cover their costs the Reserve Banks or the government must be prepared to subsidize them during such a period.

All of these conditions could be satisfied with very little fundamental change in existing institutions and customs. On the other hand, the nationalization of the banks would not impede the prosecution of the proper monetary policy, and could, indeed, only aid it. For if all the banks were nationalized and formed into one state monopoly, three of the difficulties discussed above would be capable of direct and immediate solution. In the first place, it would no longer be possible for variations in the member banks' cash reserve ratio to affect the total amount of money. For a unified National Bank could through its own purchases and sales of securities control the total amount of money directly; it would no longer rely upon the indirect effects of its action upon other banks. Secondly, the problem of excessive use of the rediscounting privilege by private independent banks borrowing to make a profit would automatically be solved. Thirdly, such a bank could concentrate solely on exercising the desired control of interest rates through varying the total supply of money. It would attempt to cover its costs by lowering the rate of interest which it offered to pay on its deposit liabilities; but the effect of banking action on the total volume of industrial employment is so important that the making of a profit would be a secondary consideration. If the bank in any period could not carry out the requisite monetary policy without making a loss, it would be necessary for the government to meet this loss from the budget. As we have seen, any loss is improbable and would, in any case, not be very considerable; and such a loss is a small price to pay to cure or even to mitigate unemployment.

We may conclude that the nationalization of the banks would in certain respects simplify the adoption of the proper monetary policy. But the proper monetary policy *can* be carried out with a minimum of change in the present legal position of the banks. Two morals are to be drawn from this conclusion. In the first place, the question of the nationalization of the banks must be decided largely on grounds other than those which are relevant here.[1] In many respects the case for the nationalization of the banks is the same as the case for the nationalization of any other industry; this case is examined in Parts II and III. Secondly, it is not necessary to wait for any change in the legal position of the banks before banking policy is used vigorously for the prevention of unemployment. Indeed nothing is more important than the realization that for this purpose all that matters is what policy the banks pursue; who owns or controls them matters only in so far as it affects that policy.

1. The important practical question as to whether chain or branch banking should be permitted or encouraged must also be decided largely on grounds irrelevant to the present discussion. From the point of view of a policy designed to mitigate unemployment, however, it is essential that banks should not fail during depression, and it seems probable that reform along these lines would make failure less likely. As much could be accomplished, with the thousands of small banks which exist at present, by a genuine and safe scheme of deposit insurance in extension of the plan adopted during the depression as an emergency measure and made permanent in the Banking Act of 1935.

V

THE PLANNING OF PUBLIC WORKS

It must not be thought from what has already been said that no action other than the monetary action already described will be necessary to preserve a high level of employment. This is almost certainly not the case; for the working of monetary action may be too weak and too slow, and there are other important features of a slump which we have not yet noticed. It is appropriate to outline the course of a slump in order to see why it is not always certain that the monetary authorities can prevent it merely by lowering interest rates.

Let us suppose that for some reason or another—e.g. because some particularly important work of capital development is completed—there is an initial fall in expenditure on capital goods. This will mean, in the absence of monopoly or price 'rings,' that their price begins to fall. The fall in the incomes of those producing these capital goods will mean a decrease in expenditure on consumption goods, so that the price of consumption goods also falls. For the same reason industry as a whole will become less profitable, so that the price of common stocks will fall. But this downward movement in all money prices will itself cause a strong incentive to reduce money expenditure still further; for when prices are falling every one will wish to postpone expenditure and to hold money in anticipation that goods can be purchased more cheaply in the future. In particular, merchants will sell stocks of goods and will postpone their replacement, since they are falling in money value. Companies will postpone investment in machinery, both because industry is less profitable and because they expect to be able to purchase machines at a lower price in the future. Private individuals, since the price of common stocks is falling, will sell them and hold money instead, and

43

may postpone their purchases of durable consumption goods such as motor cars in the hope that they will become still cheaper. All these factors will add still further to the fall in prices.

The depression might possibly have been prevented at the outset if the banks had immediately and drastically lowered interest rates. For this would tend to cause business men to borrow money for further capital development, and consumers to spend a larger proportion of their incomes. But there are three reasons why banking action designed to lower interest rates may not be sufficient alone. In the first place, the purchase of securities by the banks will only affect the rate of interest on industrial securities after a lapse of time (cf. Chap. III, pp. 31–3), so that some immediate diminution in expenditure on capital development will be hard to avoid. Secondly, even if interest rates all fall at once, it will take time for business men to plan the new development schemes which have now become profitable. Thirdly, if for either of the previous reasons the banking policy does not have an *immediate* effect on expenditure on capital goods, prices will begin to fall; and as soon as prices begin to fall, the rate of interest itself will lose much of its power of control over the amount spent on new capital goods. People will postpone expenditure on capital development even if the rate of interest is low; for they will expect to be able to install the equipment at a lower cost in the future. When commodity prices are falling, merchants will be unwilling to hold large stocks of goods even if the rate of interest at which they can borrow money is very low; in the expectation of a fall in money prices they will postpone their orders for goods and reduce their stocks to a minimum.

But if at this point Federal, State, and municipal governments decide to borrow for public works and so spend more on capital goods, they will thereby stop the fall in the price of capital goods. Such action will maintain expenditure on consumption goods by those producing capital goods, and will therefore stop the fall in the price of consumption goods. Such extra expenditure on public works should be undertaken on a sufficient scale to prevent prices falling. It need only last sufficiently long to enable the banks by lowering interest rates to stimulate expenditure by ordinary private business again, and then the expenditure on public works can be diminished, as that of private business increases. There should, therefore, be large schemes of capital development planned beforehand in such a way that they may be immediately speeded up as soon as a slump starts. As far as possible capital expenditure on prisons, hospitals, schools, asylums, waterworks, drainage, afforestation, housing, town and regional planning, docks, harbors, railways, roads, street railways, bus services, gas, electricity, and any other services under public control should be planned ahead by the government authorities. These plans should be so devised that the maximum amount of expenditure can be undertaken immediately or—perhaps at some inconvenience—put off to a later date.

This does not involve inventing jobs which would not otherwise be undertaken. The reduction of interest rates by monetary policy should be the main permanent instrument of control, and increased expenditure on public works above the normal should be regarded as only a temporary measure. It may be, for instance, that full employment is being maintained with a rate of interest of 5 per cent and with an expenditure of $1,000 millions a year on public works. If, however, the normal amount which governments would spend on public works, if they were not concerned with the effect upon employment, is only $500 millions, then the rate of interest is too high. For the governments must in this case be speeding up their plans or simply creating relief works to maintain an expenditure of $1,000 millions, and they must continue to do so until the rate of interest is lowered. In this situation the banks should increase the amount of money and reduce the rate of interest, thereby stimulating the amount of capital development undertaken by private business and also raising the 'normal' figure of public works expenditure; for, as we saw in Chapter II of this Part (pp. 17–18), normal expenditure on capital development by governments will be stimulated by a fall in interest rates. As capital development undertaken by private enterprise is stimulated, the expenditure on capital development by public authorities may be reduced towards the normal level. There must, therefore, be careful co-ordination between monetary policy and public works policy. As soon as a depression starts, governments should speed up their expenditure sufficiently to prevent it; and the monetary authorities should lower the rate of interest, and should continue to do so as long as public works expenditure has to be maintained at a figure above the normal.

We must examine the effect of this policy on the budgetary position of Federal, State, and municipal governments. We have argued that the expenditure which governments would normally undertake over a period of years should be so distributed over those years that more than the normal amount is being undertaken at one time and less than the normal at another. There is bound to be some disadvantage and some cost to the community in spreading this expenditure unevenly; and we have suggested that governments should spend more in bad times, when it is difficult for them to raise money by taxation, and less in good times, when it is easy for them to obtain a budget surplus. We must now face this problem. Granted that governments should spend more in bad and less in good times, how are they to raise the necessary funds in bad times and what should be their budgetary policy in good times?

By spreading their expenditure over a period of years in the way suggested, there will be certain economies in the actual cost of the work undertaken, to be set against the disadvantages of not spreading their expenditure exactly as they would otherwise have done. When times are bad, prices are likely to be lower than when times are good; for the money demand for goods in general is lower in bad times than in good times. They will therefore be buying on a large scale when prices are low, and buying little when prices are high, so that the cost of the public works undertaken over a period of years will be less than it would have been if the development were undertaken at a steady rate. It must be recognized, however, that the more successful their policy, the less important will this economy be. If the policy is completely successful in preventing slumps and booms, there will be no considerable fluctuations in total expenditure, and so no fall in prices when governmental expenditure is above the normal, and no rise in prices when expenditure is below the normal. There is another economy which they will gain in any case. If the monetary authorities are properly lowering interest rates in bad times and raising them in good times, governments will be in a position to borrow money on better terms in bad times than in good times. From the financial point of view they should borrow for their works in bad times, when they can do so cheaply, and should use any surplus funds which they may have in good times to pay back what they have borrowed; for in good times, when the rate of interest is high, the price of fixed interest securities will be low and governments will be able to buy back their own securities at the lowest possible price.

This policy has other advantages, and to develop the argument we must discuss budgetary problems in somewhat more detail. The receipts of any government—Federal, state, or municipal—can be divided into three heads:

(a) its receipts from taxation;
(b) its profit on any concerns which it owns—e.g. the profit from municipal busses or the profit on the Post Office—and
(c) the amount which it borrows, which we will call its budget deficit.

A government's expenditure can also be divided into three heads:

(a) its current expenditure on the maintenance of existing services;
(b) its expenditure on capital construction; and
(c) the repayment of any sums which it has borrowed in the past, which we will call its budget surplus.

A government's current expenditure includes expenditure on interest on any sums borrowed in the past, on defense, on education, on police, on unemployment benefit, etc., in so far as this expenditure does not involve capital development. Its capital expenditure includes all expenditure on capital development, such as the construction of new roads.

A government's tax receipts and profits will automatically fall in bad times. The receipts of the government, for example, from income tax and surtax do not depend solely upon the rate of tax levied on each dollar of income, but also upon the amount of income that there is to be taxed, so that in a period of bad trade when money incomes have fallen to a low figure, the receipts from these taxes will be low. At the same time the government's current expenditure will automatically rise in bad times. For example, expenditure on relief directly or indirectly caused by unemployment is an important item in the budgets of Federal, State, and municipal governments, and this sum will rise in bad times. This may be offset to some extent by the fact that in bad times prices are likely to be lower than in good times, so that economies may be achieved in some items of current expenditure by purchasing at lower prices. But experience shows that in bad times most governments find it at the same time more difficult to raise revenue by taxation or from state enterprise, and also more difficult to resist claims for increased current expenditure.

In spite of this we have suggested that capital expenditure should be at its highest in bad times, so that the government's budget surplus will fall to a low figure or be turned into a deficit. This is, in fact, a sound policy even from the purely budgetary point of view. A temporary increase in capital expenditure by governments may be necessary to prevent a depression; and, we have argued, the prevention of a depression will itself prevent a fall in ordinary revenue and a rise in their current expenditure. If an increase in capital expenditure causes revenue to be greater and current expenditure to be less than it otherwise would have been, the real cost to the budget of the increased capital ex-

penditure is the sum necessary for this expenditure minus the
rise in revenue and the fall in current expenditure due to the
increased trade activity caused by the capital expenditure. From
the strictly budgetary point of view the government, when it is
contemplating the expenditure of an additional $100 millions on
houses, should subtract from this cost the decrease in its expenditure on unemployment relief and the increase in its receipts
from income tax due to the fact that this extra expenditure will
increase employment and taxable income. In this respect the
government's budget differs from that of an individual. If
Mr. Smith spends more on developing his business, he may indirectly increase the amount spent on his own product, and so
the size of his own income, by increasing the purchasing power of
those who are employed on the development work. But since
Mr. Smith's product is only one among a very large number on
which the increased purchasing power may be spent, he will
quite rightly neglect this as of no importance in his calculations.
But the government knows that for every extra dollar of income
its tax receipts will rise and that for every extra man employed
its expenditure will fall, and it should therefore take account of
the increased tax receipts and reduced expenditure on unemployment relief which will be caused by its capital expenditure. The
cost to the budget of increased public works expenditure is less
than the actual sum which must be spent directly on these works.

Granted that expenditure on public works should be increased
in bad times, why should the necessary funds not be raised by
taxation, e.g. by raising the income tax or by the imposition of a
sales tax, instead of by borrowing? The answer is that if these
extra funds are raised by additional taxation, the taxpayers may
meet this burden by reducing their expenditure on consumption
goods. In as far as this happens, nothing will be achieved by the
public works policy; for the increased governmental expenditure
will be offset by the diminished expenditure of private individuals on consumption goods, and the total demand for commodities will remain unchanged. It is also possible that the higher

rates of taxation will diminish the net return which can be expected on business extensions and so discourage private individuals from borrowing money for expenditure on capital development.[1] If governments raise the necessary funds by borrowing, these disadvantageous effects can be avoided, provided that the banks prevent any rise in interest rates. For, provided that interest rates do not rise, private individuals will have no incentive to contract their expenditure on capital development; and since they are not being taxed more heavily, they will not restrict their expenditure on consumption goods.

Governments should therefore plan their budgets so that in years of full employment their receipts from taxation and from trading profits are sufficient to cover both their current expenditure and their 'normal' expenditure on capital development and to leave that budget surplus which on other grounds it is considered proper to devote to debt redemption. While a public authority can properly plan to reduce its debt at a certain rate over a period of good and bad years, it should allocate a large sum to debt redemption in good years and should be willing, if necessary, to face a budget deficit in bad years.

At present the Federal government budgets for the same sinking fund (i.e. for the same budget surplus for debt redemption), in good years and bad years alike—though the force of circumstances has made it impossible for this to be maintained except as an accounting device during the last depression. We have shown that the government should budget for a large surplus in good times and for a small surplus or for a deficit in bad times. If the surplus of good times is sufficiently great, the debt will be reduced just as quickly in this way; and at the same time the government will be pursuing a policy which is more easily maintained (since a surplus is more easily achieved in good times), and which will be most effective in preserving a high level of employ-

1. The effect of a high rate of income tax in diminishing the incentive to spend money on capital development is discussed in Part III, Chapter IV (pp. 253 and 254).

ment. If the banks lower interest rates in bad times, the government will be borrowing new money or buying up its own securities on a small scale when interest rates are low and the price of its securities are therefore high; and it will be buying up its own securities on a large scale, when interest rates are relatively high and the price of its securities is therefore low. A given sum spent on debt redemption over a period of years on this principle will therefore reduce more debt than if it were spread evenly over good and bad years. It should be possible to devise a scheme by means of which this principle would operate automatically. For example, the sum of two billion dollars a year might be set aside in the Federal budget to be used either for debt redemption or for public works. The whole of this sum would be spent on debt redemption when unemployment fell below a certain standard figure; but as unemployment rose above this figure part of this two billions would be used for public works. The proportion to be so used would rise on a fixed scale with every rise in the percentage of workers who were unemployed.

We have now shown the necessity for the planning of a certain amount of capital development in such a way that it can be postponed or speeded up as circumstances require. Governments must provide some incentive for the planning and execution of development on these principles. For these purposes a National Investment Board [1] might be set up with the following duties and powers:

(a) The National Investment Board should encourage or require all bodies—such as State and municipal governments, public utility concerns, and nationalized industries—over which the government has any control, to plan their capital development for some years (e.g. three to five years) ahead. The plans for the more distant years cannot be as detailed or as definite as those for the immediate future, and they would continually be subjected to detailed and even fundamental alteration. The govern-

1. Much of the work could more advantageously be done by subsidiary regional boards along the lines of the Tennessee Valley Authority.

ment should itself plan ahead its own expenditure on capital development, and should inform the National Investment Board of these plans.

(b) The National Investment Board should invite any private industries of importance to co-operate in the scheme by planning their development ahead for a period of years and by supplying to the Board information about the size and nature of these plans.

(c) Each body or industry co-operating in the scheme should be requested to plan its development on the assumption that there will be full employment in the future and the full normal purchasing power associated with full employment. For if the government is successful through its banking and public works policy in preventing depressions, this assumption will be justified. This does not mean that each body should assume that there will be no fluctuation in the demand for its services or its product; each body must judge in what way changes in taste, in population, or in the cost of alternative services, will affect the relative demand for its own product. But they should plan for that development which would be justified in the absence of a general depression of trade activity. At first it will be difficult to get bodies to accept this principle. But it is desirable that it should be adopted as far as possible, since it will help greatly to stabilize at the proper figure the amount which people plan to spend on capital development. The more vigorously and successfully the government prosecutes the different policies suggested in this Part to preserve a high level of employment, the more readily will different bodies plan their future expenditure on this assumption.

(d) Assuming that full consumers' purchasing power is maintained, the amount of capital development that any concern will undertake depends upon the rate of interest at which money can be borrowed. We have seen in Chapter II of this Part that this is true not only of industries producing goods for sale, but also of public authorities providing communal services. Each body in preparing its plans should indicate to the National Investment Board at what rates of interest the different parts of its plan would be worth undertaking, so that the Board can know how much development would be undertaken at 5 per cent interest rates, how much more if the rate were only 4 per cent, how much more if the rate fell to 3 per cent, etc. For it can then inform the banking authorities how much the rate of interest must be lowered to stimulate expenditure on capital development by a certain amount. In Chapter VIII of Part II (p. 208) we shall discuss the principles upon which public bodies in charge of nationalized concerns should assess the rates of interest at which different blocks of capital development are justified; and we shall conclude that the nationalization of monopolistic concerns will help to reduce unemployment, because from the community's point of view a larger expenditure on capital development by such concerns is justified at the current rate of interest than would be undertaken if they were left in private control.

(e) The amount of capital development undertaken in any one year can be varied in another way. For example, with the rate of interest at 4 per cent or lower it might be worth while spending $3 billions on the electrification of the railways. It would still remain to decide whether $1 billion should be spent each year for three years or $600 millions each year for five years. Each body should be required to draw up its plans in such a way that the expenditure worth undertaking at any given rate of interest is as far as possible capable of being concentrated in a few years or spread over a number of years. The National Investment Board should be informed of the extent to which such variations can be made, and will then be in a position to vary the amount of money spent on capital development by recommending the postponement or speeding up of such expenditure.

(f) Finally some inducement must be offered to those bodies which are not in the direct control of the Federal government to plan and execute their capital development on these principles. Where the government already subsidizes State and municipal governments and industries like the merchant marine, such subsidies might well be made conditional upon the planning of development on these principles. The principle of such subsidization might be extended. For example, the government might empower the National Investment Board to remit in whole or in part the tax payable by corporations on that part of their profits which they put to reserve if these companies will plan their development on these principles. Or the government, through the National Investment Board, might on certain conditions guarantee the interest on loans contracted by bodies which were willing to plan their development on these lines, and thus enable them to borrow at the lowest possible rates of interest. All industries which are directly controlled by the state can be required to co-operate in this scheme; and an important argument in favor of the nationalization of industries is that it would help to cure unemployment by giving the state this extra power of control over expenditure on capital development. Other arguments for and against the nationalization of industries are examined in Parts II and III; this chapter presents an argument in favor of the nationalization of those industries whose expenditure on capital development is large, if the state cannot obtain sufficient control over the volume of expenditure on capital development by other means.[1]

1. In this chapter and elsewhere in the book the words 'state' (spelled with a small letter) and 'government' are used in a general sense to refer to any political division. Where the State as opposed to the Federal government is meant the word 'State' is spelled with a capital. Wherever possible we have avoided the very important political and constitutional questions of whether the State or the Federal government is the proper agency to administer the economic policies which we find to be desirable. The administration of the policy of public works advocated in this chapter clearly calls for the co-operation of both.

VI

DIRECT CONTROL OF EXPENDITURE ON CONSUMPTION

WE have already argued in Chapter V, p. 44 above, that banking action alone will probably not be sufficient to prevent unemployment; and it was for this reason that we advocated in the last chapter the planning of public works expenditure in such a way that this block of expenditure could be speeded up as soon as a slump started. But there is reason to believe that even the combination of appropriate banking policy and planned public works expenditure may not be sufficient to solve the problem entirely. In the first place, the government may not be able to control a sufficiently large volume of expenditure on capital development unless it nationalizes a large number of industries. Secondly, even if the government has full control over a large volume of capital development, it will not be possible to plan that development in such a way that *all* of it can be postponed or speeded up at will. For example, houses and roads must sometimes be built because they are urgently needed. If a new factory is built in a town the employees must be housed and roads must be laid to the houses. Postponing or speeding-up construction would be possible only within very narrow limits. Thirdly, some time may elapse between the decision to speed up or postpone public works expenditure and the consequent change in expenditure itself. Contracts for a particular scheme of work may have been made ahead, and in any case some time must elapse before the technicians concerned can alter their arrangements for carrying out the work. These arguments can be exaggerated. The various governmental authorities already control a large volume of expenditure on capital development, and, if a determined effort were made, a large part of that development could be planned in the desired way.

But it is still possible that unemployment cannot be completely solved on these lines. This chapter is therefore devoted to the discussion of a third and less orthodox method of controlling the total volume of expenditure. The two methods which we have already discussed—namely, banking expansion and the expansion of expenditure on public works—can only fail because of a time-lag in their application or in the effect of their application. If there is such a time-lag, prices and profits will start to fall; and, as we have seen, once prices and profits have started to fall, it may be very difficult to prevent the further development of a slump. But there is one form of expenditure which should be capable of almost instantaneous expansion, and that is the purchase of consumption goods by individuals.

If, as soon as a slump started, people were given a certain amount of money to spend in any way they liked, the increase in expenditure would probably be immediately effective. We shall discuss later in this chapter how schemes of this kind might be organized. For the moment we can imagine a simple method, in order to examine the main effects of such a scheme. Suppose then that as soon as a slump starts the government prints new notes which it hands over to people to spend as they like, and that as soon as total money expenditure on commodities rises excessively [1] the state levies extra taxes, which it uses to redeem and destroy the notes which it has issued. The effect of such action would be to prevent any falling off in the demand for consumption goods during a slump, even if the total amount spent on capital goods fell off. For this new expenditure by consumers would offset the fact that the producers of additional capital goods were receiving smaller incomes from the sale of their products. But if expenditure on consumption goods does not fall off, then their prices will not fall and the profitability of their production is maintained; for these reasons the slump will not be intensified by falling prices and by the diminishing profitability of in-

1. In Chapter VIII of this Part we shall explain what is meant by an excessive rise in total money expenditure.

dustries producing consumption goods which would normally remove all incentive for capital development in a time of slump. Conversely, if total money expenditure rose excessively, consumers' incomes would be taxed and the money proceeds of the tax cancelled, so that an excessive rise in expenditure on consumption goods would be avoided even if the total amount spent on additional capital goods, and so the earnings of the producers of these goods, could not be prevented from rising. But since the demand for consumption goods would not rise, their prices and the profits to be made in their production would not rise. Thus a cumulative rise in total money expenditure would be avoided.

If this policy is adopted, the other policies which have been suggested in this Part will be made more effective. Both banking policy, by which the rate of interest is controlled, and the policy of planned public works expenditure aim directly at increasing the total amount spent on capital goods. If the total amount spent on consumption goods is directly stimulated, this will increase the profitability of the industries producing consumption goods, and will make capital development in these industries more attractive. For this reason the direct control of expenditure on consumption goods will make the control of expenditure on capital development by banking and public works policies more effective.

The simplest method by which a policy of granting direct credits to consumers might be carried out would be to place them in the hands of the unemployed to spend. For this purpose all the able-bodied unemployed would be brought under a single Unemployment Assistance Board, and no distinction would be drawn between those unemployed who are still in insurance and those who are no longer qualified for insurance benefits. For the purpose of controlling expenditure on consumption goods by this scheme, the benefits paid by the Board to the unemployed should be on as generous a scale as possible.[1]

1. The danger involved in paying benefits on too generous a scale is discussed in Chapter VIII of this Part (pp. 85–6).

In Chapter VIII of this Part (pp. 83-4) it will be argued that it is inadvisable to reduce unemployment by monetary measures alone below a certain volume, which will be called the 'standard' volume of unemployment, and which corresponds to the 'normal' and 'structural' unemployment mentioned in Chapter I, p. 3. To finance the unemployment assistance suggested above, this 'standard' volume of unemployment should be assessed on the principles outlined in Chapter VIII of this Part. Contributions should be levied on all employed workers and on all employers according to the number of workers they employ, as in the existing schemes of many States; but these contributions should be levied at such rates that they would raise just sufficient funds for the Unemployment Assistance Board to cover the expenditure on unemployment assistance if there were only the 'standard' volume of unemployment. The state need make no contribution from the budget to the funds of the Unemployment Assistance Board. When the volume of unemployment rises above the 'standard' and the ordinary receipts of the Board are no longer sufficient to cover its payments of benefit, the difference would be financed by new notes issued by the Treasury and covered by a non-interest bearing debt of the Unemployment Assistance Board to the Treasury. When, on the other hand, unemployment falls below the 'standard' volume, the normal receipts of the Unemployment Assistance Board will be in excess of its payments of unemployment benefit, and the excess of its receipts would then be used to pay off with notes its debt to the Treasury; these notes would then be cancelled. If at any time the total indebtedness of the Board to the Treasury had been repaid, any further excess of receipts over expenditure could be used by the Board to accumulate a reserve holding of notes. These notes would be withdrawn from circulation and would be available, as soon as unemployment rose above the 'standard' volume, to finance the difference between the receipts and the expenditure of the Board without increasing the note issue of the Treasury.

By giving the unemployed generous unemployment benefit and financing this benefit in such a manner that it does not reduce the purchasing power of other individuals, expenditure on consumption goods will not fall during a slump as much as it would otherwise have done. If the funds for unemployment benefit are raised by taxation, the expenditure of taxpayers on consumption goods is likely to be reduced to some extent. If the funds for this purpose are borrowed in the ordinary manner by the sale of new securities at the current rate of interest, interest rates may be kept at a higher level than is desirable, unless the securities are bought by the banks with new money created for that purpose; and in any case the Unemployment Assistance Board will pile up a debt on which interest has to be paid in the future, although the debt is not backed by any asset which yields a return. The proposed scheme not only avoids these difficulties, but also provides automatically an increasing reserve for the commercial banks as long as there is excessive unemployment, so that they will be able to extend their loans and investments and so lower interest rates without any fall in their reserve ratio. The new notes paid to the unemployed will, as they are spent, be paid into the banks by the firms receiving them, and if they are deposited by the banks with the Federal Reserve Banks their legal reserve will be expanded by an equivalent amount. The scheme will have similar advantages if the total volume of money expenditure rises excessively so that unemployment falls below the 'standard' volume. As more labor is employed, expenditure on consumption will not be excessively increased, since the expenditure of wages will only take the place of the expenditure of the unemployment benefit; and this reduction of expenditure by the unemployed will not be offset by lower taxation and so by increased expenditure by the taxpayers. Moreover, so long as the receipts of the Unemployment Assistance Board are in excess of its expenditure, the difference will cause a retirement of notes, and a reduction in the reserves of the commercial banks, which will force them to restrict the amount of money and to raise interest rates.

It may be objected that the above proposals will lead to inflation. The kind of inflation that occurred in Germany after the
War, caused by an attempt on the part of the government to
finance its ordinary expenditure by printing new notes, is to be
avoided at all costs; but the proposals outlined above cannot
lead to similar results. So long as there is a large amount of unemployed labor and of idle capital, the total amount of money
spent on goods should be increased; for, while increased expenditure on goods will cause some rise in prices, yet, so long as considerable cyclical unemployment exists, a small rise in price will
make it profitable to produce on a much larger scale. On the other
hand, an increase in the total amount of money spent on goods
is to be avoided when there is no serious unemployment of labor
and capital; for in these circumstances the increased money expenditure can only cause prices to rise.

In this respect the foregoing proposals must be sharply distinguished from an attempt to finance an ordinary budget deficit
by inflationary measures. For if a government finances a permanent budget deficit by printing more paper money, this must
lead to progressive and inflationary rises in prices as soon as all
factors of production are employed. But these other proposals
cannot lead to a progressive inflation of prices. As soon as there
is only a 'standard' volume of unemployment the issue of new
notes will automatically cease, since the receipts of the Unemployment Assistance Board will balance its expenditure; and, indeed, if there were any further increase in the money demand for
commodities leading to a further fall in unemployment, the proposed measures would cause a strong deflationary movement to
develop. These proposals are, therefore, designed to maintain
and increase money purchasing power as long as serious unemployment exists and as long as such action can cause output and
employment to increase; and they will cause equally strong deflationary measures as soon as the money demand for commodities becomes excessively great.

The plan has been outlined here in its final form. If it is started when the volume of unemployment is not greatly in excess of the 'standard' volume, there is no reason why it should be modified; unemployment benefit can be determined on the most generous lines and the contributions from workers and employers can be calculated to make the receipts and expenditure of the Unemployment Assistance Board balance with a 'standard' volume of unemployment. If, however, there is a much greater volume of unemployment at the time when this scheme is started, the final scheme should be approached by stages; for, as we shall argue in Chapter VIII of this Part (pp. 87–90), there are dangers in reducing unemployment too quickly. If, for example, the 'standard' volume of unemployment was assessed at 5 per cent of the employable population, and the scheme was started when there was 20 per cent unemployment, the contributions and benefits might be balanced first of all for a 15 per cent volume of unemployment. When this point was reached, the scales of benefit might be raised or contributions might be lowered, so that the contributions and benefits balanced for a 10 per cent volume of unemployment; and when unemployment had been reduced to this figure the scheme might be altered to its final form.

This method of financing consumers' credits has two advantages. In the first place, it gives money income in a time of slump to those who need it most, and in the second place, it provides an automatic guide to determine when consumers' credits should be paid. We shall argue in Chapter VIII of this Part that the whole object of monetary policy should be to reduce unemployment to and maintain it at a certain 'standard' volume; and this scheme automatically distributes consumers' credits to the unemployed when unemployment is above the 'standard,' and automatically draws in notes from those employed in industry and cancels them when unemployment falls below this 'standard.'

On the other hand, this scheme has one disadvantage. It is true that with this scheme a *laborer's* income and expenditure would not be much reduced if he lost his job, since his unemployment benefit would take the place of his wage. But the scheme does not prevent all reductions in expenditure on consumption goods, because the income and expenditure of *owners of property* may still fall in times of slump. Suppose that for some reason the total amount spent on additional capital goods falls off. The growth of unemployment in the industries producing capital goods will no longer cause any considerable fall in the workers' expenditure on consumption goods. But the fall in expenditure on capital goods will also reduce the profits made in those industries, so that profit makers will spend less on consumption goods. This will cause a fall in the incomes of those producing consumption goods, so that the profits earned in industries producing consumption goods will also be reduced; and in consequence these profit makers will in turn restrict their expenditure on consumption goods.

Thus the scheme which we have just outlined would not remove all fluctuations in expenditure on consumption goods; and it is therefore worth while to try to find a suitable method by which it could be supplemented. One possibility is that when unemployment rose above the 'standard' volume, the government might reduce the rates of taxation and so increase the spendable incomes of the taxpayers. The difference between the government's receipts and expenditure could then be financed by the sale to the Federal Reserve Banks of non-interest bearing securities either for newly created deposits or for newly issued notes. This would increase consumers' expenditure by the reduction of taxation without reducing the government's expenditure. The new money created by the Federal Reserve Banks would be paid by the government for its normal expenditure to persons who would probably deposit it in the commercial banks, and this would swell the cash reserves of these banks and so help with the execution of the proper banking policy. And conversely when the volume of unemployment fell below the 'standard,' the government could levy specially high rates of taxation, the proceeds of which could be used either to repay any non-interest bearing debt sold in previous periods to the Federal Reserve

Banks, or, if such debt were already all redeemed, to build up a balance of idle money either on deposit with the Reserve Banks or in the form of notes. By such means consumers' credits of any desired magnitude could be administered.

A budgetary policy of this kind suffers from two disadvantages. First there is no foolproof mechanism to determine when taxation should be diminished to allow for a budget deficit or when taxation should be increased to provide a budget surplus. With the financing of consumers' credits through the payment of unemployment benefit the creation or destruction of consumers' income is automatically brought about, as unemployment rises above or falls below the 'standard.' Consumers' credits should be financed through the ordinary budget only if the government is likely to have the power, intelligence, and courage to raise and to lower rates of taxation at the appropriate time. Secondly, even if the government had all the necessary knowledge and power to carry out the policy, there would with present budgetary arrangements be a considerable time-lag between the decision to increase or diminish consumers' income and the full effect of this decision. If there is an annual budget so that rates of taxation are adjusted only once a year, and if certain taxes are paid only once or twice a year, the actual rise or fall in consumers' income effected by the budgetary policy will be determined a year in advance. If unemployment rose unexpectedly, consumers' credits could not be arranged till the next budget; and if unemployment fell, consumers' income could not be restricted by this means till the end of the financial year. The great advantage of the finance of consumers' credits through unemployment assistance is that the benefits can be paid each week and the contributions levied each week on the workers employed during that week, so that each week the volume of consumers' credits is automatically adjusted to the existing volume of employment.

It would, however, be quite possible to extend the plan suggested above for the finance of unemployment assistance in a way which is free from these objections, and which would allow consumers' credits of any desired magnitude to be distributed. As unemployment rose above the 'standard' level notes might be issued by the Treasury and paid to all persons, whether employed or unemployed. The amount could be made to depend on the extent to which unemployment was in excess of 'standard.' For example, suppose that the 'standard' volume of unemployment was judged to be 7–8 per cent of the employable population. In any month in which unemployment was between 8 per cent and 10 per cent, fifty cents might be paid to every member of the community; in any month in which unemployment was between 10 per cent and 12 per cent, one dollar might be paid, and so on. As unemployment fell below the 'standard' level, a special tax might be levied from employers for every man employed, and the proceeds could be used by the Treasury either to redeem the notes previously issued or to hold as an idle balance which could be distributed again as unemployment increased. The tax might also be graduated. In any month in which unemployment was between 6 per cent and 7 per cent a tax of 50 cents could be levied for each man employed; in any month in which unemployment was between 5 per cent and 6 per cent, a tax of a dollar, and so on. Such a scheme would enable any desired expenditure on consumption to be financed without interfering with that relation between wage-rates and unemployment relief which was considered desirable on other grounds, and it would also allow the payments and taxes to be adjusted promptly from month to month.[1]

The objections to measures of this type that they 'really' unbalance the budget indicate, as a rule, a misunderstanding of the purposes of budget-balancing. A private individual must, over a period of years, live within his income, because if he does not he

---

1. The payment of the Soldiers' Bonus in cash in 1936 was a measure of the sort we envisage; except that our payments would be systematic and would not be restricted to veterans or any other single group. It is not important whether the payments are made by cash or check; if by check they would have to be financed by an issue of notes or non-interest bearing bonds to the Federal Reserve Banks.

will be unable to meet his obligations and must appear in bankruptcy court. A government is in a somewhat happier position; if it collects as current revenue less than it disburses it can always either borrow additional funds or, since it controls the issue of money, create new funds. The bankruptcy court is not an alternative, and if there is a sound reason for government's living within its income it must be sought elsewhere. Actually, of course, there is such a reason. An unbalanced budget creates additional private incomes and thus increases the demand for consumption goods and as a result for additional capital goods; it is, in other words, an inflationary force, and if persisted in will lead to a serious debasement of the nation's currency. Governments have learned by long and painful experience that the first rule of sound finance is a balanced budget; and nothing in the above proposals must be taken to contradict it.

To argue, however, that a government should not combat cyclical unemployment, when it exists, by permitting its disbursements to exceed its tax and profit revenues because this unbalances the budget is to sacrifice the end—which is steady incomes at a level representing full employment—for one of the means to that end. Because a budget which is unbalanced is inflationary it should, on the average over a period of years, be balanced. But in any one year there may be other and strong deflationary forces which an unbalanced budget would merely correct—in whole or in part. In another year the reverse may be the case; and the budget would have to be 'overbalanced' to counteract other forces of an inflationary character. If the 'standard' volume of unemployment is correctly estimated the existence of unemployment in excess of 'standard' is evidence that deflation has the upper hand, and should be countered. If the budget is unbalanced, in accordance with the scheme outlined above, only on such occasions, the only possible reason for balancing budgets—the prevention of inflation—will be satisfied.

At the end of Chapter I of this Part we concluded that the total amount of money spent on consumption goods could be increased in either of two ways—by an increase in the total amount spent on additional capital goods unaccompanied by any rise in the proportion of income saved, or by an increase in the amount of income spent unaccompanied by a fall in the total amount spent on additional capital goods. The second method may be accomplished by means of consumers' credits; an alternative would be to decrease the proportion of income saved. It is possible for the government to induce people to spend a larger proportion of their income. For example, by heavy estate duties or by heavy taxes on the accumulation of capital above a certain figure it could make it unprofitable to save so large a part of income. Since a major portion of saving is done by corporations in the form of accumulating reserves, the government could substantially reduce the proportion of income saved, without necessarily affecting the amount of new investment, by heavy taxation of undistributed profits. The tax of this nature imposed in 1936 seems to have had precisely this effect. Moreover, the rich save a larger proportion of their income than the poor. For this reason any increase in the equality of distribution of income will cause a fall in the proportion of income saved, by transferring income from those who save a large proportion of it to those who save a small proportion. In Chapter IV of Part III we shall discuss the effect of different forms of taxation upon the distribution of income and so upon the proportion of income which is saved. Here it is only necessary to point out that by redistributing income through taxation the state can incidentally control the total volume of expenditure on consumption goods. If a situation arises in which there is permanent unemployment, which cannot be cured by lowering interest rates through banking policy because no practicable fall in interest rates will stimulate sufficient expenditure on capital goods, then the only permanent cure of unemployment is to reduce the proportion of income which is saved. In these circumstances, therefore, a more equal distribution of income may be necessary in order to stimulate expenditure on consumption goods sufficiently to cure unemployment. Whether this situation has ever arisen can only be discovered by adopting the banking and public works policies which we have examined in this Part, and so seeing whether or not they are sufficient to cure the problem. Methods of obtaining a more equal distribution of income in order to stimulate expenditure on consumption goods are discussed at length in Part III, where we shall examine this and other reasons for redistributing income.[1]

1. Still another method of stimulating expenditure on consumption goods has been put forward by farm groups and supporters of the agricultural measures adopted by the New Deal, who argue that by increasing the incomes of the agricultural population (e.g. by restricting crops and so increasing the prices of farm products more than proportionately), and so their purchasing power, the money demand for industrial products will be expanded. We have not considered this as a cure for unemployment because the effects of the policy are so uncertain, and may indeed be the reverse of those indicated. It seems probable that the effect of a large crop will be an increase in stocks of farm products carried over, which will have the same effect on incomes and the money demand for consumption as the production of additional capital goods would have. Crop restriction, whether artificial or natural, would have the reverse effect; i.e. it would be deflationary, and would reduce the money demand for consumption goods. Statistical evidence seems, on the whole, to verify this interpretation and to contradict that of the New Dealers. The experience of the United States in the 1920's is evidence that industrial prosperity and agricultural depression may go hand in hand.

WAGES AND UNEMPLOYMENT

AT the end of Chapter I of this Part it was suggested that unemployment might be reduced by one of three methods:

(a) by stimulating the total expenditure of the community on
capital development;

(b) by increasing expenditure on consumption goods without any
diminution in expenditure on capital development; or

(c) by reducing money cost of production without allowing any
diminution in total money expenditure on capital goods or
consumption goods.

We have now discussed the two first methods; and in this chapter
we shall discuss the possibility of reducing unemployment by
reducing money costs of production. Our discussion will be confined to reductions in money wage-costs because, as we shall
show, it is the real wage-rate which is of importance in determining the volume of employment.

At first sight it seems possible to argue that a reduction in
wage-rates will reduce unemployment because it will make labor
cheaper to the employer, who will therefore employ more persons.
But one might also argue that a reduction in wage-rates will *increase* unemployment, because it will reduce the purchasing
power of labor and thereby reduce the demand for goods and so
the demand for labor. It is clear that one at least of these arguments must be wrong, and to judge between them we must distinguish between the many meanings of the phrase 'a reduction
in wages.' For this purpose a clear distinction must be drawn between—

1. the money wage-rate,
2. the money wage-bill,

3. the real wage-rate, and
4. the real wage-bill.

1. By the money wage-rate is meant the amount of money paid to a man for working a particular period of time (e.g. a week). Thus the money wage-rate may be $20 for a man's work for a week.

2. The money wage-bill means the total amount paid in wages in a period of time (e.g. a week). This quantity depends upon the money wage-rate and the number of people employed. If 10 million people are employed for a week at a weekly wage-rate of $20, the money wage-bill for the week is $200 millions.

3. The real wage-rate means the amount of commodities that can be bought with the money wage-rate, or in other words, the amount of goods which a man earns for a week's work. It depends, therefore, upon the money wage-rate and the price of commodities. It will be doubled by a doubling of the money wage-rate or by a fall of prices to half their previous level.

4. The real wage-bill means the amount of goods that can be bought with the money wage-bill and is equivalent to the total amount of goods which wage-earners can buy. The real wage-bill will be increased either by a rise in the money wage-bill or by a fall in the prices at which commodities can be bought.

A 'reduction in wages' usually means a reduction in the money wage-rate, e.g. a reduction from $20 to $15 in the wage paid for one man for a week's work; but it does not *necessarily* follow from this that the money wage-bill, the real wage-rate, or the real wage-bill will fall. Suppose that there were a reduction in the money wage-rate from $20 to $15, and that in consequence of this 15 million instead of 10 million people were employed; then the money wage-bill would rise from $20 $\times$ 10 millions or $200 millions to $15 $\times$ 15 millions or $225 millions. We cannot simply argue that a reduction in the money wage-rate will cause a fall in the money income which wage-earners have to spend; for if it did cause a sufficient increase in employment the money wage-

bill would, in fact, increase. But suppose that the reduction in
the money wage-rate caused so small an increase in employment
that the money wage-bill fell; for example, suppose that in consequence of a fall in the money wage-rate from $20 to $15, employment increased from 10 millions to 12 millions, so that the
money wage-bill fell from $20 × 10 million or $200 millions to
$15 × 12 million or $180 millions. It does not follow that the
amount of goods which wage-earners can buy—i.e. the real wage-
bill—has fallen. For a reduction in the money wage-bill from
$200 millions to $180 millions represents a 10 per cent fall in the
money wage-bill; but if the prices of commodities had fallen by
more than 10 per cent, the reduced money wage-bill could buy
more commodities, so that the real wage-bill or the real demand
of wage-earners for commodities would have risen. And there is
nothing improbable in this; for a reduction from $20 to $15 in
the money wage-rate represents a fall of 25 per cent and this
might be expected to cause some fall in costs and prices. It does
not even follow that a reduction in the money wage-rate will
cause a fall in the real wage-rate; if prices fell by more than 25
per cent when the money wage-rate was lowered from $20 to
$15—though this may be improbable—the real wage-rate would
have risen.

We have not yet proved what will, in fact, be the result of a
reduction in the money wage-rate; we have only shown that a
reduction in the money wage-rate does not necessarily involve a
reduction in the money wage-bill, the real wage-bill, or even in
the real wage-rate. We must go deeper into the connection between wages and employment; and to avoid confusion we shall
not normally speak of 'wages' or 'wage-rates' but of the money
wage-rate, the money wage-bill, the real wage-rate, or the real
wage-bill.

The number of men which any producer will employ depends
upon the real wage-rate which he must pay, or in other words
upon the connection between the money wage-rate which he must
pay and the price which he can get for his product. At any given

time a producer will have a certain fixed amount of plant and machinery; but with this plant and machinery he can produce more or less by employing more or less labor. Suppose that our producer is producing shoes, that he must offer a money wage-rate of $20 a week, and that he can sell his shoes at $5.00 a pair. How should he decide whether it is worth his while employing more labor? If he employs another man, his money wage-bill will go up by $20 a week. If by employing another man he can add 5 pairs of shoes to his output, he would increase his receipts by $5×$5.00 or $25.00, since he can sell shoes at $5.00 a pair. In this case he would find it profitable to employ another man.[1] If the producer can sell shoes at $5.00 a pair and hire labor at $20 a man a week, he is, in fact, paying a real wage-rate of 4 pairs of shoes a week. It will pay him to employ an extra man only if the employment of an additional man adds more than 4 pairs of shoes to his output since only in that case will he add something to his income. We have come to the important conclusion that the volume of employment which a producer will give depends upon the real wage-rate and the extent to which his output would be increased if he employed one man more.

This is a principle of such great importance that it is worth while studying its implications more fully. A producer with a given plant and equipment can produce more by employing more men with it. But after a certain point if he wishes to produce more he must employ more men on the same machine or on parts of his machinery which are not so efficient as the parts which he is already using; when this point is reached, the producer may still be able to produce more by employing more men, but will add less to his output each time he employs an additional man. This is illustrated in Table III.

1. The student of economics will notice that I am assuming 'perfect competition.' This assumption is made for simplicity's sake and my conclusions are not greatly affected by it. For, given the productivity function of labor and the degree of imperfection both in the labor market and the market for the product, the volume of employment will be determined by the real wage-rate, and this is the point which I am making. Imperfect competition is discussed below in Part II.

TABLE III [1]

The Average and the Marginal Product of Labor

A	B	C	D	E
Men employed	Total product	Average product of labor	Marginal product of labor	Real wage-bill
I	10	10	10	10
2	22	11	12	24
3	36	12	14	42
4	52	13	16	64
5	66	13.2	14	70
6	78	13	12	72
7	88	12.6	10	70
8	96	12	8	64
9	102	11.3	6	54
10	106	10.6	4	40

The figures in column A represent the number of men employed. The figures in column B represent the number of pairs of shoes produced a week by the firm in question. Thus we suppose that when 9 men are employed, the output is 102 pairs. Column C shows the output per man. This figure we call the *average* product of labor. Column D shows the addition to the output which is caused by employing one more man; this is called the *marginal* product of labor. Thus we see from columns A and B that if 8 men are employed instead of 7, the output will be increased from 88 to 96, an addition to the output of 8 pairs a week. In other words, the marginal product of the 8th man is 8 pairs of shoes a week, so that the figure 8 is placed in column D opposite the figure 8 in column A.

The figures in column D are important from the point of view of the employer who has to decide whether he should employ more or less men. For an employer will find it worth his

---

1. These figures are represented diagrammatically in Graphs A and B in the Appendix at the end of the book. The reader may measure any real wage-rate on the vertical axis, and read off the volume of employment at that wage-rate from the curve of marginal productivity. Thus, with a real wage-rate of $10 = OA = DC$, the number of laborers employed would be $OD = 7$.

while to employ more men if the real wage-rate is lower than the marginal product of labor and to employ less men if the real wage-rate is above the marginal product of labor. For the real wage-rate represents the amount of goods which the employer must pay to hire one more man—although the payment is made indirectly in the form of a money wage-rate having this real value; and the marginal product of labor represents the amount by which his output would increase if he employed one more man. It will pay an employer to employ another man only if the resulting addition to his output—i.e. the marginal product of labor—is greater than the real wage-rate paid to the extra man employed. If the price of shoes is $2.50 a pair and the money wage-rate is $25, the real wage-rate is 10 pairs of shoes a week. We can see from column D of Table III that in these circumstances the producer will not employ less than 7 men—or he could add more to his output than to his real wage-bill by employing one more man; nor will he employ more than 7 men—or it would be possible for him to reduce his output by less than his real wage-bill by employing one less man.

It is the marginal product of column D and not the average product of column C which is important from the point of view of deciding whether to give greater or less employment. It is true that a rise in the *average* product or output per head in relation to the real wage-rate will increase the total real profit which employers can make on each man employed. And this greater profitability of industry may affect the willingness of the employers to expand their output in the future by installing new capital equipment. But it has no effect upon the employer's immediate decision to employ more or less men with his present capital equipment. What is relevant in this connection is not the absolute size of the profit being made, but the possibility that this profit could be increased by an increase or by a diminution in the number of men employed. And, as we have just seen, it is the relation between the real wage-rate and the *marginal* product of labor which determines this.

Column D of Table III shows that the real wage-rate must fall in order that more men shall be employed, because an increase in the volume of employment causes the marginal product of labor to fall; but it does not follow that the real wage-bill will necessarily fall as well. The figures in column E represent the figures in column A multiplied by the figures in column D. We can see from Table III that if the real wage-rate is 8, 8 men will be employed; the real wage-bill in this case is therefore 8 × 8 or 64. Each figure in column E shows the real wage-bill that will be paid to the number of men shown in column A at a real wage-rate equal to the marginal product of labor shown in column D. At first in our illustration as the real wage-rate is lowered (e.g. from 16 to 14) the total amount of goods paid in wages rises (e.g. from 64 to 70 pairs of shoes a week). In this case the reduction in the real wage-rate will be more than counterbalanced by the increase in the volume of employment that would result from it. But after a certain point in our illustration a reduction in the real wage-rate will more than offset the increase in employment caused by it, and the real wage-bill will fall. Thus if the real wage-rate is reduced from 12 to 10, employment will increase from 6 to 7; but this would cause a fall in the real wage-bill from 72 to 70.

It is probable that in a depression a reduction in the real wage-rate would cause a rise in the real wage-bill. We know from statistical information that during the depression between 1929 and 1932 money wage-rates fell less severely than commodity prices. This meant that the real wage-rate had risen; and as we should expect, there followed a reduction in employment. At the bottom of the depression the real wage-rate was higher than before, so that the man who could still find a full week's employment got more for it in real goods than before the depression. But the reduction in employment had been so considerable that the real wage-bill, i.e. the total amount of goods that wage-earners could buy, had fallen heavily. It is reasonable to argue from this that the opposite process may be expected in a recovery; as prices rise more quickly than money wage-rates, the real wage-rate will fall and employment will rise. But just as a rise in real wage-rates was accompanied by such a fall in employment during the slump that the total real wage-bill was reduced, so we may expect a fall in the real wage-rate during recovery to be accompanied by such an increase in employment that the total real wage-bill will be increased.

If employers always adjust their present demand for labor in such a way that the real wage-rate is neither below nor above the marginal product of labor, it follows that, if employment of labor is left in the hands of private enterprise,[1] there are only two ways in which the number of persons employed can directly be made to increase. Either the marginal product of labor must rise or the real wage-rate of labor must fall. It is impossible to increase the marginal product of labor at will; for the marginal product of labor depends upon the efficiency of the management of the firm, the amount and form of the equipment with which labor has to work, and the technical knowledge and skill of the workers themselves. These things may change relatively slowly, but obviously they cannot be made to change immediately and rapidly simply to absorb the unemployed. The marginal product of labor will be increased by any addition to the capital equipment installed, since this will increase the importance of having more labor to operate it. The marginal product of labor will rise as laborers themselves increase their skill and ability through obtaining better education, training, or upbringing. Most technical inventions will raise the marginal product of labor, though it is possible that some inventions enable capital equipment to be used in such a way that, although there is a rise in the total output produced by a given number of men with a given amount of capital, yet the importance of having one more man at work is

1. Even if industry is nationalized, reasons are given in Part II, Chapter VIII, and Part IV, Chapter II, for believing that the state should continue to pay labor a real wage-rate equal to its marginal product. In Part III, Chapter V, suggestions are made to enable a socialist state to meet the problem of an equitable distribution of income, even if this principle of wage payment were adopted.

actually reduced. Over any period of time in which capital development and technical inventions are taking place, the marginal product of labor will almost certainly be rising. And this means that over a period of years more labor could be employed without a fall in the real wage-rate, or that a rise in the real wage-rate could take place without a fall in the volume of employment.

But at any one moment of time the marginal product of labor is given and cannot be immediately altered. In order, therefore, to increase immediately the volume of employment by an appreciable amount, the real wage-rate must be reduced.[1] But the real wage-rate may be reduced either by a rise in the price of commodities or else by a fall in the money wage-rate unaccompanied by a corresponding fall in prices.

What has been said in this chapter may seem unconnected with, if not contradictory to the arguments of Chapters I to VI. But this is not the case. In Chapters II to VI we were discussing methods whereby the total amount of money spent on commodities might be increased—i.e. by a lowering of the rate of interest or by increased public works expenditure or by consumers' credits. This increased expenditure of money on commodities will raise the price of commodities, and this—provided that the money wage-rate is not raised—will lower the real wage-rate, which will cause employment to increase. Thus the methods discussed in Chapters II to VI all turn out to be methods of lowering the real wage-rate; what we have now to discuss is whether a reduction in the money wage-rate will have the same effect.

1. Certain exceptions to this rule are discussed in Chapter IX of this Part, and there are others. It should be noted that, strictly speaking, we mean by 'real wage-rate' in this context the amount of the product of industry in general which can be purchased with the money wage-rate. A reduction in the real wage-rate in this sense would not necessarily, but in any actual case would very probably, also involve a reduction in the real wage-rate measured in terms of those goods and services upon which laborers spend their incomes. It should also be noted that exceptions to the general rule stated in the text are possible where competition is imperfect in either the labor market or the markets for products; their implications will be discussed in Part II.

Whether a reduction in the money wage-rate will cause an increase in employment depends upon whether it will cause the real wage-rate to fall. This is the precise question to which we must now turn our attention.

Unfortunately no precise answer is possible. The effects of a reduction in money wages are complex and diverse, and it is almost impossible to assess the relative importance of different effects. There are two reasons why a reduction in money wage-rates might be expected to reduce real wage-rates and so increase employment:

(a) If wage-rates were reduced, say, by 10 per cent, and if in consequence all prices were also to fall by 10 per cent, then the real wage-rate would be unchanged; and, as we have seen, there would be no change in employment and output. But with prices 10 per cent lower the total value of incomes and of business turnover would be 10 per cent lower, with the result that people would need to hold less cash in their pockets and less on deposit with the banks, and that each business would need to hold less money against its ordinary transactions. Some of the superfluous cash would doubtless be deposited with the banks; which would induce them, as we saw in Chapter III, to increase their deposits by lending more or by purchasing securities. In so far as people were holding larger deposits than they needed for ordinary purposes they would probably invest some of them in securities. This purchase of securities by the banks and by the public would drive up the price of securities, and so lower the rate of interest, which would cause, in the way outlined in Chapter II, an increased output of additional capital goods and thereby increased monetary expenditure on commodities in general. It seems, therefore, that if all money wage-rates were reduced by 10 per cent that prices would in fact fall by less than 10 per cent, so that there would be some decrease in real wage-rates and some expansion in production and employment.

(b) If producers do not expect prices to fall by as large a proportion as the reduction in wage-rates, they will have, at least temporarily, an incentive to produce more, since costs have fallen relatively to expected prices. For the same reason they may expect to earn larger profits on their capital equipment, which, as we saw in Chapter II of this Part, would stimulate their expenditure on additional capital goods even if the rate of interest had not fallen. This extra expenditure on capital equipment would in itself maintain incomes and expenditure, which in turn would help to maintain commodity prices and would thus justify the producers' expectations that prices would not fall, so that the increase in employment might be permanent.

For either or both of these reasons a reduction in money wage-rates could stimulate employment. But there is a factor which will in part offset this effect. The fall in money wage-rates would, if prices did not fall proportionately, transfer income from wages to profits; and since a much larger proportion of profits than of wages is saved, this transference would tend to diminish expenditure on consumption goods.

There are, moreover, at least three ways in which reductions in money wage-rates might have adverse effects upon employment:

(a) We have given some reasons why a reduction in money wage-rates may in the end lead to a less than proportionate fall in prices and so to an increase in employment; but even in these cases *some* fall in commodity prices is quite probable, and while this fall is taking place every one will have an incentive to hoard money and to sell goods, which are falling in money value. This will directly reduce the demand for consumption goods and for additional capital goods. But it also has serious indirect effects. As long as people desire to hoard money, balances of money will not be considered superfluous, and any fall in interest rates which may in the end result from a reduction in money wage-rates will at least be delayed. Moreover the temporary unwillingness to spend will intensify the fall in prices, and this may cause producers to take a more pessimistic view about the prospects of profits and so to restrict their expenditure on additional capital goods. In consequence it is possible that a cumulative process of depression is started.

(**b**) Secondly, and less important, any fall in the prices of commodities increases the burden of all charges which are fixed in terms of money. There are many such charges, the most important for this purpose being the payment of interest by the government on the national debt and by corporations on their bonded debt. If therefore in consequence of the reduction in wage-rates there is any fall in prices and in money (as opposed to real) incomes, higher rates of taxation will have to be levied on the reduced money incomes in order to meet the interest on the national debt, and if this taxation is levied in certain ways it will discourage enterprise.[1] In a business corporation the normal effect of a simultaneous fall in the money price offered for its product and in all money costs other than interest on its bonded debt would be a mere transference of real income from the owners of its common stock, who are entitled to the residue of the profits after meeting the fixed charges, to the owners of the debt fixed in terms of money. But if the business is depressed and the total amount of its debt fixed in terms of money is large, a reduction in the selling price of its product might make it impossible for it to meet its debts. In this case some firms might be driven into bankruptcy, with detrimental effects on output and employment.

(**c**) We have seen that a reduction in money wage-rates will have favorable effects on employment only if prices fall by a smaller proportion than money wage-rates. But this, of course, assumes that prices are maintained because, for some reason or another, consumers' demand is maintained. It is possible, however, that prices may be maintained for another reason. They may be fixed at a conventional figure, and not reduced even in the face of a fall in demand. For example, toothpaste of a certain brand will be sold at 25 cents a tube irrespective of demand

1. See Part III, Chapter IV.

within wide limits.[1] Suppose that, in the absence of such rigidity of price, a 10 per cent reduction in money wage-rates would have caused some reduction in the total volume of monetary expenditure, but so small a reduction that prices would have fallen by only 5 per cent, so that employment would have increased. If in such a case the prices of commodities had been arbitrarily prevented from falling, and producers had passively followed the practice of producing the amount ordered at these fixed prices, there would have been a reduction in output and employment because the reduced volume of monetary expenditure would purchase a smaller amount of commodities at the unchanged price.   In the real world rigid retail prices and the practice of 'producing to order' are common, and for this reason a reduction in money wage-rates may have an unfavorable effect on employment.

Because the effects of a reduction in money wage-rates are so complex and diverse as to be incalculable it is preferable to rely upon the methods suggested in Chapters III to VI for stimulating employment. These methods, while not uniformly rapid and effective in increasing employment, at least cannot be detrimental to it. There are, besides, serious practical difficulties in reducing money wages. Wage-rates tend to be conventionally rigid and in many cases are fixed for fairly long periods of time by Trade Union agreements. In a democratic state it would be impossible to reduce money wage-rates by a given percentage in all industries at once. We may conclude that, as a means of reducing unemployment, reductions in money wages are not only an inferior measure, but an impractical one.

But we may also conclude from this discussion that increases in wage-rates are unlikely, on balance, to increase employment, and that the theory which maintains that they will do so by in-

1. Tacit or actual agreements among producers are one method of fixing selling prices, but price rigidities are quite possible without such agreements. The student of economics will realize that we are here considering conditions of imperfect competition, which will be more fully discussed in Part II.

creasing 'purchasing power' is almost certainly fallacious.[1] It is true, with the exceptions already noted (see footnote, p. 76), that as long as industry is left to individual enterprise an immediate increase in employment must be accompanied by a reduction in the real wage-rate; and for this reason money wage-rates must not be raised in an attempt to offset every rise in commodity prices if unemployment is to be cured. In Part III we shall examine methods by which inequities in the distribution of income can be rectified without raising real wage-rates above the level required to maintain full employment.

1. This argument might have validity if retail prices were conventionally rigid and therefore failed to rise even though consumers' demand expanded. The reader will see that this is the reverse of the case examined above (pp. 79–80).

VIII

THE PROPER CRITERION OF POLICY

WE have shown certain ways in which the total money demand for commodities may be increased in order to absorb unemployed labor. We are now in a position to explain what are the safe limits to which a policy of expansion can be carried.

The representatives of labor—whether they be the individual laborers themselves or trade union officials—can only demand a higher or consent to a lower *money* wage-rate, though they intend thereby to raise or lower the *real* wage-rate. The workers in any trade are likely to demand a higher money wage-rate if the real wage-rate in that trade is low or if the amount of unemployment in that trade is small. For the lower the real wage-rate, the greater will be their insistence that wage-rates shall be raised; and the smaller the volume of unemployment, the smaller will be the pressure of unemployed workers seeking jobs in the trade, and so the greater will be the ability of those already employed in the trade to insist successfully upon a higher wage-rate.

Suppose that by means of the measures already discussed total money expenditure on goods, and so the prices of goods, were greatly and rapidly raised, so that in consequence there was such a fall in the real wage-rate that all the unemployed were drawn into employment. Since the reduction in real wage-rates and in unemployment would be very great, workers would probably insist on higher money wage-rates in an attempt to raise their real wage-rates again. If the workers succeeded in raising *real* wage-rates—i.e. if the monetary policy adopted did not allow a further rise in commodity prices—unemployment would grow again. If, on the other hand, a further expansion of the money demand for commodities were allowed so that commodity prices rose as rapidly as money wage-rates, unemployment would not rise again.

82

But in this case workers would not have succeeded in raising real wage-rates. Still higher money wage-rates would be demanded, and a still further rise in commodity prices would be necessary to avoid unemployment. To reduce unemployment to a very low level by the expansion of the money demand for commodities might therefore involve an inflation of money incomes and prices, proceeding with ever-increasing rapidity, since all the time workers would be raising money wage-rates in a vain effort to raise real wage-rates.

An expansion of money incomes and prices cannot be dangerous until it reduces the real wage-rate and the volume of unemployment to the point at which the general level of money wage-rates begins to rise. But even if the policy of monetary expansion is carried somewhat beyond this point there is no danger. We have already seen that as capital development takes place, the marginal product of labor will rise gradually. If the volume of unemployment is reduced by monetary expansion to the point at which money wage-rates begin to rise (but no more quickly than the gradual rise in the marginal product of labor due to capital development), there will be no need for a continuous rise in commodity prices to maintain the existing volume of employment. For if the marginal product of labor is rising by 2 per cent per annum, the real wage-rate paid to labor will be rising by 2 per cent per annum without any diminution in the volume of employment; and money wage-rates may therefore rise by 2 per cent per annum without any rise in the money price of commodities becoming necessary to prevent the growth of unemployment.

This rate at which the marginal product of labor is rising gives us a margin within which increases in wage rates could not have harmful effects. The rate could be estimated, roughly, from statistical data, and on the assumption that it would be likely to have something like the same magnitude in the future that it has had in the recent past, it could be made to serve as a practical criterion of policy. We may provisionally define unemployment as of 'standard' size when it has been just sufficiently reduced for money wage-rates to start rising at the same rate as the marginal product of labor. The total money demand for commodities should be raised so long as money wage-rates are rising less rapidly, and a policy of contraction should be adopted as soon as money wage-rates are rising at an appreciably greater rate.

This is probably the most satisfactory single practical indication of 'standard' unemployment, but like all economic criteria it must not be applied automatically, but with discrimination. What we are trying to do is to distinguish 'cyclical' unemployment, which should be corrected by monetary expansion, from 'normal' and 'structural,' which should not be. The distinction between them, as we indicated in Chapter I, pp. 3–4, is somewhat loose and arbitrary, but because the remedial measures demanded are so different it must be made. Our practical criterion will probably serve accurately enough except in periods of abnormal labor militancy, for which allowance must be made. We have assumed that the pressure to raise wage-rates will vary inversely with the extent of cyclical unemployment, and this is ordinarily the case, but it varies for other reasons as well, and it is possible that a wave of successful strikes may raise wages more rapidly than the marginal product of labor when cyclical unemployment is still considerable. This is what happened in the United States in 1936–1937, and in such circumstances the board which is administering our scheme must exercise its judgment in applying the criterion. The criterion should be interpreted as adequate where the upward pressure on wage-rates is due to the diminution in cyclical unemployment only. Stated in other words, it applies assuming conditions in the labor market to be normal, and allowances must be made when these conditions are abnormal; i.e. when labor is more or less than 'normally' militant.

There are certain ways in which the 'standard' volume of unemployment may itself be reduced, though it is not possible for it to disappear completely. In any modern state in which industrial progress and change is taking place there is bound to be some unemployment. The consumers' demand for different commodities will change from time to time, and inventions will take place, which will cause some industries to expand and others to contract. For reasons of geographic location, specialized training, and lack of knowledge of opportunities, labor will take time to shift from contracting to expanding industries, and, at any one time, some labor must therefore be unemployed. A very great rise in total money demand and consequently in all money prices would be necessary to provide full employment in the specially depressed and contracting trades; and for this reason the general level of money wage-rates would start to rise very rapidly if an attempt were made by monetary expansion to reduce unemployment literally to zero.

But, in the first place, it is possible to improve the organization of the labor market so that any laborer moving from a low paid to a higher paid occupation can find an appropriate job, learn a new trade, and move to a new district more quickly. A system of Employment Exchanges could be instituted, more or less on the English model, to bring employers seeking labor and laborers seeking jobs in contact with each other. Other measures of this sort are referred to in Part II, Chapter VII (pp. 184–5). If the organization of the labor market is improved in this way a given downward pressure on wage-rates in the trades and occupations into which labor is moving could be effected by a smaller volume of unemployment, and the 'standard' volume would thus be reduced. Secondly, the 'standard' volume would be reduced if the upward pressure on money wage-rates could be resisted so long as considerable unemployment exists. It should be realized that an immediate and considerable diminution in unemployment must be accompanied by a fall in the real wage-rate. There are other ways of securing a more equitable distribution of income which do not have this disadvantage inherent in pushing up wage-rates, and laborers and statesmen would be well advised to place greater reliance upon them.

It is because of the effect on wage-rates that the payment of unemployment benefit on too generous a scale may cause unemployment. It is sometimes held that it causes unemployment because it makes the unemployed unwilling to work; but even if this were so a remedy is available. The board which is administering unemployment benefits can refuse assistance to men who are not genuinely seeking work. This could be done much more successfully if the board were working in conjunction with a system of efficient Employment Exchanges, which could always inform the worker when a suitable vacancy arose, and thus obviate the danger that he might live on relief in idleness when he might be working. But high unemployment benefits may raise the 'standard' volume of unemployment by making those who are responsible for the fixing of money wage-rates more insistent upon raising money wage-rates, even though there is considerable unemployment; for the higher the scale of unemployment benefit, the less will those in work be concerned with the volume of unemployment when they consider their demands for higher money wages.

In Chapter VI of this Part it was suggested that a generous scale for unemployment benefit should be adopted in order to prevent the demand for consumption goods from falling off when unemployment rose; and the higher the rates of unemployment benefit, the more effective this scheme would be. The doctrine of 'Work or maintenance'—i.e. the principle that a man who is unemployed through no fault of his own should be maintained at a standard as high as he would obtain in work—is both equitable and also desirable for the purpose of maintaining the demand for consumption goods. Nothing stands in the way of the principle except that it might increase the tendency for money wage-rates to be pushed up in spite of heavy unemployment. In order, therefore, for high benefits to be practicable, it is essential that money wage-rates should not be raised so long as a substantial volume of unemployment exists; but that, in these circumstances, measures designed to obtain a more equal distribution of income should be confined to those suggested in Part III.

We have shown on what principles a 'standard' volume of

unemployment may be estimated, and have argued that when unemployment differs from this a policy of monetary expansion or contraction should be adopted to bring the volume of unemployment back to this 'standard' level; but we have not yet shown how quickly unemployment should be brought back to this level. If the 'standard' volume of unemployment is 3,000,000 and the actual volume of unemployment is 7,000,000, a policy of expansion should be adopted. But should the authorities attempt to reduce this 7,000,000 to 3,000,000 in the course of a year or in five years? Just as there are dangers in expanding beyond a certain point, so there are dangers in expanding too quickly up to that point. If an attempt is made by monetary expansion to reduce unemployment rapidly, there will be a rapid rise in prices which must cease as soon as unemployment has been sufficiently reduced. But it is extremely difficult to stop a rapid rise of prices without a subsequent fall in prices and a regrowth of unemployment. As long as the monetary expansion continues the price of consumption goods and of capital goods will be rising; and as industry is becoming more profitable, the price of ordinary shares will rise. This upward movement of prices itself provides a strong incentive for increases in expenditure. When prices are rising no one will desire to hold money, but rather to hold goods or securities, since, if bought and held for a time, they can be sold for a money profit. Every business concern will have a strong incentive to speed up expenditure on capital goods, which will be more expensive in the future; merchants will increase their stocks; business concerns will increase their holdings of raw materials; and private individuals will desire to hold ordinary shares rather than money, and may even speed up their expenditure on such durable consumption goods as motor cars in expectation that they will be more expensive in the future.

If the rise in prices is rapid, therefore, a great deal of expenditure will be undertaken solely because prices are rising; and if the rise in prices stops suddenly all this expenditure will also stop suddenly. This cessation of expenditure is likely to cause the total value of monetary expenditure not only to stop rising but actually to fall. But if the total expenditure falls, prices will begin to fall and unemployment will grow. As soon as prices begin to fall, people will have every incentive to postpone expenditure and a general slump will be hard to prevent. This difficulty can be avoided if prices are allowed to rise only slowly, and if this rise in prices becomes gradually less and less rapid until the point is reached at which unemployment has been reduced to the 'standard' volume. For in this case there will be no very great volume of expenditure being undertaken solely because prices are rising, and, in so far as such an incentive for expenditure does operate, it will be gradually and not suddenly removed.

But there is a second reason why such a policy of moderately slow expansion at an ever-diminishing rate is necessary if a subsequent slump is to be avoided. There are, broadly speaking, two reasons why new capital goods are purchased. In the first place, producers may install machinery of the same character as the machinery which they already possess, because they are employing more labor and wish to equip the new labor with the same capital equipment as the labor already employed. Secondly, producers may install machinery of a new type, because they find it profitable to employ a larger proportion of capital to labor. If the demand for consumption goods is increasing and there is unemployed labor to be absorbed, machinery of the old type will be demanded to equip the newly employed labor, even if there is no fall in the rate of interest at which money can be borrowed for capital development. For the rising demand for consumption goods itself will make it profitable to expand productive capacity. If, however, the demand for consumption goods is not expanding rapidly there will be a demand for more capital goods only if it becomes profitable to substitute capital for labor, i.e. to produce by new methods of production with a larger proportion of capital equipment to labor. Such an incentive can be provided only by a fall in the rate of interest, which reduces the cost of using capital relatively to the cost of employing labor.

If, therefore, the demand for consumption goods is allowed to increase rapidly in order to reduce unemployment rapidly, there will at first be a large demand for capital equipment of the old type to equip the newly employed labor. But as soon as the demand for consumption goods is no longer allowed to rise rapidly, the demand for capital goods of the old type will disappear. For this reason as soon as the rapid increase in money expenditure is stopped, the greater part of the existing expenditure on capital development might cease; and this in turn would cause a fall in employment in the industries producing capital goods, in the price of capital goods, and in the incomes of those producing them. This in turn would cause a fall in expenditure on consumption goods, and so a fall in employment and prices in these industries as well. The cessation of a rapid expansion would itself have led to a contraction in money expenditure and a general slump.

As soon as the demand for consumption goods is no longer allowed to expand rapidly, the demand for new capital goods can be maintained only if the monetary authorities bring about so rapid and considerable a fall in the rate of interest that a demand for machinery of new types is developed equal in magnitude to the existing demand for machinery which depended upon the continuation of the rapid expansion in the demand for consumption goods. But for reasons that we have already discussed such a possibility is remote. The banks cannot immediately reduce interest rates if people do not expect interest rates to fall; and in any case the banks can only indirectly affect the rate of interest on industrial securities, since the banks will, in the main, purchase government securities and will directly reduce the yield only on this type. But even if interest rates do fall promptly, producers cannot suddenly realize what new types of machinery have become profitable or make their plans for such alterations in their methods of production. If there is any delay in turning from a demand for machinery of the old type to a demand for new types of machinery, there will be a fall in total expenditure on capital goods and a slump will occur.

This difficulty can be avoided if unemployment is absorbed at a relatively slow rate, which diminishes as the 'standard' volume of unemployment is approached. If the demand for consumption goods and so the demand for labor is never allowed to expand at a rapid rate, there will never be a very large demand for capital of the old type to equip the newly absorbed labor; and from the very start a considerable proportion of the total demand for capital goods will have to be induced by a falling rate of interest giving an incentive to increase the proportion of capital to labor. If, moreover, there is a gradual reduction in the rate at which the demand for consumption goods is allowed to expand, the demand for old types of machinery will gradually fall off, and the fall in the rate of interest need be only gradually accelerated. There will be no point at which a *sudden* fall in interest rates is necessary in order to stimulate a *sudden* increase in the demand for new types of machinery.

These considerations lead to a simple criterion for the proper rate of monetary expansion. Suppose that there are 1,000,000 unemployed in excess of the 'standard' volume. If in every year, a certain proportion, say 10 per cent of the existing volume of unemployment is drawn into industry, the actual numbers drawn into industry each year will gradually diminish. In the first year 100,000 will be absorbed, in the second year 90,000, and so on. We may conclude that the 'standard' volume of unemployment should be estimated, and that according as actual unemployment is greater or less than this, a policy of monetary expansion or contraction should be adopted. Any expansion should, however, be controlled in such a way—through the control of interest rates, of public works expenditure, and of consumers' credits—that in each year a certain percentage (e.g. 10 per cent) of any excess of unemployment above the 'standard' is absorbed into industry. By this means it can be judged not only whether a policy of expansion or of contraction should be adopted but also whether the rate of expansion or of contraction should be altered.

IX

OTHER METHODS OF REDUCING UNEMPLOYMENT

In Chapter VII of this Part (pp. 75 and 76) it was stated that in a competitive economic system employment could not be immediately increased without an accompanying reduction in the real wage-rate; and it was implied that any reduction in unemployment must be accompanied by a reduction in the real wage-rate. Neither that statement nor that implication was altogether correct. It is the purpose of this chapter to discuss measures by which the government may cause an immediate reduction in unemployment unaccompanied by a reduction in the real wage-rate. These measures can be divided into three groups:

(a) the restriction of hours of work in order to share a given amount of work among a larger number of persons,

(b) the removal of men from the labor market, and

(c) the removal of taxes on employment or the subsidization of employment.

The first two of these methods attempt to reduce unemployment without increasing employment, i.e. to reduce the number of hours a day or the number of years in his life for which a man seeks employment, so that even if no greater total amount of work is done there will at any time be less people seeking work.

Since our present object is to show how unemployment may be reduced without any fall in the real wage-rate, it is convenient to assume that a positive monetary policy is adopted by means of which the price level of commodities is kept constant. This involves the assumption that, by means of banking control over interest rates and of governmental control over public works expenditure and consumers' credits, the total volume of money expenditure is so adjusted that no rise or fall is allowed in the general level of commodity prices. If this is done, real wage-rates will vary directly with money wage-rates; and we can therefore state our present problem by asking whether unemployment can be reduced without a fall in the *money* wage-rate. But throughout this chapter it must be carefully remembered that the measures discussed may of themselves cause some change in the total money demand for goods and so in the general level of commodity prices; we are, in fact, assuming that a deliberate and successful monetary policy is being pursued which offsets any such effect of the measures discussed. We are making this assumption solely to simplify our investigation; it is not suggested that the stabilization of commodity prices is the correct criterion of monetary policy.

In discussing the restriction of hours of work as a means of curing unemployment we must first differentiate between the hourly and the weekly wage-rate. If a man is paid $20 for a week's work of 40 hours, he is being paid a money wage-rate of 50 cents an hour. If the hours of work are reduced to 30 a week, his weekly money wage-rate will fall to $15 provided the hourly money wage-rate is kept constant, or the hourly money wage-rate will rise to 67 cents if the weekly money wage-rate remains $20. If, as we are assuming, the price level of consumption goods is kept constant, in the first case the hourly real wage-rate and in the second the weekly real wage-rate will remain unchanged.

Secondly, it must be decided how the hours worked in a week are to be cut down. Should the length of the working day be reduced? Or should the working day be as long but the number of days worked by each man be reduced? Or should a larger number of shorter shifts be worked each day, so that the working day of the factory remains the same though the working day of each man is reduced? These different methods will affect producers' costs differently. Those who are interested in this problem are referred to a report by the International Labor Office on *Hours of Work and Unemployment* published in 1933. To simplify the issues we shall suppose that the hours worked each day are unchanged, but that the average weekly hours are reduced by giving each man a complete day off every now and then. Thus suppose that the weekly hours are reduced from 48 a week to 40. If a 48-hour week were made up of 6 working days of 8 hours, and this was then reduced to a 40-hour week, the working day might still be 8 hours and the factory might still be open for 6 days in the week, but every individual man would only work 5 days out of 6. By arranging that out of every 6 men employed each man takes a day off each sixth working day, the weekly hours worked may be lowered from 48 to 40, and by means similar to these the average working hours may be reduced in any degree desired.

If all the men employed are of equal efficiency, a reduction of hours of work of this kind should make no difference to the number of men that will be at work in the factory at any time, so long as the *hourly* real wage-rate is the same. If the hourly real wage-rate, the number of hours worked a day, and the number of days in the week on which the factory is open, all remain the same, there is no reason why any change should take place in the number of men the producer employs at any one time. He still employs a certain number of men for 8 hours a day for 6 days in the week, but these men are not always the same men. If the hourly real wage-rate is unchanged, the relation between the money demand price for his commodity and his money costs will not have changed. The only change will be that instead of 5 men being fully employed and 1 unemployed, there will be 6 men employed for 5 out of 6 days. The weekly real earnings of each of these men will, however, be only five-sixths of their previous earnings.

This is a sure method of sharing the same amount of employment among more people. But if the *weekly* instead of the hourly real earnings of labor remain unchanged, the employer will have to pay the same weekly real wage as before to 6 men, although only 5 of them will be working at any one time. To him this is equivalent to a simple rise in the real wage-rate, and will cause a reduction in the number of men put to work in the factory on each day. But this does not necessarily mean that there will be an increase in unemployment.

A numerical example will make the difference clear. Suppose that 500 people are employed in a factory for 6 days a week, and that then the working week for each man is reduced to 5 days a week with such a rise in the hourly real wage-rate that the weekly real wage-rate remains constant. Since the hourly real wage-rate is raised, there will be some diminution in the total number of people at work in the factory on each day in the week. Let us suppose that for this reason the number at work on each day falls from 500 to 450. In this case 540 men must be attached to the factory: on each of the 6 days in the week one-sixth of the 540 men or 90 men will be resting and the remaining 450 will be at work. In this case although the number of men employed on each day has fallen from 500 to 450, yet the volume of unemployment will be reduced by 40, since the number of men attached to the factory will have risen from 500 to 540. But if the rise in the hourly real wage-rate, which was necessary to maintain the weekly real wage, had caused the employer to reduce the number at work in the factory on each day from 500 to 400, then the total number attached to the factory would fall from 500 to 480; and the volume of unemployment would rise by 20.

Thus a restriction in hours of work combined with a rise in hourly real wage-rates will reduce the total amount of work done; but it will decrease unemployment if the rise in hourly real wage-rates does not restrict the total volume of work done beyond a certain point.[1] We may conclude then that it is always possible to reduce unemployment by a restriction of the hours of work without any fall in the *hourly* real wage-rate, and that it

1. It will be clear to the student of economics that the result will depend upon whether the elasticity of demand for labor in terms of the hourly real wage-rate is > or < 1. If the elasticity of demand is < 1, a rise in the hourly wage-rate will cause the wage-bill to increase, and if the weekly wage-rate is unaffected more people must be brought into employment. If the elasticity of demand is > 1, the wage-bill will fall when the hourly wage-rate rises, and therefore with a constant weekly wage-rate unemployment will be increased. For a definition of elasticity see the Appendix.

may be possible to reduce unemployment in this way without any reduction in the *weekly* real wage-rate, if the necessary rise in the hourly real wage-rate does not much diminish the total number of men at work at any one time.

The second type of state action which will reduce unemployment without a fall in the real wage-rate is the removal of people from the labor market. Keeping boys in school longer or paying pensions to persons at the age of 60 if they will retire from employment will reduce unemployment without a fall in the real wage-rate by reducing the number of the young and of the old who are seeking employment. For the volume of employment given depends upon the real wage-rate and the marginal product of labor. Without any alteration in either of these quantities and therefore without any alteration in the volume of employment given, these schemes would reduce the number of people seeking work in the labor market and would so reduce the volume of unemployment.

This conclusion is, broadly speaking, true, though there are possible ways in which it may have to be modified. The financing of the education of the juveniles or of the pensions payable to people over 60 might have some repercussions on the volume of employment given at the existing real wage-rate. Taxes would have to be raised to finance the extra education or pensions. If these funds were raised, for example, by a tax levied on each worker employed, the net real wage-rate received by the worker would be reduced below the marginal product of labor by the amount of the tax. With such a tax, therefore, the real wage-rate would have to be reduced to maintain the existing volume of employment. But if the necessary funds were raised by appropriate forms of taxation—we shall discuss the different effects of different taxes at length in Chapter IV of Part III—there is no reason why the financing of these schemes, even if there is no fall in the real wage-rate, should prevent them from reducing unemployment by the number of persons withdrawn from the labor market.

But there is a second way in which this conclusion may have to be modified. These schemes will remove a certain type of labor from the labor market; the raising of the school-leaving age, for example, will remove all juveniles of a certain age from employment. The real wage-rate and the marginal product of juveniles is different from the real wage-rate and the marginal product of older persons; and if an employer is employing juveniles for a certain job, he is doing so because it is more economical. If all juveniles are removed from the labor market and if the real wage-rate of the older persons does not fall, it may not pay the employers to substitute unemployed older workers for the cheaper juveniles who are called to school. In as far as this happens, it will be employment and not unemployment that is reduced by the removal of juveniles from the labor market. It is conceivable that unemployment will actually be increased for this reason. For in certain occupations older men may be employed side by side with juveniles who are alone capable of undertaking a certain vital part of the job. If the juveniles are now removed from employment, it will not only be impossible to substitute older unemployed workers for them, but it will be necessary to throw out of work the older workers who were employed side by side with the juveniles.

But, in fact, the removal of juveniles from the labor market will almost certainly reduce the amount of unemployment at any given real wage-rate. For, in the first place, it will remove a number of juveniles, who are themselves unemployed. And secondly, it is, in the vast majority of cases, possible to substitute older men for juveniles. It may not pay employers at the current real wage-rate to fill with older men all posts vacated by juveniles who are kept at school, but it will probably pay them to fill some of these posts; and only in rare circumstances will it be necessary to throw older men out of work because they can no longer get juveniles to work with them. The removal of juveniles from the labor market will increase unemployment only if the number of older men who are thrown out of work because they can no longer get juveniles to work with them is greater than the number of juveniles previously unemployed plus the number of posts vacated by juveniles and refilled by older men.

The third way in which unemployment can be diminished without any reduction in the real wage-rate is through the removal of taxes directly levied on employment or through the subsidization of employment. By these means the real wage-cost which the employer has to pay for each man employed may be decreased without affecting the real wage-rate received by the worker. Suppose that under an unemployment insurance scheme the employer and the worker have to contribute 50 cents each a week. If the money wage-rate is $20 a week the worker receives only $19.50, since 50 cents a week is deducted from his wage as a contribution towards the unemployment insurance fund; while the employer has to pay $20.50 for every additional worker, since he must contribute 50 cents for each worker employed. This is not only true of contributions levied for an unemployment insurance fund, but also of any other contributory insurance schemes for health, pensions, etc. When the Federal social security program becomes fully operative the total amount levied in respect of each man employed will be considerable. Suppose that the $1 levied on each man employed for the payment of unemployment benefit were raised by a different form of tax which does not vary directly with the number of men employed, e.g. by a tax on industrial profits. Then the amount which an employer has to pay for each additional worker could be reduced by $1 a week without any reduction in the amount actually received by each worker, so that it would pay to employ more men at the same real wage-rate.

But this principle might be extended. Suppose that the wage-rate is $20 and that the state pays a subsidy of $2.50 a week to employers for every worker employed and raises the funds for this subsidy by a tax on profits. In fact the state is giving to employers in the form of the subsidy exactly the same amount which it takes from them in the form of the tax on profits; but nevertheless it will cause an increase in employment at a given real wage-rate. For each individual employer knows that for every additional laborer employed he will add only $15 to his costs. Since the amount which he must pay in taxation on his profits does not depend upon the number of men he employs, each employer will take on another man until the addition to his receipts from the sale of the extra product has fallen from $20 to $15. Thus the workers will get a wage-rate of $20, but will be employed up to the point at which the value of their marginal product is only $15. It is sometimes suggested that for every extra man employed employers should receive as a subsidy from the unemployment insurance fund the whole or part of the amount which would have been paid to the man if he were unemployed. And the argument of this paragraph shows that such action would cause an increase in the volume of employment at any given real wage-rate received by the worker.

There are, however, certain administrative difficulties in the operation of this scheme. In the first place, if it were simply stated that for every man employed after a certain date a subsidy of $2.50 a week would be paid, employers would immediately dismiss men in order to employ them again in the near future to qualify for the subsidy. This difficulty could be surmounted in the following way. If the scheme were started in January 1938, an arbitrary date in the past—say January 1937—would be chosen. Each employer would be told that for every man employed above the number he was employing in January 1937 he would receive the subsidy from the unemployment insurance fund. If this were done, no one would have an incentive to dismiss men in order to qualify for the subsidy on a larger number of workers.

There is a second difficulty of the same nature. In order that the funds paid in subsidy of wages should be most profitably used, they should be paid only on the wages of those workers who would not have been employed had the subsidy not been paid. In the course of time some industries will expand and others will contract, because of inventions which substitute oil for coal or motor cars for carriages, or because of changes in taste and fashion, which diminish the output of crinolines and increase that of athletic shorts. Further, even if there is little change of this kind as between different industries some firms will decline owing to change of management leading to decay, while others will expand; some firms will disappear entirely, and others will take their places. For this reason as time goes on there will be less and less employment in the actual firms in existence in January 1937—or whatever date is chosen as the fixed reference date —and more and more employment will be given in new firms or in old firms which have expanded since the fixed reference date, so that a number of employers will qualify for the subsidy on a large amount of labor which they would in any case have employed. After a considerable period of time the vast majority of employment might qualify for the subsidy, which could no longer, therefore, be met out of the ordinary unemployment insurance fund.

The only way to overcome this difficulty would be to revise the fixed reference date from time to time. But the more frequently the reference date is revised, the less effective will the subsidy become. If, for example, an employer was employing 100 men in January 1937, he might employ 110 men in January 1938 because he is promised a subsidy of $2.50 a week on each man employed in addition to the number employed in January 1937. It is possible that in January 1939 little change has taken place in his position and that he would again be willing to employ 100 men without the subsidy or 110 with the subsidy of $2.50 a week on each of the additional 10 men. But if the fixed reference date has been changed from January 1937 to January 1938, he will be promised a subsidy only on any men he employs in addition to the 110 he was employing in January 1938. In these circumstances he would qualify for no subsidy and would reduce his employment again to 100. It is impossible to discover exactly how many men each employer would have employed at each date without a subsidy and then to offer the subsidy on every additional man employed. Some arbitrary reference date must be taken, and this date must be revised from time to time, though the scheme will be less efficient than it would be if all the necessary information could be obtained. But in spite of these defects a scheme of this kind might be an important aid in reducing unemployment without reducing the real wage obtained by the workers.

We have seen that it is possible to reduce the volume of unemployment without a fall in the hourly real wage-rate by restricting the hours of work worked by each man, by taking some persons off the labor market, and by removing taxes on employment or by subsidizing employment. But there is an important reason for being very careful about the use of these methods. In order that people shall be as well off as possible, they must choose the proper balance between work and leisure, and, as we shall argue in Part IV, Chapter II, this balance will be affected by all the policies outlined in this chapter. There may be special reasons for adopting these policies in order to alter the balance between work and leisure, but where the effects on this balance are objectionable it would be best not to adopt them in order to reduce the volume of unemployment. Unemployment can always be reduced by expanding the total money demand for commodities by the measures suggested in Chapters II to VI of this Part; and the decision whether to employ these other methods in a supplementary capacity can be made on the basis of their merits as devices for achieving the right balance between work and leisure.[1]

1. In Part II, Chapter VII, other ways in which employment can be increased without any reduction in the real wage-rate will be discussed. In industries in which the labor market or the market for the product is imperfect, the removal of the imperfection will increase the employment available at a given real wage-rate. No exception can be taken to the raising and fixing of wage-rates by Trade Unions in cases in which the labor market is imperfect provided that the wage is fixed at a level which permits the attainment of full 'standard' employment.

Part II

COMPETITION AND MONOPOLY

I

THE MEANING OF PERFECT COMPETITION

IN Part I of this book we discussed how all the factors of production may be brought into employment. In this Part we shall assume that all the factors of production are employed at making something, and shall discuss how they may be attracted to the production of those things which consumers most desire. Our first task is to see what determines which things will, and which things will not, be produced in an economic system in which there is competition between producers and in which property is owned and economic decisions are made by private individuals.

A great deal is written about the advantages of competition. The theoretical arguments in favor of such a system are strong and must be carefully studied; but most of these arguments rest upon a tacit assumption that there is 'perfect competition' in the economy. We must, therefore, at the outset explain what is meant by perfect competition, in order to understand the advantages of such a system. In Chapters IV to VI of this Part we shall study how competition in the real world departs from the perfection of the theoretic system discussed in this chapter.

The study of a perfectly competitive system is important for two reasons. First, it is impossible to understand the many arguments which are based on the tacit assumption of perfect competition unless we know exactly what a perfectly competitive system implies. But secondly, apart from giving an understanding of the text-book system, this study reveals certain fundamental principles which it is important to understand before choosing between different economic policies.

Economic activity is made up of a process of buying and selling commodities and services. These may be bought with and sold for money or exchanged for other things, i.e. bought with and sold for other commodities. The price of one thing is the amount of other things which can be obtained for the thing sold, and this price is usually expressed in a modern economic system in terms of money. Consumers and producers buy and sell commodities for money. Laborers and employers buy and sell the services of labor, and the money wage-rate is the price of labor. Lenders and borrowers buy and sell the use of a loan of money for a period of time, and the price of a money loan is the rate of interest which is paid for it.

We say that competition is perfect when two conditions are fulfilled:

1. when there is no artificial restriction upon the movement of factors of production from occupation to occupation in search of the highest reward, and

2. when no single unit of control—i.e. no single individual or corporation which is deciding to buy or to sell something— can by its own action appreciably affect the price of the thing bought or sold.

1. The first condition implies that there are no artificial restrictions preventing labor from moving from a low paid to a highly paid occupation, or preventing owners of capital and land from lending these factors to those producers who offer the highest rate of interest or rent, or preventing producers of raw materials from selling their products to those who offer the highest price for them, or preventing new producers from setting up a firm in any industry in which the highest profits are to be obtained. We may give two examples of the artificial restrictions which we are at the moment assuming away. First, a Trade Union or professional body may limit the number of new persons who can enter a particular occupation by restricting the number of apprentices or by charging unnecessarily high entrance fees to the profession, in order to maintain earnings in the occupation above the level of earnings in similar occupations. Secondly, the

state may limit by license the number of producers who are allowed to produce a certain commodity.

2. The second condition needs more consideration. It implies that there is a large number of buyers and a large number of sellers, buying and selling identically the same article or service and each knowing the price at which others are buying and selling. An example will make this clear. Suppose that there is a large number of independent farmers producing wheat of a given quality and a large number of independent buyers of wheat, and that every farmer knows the price which every buyer is paying and every buyer knows the price at which every farmer is selling. The first consequence of these conditions is that all wheat will be sold at the same price at any given time. For if different prices were quoted in the market, the farmers would sell their wheat only to the buyers who were offering high prices, while buyers would purchase only from the farmers charging low prices, and all differences in price would be abolished.

But the second and more important result of these conditions is that no producer or consumer could affect the price of the commodity by his own individual action. If there is a large number of consumers of an article, no single consumer is purchasing an appreciable proportion of the product, so that no single consumer can affect appreciably the total demand for the product by varying his own purchases. If there were a million consumers of bread each consuming a loaf a week, and if one consumer decided to increase his consumption by 100 per cent and to consume two loaves instead of one, the total demand would only rise from 1,000,000 to 1,000,001 loaves a week. This increase in demand, though by no means negligible from the point of view of the single consumer, would be negligible from the point of view of the total demand for bread and would therefore exert a negligible effect upon the price of a loaf. Experience bears out this conclusion. No individual consumer of bread argues that if he increases his demand he will increase the total demand for bread and so raise the price; each decides how much he will buy at current prices, assuming quite correctly that his demand being but a drop in the ocean will have no effect upon the price of bread. The same is true of the producers of bread. If there is a large number of them —say a million producers each producing the same output—a 100 per cent increase in the output of one of them will only cause a millionth increase in the total supply and will therefore have a negligible effect upon it, and so upon the price of bread. Each producer will decide how much to produce at the current market price; no one of them will expect variations in his own supply to affect the market price.

This result would follow irrespective of the sort of thing exchanged. If there is a large number of independent employers and workers, buying and selling labor of the same efficiency, with knowledge of the wages which other employers are offering and other wage-earners are demanding, no single employer will be able to affect the wage-rate of this labor by employing more or less men, nor will any one worker be able to raise or lower the wage-rate by offering less or more labor. If there is a large number of borrowers and lenders of capital, knowing the rates of interest at which loans are being made, no one of them alone can affect this rate of interest by offering to borrow or lend more or less. This does not imply that if all the buyers of a commodity decide to buy more of it, or if all the sellers decide to supply less of it, the price will not rise; it merely implies that in a perfectly competitive system no single buyer or seller will think that his own action will have any effect on the price of the commodity. Nor does this imply that a consumer or seller of a commodity will never expect a change in its price. A farmer in a perfectly competitive system will properly expect a fall in the price of wheat if he thinks that a large number of farmers are likely to put more wheat on the market than before; perfect competition simply implies that no single farmer will think that he can prevent, or in any way affect, this fall in price by restricting his own output.

We may draw certain important conclusions from this definition of perfect competition. We may first ask on what principles an individual consumer will spend his income in order to get as much out of it as possible, if he knows that he is unable to affect the price of any commodity which he buys. Suppose that an individual consumer, with given tastes and needs, has an income of $10 a week to spend on commodities, and suppose that there are only two commodities on which he can spend this income—loaves of bread which cost 10 cents a loaf and tea which costs 25 cents a pound. (I take these figures for their convenience, not for their probability.) Suppose that he is buying 50 loaves of bread a week at 10 cents each and 20 pounds of tea a week at 25 cents a pound. Is he getting as much satisfaction as possible out of his income? It might at first sight be thought that since he is spending half his income on each commodity, he will be getting as much as possible out of his income only if the *total* satisfaction which he gets from the 50 loaves a week is the same as the *total* satisfaction which he gets from the 20 pounds of tea a week. But this is not necessarily so. Since the price of a loaf of bread is 10 cents and of a pound of tea 25 cents, the consumer can have $2\frac{1}{2}$ more loaves of bread a week if he gives up 1 pound of tea a week. He can increase the total satisfaction which he gets out of his income by buying more bread and less tea if the gain from having $52\frac{1}{2}$ instead of 50 loaves of bread a week is greater than the loss from having 19 instead of 20 lb. of tea a week, regardless of the total satisfaction which he is at present getting from the 50 loaves of bread or the 20 lb. of tea.

Suppose that it does pay him in this way to spend 25 cents more on bread and 25 cents less on tea each week. Will it pay him to spend still less on tea and still more on bread? He can still obtain $2\frac{1}{2}$ more loaves a week for the loss of 1 lb. of tea a week; and it may still pay him to reduce his weekly consumption of tea by a further pound from 19 to 18 in order to increase his weekly consumption of bread from $52\frac{1}{2}$ to 55 loaves. But this transference of expenditure from tea to bread will pay him less than before. For the gain from having 55 instead of $52\frac{1}{2}$ loaves of bread a week will be less than the gain from having $52\frac{1}{2}$ instead of 50 loaves a week, because the more loaves he has the less will he want additional loaves; and at the same time the loss due to having 18 instead of 19 lb. of tea a week will be greater than the loss due to having 19 instead of 20, since the less tea he has the more will he feel the loss of a further pound. At some point, therefore, as he buys more loaves and less tea, he will find that the loss of another pound of tea a week would be greater than the gain from another $2\frac{1}{2}$ loaves of bread a week. At this point he cannot gain by buying more bread and less tea.

It follows from this that if factors of production are moved from producing one commodity to producing another commodity in circumstances in which there has been no change of consumers' tastes or needs, the price of the commodity produced in smaller quantity will rise while the price of that produced in greater amount will fall. If a certain amount of tea is being produced and bought by consumers for 25 cents a pound, while a certain amount of bread is being produced and bought by consumers for 10 cents a loaf, consumers will be buying tea and bread in such amounts that to each consumer 1 lb. more tea is worth $2\frac{1}{2}$ loaves more bread. If now more tea and less bread are produced, consumers will have to purchase more tea and less bread. But if they have more tea and less bread the importance of having 1 lb. more tea will be reduced, while the importance of having 1 loaf more bread will be increased. This means that if the tastes and the income of consumers have not changed, an increase in the total supply of tea will cause a reduction in the price which consumers will give for it; on the other hand, a diminution in the total supply of bread will cause consumers to pay a higher price for each loaf.

This analysis is easily extended to cover the realistic case in which the consumer can choose between a large number of commodities which are offered in the market at different prices. The consumer will maximize the satisfaction which he obtains from his income if he buys all commodities in such amounts that the marginal utilities of the commodities are in the same proportion as their prices. By the marginal utility of a commodity is meant the extent to which a consumer's satisfaction would be increased if he had one unit more of that commodity; and we have just shown that consumers will get the most out of their incomes if they purchase commodities in such amounts that the proportion between the prices of any two commodities is the same as the proportion between the importance of having a unit more of these same commodities.

We can express this same fact in a slightly different way, which is simpler for certain purposes. Each consumer should distribute his expenditure upon different commodities in such a way that he could not satisfy his needs more fully by spending $1 less on one commodity and $1 more on another. The amount by which a man's satisfaction is increased if he spends one more unit of money on tea at the current price of tea may be called the marginal utility of money spent on tea. We may now restate the condition in which a consumer will obtain the greatest possible satisfaction from the expenditure of a given income: he should spend his money in such a way on the different commodities that the marginal utility of money spent on each commodity is the same. The importance of having one dollar's worth more tea must at current prices be the same as the importance of having one dollar's worth more of any other commodity.

We can next discuss the results of perfect competition upon the conditions of production and sale, and for this purpose we must distinguish between the average cost of production of a commodity and its marginal cost of production. By the average cost is meant simply the cost per unit of output—including in the cost all the six items enumerated in Part I, Chapter I, p. 5, namely, the wages, interest, rent, cost of raw materials, cost of maintenance of the capital equipment, and a sufficient profit to induce the owners and managers to undertake the effort and risks involved in the business. By the marginal cost is meant the amount which is added to the total costs of a business by producing one more unit of output. The result of perfect competition is that the price of each commodity will be equal both to its average and to its marginal cost of production.

If producers are free to move from one occupation to another, each commodity will tend to be supplied in such amounts that its price is equal to its average cost of production. If the price offered for a commodity were above its average cost of production—which includes the 'profit' to producers necessary to make them continue production—new producers would enter this occupation in which abnormally high profits can be made. The total output would increase, and so the price offered for the product by consumers would fall. If, on the other hand, the price offered for a commodity were below its average cost of production, the existing producers would be making a loss, and would therefore move into other occupations; and this would continue until the total output was reduced and the price offered by consumers was therefore raised as high as the average cost of production of the commodity.

Two additions must be made to this argument. First, it may appear unreal to assume that if one commodity is being produced at a loss there are necessarily others which are being produced at a profit. May it not be true that in a trade depression every commodity is being produced at a cost which is above the price obtainable in the market for that commodity? May it not be that at other times every commodity, or nearly every commodity, is being sold at a price above its cost of production? In a depression, therefore, since there may be no profitable commodities to produce, producers will have no incentive to turn from the production of unprofitable commodities; and if all commodities are being produced at costs lower than the prices at which they can be sold, new producers will not necessarily come in to increase the supply of every commodity which is being sold at a profit. But we are assuming that by the policies suggested in Part I the total money demand for commodities in general is properly adjusted to their money costs of production; and in this case if some industries are depressed and making losses, there will be others that are at the same time more than covering their costs of production. The policy of Part I will bring it about that the whole of industry will neither be making losses nor profits, while the existence of perfect competition will *in these circumstances* constantly tend to remove losses and profits in each individual industry by permitting and encouraging movement from unprofitable to more profitable occupations.

Secondly, the shift of producers from industries making losses to those making profits will not be immediate even in a perfectly competitive system. Manufacturers will have invested capital in the form of durable equipment in different industries, and it is neither possible nor profitable to shift from one to another more quickly than the capital can be moved from the first to the second industry. The transference of fixed capital goods such as factories and machinery from a depressed to a prosperous industry will take time, because existing machinery in the depressed industry takes time to wear out, while new machinery for the prosperous industry takes time to construct. Let us suppose that in coal mining only 2 per cent and in automobile manufacture 6 per cent is earned on capital. It is profitable to shift capital from the coal mines to motor car firms. But in the coal mines the capital takes the form of shafts, trucks, props, elevators, etc., none of which is of any use in a firm producing cars. The shift of capital from coal mining actually takes place when those who direct the coal mines refrain from using money to replace these capital goods when they wear out, and invest these sums either directly in some other business or in securities which earn a higher rate of interest. The actual equipment of the motor car industry can only be increased when sufficient time has elapsed for labor, land, and capital in the engineering trade to produce more machinery for the use of motor car manufacturers. But though the shift of producers from one industry to another may take some time, in a perfectly competitive system in which the factors of production are free to move it will in the end take place, and all commodities will tend to be sold at prices equal to the average cost of production.

In perfect competition the price of each commodity will tend to be equal to its marginal cost as well as to its average cost of production. In order to maximize his profit each producer will produce more so long as what he adds to his costs by producing another unit—which we call his marginal cost—is less than what he adds to his receipts by selling another unit. In perfect competition no single producer can affect the price offered for his product by selling more, so that by selling an extra unit he adds to his receipts the price of that extra unit. In perfect competition each producer of each commodity will therefore extend his production until the price offered for his product is equal to the amount which he must pay for the additional factors of production required to produce an extra unit, so that the price of each commodity will tend to be equal to its marginal cost of production.

But is it certain that in perfect competition the price of a commodity can be equal both to its average and to its marginal cost? An individual unit of production, which we will call a 'firm,' may be too small or too large to be producing in the most efficient manner. If a firm is too small, it cannot reap the advantages of 'mass production.' It does not pay to put in certain efficient types of machinery which are large and costly unless the output of the firm using that machinery is sufficiently great to insure that it will be fully used; and once the machinery has been installed, a large output can be produced with it without adding to the costs proportionately, since the single block of machinery can serve a large as well as a small output. Even in occupations in which mechanical methods are not important, there must be at least one man with a minimum amount of capital and land, and this 'one-man firm' can, up to a point, produce more without a proportionate increase in total costs. On the other hand, when firms become too large, the average cost of production is likely to rise because the firms become too unwieldy for a single management; for some single person must be responsible for the final decisions and for the co-ordination of the different branches of every business unit. At some point after the economies of large-scale production have been well utilized, and before the firm has become too large for a single management, the average cost of production will be a minimum. When the output has reached this size, we may say that the firm is of the 'optimum' size.

In perfect competition the individual firms will tend to be of this optimum size. If the demand price ruling in the market were below the average cost of a firm of the optimum size, no firm in the industry could cover its costs. Firms would leave the industry and the total output put on the market would diminish until the demand price had risen to cover the average cost of firms of the optimum or most efficient size. If, on the other hand, the demand price were higher than the average cost of a firm producing the optimum output, firms in this industry could make a profit over and above their costs by producing an output near their optimum output and selling it at a price higher than its cost. In consequence new firms would be attracted to the industry and the total output would increase until the demand price had fallen to the average cost of a firm producing the optimum output.

Perfect competition would therefore cause the price offered for the commodity to be equal to the cost of production of a firm of the most efficient size. Any firm which produced more or less than this optimum output would make a loss, since its average cost would be raised above the market price of the commodity. In these conditions each firm would tend to be of the optimum size; for only a firm of the most efficient size could cover its costs.

It can, however, be shown that when a firm is of the optimum size, its average cost will be equal to its marginal cost of production. The relationship between average and marginal costs can be explained by means of an analogy. Suppose that a pitcher has an earned run average of 3 runs per game. If, by pitching an additional game, he brings this average down, he must have permitted fewer than 3 earned runs—i.e., he must have added to the total runs he had allowed to date less than his existing average. If he does not change his average, he must have allowed precisely 3 earned runs. If, finally, he raised his average, he must have allowed more than 3. In the same way suppose a producer to be producing a certain output at an average cost of $3 per unit. If by producing another unit of output the producer causes the cost per unit of output to fall, he must have added something less than $3 to his total costs by producing the extra unit; if he causes no change in the cost per unit of output, he must have added exactly $3; and if he causes his average cost to rise, he must have added more than $3 to his total cost. The marginal cost is only another term for 'what a producer adds to his total costs by producing another unit.' So long, therefore, as a firm's average cost can be lowered by an increase in output, the marginal cost is below the average cost; if a firm's average cost would be unchanged by an increase in output, the marginal cost is equal to the average cost; and as soon as an increase in output would cause a rise in a firm's average cost, the marginal cost is higher than the average cost. A firm is, however, of the optimum size when its average cost has just ceased to fall and has not started to rise, so that at this point the marginal cost must be equal to the average cost. And, as we have already shown that in perfect competition a firm will be of the optimum size, we may conclude that in perfect competition firms will be of that size at which the price of the product can be equal both to the marginal and the average cost of production.[1]

The argument that in perfect competition the price of each product will be equal to its marginal cost can also be expressed by saying that each factor of production will be paid a reward equal to the value of its marginal product. We have already explained in Part I, Chapter VII, what is meant by the marginal product of labor. If a producer of shoes, by employing one more man with an unaltered amount of the other factors, can produce

---

[1]. See the Appendix for a discussion of the relations between average and marginal quantities. Graph I, p. 143, shows the equilibrium position.

2 more pairs of shoes a day, then the marginal product of labor is 2 pairs of shoes a day. Similarly, if by employing one more machine with the same amount of labor and land he can produce 3 more pairs of shoes a day, then the marginal product of a machine is 3 pairs of shoes a day. The marginal product of any factor of production in any industry is the amount by which the output would be increased if one more unit of that factor of production were employed with the same amount of the other factors of production. The value of the marginal product of any factor is the price at which its marginal product can be sold in the market; if the marginal product of labor in the shoe industry is 2 pairs of shoes and if shoes sell at $2.50 a pair, the value of the marginal product of labor in this industry is $5.

If there is perfect competition, a producer will employ each factor up to the point at which the price which he pays for the factor of production is equal to the value of the marginal product of that factor. The reader is referred to pp. 70–75 of Part I, Chapter VII, for a full discussion of this point; here we may summarize the conclusion of that section. What an employer gains by employing another man is the price at which he can sell the additional output due to his employment, i.e. the value of his marginal product, less the cost of employing another man, i.e. the wage-rate of labor. In a perfectly competitive system, therefore, every employer tends to employ more labor so long as the wage-rate is below the value of the marginal product of labor, and to dismiss labor if the wage-rate is above this value. The same argument applies to land and capital. A producer will, for example, put in more capital in the form of machinery, if the annual cost of interest and maintenance of the machine is less than the value of its marginal product.

The marginal product of any particular factor of production falls as more of it is employed, but rises if there is an increased employment of the other factors with which it co-operates in production. This fact is of great importance in the development of our argument. If a producer has much machinery and land but little labor, the marginal product of machinery and land will be small and the marginal product of labor will be great; for he will be able to add little to his product by taking on still more machinery and land, but it will be important to have a larger labor supply to work the machinery. But if he had much labor and little land and machinery, the productiveness of another laborer would be small, as the machinery and land would already be overcrowded; while it would add considerably to the product to take on more machinery and land to employ with the excessive labor force. For this reason the marginal product of any factor depends not upon the absolute amount of that factor employed, but upon the proportion between the amount of that factor and the amount of other factors employed.

We have seen that in perfect competition more of each factor of production will be employed in each industry until the reward paid to the factor is as great as the value of its marginal product. If, therefore, the factors of production are free to move from the occupations in which their earnings are low to those in which their earnings are high, they will move from industries in which the values of their marginal products are low to those in which the values of their marginal products are high. This movement of factors will go on so long as there is any difference in their earnings, so that perfect competition will cause the value of the marginal product of each factor to be the same in every industry. Suppose that the value of the marginal product of labor is higher in industry A than in industry B. This means that higher wages will be offered in industry A than in industry B, and labor will tend to move to industry A. But two things will happen. In industry A the marginal product of labor will fall as more is employed with the given equipment in that industry, and at the same time the price paid for the product of industry A will fall as more of it is produced and offered for sale. For both of these reasons the value of the marginal product of labor will fall in industry A. The opposite will happen in industry B. As labor moves from that industry and less is produced there, the marginal product of labor will rise and the price offered for the product will rise. There will be a double set of influences lowering the value of the marginal product of labor in industry A and raising its value in industry B, and the movement of labor to industry A will continue until the value of its marginal product is the same in each industry.

These conclusions would, of course, be true only if there were *no* restriction on the movement of factors of production between different industries. But even if all unnecessary restrictions of movement (such as legal restrictions or ignorance of the possibilities of moving to a job in which wages were higher) were removed, an unavoidable economic cost may be involved in such movement. Labor will be attracted from industry B to industry A only if the wage offered in industry A is so much greater than the wage offered in industry B that the increase in earnings offsets any cost involved in this movement. Suppose that it costs a laborer $500 to move to industry A from industry B, because the change involves moving to another city or learning a new trade. Suppose, further, that the value of the marginal product of labor in industry A, and so the wage offered in industry A, is $30 a year greater than the value of the marginal product of labor, and so the wage offered to labor, in industry B. Then the expenditure of a capital sum of $500 on moving would raise his earnings by $30 a year, and this represents a yield of 6 per cent on the money invested in the move. Only if the laborer could borrow money at a rate of interest lower than 6 per cent would the move be worth his while. We should restate our previous conclusion more accurately by saying that in perfect competition the difference between the values of the marginal products of any factor of production in any two industries cannot remain greater than the cost of movement of that factor between the two industries; and we must reckon this cost as the interest which would have to be paid on the sum borrowed to finance the move. For this reason, even in a perfectly competitive community, any existing distribution of factors of production either among different occupations or among different districts tends to be continued even though this distribution of the factors of production was due in the first place to chance or to historical causes which are no longer of importance. In future when any argument is based on the statement that one factor will move to one industry from another because the reward offered for it is higher in the one industry than in the other, the passage must be understood to be subject to this modification. This modification will be expressly mentioned only when it makes an important difference to the argument.

NOTE ON TERMINOLOGY

The economists who have developed the analysis of 'monopolistic' and 'imperfect' competition in recent years have used very different terms to describe the different conditions in which production is carried on; and the selection of appropriate terms to describe the categories which we use in this Part has therefore been difficult. Readers who are familiar with Professor Chamberlin's *Monopolistic Competition* will observe that our definition of 'perfect' competition is intermediate between Professor Chamberlin's definitions of 'perfect' and 'pure' competition; it is not only 'pure' in Professor Chamberlin's sense of being free of monopolistic elements, but is also perfect in one other particular, namely, in the absence of artificial restrictions on the movement of factors of production from one industry to another. Conversely our definition of 'imperfect' competition is considerably broader than Professor Chamberlin's definition of 'monopolistic' competition; for it includes cases of 'pure' competition where there are artificial restrictions on the movements of factors, and also the categories which Professor Chamberlin designates 'pure monopoly,' 'duopoly' and 'oligopoly,' and 'oligopoly plus monopolistic competition.' Although there is much to be said for the descriptive accuracy of the term 'monopolistic' competition, it was thought that the use of Professor Chamberlin's term in a sense very different from that in which he uses it would increase rather than diminish the present unfortunate confusion of terminology in this field of economics. In subsequent chapters the term 'monopolistic' will be used to describe conditions which do not conform to those of 'perfect competition' in our sense.

II

THE ADVANTAGES OF PERFECT COMPETITION

IN the last chapter we explained the meaning of perfect competition and outlined the principles on which the factors of production would be distributed among different occupations in a perfectly competitive system. In this chapter we shall show that such a system has three fundamental advantages. First, it would be impossible by producing more of one thing and less of another to make any one consumer better off without making other consumers worse off.[1] Secondly, output would be maximized in the sense that it would not be possible with a given amount of the factors of production to produce more of one commodity without producing less of some other. Thirdly—an advantage which is really only a particular case of the second—each individual firm would be of the most efficient size.

The first advantage—that it would not be possible by producing more of one thing and less of another to make any one consumer better off without making other consumers worse off—follows from these two facts:

(i) that each consumer spends his money on the different commodities in such a way that the marginal utility of the money spent on each commodity is the same, and

(ii) that each factor of production moves into that industry in which the value of its marginal product is highest.

Let us consider again the production and sale of two commodities, bread and tea. Each consumer spends his money in such a way that the marginal utility of the money spent on each com-

---

1. This is a necessary but not a sufficient condition for maximum total satisfaction. For it might be possible to increase total satisfaction by altering production in such a way that some consumers would be better off, others worse off.

modity is the same, so that each consumer would be just willing to give up an amount of bread which sells for $1 in exchange for an amount of tea which sells for $1. Any one consumer would therefore be better off if he were given an amount of tea which at current prices sells for more than $1 in exchange for an amount of bread which at current prices sells for $1. Thus it would be possible for one consumer to be better off without any reduction in the welfare of other consumers, if it were possible for the community to produce an amount of tea which at current prices sells for more than $1 by giving up no more than an amount of bread which sells for $1. But such a change in the output of different commodities would be brought about automatically by the forces of competition if it were possible. For suppose that it is possible by shifting a unit of labor from the bread to the tea industry to produce an amount of tea which at current prices sells for more than $1 at the sacrifice of an amount of bread which sells for $1. The value of the marginal product of labor must be higher in the tea industry than in the bread industry, so that labor will automatically be attracted from the bread industry to the tea industry; or, in other words, the marginal cost of an amount of tea which sells for $1 must be less than the marginal cost of an amount of bread which sells for $1. But in perfect competition, as we have seen, the factors of production will be automatically so distributed among different occupations that the value of the marginal product of each factor is the same in every industry, and the marginal cost is equal to the price of the product in every industry.

This is still true if we take into account the fact that a factor of production will move from one industry to another only if the value of its marginal product in the one industry exceeds the value of its marginal product in the other by more than the cost of movement. Suppose that the value of the marginal product of labor is $30 a year greater in the tea industry than in the bread industry, that it costs a laborer $500 to move from the one to the other, and that the rate of interest is 8 per cent per annum. In

these circumstances labor will not move to the tea industry, because although its earnings would be raised by $30 a year it would
lose $40 a year in interest on the cost of movement. Yet it may
seem that in these circumstances it would be possible to improve
one consumer's position without making any other consumer
worse off; for the shift of a unit of labor from the bread industry
to the tea industry would increase the output of tea by an amount
which at current prices sells for $30 more—and is therefore worth
$30 more to the consumer—than the amount by which the out-
put of bread would be reduced. But the production of a certain
amount more tea involves not only the use of one less laborer in
the bread industry but also the use of $500 less capital in some
industry or another; [1] for $500 must be invested in the cost of
moving the laborer. In perfect competition the price offered for
capital will measure the value of its marginal product. If, therefore, the rate of interest is 8 per cent, the use of $500 less capital
in any industry will diminish the annual output of that industry
by an amount which sells for $40. If, therefore, one unit of labor
were moved from the bread industry to the tea industry, two
things would happen: there would be an increase in the output
of tea, worth $30 more to consumers than the reduction in the
output of bread; but because of the investment of $500 capital
in the cost of moving, the output of some other commodity would
be reduced by an amount worth $40 to consumers. Allowing for
both these facts, it would not be possible to improve the position
of one consumer without worsening the position of others. This
would be possible only if the interest on the cost of movement
were less than the increase in the value of the marginal product
of the factor due to the move; but these are just the conditions in
which the automatic forces of competition will themselves produce the desired movement of factors.

1. The reader is reminded that we are arguing on the assumption that full
employment is being maintained by the measures discussed in Part I, so
that it is impossible to spend $500 on moving a worker without less of some-
thing else being produced. When there is unemployment the value of what
a laborer employed in one industry would produce elsewhere may be zero.

The second advantage of perfect competition is that the factors of production will always be employed in the most efficient combinations in different industries, so that if there is full employment it will be impossible to produce more of one commodity without producing less of some other. This can best be shown by an example. Let us imagine that by moving labor from the production of tea to the production of bread, and at the same time moving capital from the production of bread to that of tea, it is possible to produce as much tea and more bread than before. This can only be the case if the ratio between the marginal products of labor and of capital in the one industry is different from the ratio between the marginal products of labor and of capital in the other industry. Suppose that in the bread and tea industries the marginal products of labor and capital are as shown in Table IV.

Table IV

The Ratio between the Marginal Products of Two Factors Differs in Two Industries

BREAD INDUSTRY

Marginal product of labor	.	.	. 4 loaves a day
Marginal product of capital	.	.	. 4 loaves a day

TEA INDUSTRY

Marginal product of labor	.	.	. 1 lb. a day
Marginal product of capital	.	.	. 3 lb. a day

By shifting one unit of labor from tea to bread the output of tea will be reduced by 1 pound a day, and the daily output of bread will be increased by 4 loaves. If at the same time one unit of capital is shifted from producing bread to producing tea, the output of bread will fall again by 4 loaves, and the output of tea will rise by 3 lb. a day. The combined result, therefore, of these two shifts is that the output of bread remains the same, while the output of tea rises by 2 lb. a day. The factors of production were not being used in the most efficient proportions, since by using a larger proportion of labor to capital in producing bread and a smaller proportion in producing tea the output of tea could be increased without diminishing the output of bread.

Perfect competition would automatically readjust this position, if it existed. In perfect competition each factor will be paid the value of its marginal product, so that in the circumstances illustrated in Table IV a unit of capital in the bread industry would be paid the same as a unit of labor, whereas in the tea industry a unit of capital would be paid three times as much as a unit of labor. Capital would be attracted into the tea industry and labor into the bread industry. And this movement would continue so long as the ratio between the marginal products of capital and labor was higher in the tea industry than in the bread industry.

But as labor moved into the bread industry and capital left it, the marginal product of labor would fall and that of capital would rise; for when a large proportion of labor to capital is employed, it becomes less important to have one more unit of labor and more important to have one more unit of capital. Similarly, as capital moves into the tea industry and labor leaves it, the marginal product of capital will fall and the marginal product of labor will rise. The movement of the factors of production will therefore raise the marginal product of capital in the bread industry and lower it in the tea industry. At the same time it will lower the marginal product of labor in the bread industry and raise it in the tea industry. We shall then reach a situation of the kind shown in Table V.

TABLE V

The Ratio between the Marginal Products of Two Factors Is the Same in Two Industries

BREAD INDUSTRY

Marginal product of labor . . .	3 loaves a day
Marginal product of capital . . .	5 loaves a day

TEA INDUSTRY

Marginal product of labor . . .	$1\frac{1}{2}$ lb. a day
Marginal product of capital . . .	$2\frac{1}{2}$ lb. a day

In these conditions, in both industries the marginal product or the reward of labor is three-fifths of the marginal product or the reward of capital, and competition will not cause any further change in the proportions in which labor and capital are employed in the two industries. But these are precisely the conditions in which it is impossible to produce more of one commodity without producing less of the other. Suppose that 5 units of labor are shifted from the bread industry to the tea industry; the output of bread will fall by 15 loaves and the output of tea will rise by $7\frac{1}{2}$ lb. Since the marginal product of capital is 5 loaves, it will be necessary to shift 3 units of capital into the bread industry to make the output of bread rise again by 15 loaves, and so prevent any net fall in its output. But the loss of 3 units of capital from the tea industry will cause the output of tea to fall again by $7\frac{1}{2}$ lb. to its previous level. Thus when the ratio between the marginal products of the two factors is the same in both industries, it is impossible to increase the output in one industry without reducing the output in the other.

It must be realized that Table V only shows that the payment of a unit of labor will be three-fifths of the payment of a unit of capital in the tea industry and in the bread industry; it does not show that labor and capital will be getting the same payments in each industry. This will be so only if the demand price of a pound of tea is twice that of a loaf of bread. Suppose that the price of a pound of tea is 20 cents and that of a loaf of bread 10 cents. Then the payment of a unit of labor in the bread industry will be $3 \times 10c$. and in the tea industry $1\frac{1}{2} \times 20c$.; i.e. 30c. in both industries. The payment of a unit of capital will be $5 \times 10c$. in the bread industry and $2\frac{1}{2} \times 20c$. in the tea industry, i.e. 50c. in both industries. But if the price of a loaf is 5 cents, and that of a pound of tea 30 cents, labor will be paid $3 \times 5c$. or 15c. in the bread industry and $1\frac{1}{2} \times 30c$. or 45c. in the tea industry; while capital will be receiving 25c. in the bread industry and 75c. in the tea industry. In this case both labor and capital will move from the bread to the tea industry, where their earnings are higher. The output of bread will fall and its price will rise, while the output of tea will increase and its price fall. The factors of production will continue to move from the bread industry to the tea industry until the price of bread has risen and that of tea has fallen sufficiently to enable each factor to earn the same in each industry; but it will, of course, follow that the ratio between their earnings in each industry is the same. In other words, perfect competition will cause the ratio between their marginal products in each industry to be the same; and we have seen that this is the condition in which it is impossible to increase the output of one commodity without diminishing the output of another.

This result is not modified by taking into account the fact that factors of production will only move from one occupation to another if the difference in their earnings more than covers the cost of movement. Suppose that in the tea industry the value of the marginal products of both capital and labor is $1,000 a year, while in the bread industry the value of the marginal product of capital is $1,000, but the value of the marginal product of labor is only $970 a year. Here is a case in which the shift of a unit of capital from the tea to the bread industry together with the shift of a unit of labor from the bread to the tea industry would increase the output of bread without reducing the output of tea. For there will be no change in the output of tea, in which the marginal products of labor and capital are the same; and the output of bread will be increased, because an additional unit of capital adds more to the product than is lost through the disappearance of one unit of labor. Suppose, however, that it costs labor $500 to move from the bread to the tea industry; and suppose further that the rate of interest is 8 per cent, so that the cost of movement of labor can be represented by $40 a year. It will not pay labor to move from the bread industry to the tea industry, because the rise of $30 a year in labor's earnings would be more than offset by the fact that it costs $40 a year to move. But in these circumstances the shift of capital from the tea industry to the bread industry with a corresponding shift of labor from the bread to the tea industry will no longer cause the output of bread to increase without any diminution in the output of tea. It is still true that if one more unit of labor and one less unit of capital is used in the tea industry the output of tea will not be changed. But in the bread industry, while as before there will be one less unit of labor and so a reduction in output worth $970, there will not be one more unit of capital available to increase the output by an amount worth $1,000. For although one less unit of capital is needed in the tea industry, $500 of this capital must be invested in the cost of shifting labor from the bread to the tea industry; and since the marginal product of capital is 8 per cent, this in itself will cause the output of bread to be reduced by an amount worth $40. Only if the marginal product of capital, and so the rate of interest, were less than 6 per cent, would a net increase in the output of bread be possible without any change in the output of tea. But if the rate of interest were lower than 6 per cent, it would pay labor to shift from producing bread to producing tea.[1]

Finally, in a system of perfect competition each individual firm will be of the most efficient size. We have already proved this by showing in Chapter I of this Part (p. 111) that the freedom of producers to move from one industry to another will cause the price of each product to be equal to the average cost of production of a firm of the optimum size, so that each firm must be of the optimum size in order to cover its costs.

1. In reality the rate of interest at which workers could borrow money to move to another occupation would be much higher than the rate at which capital could be borrowed for investment in industry. But this is one of those 'artificial' restrictions on the free movement of capital from one use to another, which at the moment we are assuming away.

III

THE DISADVANTAGES OF PERFECT COMPETITION

IN the remaining chapters of this Part our attention will be turned to a criticism of *laisser-faire*.[1] By *laisser-faire* we do not necessarily mean an economic system in which there is perfect competition; we mean simply an economic system in which there is a minimum of state interference. We shall see in Chapters IV and V of this Part that the absence of such interference does not necessarily lead to perfect competition. Our criticism of *laisser-faire* therefore will fall into two parts: the first, which we shall undertake in this chapter, showing that even if there is perfect competition there are disadvantages to be set against the three advantages which we have discussed in the last chapter; the second, which we shall undertake in Chapters IV to VI of this Part, showing that *laisser-faire* in many cases does not lead to perfect competition and therefore does not necessarily lead to the three fundamental advantages of perfect competition.

It is hardly necessary to point out, as a criticism of a system of perfect competition, that there are certain activities which for one reason or another cannot be performed by private individuals. There are three functions of government, namely, defense, police, and the administration of justice, which require the purchase and sale of goods and services by the state, and which for obvious reasons cannot be left to the free play of competitive forces: individual citizens cannot be left to buy and sell justice in competition. Government interference with a competitive system in order to raise money by taxation for the communal satis-

1. In Part I we have already suggested certain ways in which governments should intervene in economic affairs in order to prevent unemployment. The remaining chapters of this Part suggest reasons for state interference of a different kind.

faction of these needs is clearly justifiable. How much should be spent by the state on these services is mainly a political question, into which we shall not enter; but there are certain obvious economic considerations to be taken into account in making these decisions. For example, a rich community, in which the real income of the average individual is high, can properly afford to spend more than a poor community on the provision of an efficient system of police and justice, because the use of men and commodities for the provision of extra efficiency in these services, rather than for the provision of commodities and services supplied by the ordinary competitive processes, will entail a smaller burden on a rich than on a poor community.

Apart from this there are three main criticisms which can be directed against an economic system of perfect competition combined with freedom of movement for the factors of production. The first is that it would not bring about the production of those commodities which are most beneficial to consumers in so far as consumers fail to distribute their expenditure 'wisely' among different commodities. If consumers did consider carefully the importance of having a little more of this and a little less of that, and if they did know what was best for them, perfect competition and freedom of movement of the factors of production might cause the economic resources of the community to be set to work on the production of commodities in amounts which satisfy their needs most fully. But do consumers really know what is best for them? This criticism depends upon fundamental questions of psychology and politics, which it is my desire to avoid in this book. But the question is of such great importance in the formation of economic policy that it is well to discuss the problem shortly, although the conclusions reached are largely a matter of personal opinion. Do individuals know better than the state or some other semi-official body what is best for them? Obviously in certain cases they do not. A man who is ill will go to the doctor for a prescription; he will not choose his own medicine at the corner drug store. But this is not a case for interference with the workings of perfect competition. For the consumer, realizing that he does not know the 'marginal utility' of different drugs, will inquire of some one who does know. It is only in cases in which the consumer does not know what will satisfy him most, but thinks that he does, that a case can be made out on these grounds for interfering with the free choice of consumers. There are many cases in which this may be true. While a man who is ill may go to a doctor rather than prescribe medicine for himself, he may underestimate the importance of spending money on medical services as a whole. He may put off going to the doctor until an ailment is well advanced under the misapprehension that nothing much is wrong, or he may habitually underestimate the risks of his falling ill and fail in times of health to put aside sufficient to meet the probable medical costs which he must face in times of sickness. If people habitually spend too little on medical advice, there is a strong case for some form of state subsidization of medical services or for the state provision of compulsory insurance against illness. Or again people may underestimate the advantages of education and the state may be a better judge than the majority of people as to how much should be spent on this service; if this is so, there is a strong case for interference by the state to make education cheaper to people than it actually is.[1] Or drug addicts may, at the moment that the desire for the drug seizes them, greatly overestimate the advantages to be gained from the drug. Here again the state has a strong reason to interfere with perfect competition by means of a prohibition or limitation of the sale of the drug.

Whether the reader agrees with these particular examples or not, there are occasions on which the individual consumer either loses control of himself or else is ignorant, so that he does not spend his income in the way that satisfies him most. It may be agreed in principle that in these circumstances the state should

---

1. That this is by no means the only argument in favor of subsidizing education will become apparent when the distribution of the national income is discussed in Part III.

interfere if it is likely to know better than the individual how his need may best be satisfied, and that it should control his purchases by means of taxes, subsidies, prohibition, rationing, etc. But in many cases of this kind what is most desirable is state action designed to remove the consumer's ignorance. For instance, should the consumer buy pasteurized milk? Some persons hold the view that pasteurizing milk diminishes the chance of it causing tuberculosis, while others believe that it increases the risk of rickets. Can the ordinary consumer properly decide whether to pay a certain amount extra for pasteurized milk? Mrs. A may buy pasteurized milk, though it costs her more, because Mrs. B tells her that Mrs. C's daughter died of tuberculosis and did not drink pasteurized milk. Mrs. D may avoid pasteurized milk because Mrs. E tells her that Mrs. F's son suffered from rickets and always drank pasteurized milk. Do Mrs. A and Mrs. D really have sound reasons for their choice? Could not the state intervene with advantage, put the question to the decision of expert opinion, and compel Mrs. A or Mrs. D to change her habit of life? If the answer of the experts were overwhelmingly in favor of the one course or the other, there would be a strong case for such action. But quite possibly expert opinion would say that there is a certain added risk of tuberculosis if milk is not pasteurized and a certain added risk of rickets if milk is pasteurized. In these circumstances it is extremely important that the state should discover the most reliable answer to the question and make every effort to inform Mrs. A and Mrs. D, so that they know what are the risks involved. Mrs. A can then decide best for herself whether she thinks that the extra amount which she pays for pasteurization of her milk is worth the lessened risk of tuberculosis and the greater risk of rickets.

To state briefly my own opinion, there is a case for direct state interference with the consumer's choice in those cases in which it is probable that the consumer will otherwise buy something which is definitely harmful to himself or neglect something which is of benefit. There is a strong case, where technical ignorance is likely to affect the consumer's choice, for the promotion by the state of expert investigation in order to inform public opinion. But in the majority of commodities consumers should retain their freedom of choice. Whatever economic system may be adopted, there will be a definite loss involved if for the vast majority of commodities some mechanism analogous in its effect to price competition is not maintained; otherwise it would always be possible to satisfy consumers' needs more fully by shifting the factors of production from one industry to another to produce more of one commodity and less of another.

The second main criticism is that the extra cost to the community of providing one more unit of a particular commodity may not always be the same as the extra cost to the individual producer. The costs to the community of providing more of a commodity may be greater than or less than the costs to the individual producer, and we may explain the possibility of such differences by means of illustrations. Let us first take a case in which the cost to the community is greater than the cost to the individual producer. Let us suppose that factories in one industry in a certain district cause a great deal of smoke in the course of their activities, and that this annoys private residents and other producers in the district. The private residents and other producers will have either to put up with dirty conditions of life and work or will have to spend more on cleaning their clothes, rooms, and offices. The cost to the community of producing the product of the smoky factory is the cost to the individual firm producing it—let us say this is $10 a unit—plus the extra amount which other persons in the district must spend on removing the dirt caused by the excessive smoke; and let us suppose this amount to be $2 for every unit of the commodity produced. (Even if these other persons do not actually spend extra money on cleaning up the dirt left by the smoke-polluted air, they will lose in welfare because of their dirty conditions, and some allowance must be made for this.) Since the cost to the individual producers of producing one more unit of the commodity is $10, competition will cause this commodity to be sold in the market for $10. But it costs the community $12 to produce another unit of the commodity.

This commodity will be produced and sold in quantities greater than are advantageous to the community. For since it will sell for $10, consumers will buy it up to the point at which the importance of having one unit more of it will be the same to them as the importance of having one unit more of other commodities which cost the community $10 to produce; whereas if consumers are to get the greatest possible satisfaction from the use of the existing factors of production, they should purchase it only up to the point at which the importance of having one unit more of it is the same as the importance of having one unit more of other commodities which cost the community $12 to produce. There is a case for interference by some public body to make the producers of this commodity bear the cost of the smoke, either by insisting on the use of devices which will prevent the excessive smoke or else by taxing this commodity $2 a unit. The choice between these methods will depend among other things upon whether the cost of smoke-abatement devices is greater or less than $2 a unit of output; if the cost is less than this figure then the insistence on smoke-abatement devices is preferable to the tax.

Next we may give an example of a case in which the cost to the community of producing a particular commodity is less than the cost to the individual producer concerned. Suppose that a farmer or landowner is considering the advantages of draining a particular piece of land and that in order to undertake this work he must borrow $1,000 at a rate of interest of 5 per cent. If the drainage would add an amount to his annual crop which he could sell for $40 a year, it will not be worth his while to undertake the development. And if this is the whole result of his action it is best for the community that he should not undertake the work; for the fact that 5 per cent is being offered by other persons for capital means that other persons can find uses for an extra capital sum of $1,000 which will add to their output an amount which consumers value at $50 a year. But it may be that the draining of this farmer's land will indirectly help to drain the land of a neighboring farmer, and will therefore add an amount to his neighbor's output which consumers value at $20 a year. If this is the case, the investment is desirable; for its marginal product is 6 per cent from the point of view of the community. But the farmer himself will not undertake it. In this case there is an argument in favor of intervention by the community to encourage production beyond the limits which will be brought about by perfect competition; and this can be done either by legal arrangements by which the individual farmer can obtain compensation from his neighbor for the advantages conferred upon him by the investment, or else by a subsidy paid by some official body on this type of investment.

There is a third criticism of perfect competition which is far-reaching in its effects. There is no reason to believe that a perfectly competitive economic system will distribute income among different consumers in the most desirable way. This objection to competition is only mentioned at this point, because the whole of Part III is devoted to its discussion.

IV

IMPERFECT COMPETITION BETWEEN SELLERS

In Chapter II of Part II of this book certain fundamental advantages of a perfectly competitive economic system were discussed. It is the object of this and the following chapters to demonstrate that, even if there is no government interference in economic matters, conditions of competition in the real world are not perfect, and that for this reason the advantages claimed for a competitive system in Chapter II of this Part in actual fact only apply with considerable modification. An attempt will then be made to discuss the way in which the disadvantages due to the imperfection of competition may be removed.

On page 102 we stated that for competition to be perfect, no single buyer or seller must be able to exercise any appreciable control over any price. It was argued that, for this to be so, the following three conditions must be satisfied:

(a) there must be a large number of independent sellers;
(b) there must be a large number of independent buyers; and
(c) the market for the commodity must be perfect in the sense that every buyer must buy from the seller who is offering the lowest price and every seller must sell to the buyer who is offering the highest price.

It is the object of this chapter to investigate the conditions in which a single seller will be able to affect the price of the commodity by selling more or less of it. In the next chapter we shall investigate the conditions in which a single buyer of a commodity can affect its price.

A single seller of a commodity will be able to affect the price of the commodity if there is not a large number of sellers of that commodity. In that case each seller will be selling a large proportion of the total output of the commodity and will thus appreciably affect the total supply of the commodity by selling more of it. If there were only two producers of motor cars, each one producing half the total output, either of them would increase the total output of cars by 5 per cent if he increased his own output by 10 per cent. In these circumstances neither of the producers would assume that the price of cars was unaffected by the number of cars which he produced, since he would realize that if 5 per cent more cars are to be bought the price at which they are offered to the purchasers must be lowered. This would be true even if there were a perfect market for the sale of cars in the sense that both producers were producing identically the same product and the consumers always bought from the producer who offered cars at the lower price.

Even if there is a system of complete *laisser-faire*, the number of independent producers of a commodity will not necessarily be great. The most obvious case of this is when the legal ownership of a particular raw material is in one or a few hands. In this case the single owner, or any one of the few owners, could appreciably affect the total supply of the raw material and could therefore control its price within certain limits. By restricting the supply of this commodity the producer could raise the price above the cost of its production and so make a monopoly profit, i.e. an income which is greater than would be necessary to induce him to continue producing that amount of the product if he were unable to control its price. In other circumstances the fact that he was making such abnormal profits would induce other producers to enter this line of business, so that the number of producers would grow and the price would be reduced to the cost of production of the commodity. But such action is impossible when the production is in the hands of a few and there are no other supplies of it to be developed. There are probably few if any cases in which there is only one or a very limited number of natural sources of supply of a raw material. But even if there were a large number of such sources of supply, an artificial monopoly of this kind could be created if all, or a large proportion, of the owners of such sources agreed together to restrict the supply, so that a large proportion of the available sources were brought under a single ownership or a single unit of control. If all the owners of coal mines agreed together to restrict their output and so to raise the price of coal, each would be able to gain by the fact that the price of coal was raised above its cost of production; and the high profits of coal mining could not attract new persons into the industry, simply because there were no other coal fields.

It might appear that apart from this possibility the number of independent producers competing in the production and sale of any commodity could not be successfully restricted unless the state restricted by law the number of persons who are allowed to produce. Otherwise as soon as any artificial restriction of supply by a combination of the existing producers caused a rise in the price of the commodity above its cost of production, the abnormal profits so earned would attract other producers into this line of business, so that the production would again fall into the control of a large number of independent producers. But this is a mistaken view. There is another reason why a small number of producers may maintain a monopoly position, and this reason is by far the more important in the modern world.

It has already been argued in Chapter I of this Part (pp. 110–11) that there is an optimum size for a firm, that as the output of the firm grows up to this optimum output the average cost of production will fall, and that as the output grows beyond this optimum amount the average cost of production will rise. In industries in which the technical economies of large-scale production are very important, the total demand for the product of the whole industry may be small in relation to the optimum output of a single firm. It may be that one or two firms of the optimum size would produce sufficient to satisfy the whole of the consumers' demand for the product; and in some cases the total consumers' demand may be less than the optimum output of a single firm. In such cases the absence of government interference will not lead to competition between a large number of independent producers.

This point is made clear by the following examples. Automobiles, to be produced at the lowest possible average cost, must be produced on a large scale; and it follows that if there were a very large number of independent producers no one of them would be producing on a sufficient scale to reduce the average cost of production to a minimum. In these circumstances any one of the producers by producing more could lower his costs, sell at a lower price, and drive out some of his rivals; and this process would continue until there were only a few producers left in the market. But as soon as there are only a few producers left, each one of them will be producing an appreciable part of the total output of cars and each one of them will therefore affect the price of cars by producing more or less. In the end there will be a small number of producers of motor cars, each one of whom may be selling cars at a price higher than the cost of production. Each one of them may be unwilling to produce more, because by doing so he would appreciably increase the total output of cars and would so lower the price of cars that he would thereby reduce his own profit. No new producers of cars may be willing to enter the industry, although the profit made in it is abnormally high. For each new entrant would know that in order to produce at a low cost and so to share in these abnormal profits he would have to produce on a very large scale. He would realize that this additional output of cars would have a considerable effect on the total output of cars and would therefore cause a considerable fall in their price. He would realize that, while his entrance into the business would remove the abnormal profit of those already in the business, it would also so lower the price of cars that he too would be unable to cover his costs.

In many cases single and complete monopolies may exist for these reasons. In the case of the generation of electrical current a large capital outlay on plant must be incurred to set up a generating station. For this reason the average cost of production of the current will be high unless the current is produced on a sufficiently large scale to enable the plant to be fully utilized. Similarly, a railway involves investment in a large capital equipment of stations, tunnels, embankments, road bed, etc., and a small volume of traffic over the railway is costly, since it has to bear the whole of these capital costs. But any additional traffic will add little to the total costs of providing the extra service. In these circumstances a single company generating electricity or a single railway may be able to charge a price for its service higher than its cost. It may not pay any one to set up a second company to compete with the existing monopoly; for the formation of the second company would involve a similar heavy capital outlay, and would therefore need a similarly large volume of sales to produce its service cheaply, and to double the service might so lower the price which could be charged for it that the new company would be unable to cover its costs.[1]

But each individual producer may be able to affect the price of his product, not only because there are few producers but also because the market in which the product is sold is imperfect. The market in which a commodity is sold is said to be imperfect if the consumers of that commodity do not invariably purchase it from the sellers who are offering it at the lowest price. The main reasons for an imperfect market are:

(a) the existence of transport costs;
(b) lack of knowledge or inertia on the part of the consumers; and
(c) differences—whether real or imaginary—in the quality of product which each individual producer is selling.

1. Even if there were sufficient traffic to allow two competing railway lines to be profitably operated, yet there would be important economies of operation to be achieved by a combination which brought the two lines under a single management. For the two lines would not go by exactly the same route and it would be important to arrange (e.g.) the time-tables on the two lines in such a way that all the possible connections were made in the most convenient way. In the case of railways, therefore, however great the traffic may be, there are important economies to be obtained from a *single* control of the whole system in any district.

For any of these three reasons any one individual producer of a particular commodity may considerably affect the price of his product by selling more or less of it, even if there are a large number of other producers also producing the article in question. Any one of these three things may give a particular producer the support of customers whose purchases do not depend entirely upon the price which he is charging, and who thus form a special market for his product, to some extent independent of the prices charged in the rest of the market for the commodity.

(a) If the producers of a commodity are situated in different parts of the country, and if the cost of transporting the commodity from the factory to the consumer makes up a considerable part of its total cost to the consumer, each producer will affect the price of his own product by selling more or less of it. Each producer will possess a semi-independent market, composed of the consumers nearest to his factory and protected by the cost of transport of his rivals' goods into this area. Only by reducing appreciably the price charged at the factory can he persuade those consumers who live near his factory to increase their purchases considerably; and only by a similar reduction in the price charged at his factory will he be able to invade that part of his competitors' markets, which is geographically most remote from their factories and geographically nearest his own. In the absence of transport costs a quite inconsiderable reduction in price would be sufficient to attract a large volume of custom from his many competitors. Similarly, if transport costs are heavy, each producer could raise the price of his product without losing his whole market. The consumers situated near him might buy less because the price was higher, but would still buy from him rather than from his competitors. For this reason perfect competition is non-existent in nearly every industry; but if producers happen all to be situated in the same district, or if the cost of transport of the commodity is small in relation to its cost of production, the imperfections of competition due to this consideration are negligible. When production is geographically widely distributed and costs of transport are important relatively to costs of manufacture, each independent producer can exercise considerable control over the price of his product.

(b) Lack of knowledge on the part of consumers of the prices at which a commodity is being sold by different producers is another important reason why each producer may be selling in a partially independent market. There may be a large number of producers of an exactly similar article selling in conditions in which transport charges are unimportant; but if most consumers have very imperfect knowledge of the prices charged by each firm, a single producer may have to lower his price appreciably in order to be able to sell more. A lowering of his price will cause those consumers who are already purchasing from him to purchase somewhat more, and will attract from his rivals all those consumers who realize that they can now obtain the product cheaper from him. But if most of his rivals' customers do not realize that he has lowered his price, he will have to lower his price considerably to expand his sales by a given amount. Similarly, if he raises his price, he will not lose the whole of his market. Sheer force of habit also plays a part in attaching consumers to particular producers. Many people simply do not try to find cheaper sources of supply; either because it does not occur to them to do so, or because they do not consider the possible gains worth the trouble involved.

(c) The most important reason for an imperfect market is the existence of real or imaginary differences in quality and type in the article produced by each individual firm. There may be a large number of independent producers of canned fruit, but there may be differences in quality or taste of the products of the different firms. Such differences will mean that each producer has a partially independent market for his own product. If one of them puts more canned fruit on to the market, his increased output may have no appreciable effect upon the total amount of fruit offered for sale; but in order to sell his increased output he must nevertheless offer it at a considerably lower price.

For such a reduction in price will be necessary either to persuade those who are already purchasing his product to purchase more, or else to attract from his rivals those customers who prefer the particular quality or taste of other producers' fruit. Whereas, if there were no such differences in quality, a quite inconsiderable reduction in price below that charged by his competitors would suffice to attract any amount of custom which he desired. And, similarly, he could charge a higher price without losing all his custom to his competitors, since some of his customers will prefer his particular brand even at a higher price. These real or imaginary differences in quality are very important in the modern world in the purchase of chocolate, drugs, motor cars, furniture, cigarettes, clothes, and innumerable other articles.

In all the cases which we have examined in this chapter the individual producer will appreciably affect the price of his product by putting more or less of it on the market. In order to maximize his profit (or to minimize his loss) a producer will always produce and sell more so long as what he adds to his costs by producing an extra unit—which we have called his marginal cost—is less than what he adds to his receipts by selling an extra unit—which we will call his marginal receipts. In perfect competition the producer can sell more without any considerable effect upon the selling price of his product, and in this case, therefore, by selling an extra unit he will add to his receipts the price of that unit, so that in perfect competition the producer will produce more so long as his marginal cost is lower than the price of his product. In imperfect competition the producer will again produce more so long as his marginal cost is less than his marginal receipts; but in imperfect competition his marginal receipts will be less than the price of his product. For in imperfect competition he must lower his price in order to sell more; and this price reduction will affect the amount which he receives for all the units which he is already selling, so that by selling one more unit he will add to his receipts a sum equal to the price of the extra unit sold minus a reduction in price on all the units which he is already selling. He will therefore stop producing at some point before the price of his product has fallen to the level of its marginal cost.

This distinction between perfect and imperfect competition is illustrated in Tables 1, 2 (a) and 2 (b) on Chart I at the end of the book. Table 1 represents the cost conditions of a single producer. The figures in column A represent his daily output and the corresponding figures in column B represent the average cost of production when the amount shown in column A is being produced. Thus if 4 units a day are produced, the cost per unit is $25.25. The figures are chosen so that the average cost falls at first as the output is increased until, when the firm is producing 10 or 11 units a day, the cost per unit is at a minimum of $20. Up to this point the economies of mass production are predominant; but after this point the firm becomes too large for a single management and the average cost rises as the output increases. The marginal cost of production is calculated by means of columns C and D of Table 1. The figures in column C show the total cost of producing the daily output shown in column A, and are obtained by multiplying together the corresponding figures in columns A and B. Thus since 4 units a day are produced at a cost per unit of $25.25, the total cost of producing 4 units a day is $101. The figures in column D show the marginal cost of production. We see from column C that if 4 instead of 3 units of output are produced, the total cost will rise by $20—from $81 to $101—so that the marginal cost of producing the 4th unit of output is $20, and $20 is shown in column D opposite the 4th unit of output. Thus each figure in column D is obtained by subtracting the previous figure in column C from the corresponding figure in column C, and the result shows by how much the total cost is increased by adding one unit to the output. It is to be observed from Table 1 that the marginal cost in column D is always below the average cost of column B so long as the average cost is still falling, and rises above the average cost as soon as the average cost starts rising.

We have already shown in Chapter I of this Part (p. 112) why this must be so.

Tables 2 (a) and 2 (b) on Chart I represent the selling conditions for this firm's output. In both tables column A shows the output sold, column B the price at which this output can be sold, column C the total receipts for the sale of that output, and column D the marginal receipts or the amount by which the total receipts are increased by selling one more unit of output. Thus the figures in column C of Tables 2 (a) and 2 (b) are obtained by multiplying the output of column A by the selling price of column B. The figures in column D show the amount by which the figure in column C is increased through the sale of the last unit of output; thus in Table 2 (b) 8 units can be sold for a total amount of $176 and 7 units can be sold for $161, and the difference of $15 is shown in column D against the 8th unit of output. Table 2 (a) represents conditions of perfect competition in the sale of the output so that the price of $20 can be obtained for each unit of the commodity however much or little is sold; in this case whatever his output may be, the producer can add $20 to his receipts by selling one more unit, so that the figures in columns B and D are the same. In Table 2 (b), however, which represents conditions of imperfect competition in the sale of the product, the producer must lower his price in order to sell more. In this table, therefore, the marginal receipts in column D are always lower than the corresponding price in column B, since by selling an extra unit of output the producer will add to his receipts the price of the extra unit minus the fall in price on all the units which he is already selling.

We have already argued that to maximize profits or to minimize losses a producer will always sell more so long as his marginal cost is lower than his marginal receipts. To illustrate the effect of this in conditions of perfect competition we must compare column D of Table 1 with column D of Table 2 (a). We can see that the producer—if he produces anything—will produce 11 units, since his marginal costs are lower than his marginal receipts for 8, 9, or 10 units, and are higher than his marginal receipts for 12, 13, or 14 units; and from column D of Table 1 and column B of Table 2 (*a*) we see that at 11 units of output his marginal cost is equal to the price of his product. To illustrate conditions of imperfect competition we must compare Tables 1 and 2 (*b*). We can see from column D of Table 1 and column B of Table 2 (*b*) that, as before, the producer's marginal cost is equal to the price of his product for 11 units of output; but by comparing column D of Table 1 with column D of Table 2 (*b*) we can see that he will produce only 7 units, since beyond this point his marginal cost rises above his marginal receipts. At this output, however, his marginal cost, which is $15.50, is considerably below the price of his product, which is $23. This illustrates the fact that in perfect competition the marginal cost will tend to be equal to the price of the product, whereas the marginal cost will be below the price of the product if the second condition for perfect competition (mentioned on p. 102 above) is not fulfilled; i.e. if the individual firm can influence the price of its product by selling more or less of it. In the particular numerical illustration which we have chosen the average cost is also less than the price, so that the firm is making an abnormally high profit. This is likely to be the case if the first condition for perfect competition (mentioned on p. 102 above) is not fulfilled; i.e. if new firms are not free to enter the industry in which abnormal profits are being made. If they were free to do so their entry would reduce the demand for the product of each firm already there until the average cost was just equal to the price. In other words the *marginal* cost will be below the price if each individual firm can affect the price of its product by selling more or less; and the *average* cost will be below the price if new firms cannot enter the industry. These two conditions do not necessarily go together.

[The distinction between perfect and imperfect competition in the sale of the product, and the relationships in each case between costs and receipts, may be illustrated by means of

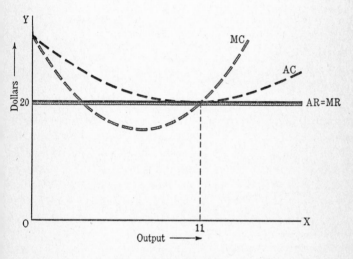

GRAPH I. *Cost and Demand Conditions in a Firm:*
PERFECT COMPETITION.

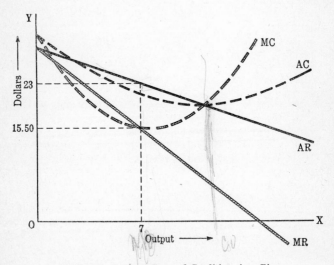

GRAPH II. *Cost and Demand Conditions in a Firm:*
IMPERFECT COMPETITION.

two simple graphs.[1] On Graph I, which represents perfect competition, the cost conditions given in Table 1 and the demand conditions given in Table 2 (*a*) have been plotted. The curve AC represents average costs per unit of output, and first falls and then rises as output increases. The curve MC represents marginal costs; it falls at first more steeply than the average curve, and then rises more steeply, cutting the average curve at its minimum point; i.e. where the size of the firm is 'optimum.' The demand curve AR, which shows the price—or average receipts; i.e. receipts per unit of sales—at which different outputs can be marketed, is a horizontal straight line, since where competition is perfect in the sale of the product the market price is not affected by a change in the output of a single firm. The marginal receipts curve MR, for reasons which are fully explained in the Appendix, coincides with the demand or average receipts curve. The manager of the firm will extend his production so long as marginal cost is less than marginal receipts. When they become equal; i.e., at 11 units of output, where the marginal cost curve cuts the marginal receipts curve, he will find it profitable to produce neither more nor less, and will therefore be in equilibrium. Since there is also free entry into the industry which produces this product, there will be a tendency for average cost to be equal to average receipts at this same point. For if it were less new firms would be attracted by the resulting profits and their entry would force down price, or average receipts, until it was equal to average cost. Conversely, if average cost were greater than average receipts, firms would tend to leave the industry because of their losses until the two again became equal. On Graph I the final position of equilibrium is shown, with all four curves intersecting at a single point.

On Graph II, which represents imperfect competition, the cost conditions are the same, but the demand conditions are those given in Table 2 (*b*). Price, or average receipts, which is

1. As we pointed out in the Introduction the reader who objects to geometry may ignore the graphs and the descriptive material printed in brackets. The graphs are alternative to the arithmetic examples; and do no more than present the same material in a different form. Those who do not object to geometry will find them useful because they simplify the exposition. An Appendix on the use of the diagrammatic method in economics is added at the end of the book, and readers who intend to use the graphs are urged to study it at this time, before attempting to understand the graphs in the text.

represented by the curve AR, falls as output is increased, and
the marginal receipts curve MR, which is derived from it,
falls more rapidly. The manager of the firm will, as in the
previous case of perfect competition, extend production so
long as marginal cost is less than marginal receipts; where,
at 7 units of output, the marginal cost and receipts curves
intersect, he will find that it pays to produce neither more nor
less. At this output, it will be noted, the marginal cost ($15.50)
is considerably less than the price ($23). This is invariably the
case where competition is imperfect. It will also be noted that
at this output the curve of average receipts AR lies above the
curve of average cost AC, which means that the firm is making
abnormal profits. If there is not free entry of firms into the
industry these may persist indefinitely. But if competition is
imperfect only in the sense that each firm can influence the
price of its product, while factors of production move freely
from occupation to occupation, these abnormal profits will
tend to disappear as a result of the entry of new firms. The
effect of such entry will be that the demand curve AR for the
product of each firm will be depressed until, directly above the
point of intersection of the marginal cost and receipts curves,
it is a tangent to the average cost curve.[1]]

In Chapter I of this Part (pp. 113–14) it was argued that in
conditions of perfect competition every producer would employ
each factor of production up to the point at which the wage of the
factor of production was just equal to the value of the marginal
product of that factor, i.e. to the price at which the additional
output due to employing the last unit of that factor could be sold.
We argued that this was so because a producer by employing
one more man would add to his cost the wage of one man and
would add to his receipts the price at which the extra product
could be sold, so that he would go on employing more men so
long as the wage-rate was lower than the price of this extra
product and would dismiss men if the wage-rate was higher than
the price of this extra product. But this is no longer true when

1. The reader who is interested may learn the reason for the marginal curves
   intersecting directly beneath the point of tangency of the average curves
   by studying the section on 'elasticity' in the Appendix.

competition is not perfect and when, by selling more of his product, the producer will cause its price to fall. The producer will still employ another man so long as he adds more to his receipts than to his costs, and he will still add to his costs the wage of one man; but he will no longer add to his receipts as much as the price at which the extra product can be sold, since the sale of a larger output will cause a reduction in the price received for the output which he is already selling.

This point is illustrated in Tables 6 (*a*) and 6 (*b*) on Chart II, at the end of the book.[1] Table 6 (*a*) illustrates perfect competition and Table 6 (*b*) imperfect competition in the sale of a producer's output. In both tables column A shows the number of men employed in a firm, and column B the output which will be produced with each quantity of labor. In both tables if 22 men are employed 904 units of the article will be produced. Column C shows the amount by which the total output shown in column B is increased by the employment of the last unit of labor. In both tables since 22 men produce 904 and 23 men produce 948, the 23rd man adds 44 units to the output, so that the marginal product of labor is 44 when 23 men are employed. Column D shows the price at which the product can be sold. In Table 6 (*a*) we are assuming perfect competition, so the producer cannot affect the price of his product, which is $1 irrespective of his output. But in Table 6 (*b*) we are assuming imperfect competition, so that the producer will cause the price to fall as he sells more. Thus, if he produces 1,170 units, he can sell them at $1.04 each, whereas if he produces 1,200 units, he must reduce his price to $1 to sell them. Column E shows the value of the marginal product of labor or the price which can be obtained for the extra output of the unit of labor employed. Since the employment of a 23rd man adds 44 units to the output, and a unit can be sold for $1 in Table 6 (*a*) and for $1.28 in Table 6 (*b*) when 23 men are employed, the value of the marginal product of the 23rd man in

1. It is also illustrated diagrammatically on Graphs III and IV in the next chapter, p. 156.

Table 6 (*a*) is $44 (i.e. 44×$1) and in Table 6 (*b*) is $56.32 (i.e. 44×$1.28). The figures in column E are thus obtained by multiplying the marginal product shown in column C by the price shown in column D. In both tables column F shows the total receipts for the sale of the output and is obtained by multiplying the output in column B by the price in column D. Column G shows the marginal value of labor to the employer or, in other words, the amount added to the total receipts by employing one more man. In Table 6 (*a*) the total receipts are $904 when 22 men are employed, and $948 when 23 men are employed, so that the addition to the receipts due to employing a 23rd man is $44. Each figure in column G in both Tables is obtained by subtracting from the corresponding figure in column F the previous figure in column F, i.e. it shows by how much the total receipts are increased by employing the last man.

In perfect competition (Table 6 (*a*)) the figures in column E and G are always the same, whereas in imperfect competition (Table 6 (*b*)) the figures in column E are always greater than the corresponding figures in column G. In other words, in perfect competition the amount added to total receipts by employing one more man is the price at which the extra output can be sold. In imperfect competition the amount added to total receipts by employing one more man is less than the price at which the extra output can be sold, because all the units of output which are already being sold must now be sold at the lower price which is necessary to sell the greater output. If competition is very imperfect, a producer by producing and selling more may actually cause his total receipts to diminish. This is illustrated by the last six figures in column G of Table 6 (*b*). If 28 men are employed, 1,138 units can be produced and sold at $1.08 each for $1,229.04; whereas if 29 men are employed, 1,170 units can be produced and sold at $1.04 each for $1,216.80. Although employing a 29th man would add 32 units to the output, each of which consumers value at $1.04, it would actually cause the producer's total receipts to fall by $12.24; for the fall in the price at which the product can be sold outweighs the fact that a large product is being sold.

A producer will employ more labor so long as the consequent addition to his costs is less than the addition to his total receipts. The figures in column G in Tables 6 (a) and 6 (b) measure the amount added to total receipts by the employment of the last unit of labor. If we suppose that the wage of labor is $30, then in perfect competition (Table 6 (a)) the producer will employ 30 units of labor, since for all amounts of employment less than this the figure in column G of Table 6 (a) is greater than $30. But in imperfect competition, if the wage-rate is $30, the producer would employ only 21 instead of 30 men; for the figures in column G of Table 6 (b) show that, if he is employing less than 21 men, the producer will add more than $30 to his receipts by employing another man, whereas as soon as he is employing 21 men he would add less than $30. In the case of perfect competition the wage-rate of $30 was equal to the price at which consumers would buy the extra output due to employing the last or 30th man. But in the case of imperfect competition the wage-rate of $30 will be less than the value of the marginal product of the last or 21st man; the 21st man will add 48 units to the output, for which consumers will pay a price of $1.36 per unit, or $65.28 for the 48 units.

This argument applies to all the factors of production. We may conclude that when there is imperfect competition among producers for any of the reasons which we have examined, the producer will not employ factors of production up to the point at which the value of their marginal product is equal to the price paid for the factor, but will stop at some earlier point when the value of the marginal product of the factor is in excess of the price of the factor.

Finally, there is one other phenomenon which may occur in consequence of imperfect competition in the sale of a product. A producer who exercises some monopoly control over a market may be able to discriminate between different classes of consumers and charge a higher price to one set of consumers than to another. Such discrimination between consumers could not take place if competition were perfect; for individual competitive producers would always transfer their sales from the lower-priced market to the higher-priced market, until all consumers were paying the same price.

A monopolist will be able to charge different prices to different consumers if for one reason or another it is difficult for consumers to sell the product to each other after it has been bought from the producer. An example is provided by doctors' services. Doctors charge more to the rich than to the poor, and to the credit of the profession they do not themselves break down this practice, as they would if each individual doctor tried to build up a practice containing only rich patients. If each did try to do this, the fees charged to rich and to poor would soon be very similar. The doctors thus act as monopolists, although not in this case as monopolists attempting to obtain a maximum income. This monopoly discrimination cannot be broken down by the consumers, i.e. the patients, since a rich man with an ailment cannot send a poor man to the doctor to obtain the diagnosis and cure at a low price for him. If, however, a monopolist tried to discriminate in prices charged for some durable commodity easily resold, such a practice would very quickly be broken down through organized resale of the commodity on the part of those consumers who were charged little to those who were charged much.

It may be of interest to give some examples of such price discrimination in the modern world. Electric current is normally sold at a lower price for certain uses than for others, although the current sold is in each case identical. Often a low price is charged for current used for power by an industrial concern, a higher price for current used for domestic heating or cooking, and a still higher price for domestic lighting. Railways usually make different freight charges for providing similar transport services according to the nature of the commodity carried, although the cost of providing the transport may be the same for each commodity. A monopolized industry may dump its product abroad in the sense that it sells the product abroad at a lower price than that charged to the home consumer. This will be possible only if there are considerable costs of transporting the product back from the foreign country to the home market or if the latter is protected by a tariff on imports.

Where it is possible for a monopolist to discriminate in the prices charged for the product to different groups of consumers, a simple principle will determine to which group of consumers the product will be sold at a high price and to which at a low price. Let us suppose that a monopolist is able to divide the consumers of his product into two groups, which for one reason or another are unable to sell his product to each other. It may be that one group of consumers will not buy much less if the price is raised or much more if the price is lowered, while the other group of consumers will buy a good deal less or more. The demand of the first group of consumers is said to be less elastic, i.e. less sensitive to price changes, than the demand of the second group of consumers.[1] The monopolist will charge a higher price to the consumers whose demand is less elastic than to the consumers whose demand is more elastic. For by raising the price to the first group of consumers he will not restrict his sales so much; while if he raised the price to the second group of consumers to the same extent, he would lose a great deal of their custom and so lose more by the reduction in sales than he gained by the fact that the price was higher.

We find that it is on this principle that a monopolist does discriminate in practice.[2] Thus, a railway will probably charge more for the transport of commodities which are expensive and costly to produce in relation to their weight and bulk, than for

1. For an illustration of this case see the section on elasticity and Graphs E and F in the Appendix.
2. In some cases differences in the prices charged by monopolists in different markets are due to real differences in costs of production. This does not constitute 'discrimination' in the sense in which we are using the term.

the transport of commodities of similar weight and bulk which are cheaper to produce. For, in the first case, the cost of transporting the commodity will constitute a small part of their total price to the consumer, so that a rise in the cost of transport of such goods will not affect their prices very appreciably and so will not greatly affect the demand for them or for their transport. Whereas if the cost of transport of a commodity constitutes a large part of its price to the consumer, a rise in the charge for its transport would cause a significant change in its price and so a relatively large fall in the demand for the product and for its transport.

Similarly, a producer will sell his product less cheaply at home than abroad if his home market is a protected one in which the demand is fairly inelastic while in the foreign market he must meet competition of foreign producers which makes the demand for his product elastic. Several of the schemes proposed for assisting American agriculture embody this principle. The demand for wheat at home is inelastic, and the price could, to the advantage of producers, be raised. In the world market, however, the competition of wheat from Canada, Argentina, and elsewhere makes the demand for American wheat elastic, so that a lower price is more remunerative. A co-operative Wheat Marketing Board to which all wheat producers adhered could increase farmers' net revenue, assuming no retaliatory measures abroad against dumping, by discriminating between the two markets.

To summarize the effects of imperfect competition in the sale of a product: the commodity will be sold at a price higher than its marginal cost of production and—what is really the same thing—the factors of production hired by producers will be paid less than the value of their marginal products. Moreover, if the producer can distinguish in his sales between different groups of purchasers who cannot sell the product to each other, he will charge higher prices to those consumers whose demand is less sensitive to changes in price than to those whose demand is more sensitive to changes in price.

V

IMPERFECT COMPETITION BETWEEN PURCHASERS

In the last chapter we examined the conditions in which individual sellers will affect the price which they can charge for their product by selling more or less of it. We have next to see in what conditions an individual purchaser will be in a position to affect the price of the commodity bought and to examine the effects of such imperfection of competition among purchasers.

We have already seen that no single purchaser will be able to affect the price of the commodity which he purchases provided: (1) that there is a large number of independent purchasers, so that no single one of them can appreciably affect the total demand for the commodity; and (2) that the market in which the commodity is bought is perfect in the sense that sellers will always desert those purchasers who offer lower prices in favor of those who offer higher prices.

These conditions are usually fulfilled in the case of the purchase of finished consumption goods; for there is normally so large a number of competing purchasers of such goods that no single individual purchases a considerable proportion of the total supply even of a single seller. Thus, the final consumer in buying meat, tea, bread, books, phonograph records, a bicycle, or a motor car has normally little or no power of influencing the price at which he can buy any of these articles. As far as he is concerned, the price at which he can buy them at any moment of time is fixed. He cannot affect considerably the sales even of his own particular supplier. But in the cases in which one consumer buys a large proportion of the output of one individual producer, who has not the opportunity of selling his product at the same price to other consumers, it will be possible for the consumer to exercise an effect upon the price of this commodity by increasing or decreasing his purchases. Thus, a person who buys a large proportion of the eggs produced by a single farmer who for one reason or another is unable to sell his eggs to others at the current market price, may be able to force down the price he pays for eggs by reducing the number he is willing to buy. But in the purchase of finished consumption goods this state of affairs is exceptional; every consumer knows that for the vast majority of the articles he buys he cannot affect the price significantly by buying more or less.

In the case of the purchase of factors of production (e.g. the hiring of labor or the purchase of raw materials) the individual purchaser can more frequently affect the price of the factor by varying his own individual demand. For, in the first place, it is more likely that there will only be a small number of purchasers of any given factor, and, in the second place, it is more probable that those who sell the factors of production will be unable to offer their services to other possible purchasers at the same price as before if the present purchaser restricts his demand.

Suppose that there is an industry (e.g. the manufacture of motor cars) which purchases a very large proportion of the total output of some raw material (e.g. rubber of a certain type and quality), and that this industry is monopolized or in the hands of very few independent producers. If one of the producers of motor cars decides to produce more and for this purpose to buy more rubber, he will realize that his increased demand for rubber will have an appreciable effect upon the total demand for rubber and may therefore cause its price to rise. Conversely, he may be able to force down the price of rubber by restricting his own purchases, which are an appreciable part of the total purchases of rubber.

Cases of this sort may exist; but the individual purchaser of a factor of production is more likely to be able to affect the price of the factor purchased because it is difficult for that factor to move to other purchasers or employers. Even if there were a large number of independent producers of motor cars, each individual producer would be able to affect the wage-rate paid to his labor by employing more or less men if he were the only manufacturer in a particular district employing that type of labor, or if motor mechanics were ignorant of the wage-rates paid in firms other than the firm in which they are employed. A considerable reduction in the wage-rate offered by the particular employer would cause some persons to move into other jobs in the same district or to move to similar firms in other districts. But the employer would not lose the whole of his labor supply. Some of his employees might find it too costly to move into other districts or other trades, or might not realize the opportunities of earning higher wages in other occupations or districts. Similarly, he might have to offer a considerably higher wage in order to attract more labor, because the wage offered must be raised enough to make up for the cost to labor of transferring itself from other less well-paid districts or other less well-paid occupations in the same district. If the mobility of labor between different firms is not perfect, the individual employer may be able to pay a considerably lower wage-rate without losing all his hands, and may be obliged to raise the wage-rate considerably in order to attract more men to his employment.

Whether imperfect competition between the purchasers of factors of production is due to the fact that there is a small number of purchasers or to the lack of complete mobility of the factors between the purchasers, the individual purchaser will raise the price of the factor by buying more of it and can lower the price by buying less. In these circumstances the individual producer will not employ the factors of production up to the point at which the price paid to the factor is equal to the value of the marginal product of that factor. In order to maximize his profit the producer will take on additional units of a factor so long as what he adds to his costs is less than what he adds to his receipts by the sale of the extra output. If the producer must offer a higher wage-rate in order to employ more labor, then by employing one more unit of labor he will add to his costs more than the wage of that unit; for he will add to his costs the wage-rate of the new unit of labor plus the rise in the wage-rate paid to all the labor he is already employing. Thus, even if there were perfect competition in the sale of his product, in cases where the producer must offer a higher wage-rate to attract more labor he will stop employing more when the wage-rate is still considerably below the value of labor's marginal product.

This result is illustrated in Tables 7 (a) and 7 (b) on Chart II at the end of the book. Table 7 (a) represents the position of an employer who hires his labor in conditions of perfect competition, and Table 7 (b) the position of an employer who hires his labor in an imperfect labor market. In both tables column A shows the number of men employed, column B the wage-rate paid when that number is employed, column C the total wage-bill, which is obtained by multiplying each number employed by the wage-rate paid, and column D the marginal wage-cost or the addition to the total wage-bill which is caused by taking on one more man. Thus from Table 7 (a) it is clear that if the wage-rate is unaffected by the size of the employer's demand for labor, the addition to costs due to taking on one more man (column D) is the same as the wage-rate paid (column B). But from Table 7 (b) it can be seen that when an increase in the demand for labor causes a rise in the wage-rate, the individual employer by taking on one more laborer will add to his wage-bill more than the wage-rate of the additional laborer employed. In Table 7 (b) 25 men can be employed at a wage of $20 and 26 men at a wage-rate of $22 so that the total wage-bill will rise from $500 to $572 if a 26th man is employed. Thus the marginal wage-cost of the 26th man is $72, which is considerably greater than the wage-rate of $22 which is paid when 26 men are employed. In these conditions a 26th man will be employed only if his employment adds to the receipts of the firm as much as $72, although the wage-rate is only $22.

We have shown in the last chapter that when a product is sold in conditions of imperfect competition, labor will be paid an amount less than the value of its marginal product because the producer will add to his receipts by employing another unit of labor something less than the price at which additional output is sold. This is illustrated in Table 6 (*b*). We have now shown that if labor is hired in conditions of imperfect competition, it will receive less than the value of its marginal product because the employer will add more to his costs by employing one more man than the wage of that man. This we have illustrated in Table 7 (*b*). It is, of course, possible that in a particular case the conditions of competition are imperfect both for the sale of the product and for the hire of labor. In this case labor will receive a wage which is lower than the value of its marginal product for two reasons: the addition to costs due to take on another man will be more than the wage of that man, and at the same time the addition to receipts due to the sale of the extra output of the additional man will be less than the value of that extra output.

There are in fact four possible combinations:

1. If there is perfect competition both in the sale of the product and in the hire of labor, producers will employ more labor so long as the marginal value of labor in column G of Table 6 (*a*) is greater than the marginal wage-cost in column D of Table 7 (*a*). In these circumstances 30 men will be employed; the value of the marginal product of labor will be $30 as can be seen from column E of Table 6 (*a*), and the wage-rate will be $30, as can be seen from column B of Table 7 (*a*).

2. If the market for the sale of the product is imperfect, while labor is hired in conditions of perfect competition, we must compare Tables 6 (*b*) and 7 (*a*). More men will be employed so long as the marginal value of labor in column G of Table 6 (*b*) is greater than the marginal wage-cost in column D of Table 7 (*a*). In this case 21 men will be employed, and it is seen from column E of Table 6 (*b*) that the value of the marginal product of labor will be $65.28 and from column B of Table 7 (*a*) that the wage-rate will be $30.

3. If the product is sold in conditions of perfect competition, while labor is hired in conditions of imperfect competition, we must compare Tables 6 (*a*) and 7 (*b*). More labor will be taken on so long as the marginal value of labor in column G of Table 6 (*a*) is greater than the marginal wage-cost in column D of Table 7 (*b*). In this case only 20 men will be employed, and it is clear from column E of Table 6 (*a*) that the value of the marginal product of labor is $70 and from column B of Table 7 (*b*) that the wage-rate is $10.

4. Finally, if there is imperfect competition both in the sale of the product and in the hire of labor, we must compare Tables 6 (*b*) and 7 (*b*). Employment will only be increased so long as the marginal value of labor in column G of Table 6 (*b*) is higher than the marginal wage-cost in column D of Table 7 (*b*). In this case, then, only 19 men will be employed, the value of the marginal product of labor will be $74.88, and the wage-rate only $8.

[These four possible combinations can also be illustrated graphically. That of perfect competition in both the product and labor markets is shown in Graph III. The curve VMP, representing the value of labor's marginal product, is obtained by multiplying the marginal product of labor for each number of laborers employed by the price of the product. The curve of the marginal value of labor coincides in this case with the curve of the value of labor's marginal product because, as we have shown, the marginal value of labor is equal to the value of labor's marginal product when the market for the product is perfect. The wage-rate or cost per unit of labor is represented by the curve AC (average cost); and since the wage-rate is independent of the number of laborers hired AC is a straight horizontal line. The curve MC showing the marginal cost of labor coincides with it (for reasons explained fully in the Appendix). The point of intersection of the two marginal curves reveals that 30 laborers will be employed at a marginal cost equal to the wage-rate of $30.

The second combination—imperfect competition in the market for the product coupled with perfect competition in the labor market—is illustrated by Graph IV. Here the mar-

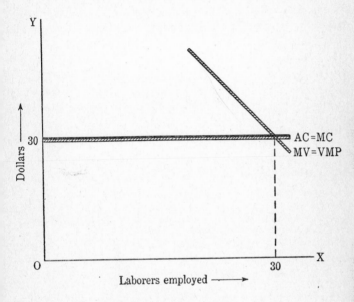

GRAPH III. *The Demand for Labor in a Firm:*
PERFECT COMPETITION *in Sale of Product and Hire of Labor.*

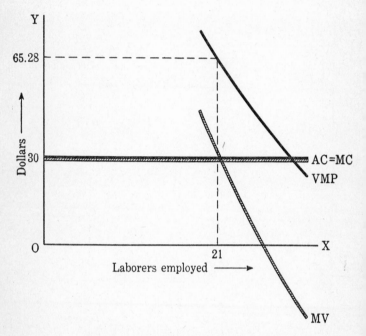

GRAPH IV. *The Demand for Labor in a Firm:*
IMPERFECT COMPETITION *in Sale of Product and*
PERFECT COMPETITION *in Hire of Labor.*

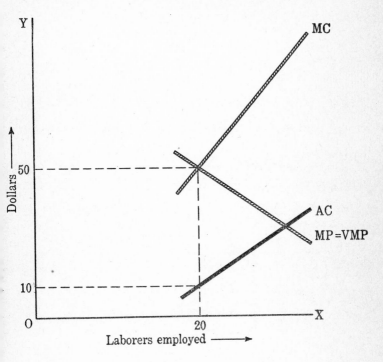

GRAPH V. *The Demand for Labor in a Firm:*
PERFECT COMPETITION *in Sale of Product and*
IMPERFECT COMPETITION *in Hire of Labor.*

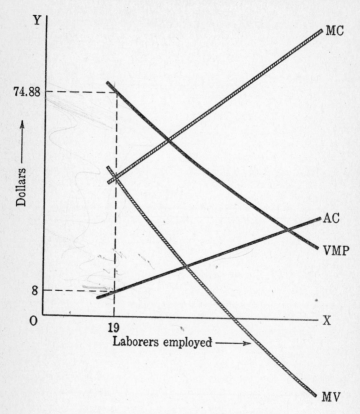

GRAPH VI. *The Demand for Labor in a Firm:*
IMPERFECT COMPETITION *in Sale of Product and
Hire of Labor.*

ginal value of labor MV is less than the value of labor's marginal product VMP, for the hiring of each additional laborer involves the employer in a loss on the whole of his previous output due to the lower price at which he must offer it. The point of intersection of the curve of marginal cost and marginal value shows that 21 men will be employed at a wage-rate of $30, although the value of the marginal product of labor is still as high as $65.28.

Graph V shows perfect competition in the market for the product with imperfect competition in the supply of labor. The hiring of each additional unit of labor involves the payment of a higher wage-rate, with the effect that the average cost of labor curve AC, which represents the wage-rate, rises as employment increases, and that the marginal cost curve MC rises even more rapidly. The point of intersection of the marginal curves is accordingly far to the left of where it would be if, with the same wage rate, the labor market were perfect.

It would be possible, similarly, to draw a graph showing the demand and supply conditions when competition is imperfect in both markets. The MV and VMP curves of Graph IV would have to be combined with the AC and MC curves of Graph V. The point of intersection would clearly be farther to the left, and the divergence between the wage-rate and the value of the marginal product greater, than in either of the graphs showing imperfect competition in one market only.]

The foregoing argument applies to all factors of production hired by employers, so that any factor of production will be paid less than the value of its marginal product if the product is sold in conditions of imperfect competition or if the factor is hired in conditions of imperfect competition. We may add that the extent to which any factor of production is paid less than the value of its marginal product would be increased,

(1) if competition in the sale of its product became less perfect, i.e. if the price at which the product could be sold became more sensitive to changes in the amount put on the market by the individual producer, and

(2) if competition in the purchase of the factor became less

perfect, i.e. if the wage paid by the individual employer became more sensitive to changes in the amount of the factor employed by the individual employer.

The extent, therefore, to which any factor of production is paid less than the value of its marginal product will differ in different occupations, according as competition is more or less perfect in different occupations both in the sale of the products and also in the purchase of the factor.[1]

1. The tables and the diagrams illustrate these *relations* between the marginal product and the wage of a factor, and care should be taken not to deduce from them more than this. They do *not* show that employment in an industry will become less if competition in the market for the product or the factor becomes less perfect, but merely that marginal product will exceed the wage-rate by an amount dependent upon the degree of imperfection in the two markets. It is not suggested that imperfect competition causes unemployment, nor has it been proved that the restoration of perfect competition, where that is possible, would alleviate it, although in the normal case it probably would to some extent. Only if the curve of marginal productivity and the wage-rate were the same in the two cases would employment necessarily be less with imperfect competition.

VI

THE DISADVANTAGES OF MONOPOLISTIC CONDITIONS

In Chapter II of this Part it was argued that, if there were perfect competition, a given amount of the factors of production would be employed in such a way

(i) that no individual consumer's needs could be better satisfied without a reduction in some other consumer's welfare,

(ii) that no commodity could be produced in greater amount without a reduction in the production of some other commodity, and

(iii) that each individual firm would be of the most efficient size.

In Chapters IV and V of this Part, however, it was argued that the absence of state interference in the economic sphere does not necessarily lead to perfect competition. We have therefore to see to what extent these three fundamental advantages of competition are modified by the fact that competition is not perfect. This is the task which we shall undertake in this chapter.

The first important advantage of perfect competition was that the factors of production would be used in different occupations in such a way that the consumers' needs were best satisfied. For in perfect competition each factor is offered in each occupation a reward equal to the value of its marginal product, which measures the price which consumers are willing to pay for the additional output of the factor. But in the real world in conditions of imperfect competition the factors of production will not automatically flow into those occupations in which their output is most desired by consumers. In an industry which is producing in conditions of highly imperfect competition the reward offered for a factor of production will be much below the price offered by consumers for the marginal product of that factor: in an industry which is perfectly, or very nearly perfectly, competitive the reward offered for the factor will be nearly as great as the price offered by consumers for the marginal product of the factor. In this case consumers' needs could be better satisfied if factors of production were compelled to move from the highly competitive to the very imperfectly competitive industry; for consumers would lose in the first industry an output for which they offered a price about equal to the reward of the factor, and would gain in the second industry an output for which they were offering a price considerably in excess of the reward of the factor.[1]

This point can be illustrated by means of an example. Suppose that the marginal product of labor in the production of tea is 1 lb. and in the production of bread is 1 loaf, and that the price of a pound of tea is 10c. and of a loaf of bread is 20c. Consumers' tastes would be better served if labor were shifted from the production of tea to the production of bread, since for each unit of labor so shifted consumers would lose 1 lb. of tea valued at 10c. and gain 1 loaf of bread valued at 20c. In perfect competition this shifting would occur, because labor would be being offered twice as much in the production of bread as in the production of tea. In imperfect competition this would also happen if competition were equally imperfect in both industries. The reward offered to labor in each industry might be equal to half of the value of its marginal product, and in these circumstances labor would shift from producing tea to producing bread until the value of the marginal product of labor was the same in each occupation. But if competition were more nearly perfect in the tea industry than in the bread industry, factors might be offered rewards equal to three-quarters of the value of their marginal products in the tea industry and to one-quarter the value of their marginal products

1. Strictly speaking, consumers *could* gain in the second industry a more valuable output than they lost in the first; and *would* if steps were taken, along lines to be suggested in the next two chapters, to insure that the factors were effectively utilized in the imperfectly competitive industry to which they were moved.

in the bread industry. Then in the numerical example quoted above, labor would be offered $7\frac{1}{2}$c. (i.e. $\frac{3}{4} \times$ 10c.) in the tea industry and only 5c. (i.e. $\frac{1}{4} \times$ 20c.) in the bread industry. The factors would actually be attracted from producing bread to producing tea, although the consumers would be better served if they moved from producing tea to producing bread, where the price offered by consumers for their marginal product is twice as great. If there are different degrees of imperfection of competition in the sale of different products, more factors ought to be employed in those industries in which competition is abnormally imperfect and less in those industries in which competition is most nearly perfect.

We saw at the end of Chapter IV of this Part that monopolistic sellers may be able to discriminate in the prices charged to different groups of consumers for the same product. In this case, though it may be that production is greater than if the monopolist had not the power of discrimination, it is certain that the factors hired by the discriminating monopolist will not be used in the most advantageous way, for the marginal products of those serving the dearer of his markets will be greater than the marginal products of those serving the cheaper. Suppose that a co-operative Dairy Association, to which all milk producers in a given area belong, attempts to increase its revenue by selling milk for manufacturing into cheese more cheaply than milk for liquid consumption.[1] Each pint of milk costs the same to produce; but because different pints are sold at different prices consumers' needs are not most effectively served. For without using more factors, consumers could be made better off if more milk were sold in liquid form and less to be manufactured into cheese. The price which consumers pay for a pint of liquid milk measures the degree to which they would like one more pint to drink; while

1. On the theory, doubtless correct, that the demand for milk for manufacturing purposes is more elastic than the demand for milk for liquid consumption. Most co-operative associations of dairy farmers in this country do discriminate in precisely this way, as does the English official Milk Marketing Board.

the price paid for a pint of milk to be made into cheese measures (indirectly through the price offered for cheese) the extent to which consumers want one more pint of milk in the form of cheese. If, therefore, the price of milk sold in its liquid form is higher than the price of milk sold in the form of cheese, consumers would be better off if they had one more pint of milk to drink at the cost of having one less pint of milk in the form of cheese. Only if the price of a commodity is the same for every purpose for which it is purchased will consumers use the available supply in such proportions between the different uses that no advantage can be obtained by using more of it in one use and less of it in another.

The second fundamental advantage of perfect competition was that the factors of production would automatically be used in such proportions in different industries that it would be impossible to increase the output of one industry without reducing the output of some other. It was argued on pp. 120, 121 that production will be maximized in this sense if the ratio between the marginal products of the different factors is the same in every industry. In Table IV on p. 120 the situation was illustrated by supposing that in the bread industry the marginal products of labor and capital were the same, viz. 4 loaves a day, while in the tea industry the marginal product of labor was 1 lb. a day and the marginal product of capital was 3 lb. a day. It was shown that if a unit of labor moved from the tea industry to the bread industry and a unit of capital from the bread industry to the tea industry, the output of tea would be increased by 2 lb. a day while the output of bread would remain unchanged. It was argued that perfect competition combined with free movement of the factors of production would cause the desired shifting of the factors of production. For the proportion of labor to capital employed would diminish in the tea industry, where the marginal product of labor and so its reward were only one-third that of capital: whereas a higher proportion of labor to capital would be used in the bread industry where the marginal products and so the rewards offered for the factors were the same.

But this shift of factors would not necessarily take place if competition in the purchase of labor were more imperfect in the bread industry than in the tea industry, or if competition in the purchase of capital were more imperfect in the tea industry than in the bread industry. Suppose that there is perfect competition in the sale of both tea and bread, that there is perfect competition in the hiring of capital in both industries, and that there is perfect competition in the hiring of labor in the tea industry but not in the bread industry. In these conditions both the factors of production will be offered rewards equal to the value of their marginal products in the tea industry; whereas in the bread industry capital will be offered a reward equal to the value of its marginal product, while labor will be offered a reward less than the value of its marginal product. Thus, if the price of a loaf were 3c. and of 1 lb. of tea were 4c., we can see from Table IV that the value of the marginal product of capital in the bread industry will be 4×3c. or 12c. and in the tea industry also will be 3×4c. or 12c. The value of the marginal product of labor in the bread industry will also be 4×3c. or 12c., but in the tea industry will only be 1×4c. or 4c. A unit of capital will be paid 12c. in each occupation. Labor will be offered 4c. in the tea industry, where competition in the labor market is perfect, and something less than 12c. in the bread industry, where there are monopolistic conditions. If there is sufficient imperfection in the labor market in the bread industry (i.e. if the individual producer of bread is obliged to offer a considerably higher wage-rate to attract more labor), it is possible that labor is paid a wage of only 4c. in the bread industry, although the value of its marginal product is as high as 12c. In these circumstances the position shown in Table IV would continue unchanged, since labor as well as capital would be offered the same rewards in both industries.

For this reason, if there are two industries, in one of which there is considerably less perfect competition for the hiring of labor, while the same degree of competition exists in both industries for the hiring of other factors, the production of the two industries will not be maximized. Producers in the industry in which there is great imperfection in the hiring of labor will have a particularly strong motive to use a small proportion of labor to other factors in order to avoid raising the wage-rate by employing more labor. In such an industry, therefore, the ratio between the marginal product of labor and the marginal product of other factors will remain unusually high. And these are just the circumstances in which by using a larger proportion of labor to other factors the output of the commodity concerned could be increased without diminishing the output of other commodities.

The third fundamental advantage of perfect competition was that all the individual firms would be of the optimum or most efficient size. We argued in Chapter I of this Part (p. 111) that in perfect competition, if a firm is producing less than the optimum output, forces will operate which will induce it to expand. But if competition in the sale of its product is imperfect, it may not expand; for although it would lower the average cost of its product by producing more, the fact that it would have to lower its price to sell more might outweigh this, so that it would diminish its profits by doing so. In imperfect competition it is quite probable that in a particular industry there will be a number of firms each just covering its costs and each producing an output below its optimum output. No one of them may have an incentive to expand because to do so would cause the price obtained for the product to fall much more quickly than its costs. And in these circumstances there is, prima facie, a loss to the community; for if the same total output of the commodity were produced by a smaller number of firms, each firm could produce at its capacity output and so at a lower cost, and in this way the same output could be produced at a lower total cost.

Thus in conditions of imperfect competition it may be possible to obtain more efficient conditions of production by concentrating the output of an industry on a smaller number of firms. But in pointing this out we have raised a complex issue. The reason why the concentration of output does not necessarily take place is because any one of the firms would have to sell its output at a lower price in order to sell more. An individual firm will have to lower its selling price in order to sell more either if there are only a few firms in the industry each producing a large proportion of the total output of the industry, or if there is an imperfect market for the product.

An imperfect market for the industry's product exists if for one reason or another the consumers do not consider the output of each firm to be identical, but prefer the product of one firm to that of another, so that they will only change their custom from one supplier to another if their preference is overcome by a sufficiently large margin between the prices at which the two suppliers are offering their products. But—and this is the point of vital importance—this buyers' preference may be of two kinds, 'irrational' or 'rational.' If it is irrational, it is due to inertia or lack of knowledge on the part of consumers. Consumers may prefer A's goods to B's goods mistakenly, either simply because they are in the habit of buying A's goods or because they think wrongly that A's goods are superior to B's goods. If the buyers' preference is rational, they prefer A's goods to B's goods for good and rational reasons, such as differences in transport costs or in the qualities of the products. The test is simply this. If a consumer were forced to have B's goods instead of A's goods, would he be worse off as a result of the change?[1] If, in fact, he would be worse off, the buyer's preference is rational; if not, it is irrational.

If the failure of an imperfectly competitive industry to concentrate its output on a sufficiently small number of firms is due either to the fact that there are only a few firms in the industry, or to the fact that irrational buyers' preference exists in the

---

1. He would be worse off unless his satisfaction was increased by enough to compensate for any costs (e.g., the breaking of old friendships) involved in transferring his custom.

Note that we are using the terms 'rational' and 'irrational' in a very special and technical sense. A person who pays an unnecessarily high price because he doesn't bother to investigate other sources of supply is behaving 'irrationally' by our definition, although *from his own point of view* his action might be perfectly sensible.

market for the product, then the community clearly gains by the concentration of the industry's output on a smaller number of firms. For in these cases consumers lose nothing by being offered a smaller choice of products, and there is an economy of production obtained from the concentration. But if the failure to concentrate output is due to the existence of rational buyers' preference, it is not certain that the concentration of output is to the community's advantage. If some firms are closed down, some consumers will be forced to transfer their custom to other firms, although they had a rational preference for the products which they were previously buying. There will therefore be a certain loss of consumers' satisfaction which must be set against the increased efficiency of production. We must therefore determine in what circumstances there will be a net gain by concentrating output on a smaller number of firms.

We must at this point introduce an idea which we have hitherto avoided, namely, 'the marginal product of management.' Just as we have spoken of the marginal product of labor, or capital, or land, so we may speak of the marginal product of management. The marginal product of labor was defined as the amount by which output would be increased if one more unit of labor were employed, *the amount of the other factors of production remaining unchanged*. In an exactly similar way we may define the marginal product of management as the amount by which the output of an industry would be increased if one more unit of management were used in that industry together with the same amount of the other factors of production, i.e. if there were one more firm in that industry, while the total amount of the other factors employed in that industry was constant. Suppose that there are 9 firms in an industry, each employing 100 units of labor and capital. Then the marginal product of management in that industry is the amount by which the output of the industry would be increased if the 900 units of labor and capital were employed by 10 firms each employing 90 units of the other factors, i.e. if the number of units of management increased by one from 9 to 10.

It follows that the value of the marginal product of the management of a particular firm is equal to the total value to consumers of the output of that firm minus the value of the marginal product which could be produced in other firms by the factors now employed in the particular firm. For the closing down of this firm together with the transference of the hired factors to other firms will inflict a loss on consumers equal to the total value to them of this firm's output minus the price offered by them for the marginal product of the hired factors in the other firms to which they are transferred.

If there is no rational buyers' preference for the product of a particular firm over the product of other firms in the same industry, and if the number of firms in the industry is large, the total amount spent by consumers on the firm's output will measure the total value to them of the firm's output. If, therefore, the firm was closed down and the hired factors were transferred to other firms in the same industry, the net loss to consumers—and so the value of the marginal product of the management of this firm—would be equal to the amount spent on this firm's output minus the value of the marginal product of the hired factors when employed in the other firms. Since the management of the particular firm will receive a reward equal to the amount spent on the firm's output minus the amount paid by it to the hired factors, it follows that if it must pay rewards to the hired factors as great as the value of their marginal products in other firms—which will be the case in perfect competition, since the other firms will be offering rewards as great as the value of their marginal products—the management will receive a reward equal to the value of its marginal product. But if it can pay rewards to the hired factors lower than the value of their marginal products in other firms—which will be the case in imperfect competition, since the other firms will be offering rewards lower than the value of marginal products—the management will receive a reward greater than the value of its marginal product; and the excess of the reward of management over the value of its marginal product will be exactly equal to the deficiency of the rewards paid to the hired factors below the value of their marginal products in other firms. We may conclude, therefore, that in the absence of rational buyers' preference for the product of any particular firm, both management and the hired factors will receive rewards equal to the value of their marginal products in conditions of perfect competition, while in conditions of imperfect competition the hired factors will receive less than the value of their marginal products and management will receive just so much more than the value of its marginal product.

Since at any one time there is only a limited amount of business ability—i.e. of the factor 'management'—available in the community, it, like every other factor, should be used in different occupations up to the point at which the value of its marginal product is the same in every occupation. Management should therefore move from those industries in which the value of its marginal product is low to those in which it is high. The state should interfere with the automatic distribution of factors of production among different occupations in order to shift those factors which are hired by the management from the less to the more monopolistic industries, where they are offered much less than the value of their marginal products, and to shift management from those industries which are more to those which are less monopolistic. In other words, in the more monopolistic industries there should be more land, labor, and capital concentrated among fewer firms, and in the less monopolistic industries there should be less of the hired factors spread over a larger number of firms.[1]

It may at first appear paradoxical to conclude that there should be *fewer* firms in the *more* monopolistic industries, since monopoly

1. Cases may arise when the transference of hired factors to the more monopolistic industries will not be necessary. For the reduction of the number of firms in the industry may so increase the efficiency with which the factors already there are used, and thereby the product, that the values of the marginal products of the factors will fall below the values of their marginal products elsewhere.

is naturally considered to exist only when the number of independent sellers is too few. But it must be remembered that this argument is based on the assumption that all factors of production including management have been free to move to the industries in which they can earn most. Of course, a monopoly may also exist because the right to produce a certain commodity is restricted by law to one producer. In this case the management will be earning more than management can earn in other industries, and if such legal restrictions were the only cause of monopoly, the removal of these restrictions would cause more firms to come into the industry. In this case more firms *should* come into the industry until perfectly competitive conditions have been restored, in which case both the reward and the marginal product of management will be the same in every industry.

But as we saw in Chapter IV the chief reasons for monopolistic conditions, which enable each firm to affect the price of its product, are not legal restrictions on entry into an industry. There may, for example, be a very large number of independent drug stores in a district, each of which has a very small turnover and is therefore of less than the most efficient size. None of them may be able to expand profitably at the expense of the others, because each has a special semi-independent market protected by the irrational goodwill of its customers. The management of each store may be receiving a reward no greater than similar management in other occupations, because it is perfectly open for more people to set up drug stores and they will do so as long as an abnormally high reward for management is obtainable in that occupation. Yet each store is monopolistic according to our definition, since each could sell more only by offering its goods at a considerably lower price. In cases of this sort, where irrational preferences exist and the unrestricted movement of the factors of production will not in itself remove all monopolistic conditions, governmental measures designed to shift management from the more to the less monopolistic industries should no longer appear paradoxical.

In the next two chapters we shall discuss possible ways of re-

moving the disadvantages which are due to monopolistic conditions; but it is worth while pointing out here one way in which
(so long as there was no rational buyers' preference) it could be
insured that there were the correct number of firms in each industry. We have seen that, if the hired factors of production are,
in every firm, paid rewards equal to the value of their marginal
products, the management will also receive a reward equal to
the value of its marginal product. If, therefore, some method of
control were devised to insure that all *hired* factors of production
were offered rewards equal to the value of their marginal products, management also would receive the value of its marginal
product. In consequence, if there were no rational buyers' preference and if all factors were free to move in search of the highest
rewards, management would automatically go into the industries where it was most needed and the number of firms in each
industry would be the optimum.

But these arguments unfortunately do not apply when buyers'
preference is rational.[1] Where rational buyers' preference exists,
the products of the different firms in the industry must differ in
some significant way. In other words, when there is no rational
buyers' preference, we may say that each firm is producing identically the same commodity, but where there is rational buyers'
preference, each firm is producing a different commodity. If one
among many firms producing identically the same commodity
stopped production, the total loss to the consumers could be
measured by the marginal utility of the money spent by the consumers on the product of that firm. But if there is only one firm
producing a single commodity and this firm ceased production,

1. It should be noted that while the rationality of buyers' preference *may*
make it undesirable to interfere to achieve the third advantage of perfect
competition (i.e. firms of optimum size, see p. 159 above), it can never
make it undesirable to interfere to achieve the first two advantages. As long
as the values of the marginal products of factors are different in different
occupations, whether the difference arises as a result of rational or irrational preferences, it will benefit consumers to secure a movement of factors
between industries which will equate them. The only question which
arises is whether, within each industry, firms should be so reduced in numbers as to be of the technically most efficient size.

the total loss to consumers is greater than the marginal utility of the money spent on the commodity.

This can be made clear by an example. Suppose that there are 100 consumers each consuming 100 loaves of bread at 5c. a loaf. Then the total output of bread will be 10,000 loaves selling at 5c. each. If these loaves are produced by 100 independent firms and one firm ceased production, each consumer would have only 99 instead of 100 loaves. Each consumer will lose five cents worth of satisfaction by having only 99 instead of 100 loaves, and the total loss to consumers can therefore be measured by the marginal utility of the $5.00 which was being spent on the output of the firm which has now ceased production. But if all the 10,000 loaves were produced by a single firm which ceased production, the total loss to consumers, who would now have no bread at all and so might starve, would be very much greater than 100 times the loss caused by the disappearance of one hundredth part of the total output. The amount of money spent on the total output of a commodity does not measure the total loss in which consumers would be involved if that commodity were not produced at all, although the price of a commodity does measure the loss in which consumers would be involved if one less unit were produced.

In order to deal with our present problem we must know how to estimate the loss to consumers of being deprived of the *whole* of the supply of one commodity. We can do this by means of Table 4 on Chart I at the end of the book. In this table column A shows the total output of a commodity demanded by consumers, and column B shows the price which they will be willing to pay for every amount of the commodity which they consume. Naturally this price falls as they consume more. Column C shows the total amount spent by consumers on different amounts of the commodity, and the figures in column C are therefore obtained by multiplying together the corresponding figures in columns A and B. Column E shows the total amount which consumers would pay for each amount of the commodity shown in column A if they were offered the choice between having that amount or none at all.

The figures in column E are calculated in the following way. We can see from column B that consumers will purchase 1 unit if the price is $25. It follows immediately that consumers will give $25 for 1 unit rather than go without it, so that the corresponding figure in column E is also $25. Column B shows that when the price falls to $24 the consumers will buy 2 units instead of 1 unit. When the price is $24, consumers are perfectly free to buy 1 or 2 units of the commodity. The fact that they buy 2 instead of 1 means, as we have already argued in Chapter I of this Part, that to have a second adds an amount to their satisfaction which is worth $24. But since to have 1 rather than none added $25 worth of satisfaction, while to have 2 instead of 1 added $24 worth of satisfaction, clearly to have 2 instead of none adds $49 (or $25+$24) worth of satisfaction. The consumers would pay anything up to $49 in order to have 2 rather than none. Similarly, column B shows that when the price falls to $23, the consumers, who are free to buy as much as they like at this price, buy 3 instead of 2 units. To have a 3rd must therefore add $23 to their satisfaction. But since, as we have seen, they would pay anything up to $49 to have 2 units instead of none, they would pay anything up to $72 (or $49+$23) to have 3 instead of none, since a 3rd unit adds $23 worth to their satisfaction. Thus $72 is entered in column E against the 3rd unit of consumption. Each figure in column E is obtained by adding the corresponding figure in column B to the previous figure in column E. The price of a commodity measures its marginal utility to consumers, i.e. the amount which is added to the consumers' satisfaction by having one more unit of the commodity, so that the total value of any amount of a commodity to consumers is obtained by adding the price at which they will purchase the last additional unit to the total value of the previous number of units purchased.

In using Table 4 of Chart I there are two points which must be borne in mind:

(i) The table must show the prices which consumers would actually pay for different amounts of the particular commodity on the assumption that they continue to purchase approximately the same amounts of every other commodity. For it is only in these circumstances that the price measures the importance to consumers of having one more or less unit of this particular commodity. It was assumed in the two paragraphs above that such a schedule of prices is identical to the schedule which an individual firm, producing the whole supply of a commodity, can expect to obtain, or can in fact obtain, for different quantities of output. In fact the two schedules may differ considerably. For if there are a few other firms producing commodities which are close substitutes for this particular commodity, the firm in question by producing more or less of its own product may cause the other competing firms to alter their output.[1] In this case the schedule of prices which an individual firm can expect to obtain for different amounts of output differs from the schedule of prices which consumers *would* pay for different amounts of its output if there were no change in the quantities of the products which other firms put on the market. The former schedule will determine the firm's output; the latter is relevant for our present purpose.

(ii) It is assumed that the commodity in question is one upon which individuals spend only a small proportion of their total income. For if this were not so, a rise in the price of this single commodity might significantly increase to consumers the importance of their money income; and since in this case the marginal utility of money would depend upon the price of the commodity, the money price paid for it would no longer form a stable measure of its marginal utility.

We can now see the difference between the value of the marginal product of management in an industry in which there are many firms producing identical commodities, and the value of

1. The student of economics will observe that this is the case where 'duopoly' or 'oligopoly' elements are present.

the marginal product of management in an industry in which there is rational buyers' preference for the product of different firms, so that each firm is, in fact, producing a different commodity. In both cases the value of the marginal product of management is the net loss to consumers due to the closing down of the single firm and the concentration of the hired factors on the remaining firms. In both cases it can therefore be measured by the total value to consumers of the output of the single firm minus the price offered by consumers for the marginal product of the hired factors in the existing firms to which they are transferred. But in the case of an industry in which there are a large number of firms producing identically the same commodity, the output of a single firm represents only a small part of the total output of the commodity, and the price paid for the output of this firm can be taken to measure the total value to consumers of the firm's output; whereas in the case of a single firm producing the whole output of a single commodity, the total amount spent on the firm's output is less than the total value of that output to the consumers. For consumers would be willing to pay a larger amount than they do for the whole output of a commodity rather than go without it altogether.

If it could be arranged that all hired factors were paid rewards equal to the value of their marginal products, the actual rewards received by the management of firms in industries in which there were a large number of firms producing the same commodity would be a true measure of the value of the marginal product of management. In these circumstances management should move to the industries in which it received most. But if the question arises whether a single firm should be set up to produce a new commodity, or whether a single firm which is producing the whole output of a particular commodity should be closed down—and this case includes the setting up or closing down of one firm in an industry in which there is rational buyers' preference—the principles involved are different. If all hired factors are paid rewards equal to the value of their marginal products in other occupations, the management of a single firm producing the whole output of a commodity will receive something less than the value of its marginal product. For the value of its marginal product is equal to what consumers would be willing to pay for the firm's output, rather than have none of the commodity, minus the amount paid to the hired factors; and this is greater than what is spent on the product minus the amount paid to the hired factors. A new firm should therefore be set up to produce a new commodity if the value of the marginal product of management reckoned in this way is greater than the value of the marginal product of management in other industries.

If it could be assured that the hired factors of production were paid rewards equal to the value of their marginal products, the movement of every factor of production, including the factor management, to those occupations in which it was earning the highest reward, would bring about the most desirable distribution of resources among the different *existing* occupations, but would not serve to show whether a new commodity should be produced or whether an existing commodity should in future not be produced at all. The ordinary pricing principles, which we examined in Chapters I and II of this Part, will serve to determine how much of each commodity should be produced, if any at all is produced, but will not serve to show whether a particular commodity should be produced or not.

We may, however, make certain statements about this decision. A new commodity should always be produced if there is any output of that commodity for which the total expenditure on the commodity would cover its costs, where these equal the value of the marginal products of the factors elsewhere. For, as we already have shown, the total value to consumers of the output of a new commodity is always greater than the total amount spent on it. Consequently, if the total amount spent on it is sufficient to cover its costs, the total value of the commodity to consumers will be more than sufficient to cover its costs. But even if there is no output of the commodity for which consumers would offer a price sufficient to cover its cost of production, it may nevertheless be desirable to produce the commodity. This is illustrated by a comparison of Tables 1 and 4 on Chart I at the end of the book. Let us suppose Table 1 represents the conditions of production of a new commodity by a single firm, and that column B of Table 4 shows the price which consumers will pay for the corresponding outputs of the firm. By comparing column B of Table 1 with column B of Table 4 we can see that for every output the average cost of production is higher than the price which consumers will pay for the product. But by comparing column C of Table 1 with column E of Table 4 we can see that for all outputs between 6 and 11 units the total value to consumers of the commodity is greater than the total costs incurred in its production. The commodity should, therefore, be produced.

Thus monopolistic conditions may involve waste for two reasons: because the output of an industry may not be concentrated on the correct number of firms, and because the pricing system alone will not suffice to show whether or not a single new firm should be set up to produce a new commodity or a new brand of an old commodity.

We have shown that the existence of monopolistic conditions may modify all the three fundamental advantages of perfect competition mentioned in Chapter II of this Part. It will be clear from this discussion that a large number of the so-called wastes of competition are more properly to be called 'wastes of monopolistic conditions'; and it may be of use to enumerate a number of particular ways in which these wastes may show themselves.

(a) One 'waste of competition' which is only possible when competition is imperfect is expenditure on advertising, salesmen, etc., with a view to increasing sales. If in any industry no firm produced an appreciable proportion of the total output of a product, and if this product were standardized and sold in a perfect market, no firm would spend money on *selling* goods. It would be sheer waste to do so, as in these conditions each firm can extend its market by an inconsiderable reduction in the price of its product. But where the market for a firm's product is imperfect, so that in order to sell more it must lower its price considerably to attract custom from its rivals, it may be more economical for it to sell more not by lowering its price but by spending considerable sums on persuading its customers that its product is better than that of its rivals. If all preferences were rational and so based solely on real differences in price and quality, firms could attract custom only by cutting prices or improving quality. But if irrational buyers' preferences exist, each of two firms, selling almost the same product, may spend large sums on advertising and salesmen, and the expenditure of each firm may just offset the effect of the expenditure of the other. Yet it may pay neither of them alone to stop.

Such expenditure is clearly a waste from the community's point of view; labor, capital, and other economic resources are utilized for a purely competitive battle which has no social usefulness at all. If real differences in the product of different firms exist, advertising will serve a useful purpose if it is used simply to point out the real advantages and disadvantages of different products and so to lessen irrational buyers' preference. But, even in this case, the advertising will only be worth while if the extra satisfaction obtained as a result of the additional knowledge on the part of consumers is greater than the satisfaction obtainable from the goods which might otherwise be produced by the factors of productions used in the preparation and organization of the advertising. In the real world a large part of expenditure on selling costs is undertaken simply to attract purchasers from one firm to another or from one product to another, without in fact giving consumers any greater knowledge of the ways in which particular goods will satisfy their needs. And all such expenditure is a waste, due to monopolistic conditions in the sale of commodities.

(b) A similar waste which is due to irrational buyers' preference is expenditure on cross-transport. A firm in the north may be selling to customers in the south, while a firm in the south is selling an equally satisfying product to customers in the north. If competition were perfect, the firm in the north could sell at a better price in the north, since it would have to bear smaller transport costs on goods sold there than on goods sold in the south. But if the firm in the north had to lower its price or to spend money on advertisement to attract the northern consumers from the southern firm, it might find it more profitable to bear the transport costs rather than to change its market.

Such a waste due to unnecessary transport can be exemplified in the distribution of milk in a city. If each milk cart delivered to one or two streets instead of each cart to one or two houses in each street, the delivery of milk could be undertaken at a smaller cost. And *perfect* competition would bring this about, since each seller of milk would concentrate on one or two streets and drive out his competitors by inconsiderable reductions in the price at which he offered milk to persons in the particular district. But, in fact, an individual dairyman will not find it profitable to concentrate on a particular district, for, in order to obtain all the custom in one street, he would have to reduce his prices very considerably below his rival's to obtain his rival's custom.

(c) The failure of each firm in one industry to specialize on a line of product to which it is most suited is another waste due to the imperfections of competition. Here again if there were perfect competition so that each individual firm could sell as much as it liked of a particular type of the product without causing the price to fall, competition would automatically bring about this specialization. For each firm would in these circumstances concentrate on one type and quality of product if there were any real economies to be achieved by such action. But if each firm has to spend money on advertising or to offer considerably lower prices to attract customers, it may find that it pays better to produce a varied assortment of types and qualities to sell to its own particular customers rather than to face the cost of attracting a larger number of customers for one type of product alone.

In this case as well there is a certain waste only if the failure to specialize is due to irrational buyers' preference. If there is a rational buyers' preference for the goods of each particular firm, the concentration of the output of one line of the commodity on each firm will mean that certain firms stop producing particular lines of the product. This is equivalent to disappearance of certain distinct commodities, and the loss involved to the consumers by this must be reckoned on the principles discussed above in this chapter (pp. 170-4).

(d) Finally we may point out two particular ways in which an industry may fail automatically to concentrate the output on a small enough number of firms. In both these instances the distinction between rational and irrational buyers' preference is all-important in order to judge on the principles outlined above (pp. 170-4) how far any concentration should go. First, in conditions of imperfect competition the efficient firms which can produce at lower costs may fail to drive out the inefficient firms. Perfect competition would bring this about, since each efficient firm would produce and sell more so long as its marginal cost was below the demand price of the product; and as all the efficient firms produced more, the total output of the commodity would grow and the demand price would fall, so that any inefficient firms, whose lowest average cost could no longer be covered by the demand price, would be driven out of business. But if there were not perfectly competitive conditions, and if the efficient firms had to spend considerable sums on advertisement or had to reduce their prices considerably to attract the customers of the inefficient firms, they might well prefer not to drive out the inefficient firms, even if the prices charged by the inefficient firms were well above the marginal costs of the efficient firms.

Secondly, monopolistic conditions may prevent that standardization of commodities which is desirable for the most efficient methods of production. A large number of firms might be producing different types of radios, each producing a small output at a high cost. If only a few designs were produced, and each were produced in one firm on a large scale, the cost might be very much reduced through the economies of large-scale production. Yet there is no assurance that imperfect competition will bring about this standardization and concentration of output. No individual producer might have any incentive to start to expand his output and to produce a single design on a larger scale, since the cost of invading his rival's markets might outweigh any reduction in his average cost which he could hope to obtain by the expansion in his output.

VII

THE CONTROL OF MONOPOLY

In this chapter we shall discuss the different measures by which the state may control industry in order to remove the disadvantages of monopolistic conditions. These measures fall into five groups:

1. **Anti-Trust Laws** designed to prevent the formation of monopolies among sellers or buyers;
2. **Educational Measures** designed to remove irrational buyers' preference on the part of consumers or to remove the lack of mobility of factors of production, in so far as this is due to ignorance;
3. **Rationalization,** which aims at concentrating the output of any industry in the hands of a single but private control;
4. **Taxes and Subsidies** used to control the output of different industries; and
5. **Price Control** which aims at removing the monopolistic power of influencing prices.

1. The possibility of removing monopolistic conditions by legislation [1] making the formation of combinations illegal is limited in the modern world. A monopolist may be able to restrict supply and so to hold the price of his product above the cost because he controls the whole or a large proportion of the total supply of some natural resource. In this case a legal regulation, which effectively prevents all the owners of oil, for example, from forming an

[1]. Actual legislation in the modern world is more often designed for precisely the opposite purpose of creating monopolies (e.g.) by limiting through licenses the number of bus companies that may operate in any district. Although, as we shall argue below (pp. 186 and 187), such legislation may be justifiable in special circumstances and with special safeguards, there is a dangerous tendency for modern industrial legislation to increase rather than to diminish the power of monopolies.

agreement to hold the price of oil above its cost, may be useful in preserving the fundamental advantages of competition. Legal regulation may be useful also in preserving the free movement of factors of production from one occupation to another. A trade union or professional body may be able to restrict free entry into the trade or profession by charging unnecessarily high entrance fees or by otherwise limiting the number of entrants. Those who are already in the trade may be the only people able to train newcomers to it; or a professional body may misuse legal powers which have been entrusted to it to maintain the standards of the profession. Legal regulations preventing the restriction of entry into any occupation on any ground other than lack of the necessary professional qualifications may effectively increase the ease with which labor can move from lower paid to higher paid occupations.

But there are many causes of monopoly which such anti-trust laws cannot remove in the modern world. Nothing useful can be done by this method to prevent monopolistic conditions in an industry in which there are important economies of large-scale production. Anti-trust laws cannot insure that there will be a large number of independent railways competing between Boston and New York, or that motor cars will be produced by a large number of small independent firms. Or if legal regulations could bring this about, they would clearly be wasteful. Such measures cannot cure that imperfection in the market for the sale of a product which is due to transport costs or to buyers' preference, whether rational or irrational. Nor can they insure perfect competition in the purchase of factors of production, since they do nothing to remove either the cost of movement of labor or the ignorance of the factors as to the occupations in which they can obtain the highest rewards. In spite of such measures the most important reasons for monopolistic conditions will still remain.

2. Educational measures are of greater significance in the modern world. Such measures are of two kinds; they may give con-

sumers fuller knowledge of the real qualities of the goods which they purchase, or they may give to the owners of factors of production, and in particular to labor, fuller knowledge of the rewards offered for employment in different occupations and of the cost and methods of training for and of moving into other occupations. We may deal with these two objects separately.

If consumers' associations or a public consumers' board could test scientifically the qualities of different products and could instruct consumers in the advantages to be derived from different amounts of different commodities, irrational buyers' preference would be diminished. If a trustworthy and authoritative body were enabled to spend on consumers' research one tenth of the sums now spent on wasteful competitive advertisement, and to make its findings public, a large amount of buyers' preference would disappear. In consequence, wasteful competitive advertisement would diminish and producers would be forced to concentrate on real quality rather than on high-pressure salesmanship; cross-transport charges would diminish, in as far as they were wasteful; the concentration of output on a smaller number of more efficient firms would take place; and competition would become more nearly perfect in the case of many products, so that the price paid for the factors of production would approach more closely to the value of their marginal products.

But many reasons for monopolistic conditions in the sale of commodities cannot be touched by consumers' education. In industries in which there is room for only one or a few firms of the optimum size, consumers' education will not remove the power of each firm to influence the price of its product by varying its sales. In this case the monopolistic condition is due to the fact that the number of sellers is small, and not to the existence of buyers' preference. And in many cases in which there is a large number of independent firms producing a commodity, each firm has a semi-independent market for its product based on *rational* buyers' preference due (e.g.) to transport costs or to real differences in quality of the products; and in these cases consumers' education will not remove the fact that each firm by selling more or less can appreciably affect the price of its own product.

Educational measures include also measures designed to lessen monopolistic conditions in the purchase of factors of production. A single producer may be able to depress the price of a factor which he is purchasing either because the number of purchasers is small or because the factor purchased does not move readily from the purchaser offering a lower to a purchaser offering a higher price. Where the first of these causes is operative, and there are only a limited number of firms bidding for a given factor (e.g. a raw material), no amount of information given to the owners of the factor will remove the power, possessed by its purchaser, of depressing its price by buying less of it.

But where the second cause is operative producers have some power of control over the price of a factor which they purchase not because they are few in number but because a certain amount of this factor is closely attached to each individual producer and does not move immediately to other producers who are offering a higher price. This lack of mobility of the factor of production may, however, be 'rational' or 'irrational.' It is rational if it is based on real costs of movement. If it is costly for a worker to move from one firm to another because employment in the second firm involves costlier travel to and from his work each day, or because he must move his home to another district or learn a new skill, he will have a rational cause for not moving, unless the wage offered by his present employer falls so far below the wage offered by the alternative employer that the difference in wage more than covers the cost of movement. These rational costs of movement cannot be removed by any educational measures.

Educational measures may be made effective, on the other hand, where the factor is immobile for 'irrational' causes. Labor may fail to move because it is ignorant of the wages offered elsewhere or of the chances of employment in other occupations, or because it overestimates the cost of movement or the cost of learning a new skill, or because it is ignorant of the cheapest methods of moving or of learning a different skill, or because it cannot raise the sum necessary for the move at the current rate of interest. The owners of capital and land from ignorance of the yield of capital and land in different occupations may fail to move these factors to the occupations in which the yield is highest. Sellers of raw materials from ignorance of the prices offered for the material by different producers in different industries or in different districts may fail to desert a purchaser offering a lower price for a purchaser offering more. If the ignorance of the owners of factors of production could be removed there would be a considerable diminution in the control of individual purchasers over the price of the factors which they purchase.

Different educational measures will be proper in the case of different factors. A comprehensive system of Employment Exchanges for the purpose of giving information about jobs offered in different districts, firms, and occupations and about the rates of pay offered; the provision either through Employment Exchanges or other bodies of information about the cost and methods of learning different skills; an extension of the guidance given by schools and official bodies to juveniles entering industry concerning the prospects in each industry; the provision of industrial and commercial training courses at the lowest possible cost; the provision through public agencies of information about the cost of movement from district to district and about the cost of living in different districts; the loan of money by some public body to workers, at the current rate of interest and with appropriate sinking funds for the repayment of the capital sum, to finance the cost of movement—all these are appropriate measures to take in the case of labor.[1]

In the case of capital much is already done by the owners of capital themselves through the organization of the stock exchanges and the advice which stockbrokers can give of the yields

1. If by such measures the labor market is better organized, there will be a diminution in that part of 'standard' unemployment (referred to in Part I, Chapter VIII) which is due to the fact that some labor is always in process of moving from one job to another.

in different industries and firms. But in the case of newly floated companies which are issuing stock and borrowing for the first time, the owner of capital is often left in great ignorance about the probable profitability of the new enterprise. The organization by the government or by the stock exchange of a body which could call on technical experts in different fields to give authoritative and fair judgment about the actual prospects of a new company might be of considerable assistance.[1] The organization of the markets in which raw materials are bought and sold already provides considerable knowledge to the buyers and sellers. But any increased publicity of the actual prices paid by different purchasers would be of considerable help, and the state might give legal power to certain bodies to obtain and publish the prices at which purchases of different raw materials were taking place by different firms in different districts and in different industries.

3. We must turn now to 'rationalization' as a method of removing some of the disadvantages of imperfect competition. By rationalization is meant action taken by the state or by the majority of producers in a particular industry to bring that industry under a single control. Such action will remove many of the wastes which are due to irrational buyers' preferences between the products of the different firms in an industry. If an industry is brought under a single control, wasteful competitive advertisement between the individual firms will be directly eliminated; and it will pay the single ownership to concentrate production on the more efficient plants, to reduce the number of plants until

1. The Securities Exchange Commission could be made to develop along these lines. At present it merely requires that the relevant information about the accounts of the company and the purposes for which the funds are being raised are correctly and fully stated in the prospectus. The objection to an official body giving judgments on the prospects of new companies is that there are many unknown factors involved (e.g. consumers' demand) which even technical experts cannot accurately assess. Investors are likely to rely too much on the opinion of the official body, which could not accept responsibility, and bad feeling would follow every bad judgment. This objection would not, of course, apply if the body confined itself to giving full information in understandable form.

each remaining plant is working at capacity, to specialize each productive unit on a single line of product, and to eliminate any existing cross-transport charges.

Rationalization will therefore eliminate directly many of the so-called wastes of competition, which could be eliminated indirectly by the removal of consumers' ignorance and inertia; and in many cases rationalization is a better way of removing these wastes than the education of consumers. For such education of consumers could never be complete, and it could only remove irrational buyers' preference at considerable cost. But rationalization will remove these particular wastes without any cost and will remove them completely. This is not, however, to argue that expenditure on the provision of authoritative information to consumers is not desirable, since consumers will always have to choose between the products of different industries, whether these industries are rationalized or not. If there is irrational buyers' preference in the choice between articles produced by different rationalized industries, these industries may embark on wasteful competitive advertisement aimed at attracting custom from the one industry to the other.

But it is equally clear that rationalization alone is not a sufficient cure for the evils of monopolistic conditions. For rationalization is based upon bringing the control of an industry under a single private direction, and this will obviously increase the monopolistic power of the industry over the price charged for its product and over the price paid for its factors of production. We may conclude that while the breaking down of obvious artificial barriers to competition, the education of consumers and of factors of production, and the rationalization of industries in which irrational buyers' preference plays an important part, will together remove many wastes due to monopolistic conditions, yet these measures cannot remove the monopolistic influence over prices which will be exercised in industries in which the number of competing producers is necessarily small. Rationalization will clearly increase such monopolistic control over prices. We must turn to measures which will remove the disadvantages of monopoly in those cases in which there is not room for a large number of independent producers.

4. The use of taxes and subsidies by a public body is theoretically a complete method of removing the wastes of monopoly. All the disadvantages of monopolistic conditions can be explained by saying that while consumers' needs would be best satisfied if a factor of production were shifted from one industry to another whenever the value of its marginal product in the second industry exceeded the value of its marginal product in the first by an amount sufficient to cover the cost of movement, in monopolistic conditions this may not happen automatically. Theoretically any desired shift of the factors of production can be brought about by a system of taxes and subsidies. If, for example, it is desired to shift labor from one industry to another, a tax per worker employed may be imposed in the first industry in order to raise the cost of employing additional labor in that industry; and the proceeds of the tax may be used to pay a subsidy on each worker employed in the second industry in order to lower the cost of employing more men in that industry.

The rates of subsidies and taxes can be adjusted to shift a factor of production in any direction to any extent and yet in such a way that the tax always just covers the subsidy. Thus, suppose that there are three industries A, B, and C, and that it is desired to shift 60 units of labor from A, 40 from B, and 100 to C. A tax on labor employed in A and B used to pay a subsidy on labor employed in C is indicated. If such a tax and subsidy shifts only 80 units to C, but shifts 70 from A and 10 from B, the tax on labor employed in A must be lowered slightly and that on labor employed in B raised considerably so that a greater subsidy can be paid on labor employed in C. By adjustments of this kind, any desired shift in the employment of any factor can be achieved.

The best distribution of factors among different occupations will be achieved if factors are shifted from one to another occupation whenever the difference between the value of their marginal products in the two occupations is sufficient to cover the cost of movement. But this does not mean that the hired factors should always be shifted into those occupations in which, because of monopolistic conditions, they are paid less than the value of their marginal products. This would be true if the vast majority of industries were perfectly competitive, so that the hired factors in most industries are paid rewards equal to the value of their marginal products, while in one or two monopolistic occupations the hired factors are receiving less than the value of their marginal products. In this case it would be desirable to shift the hired factors of production from the competitive industries into all of the monopolistic industries, in which the values of their marginal products were higher. But if most occupations were monopolistic, so that the values of the marginal products of the hired factors were greater than their rewards in the vast majority of industries, it would be impossible to expand all these industries at the same time; all that is desirable is that factors should shift from industries in which the values of their marginal products are lower than the average to industries in which the values of their marginal products are higher than the average. This implies taxing the employment of the hired factors in those industries in which there is more than the average degree of competition, in order to subsidize the employment of the hired factors in those industries in which there is less.

If by such a system of taxes and subsidies the factors of production are shifted from one occupation to another until the values of their marginal products are the same in every industry, the first two fundamental advantages of perfect competition mentioned in Chapter II of this Part will be achieved. For we have shown in that chapter that if the value of the marginal product of each factor is the same in every industry, commodities will be produced in those amounts which satisfy consumers' needs best, and also it will be impossible to produce more of any one commodity without producing less of another.

The third fundamental advantage of perfect competition is

that the number of firms in each industry will be such that each firm is of the optimum size. Here again the control of monopolistic conditions by taxes and subsidies could theoretically achieve the desired result. For just as the hired factors of production can be shifted from one industry to another by this means, so a system of taxes and subsidies can be used to shift management from one industry to another, i.e. to decrease the number of firms in one industry and to increase it in another. We have already explained in the last chapter (pp. 166–74) how the value of the marginal product of management in each occupation is to be measured and how by this means it can be decided whether the number of firms is too large or too small in any particular industry. A fixed tax should be levied on each independent firm in any industry in which there are too many firms, and a fixed subsidy should be paid to each firm in the industries into which it is desired that management should move. It was argued in the last chapter (pp. 166–8) that if industry A was more competitive than the average, whereas industry B was less competitive than the average the hired factors of production should be shifted from industry A to industry B while management, if the lack of competition was not due to rational buyers' preference, should be moved from industry B to industry A. In these conditions a tax levied per unit of the hired factors employed in A, and used to pay a subsidy fixed in amount to each firm in industry A, together with a tax fixed in amount on each firm in B used to pay a subsidy per unit of the hired factors employed in B, will bring about the desired distribution of resources.

In a similar manner taxes and subsidies may theoretically be used to eliminate the wastes of competition enumerated on pp. 176–80 above. Wasteful competitive advertisement can be made unprofitable by the imposition of a heavy tax. Cross-transport charges can similarly be eliminated by a tax on wasteful transport. If because of irrational buyers' preference firms fail to specialize in particular lines of product where such specialization would bring real technical economies, a tax might be devised to rectify their wasteful practices. Finally, the reader is reminded that it was argued in Chapter III of this Part (pp. 129–31) that those wastes which are compatible with perfect competition can also be removed by a judicious use of taxes and subsidies, designed to make the marginal cost of producing anything to the individual producer the same as the marginal cost of the production to the community.

But this method of taxes and subsidies, which is theoretically so complete, has one obvious defect in operation—the difficulty which the official body administering these taxes and subsidies would have in estimating the value of the marginal product of factors in different uses, in order to shift each factor of production into that occupation in which the value of its marginal product is highest. It is important to realize exactly what this difficulty involves. The estimation of the marginal product of any factor in any occupation is a technical matter, which is dependent upon the correct judgment of those operating the firm in question. Business men will always be asking themselves and their technicians the question: 'How much should I increase my product if I employed more labor or if I installed another machine of a given type or used more of this raw material'? and they are, of course, liable to make mistakes in such matters. But no official can discover what is the business man's estimate of these 'marginal productivities' simply by inspection of what the business man does. Even if the price paid for each factor of production and the prices of all products are known, the official cannot decide whether the business man decides not to take on another unit of labor because he thinks that its marginal product is small, or because he judges that the price of his product would fall too much if he put this extra output on the market, or because he wishes to avoid increasing his demand for labor and so raising the wage-rate. Technical knowledge alone can give an approximate estimate of the marginal productivity of different factors; and since the payment of a tax or receipt of a subsidy depends upon its decision, the official cannot expect the business man to provide him with accurate estimates. The official body must either guess, or have technical experts of its own familiar with each industry, who must be continually revising their estimates of the marginal productivities of different factors; for, it must be remembered, continual technical changes are likely to take place. To guess will be unsatisfactory, while to duplicate in many industries the technical staff, one half of which is working for the owners and another half for an official body, involves considerable waste and is unlikely to lead to an easy and harmonious management of the concern. In brief, if an official body were in a position to adjust the necessary taxes and subsidies satisfactorily it would, in fact, be in a position to manage the industries itself, and direct nationalization, which we shall discuss in the next chapter, would be the obvious solution.

5. The control of prices by a governmental body is another method of control over monopolistic conditions which may theoretically bring about the desired redistribution of resources among the different occupations. We have seen that the wastes due to monopolistic conditions are all due to the fact that individual producers may have the power of raising the price of the commodity sold by selling less of it or the power of depressing the price of hired factors by hiring less of them. This power can theoretically be removed if maximum commodity prices and minimum factor prices are fixed by a governmental authority. We shall discuss the fixing of maximum commodity prices and the fixing of minimum factor prices separately.

We have argued that the resources at the disposal of the community will be most effectively used if the value of the marginal product of each factor is the same in every occupation. If, therefore, by means of price control the value of the marginal product of each factor could be made equal to its reward in every occupation, and if factors were left free to move in search of the highest rewards, the value of the marginal product of each factor would tend to be the same in each occupation. In those cases in which an individual producer can raise the price of his product by selling less, he will not employ factors such as labor up to the point at which their price is equal to the value of their marginal product; he will employ less than this, because he can raise the price of his product by producing and selling less. But if a maximum price for his product were fixed by law, this would remove his power of raising prices by restricting his output, and if the legal price were properly chosen he could be made to employ labor up to the point at which the value of its marginal product was equal to the wage-rate.

This point is illustrated by a comparison between Tables 6 (*b*) and 8 on Chart II at the end of the book; Table 6 (*b*) illustrates the position of a producer who is selling his product in monopolistic conditions, and Table 8 shows the effect of a legal maximum price for the product. Columns B and C of Table 6 (*b*) [1] show the technical possibilities of production by a certain producer, while column D shows the conditions of his selling market, i.e. the price at which he can sell the corresponding output of column B; if he can employ labor at a wage-rate of $30, he will give employment to 21 men, since column G shows that up to this point he would add more to his receipts than to his costs by employing another man. But it is clear from column E of Table 6 (*b*) that he should employ 30 men if the wage-rate of $30 is to be equated to the value of the marginal product of labor. Column D shows that for the output of 30 men, which is the volume of employment which he should give, consumers will pay a price of $1. Suppose then that some public body fixes a maximum legal price of $1 for this product; then the conditions in which the producer can sell are represented in Table 8 instead of Table 6 (*b*). Even if he employs less than 30 men and produces so small an output that consumers would be willing to offer more than $1 a unit for it, he will, nevertheless, be unable to charge more than $1. If, however, he employed 31 men and produced a larger output than consumers are willing to purchase at $1 the

1. The figures in this table have been explained at length in Chapter IV of this Part (pp. 145-7).

maximum legal price will become ineffective so that the price he could charge would fall as before to 96c. By comparing columns E and G of Table 8 it can be seen that so long as the legal maximum price is operative the conditions for the producer are made to resemble those of perfect competition (shown in Table 6 (a)), where he has no control over price and where the value of the marginal product of labor in column E is equal to the marginal value of labor shown in column G. In the conditions shown in Table 8 it will pay him to employ 30 men at a wage-rate of $30, since up to this point he can add more than $30 to his receipts by employing another man.

We can also illustrate this argument by comparing a firm's marginal cost with its marginal receipts, and by studying the effect of price control. This is done by a comparison of Tables 1, 2 (b), and 3 on Chart I at the end of the book, Table 1 representing a firm's costs, Table 2 (b) representing monopolistic conditions of sale for this firm's output, and Table 3 showing the difference made to these market conditions by fixing a maximum legal price for this firm's product.

It can be seen from a comparison of Tables 1 and 2 (b) that in the absence of a legal maximum price the firm will produce 7 units of output, since up to this point its marginal cost is lower than its marginal receipts. But it should produce 10 units of output, which it can sell at a price of $20, if it is to produce more so long as its marginal cost is less than the price of the product, i.e. so long as the rewards of the factors are less than the value of their marginal products. Table 3 represents the effect of fixing a maximum legal price of $20 for the product of this firm. The effect of such price regulation is to make the marginal receipts of the firm equal to this regulated price of $20 for every output for which this maximum price is effective, i.e. for every output for which consumers would be willing to pay a price of $20 or more. We know, however, from Table 2 (b) that, if the firm produced more than 10 units of output, consumers would not be willing to pay a price of $20, so that the price control would become ineffective; and therefore for all outputs greater than 10 the conditions of Table 2 (*b*) are reproduced in Table 3. By comparing Table 1 with Table 3 it can be seen that with the maximum legal price fixed at $20 the firm would produce the desired output of 10 units, since up to this point its marginal costs would be lower than its marginal receipts.

There is an important difficulty connected with this method of control of monopoly. In the case of industries in which the optimum size of a single plant is so large in relation to the total demand that a single plant cannot be run at its full capacity, it will not be possible simply by fixing a maximum legal price to make the price of the product equal to the marginal cost of production. For so long as the average cost of production could be lowered by operating the plant more fully, the marginal cost will be lower than the average cost of production. In these circumstances if the firm is not allowed to charge a price higher than its marginal cost of production, the price will be below the average cost of production and the firm will be unable to cover its costs, so that sooner or later it would close down entirely. This difficulty is illustrated by the comparison of Table 1 with Tables 4 and 5 on Chart I. Table 1 again illustrates the cost conditions in a single firm, while Table 4 takes the place of Table 2 (*b*) to illustrate the market conditions for the sale of the firm's product. The important difference between the figures chosen in Tables 2 (*b*) and 4 must be explained. In Table 2 (*b*) it was supposed that the desired output of 10 units was one at which the average cost of production was covered by the price offered for the firm's product. If, however, Table 1 is compared with Table 4 it will be seen that the firm should produce 9 units of output, because up to this point its marginal cost is less than the price offered for its product. But if it produces 9 units of output, it will not be able to cover its costs, since Table 4 shows that the price offered for 9 units is only $17, whereas Table 1 shows that the average cost of producing 9 units is $20.25. And if in other occupations prices are equal to marginal costs, then in this occupation more should be produced as long as the marginal cost is lower than the price of the product; for only if this is done will the factors of production be distributed in the best way between this and other occupations.

We have already shown in the last chapter (p. 176) that a comparison of column E of Table 4 with column C of Table 1 proves that this commodity should be produced. If the plant in this industry is to be used at all, it should be more fully utilized so long as the marginal cost is less than the price of the product, so that 9 units should be sold at $17. Table 5 illustrates the effect of fixing a maximum legal price of $17, which is the price at which the output of 9 units could be sold. So long as less than 9 units are sold, the legal price control is effective with the result that the figures in columns B and D of Table 5 are both equal to $17; for by selling one more unit the firm will add $17 to its receipts so long as the price is fixed at $17. But for outputs greater than 9 the legal maximum price becomes ineffective, so that the figures in columns B and D of Table 5 become the same as the corresponding figures in Table 4. If Tables 1 and 5 are compared it can be seen that if the firm produces anything at all, it will produce 9 units when the legal maximum price of $17 is fixed, since for outputs of 6, 7, or 8 units its marginal cost will be below its marginal receipts. But Tables 1 and 5 show that when it is producing 9 units, its average cost is greater than the price obtained for its product, with the result that its total costs ($182.25) exceed its total receipts ($153) by $29.25. It would not pay the firm to produce anything unless this loss were made up by a subsidy. But the combination of a legal maximum price of $17 together with the payment of a fixed subsidy to the firm of $29.25 will enable it to cover its costs and give it the incentive to produce 9 units of output. A maximum price fixed by law, and so chosen that for the amount bought at that price the marginal cost of production is equal to that price, will make a producer produce up to the point at which his marginal cost is equal to the price of his product. But in the case of any

THE CONTROL OF MONOPOLY

industry in which the total demand is small relative to the optimum output of a single efficient plant, the marginal cost will be below the average cost, and in this case price control must be accompanied by a fixed subsidy which will enable the firm to cover its total costs.

In an analogous way the power which monopolists may exercise over the prices which they pay for the hired factors of production may be removed by fixing legal minimum prices for these factors. The fixing of a minimum wage for labor will make it impossible for an employer to lower the wage-rate by employing less labor, and so long as the fixed minimum wage is effective will mean that by taking on one more or one less laborer the employer will increase or decrease his wage-costs by no more than the wage-rate of labor. In other words, such a fixed minimum wage will make the conditions for the purchase of labor correspond to those of perfect competition. This point is illustrated by a comparison between Tables 7 (b) and 9 on Chart II at the end of the book. Table 7 (b) illustrates monopolistic conditions in the hire of labor, and Table 9 illustrates the same conditions when a minimum wage of $30 is fixed. In Table 7 (b) the wage-rate which must be paid by the employer to attract 30 units of labor is $30. Let us suppose that until 30 units of labor are employed the value of the marginal product of labor is greater than $30, so that 30 units should be employed. It is clear from Table 7 (b) that if there is no control of the wage-rate less than 30 men will be employed, since by employing 29 instead of 30 men the wage-bill will be reduced by $88 and not simply by $30. But if a minimum wage-rate is fixed at $30 the conditions of the labor market become those shown in Table 9. The minimum legal wage-rate is effective for all volumes of employment less than 30, since a wage less than $30 would be sufficient to attract any volume of employment less than 30: but for volumes of employment greater than 30 the legal minimum wage-rate becomes ineffective, since a wage-rate higher than $30 must be paid to attract more than 30 laborers. In consequence, for all

volumes of employment up to 30, the conditions are now similar
to those of perfect competition (shown in Table 7 (a)); while for
volumes of employment above 30 the conditions remain monopolistic as before. But with this fixed minimum wage-rate the
employer will no longer have any incentive to employ less than
30 men simply in order to reduce his costs by reducing the wage-
rate.

[The graphical representation of the effects of fixing maximum commodity and minimum factor prices involves combining a number of graphs which we have already drawn. The
effects of fixing a maximum price for the product are revealed
in Graph VII, which contains appropriate parts of Graphs I
and II (on pp. 143 and 144 above). The average and marginal
cost curves, AC and MC and the average and marginal receipts curves AR_1 and MR_1 are the same as in Graph II
(see p. 143); they represent the cost and demand conditions of
a firm selling its product under conditions of imperfect competition. Marginal receipts are equal to marginal cost when
7 units are being produced and sold at a price of $23. By fixing
a maximum price of $20 the cost curves are unaffected, but the
receipts curves are made straight horizontal lines up to the
point where the demand price (measured by the height of AR_1)
is $20. From this point on the maximum price is ineffective,
and the receipts curves follow their former courses. The new
receipts curves are accordingly AR_2 and MR_2. The new marginal receipts curve intersects the marginal cost curve at a
point which represents an output of ten units.[1] At this point
marginal cost=price=$20, which means that perfectly com-
petitive conditions have been successfully simulated.

The effect on employment of fixing maximum commodity
prices can be seen by combining, in much the same way,
Graphs III and IV (p. 156 above). The marginal value of
labor curve MV falls so precipitously in Graph IV because the
price of the product is falling as output increases. By fixing a
maximum price of $30 for the commodity this fall can be
prevented up to the point where the value of the marginal
product (shown by the curve VMP) is equal to $30. Up to that
point, then, the MV curve will become identical to the MV

1. Instead of 11 units, as shown on Graph I. The divergence is due to the
discreteness of the units in the arithmetic table, and has no significance.

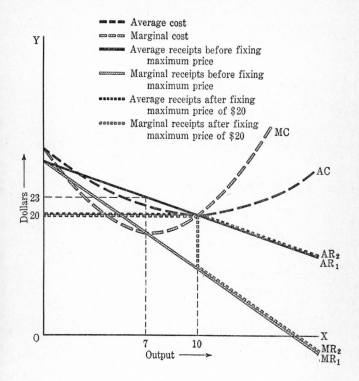

GRAPH VII. *The Effect of a Maximum Legal Price on the Output of a Firm Selling in an* IMPERFECT MARKET.

curve of Graph III, and employment will be expanded from 21 to 30, where the wage-rate is equal to the value of labor's marginal product. Beyond the point representing employment of 30 the maximum price will be ineffective, and the MV curve will follow its old course. But conditions of perfect competition will already have been secured.

Similarly the effects of a minimum wage-rate may be illustrated by a combination of Graphs III and V. In this case it is the cost curves which are made parallel to the OX axis for the significant portion of their length. If the minimum wage-rate is fixed at \$30, employment will be expanded from 20, which it was when the wage-rate, determined in the free imperfect market, was \$10, to 30, where the wage-rate is just equal to the value of labor's marginal product. Beyond this point, as in the other cases, the two cost curves will resume their former courses.]

We conclude that if a maximum price for the product is fixed at a level at which it would be equal to marginal cost of production,[1] and if minimum prices for the factors of production are fixed at the figures which would have to be paid if the factors were employed up to the point at which their rewards were equal to the value of their marginal products, the results of perfect competition can be reproduced. No producer will have any incentive to reduce output in an attempt to raise the price of his product or to reduce the rewards paid to the hired factors. In these circumstances each factor would be paid a reward equal to the value of its marginal product, and the factor would thus be distributed in the best way among the different possible occupations. In the case of commodities for which the demand was so small that a single plant could not operate at its fullest capacity, this price regulation would have to be accompanied by the payment of fixed subsidies to enable the total cost of production to be covered.

1. In the long run this would involve fixing a price equal to average cost in a firm of optimum size wherever the total demand at that price for the commodity in question was as great as the output of one such firm. In the short run, however, while factors were being transferred from or to an industry, fixing prices equal to marginal cost would involve fixing them below or above the average cost of a firm of optimum size, respectively.

If this method of control over monopoly were chosen, appropriate price-fixing bodies would have to be established. In many states such bodies exist already for the purpose of fixing prices in certain industries—chiefly the public utilities. Under the N.R.A. wages and in some cases commodity prices were fixed by the code authorities. Some states prescribe minimum wages for certain types of labor by law; and it has recently been proposed to set up a Federal body to prescribe minimum wages for different grades of labor in different regions. In some industries trade unions which are national in scope fix minimum wage-rates with employers. Where monopolistic conditions exist in the market for the finished product these price-fixing bodies diminish the incentive which firms have to curtail production to raise prices; and where monopolistic conditions exist in the labor market the wage-fixing bodies similarly diminish the incentive employers have to dismiss men simply to depress wage-rates. Such bodies, *so long as they do not fix prices and wages unduly high*, are therefore fully justified in conditions which would in any case be monopolistic, and their action makes the wage paid approximate more closely to the value of the marginal product of labor than it would otherwise do.[1]

The difficulties of this method are similar to those already discussed in connection with the control of monopoly by means of taxes and subsidies. Bodies which are fixing maximum commodity prices and minimum factor prices, in order to equate the rewards of factors with the value of their marginal products, must estimate the marginal productivities of different factors in different industries.

It is, however, relatively easy for price-fixing authorities to discover if the maximum commodity prices are too low or the minimum factor prices too high. Suppose that the relevant authority has attempted to fix a maximum price for a commod-

---

1. The fixing of wages and prices in these conditions are the two further means for reducing unemployment without reducing real wage-rates to which reference was made at the end of Part I, Chapter IX.

ity and minimum prices for the factors, which equate the prices of the factors to the value of their marginal products. If, however, the maximum legal price for the commodity has been in fact fixed below this proper level, there will be a twofold result; consumers will wish to purchase more than the proper amount of the product because its price is fixed too low, while at the same time the producers will wish to produce less than the proper amount of the product, because the lowering of the price by law has reduced the value of the marginal product of each factor below the price that must be paid for that factor. Consumers will at this price desire to purchase more than the producers are willing to produce. At the stores there will be a scarcity of goods at the ruling price, so that consumers will scramble or form lines and wait in the hope that they will be the lucky persons who will not have to go entirely without the commodity, for which at the ruling price the demand exceeds the supply. When, therefore, the price-fixing authorities observe these phenomena they will know that the price fixed is in fact too low. But if the maximum legal commodity price has in fact been fixed too high, there will be no such indications of its mistake to the price-fixing authority. For, if they have fixed too high a price, they will have taken away *some* of the monopolistic power from the producer— so long as the price fixed is lower than the price which would have been charged if there had been no control—but they will not have fixed a price sufficiently low to cause the monopolist to extend his production up to the point at which its marginal cost is equal to its price. The output will be smaller and the price of the product higher than is necessary, but there will be no means by which the price-fixing authority can tell whether this is so except by actual measurement of the marginal cost of production.

Similarly, the authorities fixing minimum legal prices for factors of production will be able to judge fairly easily if these fixed prices are too high, but will have no simple criterion by which they can judge whether they are too low. Suppose, for example, that a minimum wage-rate has in fact been fixed at a level higher than that which will equate the value of the marginal product of labor to the wage-rate. In consequence of the excessively high wage-rate more than the proper amount of labor will be attracted to this occupation, but at the same time producers will employ less than the proper amount of labor because the excessively high wage-rate has raised its price above the value of its marginal product. The result will be unemployed labor in the industry, since all the labor seeking work in that occupation at the excessive wage will not be able to find employment at that wage. But if the legal minimum wage fixed is too low, employers will be left with *some* monopolistic power of depressing wage-rates by reducing their demand for labor below that amount at which the wage-rate would be equal to the value of labor's marginal product. But the wage-regulating authority will have no means of judging whether the minimum price fixed for any factor of production is too low except by direct measurement of the marginal product of that factor.

There is one advantage of this method of price regulation over the method of taxes and subsidies. The method of taxes and subsidies cannot be used at all unless the public authority which is adjusting these taxes and subsidies directly assesses the marginal productivities of the different factors in different occupations. But by a process of trial and error use might be made of maximum legal selling prices for commodities and minimum legal buying prices for factors of production without assessing directly the marginal productivities of different factors in different occupations. If the price-fixing bodies lower the maximum commodity prices so long as there are no signs of an excess of consumers' demand over supply, and raise the minimum factor prices so long as there are no signs of unemployment, a close approximation to the correct regulation of prices might be found. At the same time it would be necessary that in industries in which the total demand is so small that a single firm could not be operated to capacity, sufficient fixed subsidies are paid to enable that firm to cover its total costs.

Even so the real difficulties of this method of control would be enormous if it was to be effective and complete. Theoretically a different legal maximum price would have to be fixed for every commodity and for every different type or quality of each commodity in the sale of which there was any element of monopoly power; and all these prices would not only have to be subject to continual revision, as technical methods of production and consumers' tastes changed, but also would have to be effectively enforced by the responsible bodies. Similarly, for every factor and for every grade and type of a given factor in the purchase of which any monopolistic element was present, a different legal minimum price would have to be fixed, revised, and enforced.

VIII

PUBLIC MANAGEMENT AND PLANNING OF INDUSTRY

In the last chapter we saw that all the suggested methods of control of industry were open to criticism, either because they were incomplete or because they were impracticable. In this chapter we shall discuss the direct management of monopolistic industries by public corporations.[1]

We have shown that the best distribution of the community's resources would be achieved if each factor were employed in every occupation up to the point at which the price of the factor was equal to the value of its marginal product. This problem would therefore be solved directly if those in control of different businesses attempted to equate the rewards of factors to the value of their marginal products rather than to maximize the profits of the business. This can be achieved if monopolistic industries are nationalized, and operated directly with this end in view. This does not involve the nationalization of any industry in which there is perfect competition, but only of industries in which there is an appreciable monopolistic element and so an appreciable discrepancy between the prices paid for the factors and the value of their marginal products. Nor does it necessarily involve public *ownership* of the capital of any industries but only public *control* or *management* of these industries. This policy could be carried out even if the capital of an industry was still in private ownership and the private owners received any profit

---

1. By a 'public corporation' we refer to an official but semi-autonomous body like the Tennessee Valley Authority or the Federal Reserve Banks; and where we subsequently refer to 'nationalization' of industry in the text we envisage administration by such a corporation, which seems better suited to the task of industrial management than a department of government like the post office.

made by the industry, provided that the managers of the industry were not responsible to the owners in their decisions how much to produce, what prices to charge for the product, and what prices to offer to the different factors. Arguments for the public ownership of capital, so that the state may receive the income from interest and profit, rest on other grounds and are discussed in Chapter V of Part III.

If all industries in which there is an appreciable element of monopoly either in the sale of the product or in the hire of the factors are brought under the management of public corporations, the managers of the concerns can aim directly at equating the price paid for each factor to the value of the marginal product of that factor. In these circumstances each factor will move automatically into those industries in which the difference made to the output by its employment is of the greatest use to consumers, provided that the following five conditions are fulfilled:

(i) that the factors move from one occupation to another so long as the cost of movement is more than offset by the increase in reward obtained;

(ii) that there is no irrational buyers' preference, so that the prices offered by any one consumer for different products does properly measure the marginal utilities of the different commodities to the consumer;

(iii) that the marginal products, to the value of which the managers equate the rewards offered to the different factors, are the true difference made to the output of the community by the employment of one more unit of the particular factor in the particular occupation;

(iv) that in as far as standardized commodities are produced by a large number of firms, more managers are allocated to, and the number of plants increased in, those industries in which the profits of management are highest; and

(v) that a new firm is set up to produce a new commodity or a new brand of an existing commodity so long as the total value to consumers of the new commodity is judged to be greater than its cost of production.

The fulfillment of the first two conditions can be assured if the state arranges for the measures designed to educate consumers and the owners of factors discussed above on pp. 182–6. The third condition will be fulfilled only if the authorities in control of each public corporation take into account the effect of the employment of more factors by themselves not only on their own output but also on other outputs. They should as far as possible assess the effect of employing a particular factor on the output of others on the principles discussed in Chapter III of this Part (pp. 129–31); and they should add the current price of any increase, or subtract the current price of any decrease, in the output of others before they assess the true value of the marginal product of the factor in order to decide what reward to offer for it.

The fourth and fifth conditions can be fulfilled if the authority in control of any industry in which there are a number of independent plants draws a distinction between rational and irrational buyers' preference for the products of the different plants, assuming that the measures directed towards the education of consumers have not entirely removed irrational preferences. In so far as it is judged that no rational buyers' preference exists, the public board in control of any industry must set up new plants so long as the profits left over to the management are greater than in other industries. For in the absence of rational buyers' preference, as we saw in the last chapter, the amount left over to management measures the value of the marginal product of management, if the other factors are paid rewards equal to the value of their marginal products. In so far as the public board considers that there is some rational buyers' preference for the output of different types of the article produced by different plants, it must determine on different principles whether to open up a new plant to produce a particular brand, or to close down an existing plant which is producing a particular brand.

It must assess what consumers would be willing to pay for the output of the particular brand rather than go without it altogether—on the assumption, of course, that they could obtain the other brands in present quantities—and must allow the production of this brand if this sum is sufficient to cover the total costs of its production including a reward for the management of the plant equal to the reward offered for similar management in other industries. There must also be some central authority to decide whether a single firm should be set up to produce an entirely new product or whether a single firm producing the whole output of a particular product should be closed down, by considering whether the total value to consumers of the commodity, assessed on the principles discussed above (pp. 171–3), is as great as the estimated total cost of producing it. Such decisions are bound to be rather arbitrary; for the estimation of the total value to consumers of a particular commodity or of a particular brand of a commodity must rest largely on guesswork and cannot be based on any prices actually ruling in the market.

The general principles of pricing, which must be observed in order to equate the rewards of the hired factors to the value of their marginal products, can be expressed by three simple rules.

(i) Those in charge of a public corporation should always expand their employment of factors and increase production so long as the price offered for the product is in excess of the current market prices of the factors which would be necessary to produce another unit of the commodity.

(ii) They should substitute one factor for another (e.g. should use more capital and less labor) to produce the same output if the current price of the factor to be thrown out of employment is greater than the current price of that amount of the other factor which is just sufficient to take its place.

(iii) A central body, like the Industrial Planning Commission referred to on p. 217 below, should insure that prices are charged for the hired factors of production which would equate, and just equate, the demand for and supply of each (i.e., which would reduce the unemployment of that factor to the 'standard' volume as defined on pp. 83-4).

In the case of industries in which the total demand is too small to enable a single plant to be run at full capacity, the marginal cost will be below the average cost, so that if the product is sold at a price equal to its marginal cost it will be selling at a loss. This difficulty can be easily met in the case of nationalized industries if the industries are not only publicly managed but are also publicly owned. For in the costs of production we include a rate of profit on the capital equipment of the industry equal to the market rate of interest, and a rent on the land used by the industry equal to the rent which this land could obtain in other uses. If the product of an industry is being sold at a price lower than its average cost, it will probably mean no more than that the industry is earning less than the market rate of interest on its capital or less than the market rent on its land. If the government owns the capital and the land, this presents no problem. It will be content with less than the market rate of interest or less than the market rent for land; but the managers of the nationalized industry will take on more capital or more land if the marginal product of such capital or land is at current prices worth more than the rate of interest or the rent which is offered for similar capital or land in other uses.[1] Difficulties would arise only if the marginal cost were so far below the average cost that to charge a price equal to the marginal cost did not enable the industry to cover the price of its raw materials, its wages, and

1. This is the principle of reckoning the rates of interest at which capital development should be undertaken by publicly-controlled industries, to which reference was made in Chapter V of Part I (p. 53). The nationalization of monopolistic industries will normally increase the capital development that is undertaken at any given rate of interest; for those in control of public corporations, unlike those in control of private businesses, will not take into account any fall in profit due to a fall in the price of the output which is already being produced in reckoning the yield of any scheme of capital development.

the cost of replacing its capital equipment as it wore out, quite apart from earning any interest on its capital or rent on its land. In this unlikely case the government would have to subsidize the industry out of taxation or out of profits earned in other public corporations.

If, however, the capital of a nationalized concern was still owned by private individuals so that it had to pay interest on bonds issued in return for the capital and land when the industry was nationalized, it might be unable to pay this interest if it charged prices as low as the marginal cost of production of the product. In this case the government would be obliged to subsidize the payment of interest to the owners of the concern.

It is often argued that it would be impossible to obtain managers for nationalized industries who would be as efficient as those who run businesses for private profit. Since any attempt to equate rewards of factors with the value of their marginal products throughout industry would eliminate many wastes, the critics of nationalization must prove not only that the managers of nationalized industries would be less efficient, but also that they would be so much less efficient that this loss in efficiency would more than offset the diminution of monopolistic wastes. The possible loss in efficiency of management due to nationalization does not depend on any increased difficulty in the technique of management but simply upon the change in the motive of management. Indeed the technical problems of management are simpler in a public corporation than in a business run for the maximization of profit. The manager of a public corporation should produce more so long as the price of a factor is less than the value of its marginal product. He will know the price of the factor and the price at which his product is selling, and has therefore only to assess the marginal product of each factor. The manager of an industry run to maximize profits must attempt to produce more so long as the addition to his costs due to employing more of a factor is less than the addition to his receipts due to employing more of that factor. He also will know the price of the factors and the price at which the product is selling; but he has to judge not only the marginal product of each factor, but also the extent to which he will cause a rise in the price of each factor by employing more of it, and the extent to which he will cause a fall in the price of the product by selling more of it. The manager of a public corporation has only a technical judgment to make, while the manager of a private business has to make the same technical judgment and in addition two market judgments.

Technically there is no reason why the salaried manager of a public corporation should make a worse judgment about the marginal productivity of different factors than the manager of a private business. The only substantial difference between them is the difference of motive. The efficiency of the manager in a public corporation must depend upon his desire to do a technical job well or upon his fear that he may lose his job if the central board in control of the corporation considers him inefficient. The manager of a private business will, if he is the owner, have the incentive of increasing his own income. The problem, therefore, turns upon the possibility of training a number of efficient managers for public corporations, moved by a professional desire to do a technical job well rather than by the desire to secure a larger personal income. But this overstates the difficulty. The managers of most large concerns are already salaried persons acting on behalf of the owners; and the real difficulty is to provide

(a) that the central board of control of a public corporation shall be able to judge efficiency or inefficiency as well as the directors of a private company; and

(b) that salaried managers shall realize that the closeness of approximation between factor prices and the value of their marginal products is as worthy a criterion of business success as the size of a firm's profit.

This problem of motive is the only serious obstacle to the elimination of waste by means of public control of industry; and it should not be more difficult to inculcate the required professional standards in the case of business management than it is in the case of other professions.

There are certain morals to be drawn from this discussion. In the first place, the success of a public corporation must not be judged by the size of the income which it is able to make; for otherwise many of the wastes due to monopoly would still continue. Syndicalist or Guild Socialist tendencies should be avoided in as far as they encourage those engaged in a particular industry to think of themselves as a separate interest, and so to attempt to run the industry with the object of making as large an income out of it as possible.

Secondly, even if all industries were publicly controlled and all capital and land were socially owned, use *could* be made of a pricing system similar to the pricing system of a competitive economy. Consumers could be left free to determine the price at which they will purchase the supplies of the different commodities put on the market by the public corporations. The prices of hired factors of production would be so adjusted—under the supervision of the Industrial Planning Commission—that the demand for each would be just equal to the supply. In the case of such factors as raw materials, where there are many identical units of each type, the determination of the price could be left to competition in a free market by the managers of the public corporations, who would buy and sell in accordance with the principles laid down on p. 207. The price of each type of labor in each region would be fixed at as high a level as was consistent with the full 'standard' employment of that type. Each section of land would be allocated by the Industrial Planning Commission to the corporation making the highest bid for it. The Federal banking corporation, acting in collaboration with the Industrial Planning Commission, would determine rates of interest for loans of different types, and at these rates each manager would determine how much development should be undertaken in his plant to equate the marginal product of capital to this rate. The rates would be fixed at a level which would secure a volume of capital development equal to the amount which income receivers would save when factors were fully employed.

These rules would suffice to determine the *relative* prices of different products and factors: and this is the important thing from the point of view of securing the best distribution of the nation's resources among different uses. By its control over the prices of factors the Industrial Planning Commission would also control the *absolute* level of money prices, and it should do this in a way which would secure reasonable stability of average money prices over fairly long periods.[1] A convenient practical method of doing this would be to fix absolutely the money price of some very important factor, e.g., the wage of unskilled labor (or the average wage if different wages were necessary in different regions), and adjust other prices to this one. Over- or underemployment of a factor other than unskilled labor would be met by raising or lowering the money price of the factor. Underemployment of unskilled labor would be countered by measures outlined in Part I (i.e., lower rates of interest, public works, consumers' credits), which would raise the general level of prices, and so lower the real wage-rate of unskilled labor. Conversely any tendency for the unemployment of unskilled labor to fall below the 'standard' volume would be countered by higher interest rates, decreased expenditure on public works, and higher taxes.

Any profits made by the public corporations (including the Federal banking corporation) not needed to subsidize losses elsewhere could either be saved, which would enable additional capital development to be undertaken, or used to reduce taxes or to pay a 'social dividend' to consumers.

Thirdly, in an economy in which industry is fully or in part under public control, use *must* be made of a system of prices for

---

1. Reasonably stable prices would facilitate economic calculations involving the future. They would also be desirable on grounds of fairness so long as any contracts were fixed in terms of money.

consumption goods and for factors of production if the best use of the community's resources is to be achieved. The resources of the community will not be most efficiently used in the service of consumers' needs unless

(a) factors of production are moved from one use to another so long as the loss of output caused in the first use is of less value to consumers than the gain in output in the second use; and

(b) factors of production are used in such proportions in the different occupations that it would be impossible, by using (e.g.) more capital to labor in one occupation and more labor to capital in another, to increase the output of one occupation without decreasing the output of the other.

Publicly-controlled industry to be efficient must conform to these two simple rules, but there are theoretically two possible methods of applying them. It is possible, by setting up a central planning commission with power to allocate the factors of production to different industries, to attempt to solve the problem without the use of a pricing system. This commission would have to discover by direct means whether a movement of factors of production from industry A to industry B would cause consumers to be better off, and whether, by shifting one factor from A to B and another from B to A, output A could be increased without diminishing output B. Alternatively, the problem can be solved if the three following conditions are fulfilled:

(a) if consumers are left free to settle the prices at which different commodities will sell;

(b) if the boards of management of each public corporation estimate the marginal product of each factor employed by them, and expand their employment of each until its price is equal to the price which consumers offer for its marginal product; and

(c) if the factors are allocated, or allowed to move freely, to those occupations in which the price offered for them is highest.

It is often considered that direct central planning is the more obvious and straightforward method. This view is entirely wrong. The problem of a general planning commission, unaided by a pricing system of the kind described, would be so complex as to be incapable of solution. If there were only two factors of production and only two commodities which could be produced, its task would be relatively simple. It might reasonably hope to discover from consumers' representatives whether consumers would be better off if they had so much more B and so much less A. By consulting the technicians in each industry it might discover whether a shift of labor from A to B and of machinery from B to A would produce more A without producing less B. But it would in fact be dealing with thousands of different products and scores of different factors of production, labor of different grades, machinery of different types, different raw materials, and land of different qualities and different locations. It would be an impossible problem to decide how much less of each of a large number of commodities could be produced if the output of other commodities—either singly or several at a time—were increased by a certain amount, and then to decide whether the consumers would be best off as they were or with any of the thousand and one rearrangements which would be possible. Moreover, no amount of consultation with engineers and technicians will enable the commission to make sure whether by shifting a little of this raw material from A to B and a little of this land from B to C, a little of this grade of labor from C to A and of this machinery from C to E, and a little of this raw material from D to E and some of this land from E to A, it is possible to increase the output of A without changing the output of any other product. But the use of a pricing system of the kind described will achieve these results.

Although a system of pricing is necessary to obtain the best use of the community's resources, there are, of course, occasions on which this must be accompanied by planning which is not solely determined by the principles of pricing outlined above. We will mention six examples of such planning.

1. There are certain services for which it is not practicable to charge prices to the consumers. As an example we may take the use of the roads for motoring. The principles of pricing would require that the authorities should levy tolls on motor cars as they used the roads, and should adjust these tolls to correspond to the marginal cost of providing roads to motorists. This is impracticable because of the inconvenience and cost involved in levying the tolls. In cases of this kind the instrument of taxation can sometimes be used so as to approximate to the correct principles of pricing. A tax on motor cars can, for example, be adjusted until it corresponds as closely as possible to the cost of road maintenance which each type of car involves.

2. There may be non-economic reasons for developing one industry or service more fully than it would be developed under the strict principles of pricing. For example, it may be decided that for military reasons a certain proportion of the country's food supplies should be produced at home, or that for social reasons a certain proportion of the population should be kept on the land. In cases of this kind the pricing system should not be abandoned; but either a tax on imported foods should be imposed or a subsidy on agricultural output should be paid to competitive agriculture; or, if agriculture is conducted by public corporations, these should be instructed to produce up to the point at which the price offered by consumers was below the marginal cost of production by a certain fixed percentage. There are two reasons why in these cases the pricing system should be retained and only modified in the ways suggested. In the first place, only in this way can any estimate be made of the economic cost involved in increasing agricultural output beyond the economic optimum; and the government must weigh the social or military advantages

against the economic loss. If a reduction of the price of agricultural products by 10 per cent below the marginal cost of production or the payment of a 10 per cent subsidy on agricultural output is found necessary to increase agricultural output by a certain amount, the government has a measure of the economic loss involved. Secondly, only through a system of prices can it be insured that the increased agricultural output is being produced in the most efficient manner. The object may be simply to increase agricultural output in general. In this case the economic loss to consumers will be minimized only if the factors of production are distributed among different agricultural occupations in such a way that it is impossible to produce more of one such product without producing less of another and that it is impossible to satisfy consumers' needs better by producing more of one such product and less of another. And this will be achieved only if consumers are free to compete for the purchase of bread, potatoes, sugar, etc., and if factors of production are moved within agriculture to the production of different agricultural products, until the value of the marginal product of any one factor is the same in every line of agricultural production.

3. There may be elements of cost which cannot easily be reckoned in the pricing system. The best example of such a case is the problem of geographic planning. When a town or region is developing, the situation of a new factory may spoil the view or other amenities of a residential area; but the exact boundaries or location of the residential area may not be known to those whose business it is to set up the factory until the factory is set up and the town has developed. There is therefore a case for imposing a town or regional plan upon the free play of the system of prices. But this planning should take place with reference to the system of prices. The authority in charge must attempt to assess any increase in costs which would be involved in forcing a factory into one area rather than another, and must weigh this increased cost against increased amenities which are expected for the residential areas.

As an instructive example of the way in which the principles of pricing should be used in geographic planning, we may take the problem of specially depressed areas. If there are areas in which unemployment is abnormally great, the question arises whether new industries should be attracted to these areas or whether surplus labor should be attracted to areas in which industry is expanding. In fact both policies should probably be adopted simultaneously. But there are simple principles of pricing by which it can be determined whether in any particular instance the new factory should move to the men or the men to the new factory. We have argued that men should be moved only if the annual interest on the capital sum which must be spent on moving them is less than the increase in the value of their marginal product caused by the move. For this reason the best distribution of men and industries between different areas can be achieved,

(a) if the real wage-rate in distressed areas is reduced until there is no abnormal unemployment in those areas;

(b) if competitive industries and publicly-controlled industries are allowed to set up new factories in those areas in which their costs are lowest; and

(c) if labor is transferred from one area to another by some official agency whenever the interest on the cost of movement is less than the excess of the value of the marginal product of labor in the new area over the value of its marginal product in the old area.

4. In an economy in which many industries are publicly controlled the government should set up an Industrial Planning Commission. For a central body would be necessary to control the markets for factors of production, as we have seen above. It would also perform the vitally important functions of organizing research for the boards of different public corporations, discovering new methods of reducing their costs, and paying individuals for new inventions which are of use to industry.

It would also be the logical body to recommend to the government when new industries should be set up to produce entirely new commodities. When it decides on the principles discussed above (pp. 171–3) that a new invention has been sufficiently developed for the production of a new commodity to be possible at a cost which will be covered by its total value to consumers, recommendations must be made to set up a new public corporation to produce the new commodity. We have already argued that such decisions must be taken without depending solely on the evidence of prices ruling in the market.

5. There should also be some centralized institution—either the Industrial Planning Commission or a subsidiary Economic Forecasting Commission—to inform those in control of private and public industries of the probable future course of different prices. When those in charge of any industry attempt to assess the yield on their plant in order to decide how much capital development they should undertake at a given rate of interest, they must take account of the future course of prices. For the yield on a machine installed now at a certain cost depends upon the prices at which the extra product can be sold in the future and on the price at which labor and raw materials can be hired in the future to operate the machine during its life. The value of the marginal product of the machine cannot be known until future prices are estimated.

There are three main reasons why the relative prices of different commodities may alter. Consumers' tastes may change, so that the demand for one commodity rises at the expense of the demand for other commodities. Technical inventions may take place which lower the cost and increase the output of certain commodities, and the resultant fall in the price of these commodities may have the further effect of causing the consumers' demand for other commodities to change. Finally, if capital development is taking place or the population is increasing, the relative demand for different commodities will change as income per head changes, and the relative costs of different products, and so their prices, will vary with changes in the relative prices of the factors of production.

It is impossible for any body to forecast changes in tastes and changes in cost due to technical discoveries. But there are many changes which can be foreseen with some degree of accuracy. The demand for new houses depends among other things upon the number of marriages. The number of marriages depends largely upon the numbers of the population which are of the normal marriage age at any time, so that it is possible to forecast with some degree of accuracy the number which will take place in the future from a study of a number of births which have taken place in past years. There may be a heavy demand for new houses now, because there is a large number of people of marriageable age now; but it may be foreseen that within five years the demand for new houses will fall off, because the number of new families seeking houses will fall. The building industry must take this factor into account in deciding the extent to which it will develop its capacity now.

The demand for railway transport will depend partly upon the price of air transport and of road transport, which in turn will depend, in part, upon the rate at which these other transport systems are developed. The extent to which the demand for one service changes will depend upon the extent to which each other service is developed; and a single Economic Forecasting Commission, which can examine the rate at which each service is developing, will be able to help those in control of any one service to estimate what will be the future demand for its service.

We may conclude that while there are many opportunities for economic planning by a state in which industry is to a large extent under public control, yet even in such a state a pricing system is essential within which such planning can be developed.

Part III

THE DISTRIBUTION OF INCOME

I

HOW SHOULD INCOME BE DISTRIBUTED ?

IF we have solved the problems discussed in Parts I and II, we shall have insured first that all the factors of production are employed, and, secondly, that they are employed in the most efficient way to satisfy consumers' needs, so that the welfare of any one consumer can now be increased only at the expense of another's. But it might still be desirable by a redistribution of income to increase the satisfaction of some even though this involved a loss of satisfaction by others. The distribution of the national income is the subject of this Part, in which we shall discuss the following three questions:

(i) on what principles income should be distributed among individuals;

(ii) to what extent the forces of competition in a *laisser-faire* economy will bring about the ideal distribution; and

(iii) in what way the state must interfere with competition in order to bring about the ideal distribution, if competition fails to do so.

In discussing the principles on which the national income should be distributed we are concerned with many questions of an ethical nature, which it is not the purpose of this book to discuss. Whether certain types of people 'deserve' more than others is not a question on which the economist can pass any significant judgment. It is held by some that people with greater ability deserve to earn more than people with smaller ability, while others hold that people with greater needs deserve more than people with fewer needs; these two principles are not necessarily compatible, since a man may have little ability and great needs or

220

great ability and few needs. It is not an economic problem to decide between these two principles, although economic problems are involved as soon as the choice has been made and means are required to give effect to the choice. But in choosing the fundamental principle upon which income should be distributed there is one important economic consideration; the larger the income of any one individual in a given situation, i.e. with unchanged tastes, knowledge, and needs, the less important will it be for him to receive a given addition to his income. This is a fairly obvious rule, to which there are probably no important exceptions. If a man possesses an income of $1,000 a year, a $500 increase in his income will add a great deal to his satisfaction; whereas if he starts with an income of $100,000 a year the $500 increase will mean a much smaller addition to his satisfaction. This fact is expressed by saying that the marginal utility of income diminishes as income increases.

It is an easy extension of this argument to say that if there are two persons *with the same tastes and the same needs*, and if there is a certain income to be distributed between them, this income will 'go farthest' and will give the greatest total satisfaction if it is equally divided between them. This argument is not ethical; it does not assert that it is just or fair to divide the income equally between the two, but only that it is *economic* to do so, since the greatest amount of satisfaction can be derived in this way.[1]

The argument can be demonstrated by means of an example. Suppose that of two men with the same tastes and needs one has $2,000 a year and the other $3,000 a year. $1 will mean more to the first than to the second, and if we give the first man $2,001

1. The term 'economic' is here being used in a sense which has the sanction of ordinary usage, i.e. that it is 'economic' to act in such a way as to obtain the maximum satisfaction from limited resources. Some writers insist that 'economics' should deal only with the means of obtaining any given end, without implying that one particular end (i.e. maximum satisfaction) is itself 'economic.' The question is merely one of definition, and any reader who objects to this use of 'economic' may substitute an adjective more to his liking.

instead of $2,000 we shall add to his satisfaction more than we subtract from the satisfaction of the second by giving him $2,999 instead of $3,000. Clearly to transfer a second $1 of income from the second to the first will also increase the satisfaction of the first by more than the satisfaction of the second is diminished. We can go on increasing the combined satisfaction of the two men in this way until both have $2,500. If we transfer another $1 from the second to the first we shall diminish the satisfaction of the second by at least as much as we increase the satisfaction of the first; and as we continue to transfer income from the poorer to the richer we shall more and more certainly diminish the satisfaction of the poorer by a greater amount than we increase the satisfaction of the richer. If, therefore, the marginal utility of income diminishes as income increases, and if there are a number of persons with identical tastes and needs and a certain income to be distributed between them, the total satisfaction to be gained from this income will be greatest if the income is equally divided.

This argument must be modified if different persons have different needs and tastes. Let us suppose that of two persons with the same tastes one has greater needs than the other, because the one has dependents to support while the other has not. If both have the same income, it will be possible to increase the total satisfaction by transferring income from the person without dependents to the person with dependents, since the man with dependents will have unsatisfied needs which are more urgent than many of the desires which the independent person is able to gratify. In this case, if we wish to make a given income go farthest, the ideal principle of distribution is that the man with dependents should receive just so much more than the man without dependents that an extra $1 would add an equal amount to both men's satisfaction.

This argument can be extended to cover the case of persons with different tastes. If one man's pleasure is to work in his garden while another's is to travel abroad, the greatest satisfaction to be obtained from a given sum to be divided between them will not necessarily be achieved by an equal division. For, if the income were equally divided, it might be possible by transferring income from the gardener to the traveller to cause an increase in the traveller's satisfaction which is greater than the decrease in the gardener's satisfaction. It is not the task of the economist to determine whether in such circumstances it is just to divide income unequally. Some people may urge that—apart from differences in needs which arise from differences in the number of dependents and in expenditure upon medical services made necessary by differences in health—the state should distribute income equally, although this division means that the man with inexpensive tastes can satisfy his desires more fully than the man with expensive tastes. For it may be held that the state should aim at providing equality of opportunity for the satisfaction of desires. The economist can, however, aid clear judgment by pointing out that there is a divergence between an equal distribution of income and that distribution which will insure that the greatest total of satisfaction is obtained from the national income.

Let us consider the case of men with different tastes more fully. It may be that the gardener with simple tastes can get a great deal of enjoyment out of a simple life, while the traveller with expensive tastes is extremely unhappy if he cannot travel. To transfer income from the gardener to the traveller, and so to distribute income less equally, would in this case both increase the total satisfaction to be obtained from the sum to be divided, and would also make both men more nearly equal in their real enjoyment of life. But it may equally well be that the gardener with simple tastes is by nature unable to get as much out of life as the traveller, who can enjoy life a great deal even with a small income, but could add to his enjoyment very considerably by having still greater opportunities. In this case to transfer income from the gardener to the traveller, and so to distribute income unequally, will increase the total satisfaction obtained, but at the same time will increase the inequality in the real satisfaction which the two men are getting from their incomes. The gardener was at the start less satisfied than the traveller because he was unable to get so much enjoyment out of the same income, and he will remain so.

These simple examples show that there is a divergence between the principles involved in distributing income—

(1) so that every one has the same opportunity of satisfying his needs;

(2) so that every one gets the same real satisfaction; and

(3) so that the total satisfaction obtained is the greatest possible.

The first involves equal money incomes, after allowances have been made for needs such as dependents and ill health; the second involves giving more income to the man who is hard to please and less to the man who is easily satisfied; and the third principle involves distributing income in such a way that the last $1 received by every one satisfies equally urgent desires.

There is a possible objection to the whole of this argument. While it may be admitted that the marginal utility of income diminishes as income increases in the case of each individual, it may be denied that the marginal utility of income to different persons can be compared. It would then be meaningless even to ask whether total satisfaction could be increased by transferring income from one person to another. If, therefore, it were decided that one man's enjoyment cannot be compared with another's, the whole foundation for any economic arguments about the distribution of income would be removed. Yet common sense demands that we should compare different men's satisfactions. If there is any meaning in saying that to take $1 from a millionaire and to give it to a starving man does more to satisfy the starving man than to dissatisfy the millionaire, then logically we must admit that the feelings of different men are commensurable. It may be that in innumerable cases there is too little evidence even to guess whether $1 means more to A than to B; but this must be because we have not got the necessary information and not because it is nonsense to attempt to compare A's feelings with B's.

The economist can therefore argue that, if it is considered desirable to maximize total satisfactions, the third principle mentioned above should be chosen. This is a purely economic judgment. We shall in what follows assume that it is desirable to make total satisfaction as great as possible and that the national income should, accordingly, be distributed in such a way that the marginal utility of income is the same to every one. The discussion of the possible methods of redistributing income according to this principle can easily be modified by the reader if he decides on ethical grounds that some other principle of distribution is to be preferred.

As we have shown, if all men had the same tastes and the same needs, this principle of distribution would involve an equal distribution of income. It is difficult to make fair allowances for differences in tastes; but there is one important difference in needs—namely the size of the dependent family—for which allowances can and should be made. In a community in which the married and unmarried are paid the same wages, poverty is concentrated on the families in which the number of children is large and in which income per head is therefore low. In order to get the more out of a given national income, this income should be distributed in equal amounts to each *person* rather than in equal amounts to each *family* regardless of its size. In what follows we shall assume that our objective is an equal distribution of income, i.e. we shall assume that needs and tastes are the same. This is, of course, not so; but methods of paying larger incomes to classes of persons with greater needs or more expensive tastes can easily be introduced by the reader into the arguments which follow. We shall discuss 'methods of distributing income more equally' instead of 'methods of distributing income so that the marginal utility of income is the same to each individual,' because this greatly simplifies the exposition of the argument, because the maximization of total satisfaction demands a much greater measure of equality than exists in the modern world, and because there are other reasons than those associated with maximum total satisfaction for believing equal incomes to be desirable.

II

INEQUALITIES OF INCOME FROM WORK

HAVING decided that—with certain modifications—income should be equally distributed, we must now discuss the causes of inequalities of income in order to show how these inequalities may be diminished. In this chapter we shall discuss the causes of inequalities in earned incomes and shall examine certain ways in which these inequalities might be modified. In the next chapter we shall show that the main cause of inequality of incomes is inequality of income from property. Subsequently we shall show how this substantial cause of inequality might be removed.

In one respect *laisser-faire* tends to bring about equality of incomes; for in competition similar factors of production tend to receive the same rewards in every industry. Labor tends to move into the industries which are paying the higher wages until the wage-rate is the same in all industries. There are, however, certain ways in which this tendency for equality in the earnings of labor will be modified in a *laisser-faire* economy.

1. The wage paid in one industry will tend to remain permanently lower than the wage paid in another in which the work is more unpleasant. For labor will move into the higher paid occupations only if the increase in earnings so obtained is more than sufficient to offset the increased unpleasantness. This modification of the tendency towards equality of earnings is, however, of no importance from our present point of view; for if the inequality of money earnings is only just sufficient to offset the inequality of unpleasantness of the work, the real welfare of labor in the two industries is equal.

2. The second reason for inequalities in the earnings of labor we have already noticed above (pp. 115 and 118); labor will not always move to the higher paid occupations because of the cost

227

of moving from one district to another or because of the cost involved in learning a new trade.

3. Inequalities in the earnings of labor may be caused by differences in the innate skill required in different industries. A first-class pianist may earn more than a first-class miner, because the skill of a pianist is more rare in relation to the demand than the skill of a miner. On the same grounds we may partly explain the facts that brain workers are paid more than manual workers and that men earn more than women. There are certain needs and desires which the manual worker is fitted to satisfy and certain others which brain workers can satisfy best; and in the existing state of affairs it happens that the number of manual workers relatively to the needs which they can best satisfy is greater than the number of brain workers relatively to the needs which brain workers can best satisfy. If there were fewer manual workers, or more brain workers, or more needs which could best be satisfied by manual work, or less needs which could best be satisfied by brain work, these two classes of work would be more equally paid.

4. The earnings of labor may be different in different occupations because of differences in opportunity for training for the higher paid types of work. The miner may be unable to become a pianist, not because he is less skilled but because he cannot afford the necessary training. These inequalities in the earnings of different types of labor, combined with the existing laws of inheritance of property, perpetuate the existing inequalities of income, since the professions in which earnings are high are more accessible to the sons of the rich than to the sons of the poor. This is undesirable not only because it perpetuates inequalities of income but also because it offends against the first of the advantages which normally result from the forces of competition. If in a competitive system a miner earns $20 and a pianist $100 a week, then the value of the marginal product of the miner is $20 while that of the pianist is $100 a week. In other words, if the miner became an equally efficient pianist, consumers would lose

something which they value at $20 and gain something which they value at $100. In these circumstances if there is no *real* difficulty in the way of the miner becoming a pianist, i.e. if each has the same innate qualities, the community would be better off if miners became pianists, so long as the cost of the necessary education was less than the consequent increase in the value of the marginal product of the worker.

5. In a *laisser-faire* economy the earnings of labor may vary in different occupations because of the existence of monopolistic conditions. These conditions may take either of two forms. In the first place, because of ignorance or inertia, labor may fail to move from the lower to the higher paid occupations. Secondly, the entry to a well paid occupation may be barred by the action of those already in that occupation. If a trade union directly limits the number of entries into a trade by limiting the number of apprentices or by holding up the wage-rate so that no new persons coming into the trade could find work there—or if a profession imposes unnecessarily high examination or entrance fees on candidates for the profession—labor employed in that trade or profession may continue to earn higher rewards than similar labor employed in other trades or professions.

The measures suggested in Chapters VII and VIII of Part II for the control of monopoly will remove the fifth cause of inequality. We have suggested there that, in order to use the factors of production most efficiently for the satisfaction of consumers' needs, measures should be taken to insure that in each occupation labor is offered a reward equal to the value of its marginal product and should be able to move to the occupations offering a higher reward, provided that the cost of movement does not more than counterbalance the increase in reward. We have suggested measures to achieve this result—such as the placing of monopolistic industries under public control, the fixing of maximum commodity and minimum factor prices, and the creation of employment exchanges to make labor more mobile between different occupations.

The fourth reason for differences in earnings—the inability of the poor to train for the occupations offering the highest rewards —is also due to the presence of monopolistic conditions, the removal of which are not only important for the solution of our present problem but also for the solution of the problem of the best use of the factors of production discussed in Part II. From our present point of view expenditure on education which will enable the sons of poor parents to earn a high income is simply one form of investment in capital for the purpose of moving labor from a lower to a higher paid occupation.

In perfect competition every one will invest capital in those occupations in which the yield on capital is higher than the current rate of interest; and if this is so, differences in the ability to earn money due to differences in the opportunity of education could not exist. The figures in Table VI are devised to illustrate this point. We suppose that a laborer without technical education can earn $1,000 a year and that the period of time over which he can earn is 50 years. (The figures are chosen because they are simple—not because they are thought to be realistic.)

TABLE VI

The Yield of Investment in Education

A	B	C	D
Expenditure on education	Annual earnings	Amortization of loan	Marginal product of investment in education
$	$	$	
0	1,000	0	..
1,000	1,500	20	48% per annum
2,000	1,900	40	38% "
3,000	2,200	60	28% "
4,000	2,400	80	18% "
5,000	2,500	100	8% "

Column A shows different expenditures on the education of this laborer; and column B shows what the annual earnings of the laborer would be if the amount in column A were spent on his education. Thus, if at the beginning of his working life $3,000 had been spent on his education, he would be able to earn $2,200 a year for the 50 years of his working life. In order to see what yield is obtained on this investment of $3,000 we must allow for the fact that the investment is not permanent but will cease to earn anything at the end of his working life. If his working life is 50 years, we must subtract $60 a year from his earnings in order that over the 50 years he shall pay back the $3,000 invested in his education. We allow, therefore, a figure of $60 a year in column C for the amortization of the $3,000 originally invested. Column D shows the marginal product of the capital invested as a fraction of the capital sum. If $1,000 is invested in his education his earnings would rise from $1,000 to $1,500, but of this increase of $500 in his annual income $20 must go to repay the capital sum of the loan. Therefore, the net amount earned on the capital investment of $1,000 is $480 a year, i.e. a rate of 48 per cent per annum. If a second $1,000 is invested in his education, his earnings will rise by $400 a year, i.e. from $1,500 to $1,900, while the amount which he must set aside to repay the capital sum of the loan will rise by $20, i.e. from $20 to $40 a year. Therefore, on the second $1,000 invested in his education a net sum of $380 a year will be earned, so that the marginal product of the investment of a second $1,000 is 38 per cent. Similarly, the marginal products of a third, fourth, and fifth investment of $1,000 in his education are 28, 18, and 8 per cent. If the laborer can borrow money at a rate of interest of 20 per cent per annum it would pay him to invest between $3,000 and $4,000 in his own education. For if he borrowed less than $3,000, the investment in his education of an additional $1,000 would add more to his annual earnings than to the annual cost of the loan. For example, by investing $3,000 instead of $2,000 he would add $300 to his annual earnings and only $220 to his annual payments for the loan. He would add $20 a year in repayment over the 50 years of the extra $1,000 borrowed and would add $200 a year in interest for the extra $1,000, because the rate of interest is 20 per cent per annum. He would gain greatly by borrowing the $3,000 for his education for he would earn $1,200 a year more than if he were uneducated and for this would have to pay $660 a year during his working life—$60 in repayment over 50 years of the capital sum of $3,000 and $600 in interest at 20 per cent per annum on the $3,000.

So long as the rate to be earned on capital invested in other lines of business, in machinery or plant, were less than 20 per cent per annum, it should pay other persons to lend to him rather than to invest in industry. And not only should such investment in education pay the laborer and the owner of property directly concerned, but also from the point of view of the best use of the community's resources this investment should take place. For if by the investment of an extra $1,000 in his education a laborer can add $280 to his net annual earnings, then the investment of capital in education will add to the output of the laborer and so to the output of the community an amount which consumers consider to be worth $280. And in order that the community's resources should be employed in the best possible manner, capital should flow into education up to the point at which the marginal product of capital invested in this way is the same as the marginal product of capital invested in other occupations.[1]

As we have seen, the self-interest of the man seeking education and of the owners of capital ought to bring this about if there is perfect competition in the lending and borrowing of money. This does not occur in the world of realities. The ignorance of those needing education about its advantages and of those owning property about the possibility of profitable investment in this field are important. But more important are the desire of the laborer for independence from the hold which such borrowing might give to others over his future life, the insecurity which owners of property would feel in such loans, and the weight of many social conventions and traditions. All these things make it

1. We are here only concerned with economic considerations. There may, of course, be non-economic reasons for pushing the investment of capital in education beyond this point.

exceedingly improbable that *laisser-faire* will of itself bring about the investment of sufficient funds in the education of the working classes.

Inequalities of earnings which occur because of inequalities of opportunity of education can be removed without fundamental interference with the competitive system. The state can provide state scholarships out of public funds, or can organize the borrowing of money and its loan to the poorer classes for the purpose of education. The training of more persons for the higher paid occupations will lower earnings in these occupations, since more persons will have to find work in them and will be employed, therefore, up to a point at which the value of their marginal product is lower than before. It will raise the wage-rate for less skilled work, since there will be a smaller supply of untrained workers. This policy will therefore work only if the higher paid workers accept lower rewards than before, so as to enable more persons to be absorbed into their occupations. Otherwise there will simply be an excess supply of and unemployment among such workers.

Even if all the causes of inequality of income due to the absence of perfect competition were removed by appropriate state action, some inequalities in earned incomes would still remain. The reasons for this are clear from the second and third causes of the inequality of the earnings of labor mentioned above: the movement of labor from one job to another may be hindered by the cost of movement, and differences in natural abilities may cause differences in earning power. We have already argued in Chapter II of Part II (pp. 118 and 119) that it is desirable to spend money on the movement of labor from one job to another —and from the economic point of view it is therefore desirable to spend money on educating people—only if the cost of the movement or of the education is less than the subsequent increase in earning power. Differences in earning power will remain, which it is not worth while removing on the principles already discussed, because the cost of removing them is greater than the differences in earning power themselves. One particular example of this is the existence of differences in man's natural abilities. A farmer may be earning less than a highly skilled surgeon because he has not the same natural abilities; and in this case it would be absurd to attempt to equalize the earnings of farmer and surgeon by training the farmer to be a surgeon at a cost which was far greater than the increase in his earning power. It may still be desirable to equalize their incomes, but more direct methods must be found.

We shall return to this problem at a later stage, but at this point we can dismiss what may at first sight appear the most obvious solution of the problem. It is sometimes argued that, in order to equalize the earnings of workers maximum and minimum legal payments for work should be fixed, which would prevent the well paid from obtaining so much and would insure that the badly paid obtained more than before. But if appropriate measures have been taken to remove the effects of monopolistic conditions, so that every factor is paid a reward equal to the value of its marginal product, such a policy would be disastrous. The fact that a low wage was paid to a laborer and a high wage to a technician would mean that the value of the marginal product of the laborer was smaller than the value of the marginal product of the technician. If the wage-rate is made equal by regulation, either the wage-rate of the laborer must be raised or that of the technician must be lowered; or else the former wage must be raised somewhat and the latter lowered somewhat. In as far as the former wage is raised by regulation, unemployment among laborers will result. For the value of the marginal product of the laborer will now be less than the wage-rate, and employers will engage fewer laborers until their marginal product has risen to the new level required by the higher wage-rate. In so far as the wage of the technician is lowered by regulation, a different but also undesirable result will follow. The demand for technicians at the lower wage-rate will be greater than before, since each employer will have an incentive to take on more technicians with his equipment of other factors; and the supply of technicians will not increase when their wage is lowered, so that at the new wage the demand for technicians will be in excess of their supply. And in these circumstances there is no means to insure that the most pressing needs of the community will be satisfied before less urgent needs.

For suppose that while the competitive wage for a technician is $100 a week, the regulated wage is $60 a week. In the new situation a technician may be engaged in any job in which the value of his marginal product is $60 or more. But there will be more jobs in which the value of the marginal product of technicians is $60 than there are technicians. This may mean that in some jobs technicians are employed up to the point at which the value of their marginal product is $120 and in others up to the point at which the value of their marginal product is $80. Competition would make this impossible because the first industry would offer a wage of $120 and the second one of $80, and the technicians would move from the second to the first. But with a regulated wage this would not happen simply because neither industry is permitted to offer more than $60. The result would be that both the first two fundamental advantages of competition mentioned in Chapter II of Part II would be lost.

III

INEQUALITIES OF INCOME FROM PROPERTY

WE have explained why competition may cause different types of workers to obtain different incomes from their work. But by far the most important reason for the inequality of incomes is inequality in the ownership of capital and land. The income of an individual is composed of his income from work and of his income from property, and equality of distribution would be achieved if each man not only obtained the same reward for labor but also possessed an equal amount of property.

But in a society in which there is freedom of bequest of property at death, the ownership of property is likely to be very unequal, because any inequalities which do exist will perpetuate and accentuate themselves. In the first place, a man who possesses much property is likely to bequeath it to his sons or to persons who are in the same income class, so that property passes from the rich to the rich and not from the rich to the poor. Secondly, those who own property are not only able to bequeath more to their sons and other dependents, but also can afford to train their sons and dependents for the higher paid professions, so that the sons of wealthier families not only inherit more property than others but are able to earn a higher income than others. Thirdly, a rich man will find it easier than a poor man to save out of his income, and so to accumulate more property, thereby increasing his income and the income of his sons still further. For these reasons any small or accidental inequalities of income are likely to be accentuated in the course of time. Some poor families by exceptional abilities, by stern and rigid thrift, or by accident may become rich; and the property of rich families may be squandered and a later generation may be poverty-stricken. But such is by no means the normal course of events. Competition, private

236

ownership, and freedom of bequest of property lead naturally to great inequalities of income.

But there is another side to this picture. For the same reasons that inequalities of income perpetuate and accentuate themselves, measures which directly increase equality by a certain amount are likely indirectly to increase equality still more. In the last chapter we suggested certain ways in which inequalities of income from work might be diminished, the most important of which was that all the most promising youths, from whatever class they might spring, should be educated for the highest paid occupations so long as the investment of money in such education would yield the current return on capital. This would greatly diminish inequalities of income from work by lowering rewards in the higher paid occupations and by raising the rewards of those who were left to compete for posts requiring little education. This primary increase in equality would tend to equalize the power of individuals to accumulate capital from their income, which in the second generation would tend to equalize the amount of inherited property. This in turn would tend to equalize the opportunity to train for the higher paid jobs and the ability to save more property. It must not be imagined that this single reform would in the end prove sufficient to cause incomes to be substantially equal; it is only asserted that any measures which directly diminish inequalities of incomes are likely to have some indirect consequences tending in the same direction.

The adoption of certain of the measures suggested in Chapters VII and VIII of Part II for the control of monopolistic conditions will also have important effect in diminishing inequalities of income due to the inequalities of income from property. It was argued in Chapters IV and V of Part II that the hired factors of production receive rewards lower than the value of their marginal products if monopolistic conditions exist either in the sale of the product of industry or in the hiring of the factors themselves. In Chapter VI of Part II we argued that in as far as the hired factors of production obtain rewards lower than the value of their marginal products the hiring factor of production 'management' receives a reward greater than the value of its marginal product. It so happens that the most important hired factor of production is labor, and that the hiring factor of production 'management' owns all or part of the capital invested in industry and receives the profit which is left over after payment of the rewards of the hired factors of production. Anything, therefore, which removes the effects of monopoly by insuring that labor is paid the value of its marginal product is likely to increase income from labor at the expense of income from property. Since the owners of property are on the average richer than the workers, this will increase the equality of incomes. As examples of the type of measure which will achieve this result, minimum wage-rates and maximum commodity prices might be fixed which would just allow full employment at real wage-rates equal to the marginal product of labor; or monopolistic industries might be placed under public corporations, which could pay the hired factors rewards equal to the value of their marginal products.

But while it is true that in monopolistic conditions the regulation of wages and of prices in the way suggested will reduce the inequality of incomes, yet it is disastrous to extend the scope of this policy beyond the point at which the results of monopoly have been removed. There are many people who argue that the most obvious way to reduce inequalities due to the inequality of income from property is to push up the wage-rate so that less is left over for profit, interest, or rent, or to restrict by law the amount which may be earned on property. These arguments imply that the wage-rate of labor should be raised even if this involves raising it above the marginal product of labor, and that interest, profit, and rent should be restricted by law even if this involves lowering the payments to capital and land below their marginal products.

If an attempt was made to increase the income which went to labor and to diminish the income which went to property by fixing a minimum wage higher than the marginal product of labor, either the attempt to raise real wage-rates would fail or unemployment would result. We have seen in Chapter VII of Part I that if a rise in money wage-rates is accompanied by an equal rise in the prices offered for commodities, there will be no decrease in employment; but in this case there will be no rise in the real wage-rate and so no redistribution of income in favor of labor. If, however, a monetary policy is adopted of such a kind that the money price offered for goods rises in a smaller percentage than money wage-rates, the real wage-rate will rise. But, in this case, labor will be dismissed until there is so much less labor employed with the existing capital and land that the marginal product of labor is raised to correspond to the higher wage demanded. Action by trades unions or wage boards or by legislation designed to raise real wage-rates by regulation cannot achieve this object without causing unemployment if the real wage-rate is already as high as the marginal product of labor.

Two qualifications of this statement must be added. In the first place, it is possible that the marginal product of labor is low because labor is inefficient, and that labor is inefficient because its wage and so its standard of living is too low to enable it to maintain its efficiency. If the wage were higher, the efficiency of labor would be greater and this might raise the marginal product of labor.[1] In these circumstances there is a vicious circle which may be broken by regulation. If a 10 per cent increase in the real wage-rate would raise the efficiency and the marginal product of labor by 10 per cent or more, then there will be a permanent rise in wages without any unemployment if the real wage is raised by regulation.

There is the possibility of a second type of vicious circle which may be broken by the regulation of wages. Real wage-rates may have to be low if the large number of people seeking work are to be absorbed into employment; but a large number of people may

1. An increase in labor's efficiency will certainly raise output per head, and it would probably—though not certainly—raise the marginal product of labor. For the distinction between the average and marginal product of labor see pp. 72–4 above.

be seeking work because wages are low. If real wage-rates are successfully raised, a smaller number will be employed; but at the same time a smaller number may seek work, because real wage-rates are higher. If the real wage-rate is raised in one occupation and not in others, labor will move towards the higher earnings and the supply of labor will be increased in that occupation. But it is by no means certain that a rise in the real wage-rate in every occupation will increase the total supply of labor seeking employment. Indeed, there is reason to believe that the total supply of labor may diminish if the general level of real wages rises. A rise in the general level of real wages can affect the total supply of labor by affecting the birth-rate, the death-rate, the age at which people start and finish their working lives, the number of members of a family who will seek work, and the length of the working week. In the long run the effect on the birth- and death-rates, which determine the size of the population, will be important. In the short run it is the other factors, which determine the proportion of the population employed and the number of hours per week worked, that will be decisive. It is difficult to generalize about the long-run effects of a rise in the level of wages. The death-rate would doubtless be decreased, since an improvement in the standard of living of wage-earners will presumably result in better health and longer average life. But so might the birth-rate be decreased, and it, as we shall see in Part IV, Chapter II, is more important in the long run than the death-rate in determining the future course of the population. The fact that the birth-rate is lower in the better paid strata of society and in nations with a high standard of life would indicate, though not conclusively, since other causes might be operative, that the long run effect of an increase in wage-rates would be a reduction in the size of the working population, or at least a diminution in its rate of increase. For a time, however, as during the 19th century, this effect might be more than counteracted by the concomitant fall in the death-rate.

In the short run the effects of a rise in wages on the proportion of the population employed and the hours per week worked are more certain; they would almost certainly decrease the total supply of labor. If the wage-rate rises, a man may either provide the same amount of work and earn more than before, or provide more work and earn a still greater increase in income, or provide somewhat less work and earn a little more than before but obtain more leisure. Experience suggests that when the wage-rate rises children will be kept at school or at home longer, because this form of leisure can now be afforded; wives will stay at home instead of going out to work to supplement the family income; men will retire from work earlier if they have been able to save more during their working lives or if their children are in a better position to maintain them; and finally, either independently or through their trade unions, workers will prefer to insist on shorter hours of work rather than on the maintenance of the existing hours at the higher wage-rate per hour. If a rise in the general level of wage-rates would for these reasons cause a decrease in the total supply of labor, it is possible that wage-rates which are already as high as the marginal product of labor may be successfully raised without creating unemployment. While the rise in the wage-rate will cause labor to be dismissed until the marginal product of labor has risen to correspond with the higher wage-rate demanded, at the same time the number of workers seeking work will be diminished. If a rise in the wage-rate causes a diminution in the total supply of labor at least as great as the diminution in the demand for labor, the regulation of wages will be successful without causing unemployment.

The raising of wages by regulation will therefore increase the earnings of labor without causing unemployment if it sufficiently increases the efficiency of labor or sufficiently diminishes the total supply of labor. But we cannot rely upon these two qualifications of the general proposition that to raise wages by regulation above the existing marginal product of labor will cause unemployment. Only in the most favorable circumstances would this not be true, and we should therefore seek other methods if we wish to interfere with the competitive distribution of income.

Let us turn to the suggestion that interest, profit, and rent should be legally restricted to prevent people from receiving too large an income from property. Such action would take the form of a combination of restrictions preventing people from lending money at a rate of interest above a certain figure, preventing companies from paying a rate of dividend upon their common and preferred stock above a certain figure, and preventing the owners of land from letting their land at rents above a certain figure per acre. Suggestions of this kind are open to grave objections. We have already seen in Part I, Chapters II and III, the important role which the rate of interest plays in regulating the total amount of monetary demand for goods in general, and have suggested that to cure unemployment the banks should lower the rate of interest in order to increase the monetary demand for goods. In times of unemployment in which the banks were finding it difficult to reduce interest rates sufficiently, it might be useful to supplement their efforts by laws analogous to the medieval laws against usury, whereby people were not allowed to lend money at a rate of interest higher than a certain figure—provided, of course, that such laws could be enforced. But the lowering of the rate of interest by legislation, or by banking action, does nothing immediately to reduce income from interest and profit combined. The object of reducing interest rates in this case is to widen the gap between the rate of profit which may be earned on capital development and the rate of interest at which money can be borrowed for such development. It is, indeed, only by increasing the net profit left to the borrower by the reduction in the interest demanded by the lender that such action would be effective in increasing expenditure on capital development and in diminishing unemployment. Moreover, if in the interests of the redistribution of income the maximum permissible rate of interest were fixed at so low a level that a larger total amount of money would be borrowed for capital development than was necessary to provide full employment, this would cause a large increase in the money demand for commodities, leading to an inflationary boom, unless the banks rationed new loans to borrowers by some means other than raising the rate of interest.

Even if an inflationary boom were prevented by the rationing of loans by the banks on other principles, the fixing of arbitrarily low maximum figures for the rate of interest on capital, for the profit that may be earned in business, and for the rent per acre of land, would cause an excess of demand for these factors of production over the existing supply of them. Suppose that the competitive rate of interest necessary to insure full employment were 5 per cent per annum, and that this were lowered by regulation to a maximum of 2 per cent per annum. This means that the output of new capital goods which was necessary to provide full employment was sufficient to enable capital development to be carried on in all occupations up to the point at which the marginal product of new capital investment was expected to be 5 per cent per annum. But if borrowers had only to pay and lenders might only receive 2 per cent, new capital goods might profitably be invested in any occupation in which the marginal product of new capital was expected to be 2 per cent or over. In these circumstances all the profitable uses of capital could not be met by the existing output of new capital goods. If there is a certain limited output of new capital goods to be distributed among all the occupations in which capital development might take place, it is only by raising the rate of interest up to the point at which the remaining profitable uses for these capital goods will just absorb the given output that it can be insured that the best use is made of them. If the rate of interest is fixed at a lower figure and the money loans for the purchase of the capital goods are rationed on arbitrary principles, there is nothing to insure that an industry in which capital development will earn only 3 per cent will not be developed, while an industry in which capital might earn 6 per cent remains undeveloped. Capital would no longer flow into those industries in which its marginal product was highest, and the first two fundamental advantages of competition mentioned in Chapter II of Part II would be lost. By a similar reasoning it can be seen that if the rent of land is fixed at a figure lower than the value of its marginal product, there is nothing to insure that the available land will be used in the most efficient way to satisfy the most urgent needs of consumers.

Similar objections apply to another method by which inequalities of income might be lessened. It is sometimes argued that the state should arrange that those commodities which are bought mainly by the poorer members of the community should be sold at prices below their cost of production, so that at these abnormally low prices the real income of the poor would be increased. This could be brought about by the subsidization of the production of such commodities, or by the nationalization of their production in order to sell them at prices lower than their cost. If this policy is adopted the fundamental advantages of competition mentioned in Chapter II of Part II would be lost. Rich men and poor men buy some of the same commodities, so that rich men would buy some subsidized commodities and poor men would buy some unsubsidized commodities. For this reason there would be a maldistribution of the factors of production among different occupations such that the rich could be better off without any diminution in the welfare of the poor, and the poor could be better off without any diminution in the welfare of the rich. Each consumer, whether rich or poor, would consume the different commodities in such amounts that the addition to his satisfaction from an extra dollar's worth of each commodity was the same. But the marginal cost to the community of a subsidized commodity would be higher than its price to consumers. If, therefore, any individual consumer, whether rich or poor, spent one dollar less on a subsidized commodity, he would release factors of production which could produce more than one dollar's worth more of an unsubsidized commodity. Each individual could therefore be better off without any diminution in the welfare of any other individual consumer, if more of the unsubsidized commodities and less of the subsidized commodities were produced.

For this reason it is preferable that all commodities should be sold to all consumers at prices equal to their marginal costs, and that any desired redistribution of income should take the form of a direct transference of income from one set of persons to another, so that every one is still free to choose between different commodities at prices which measure their marginal costs. In what follows we shall therefore consider direct methods of transferring income from the rich to the poor.

IV

EQUALITY BY TAXATION

THE taxation of the rich in order to increase the incomes of the poor is a direct method of redistributing income. It is a flexible method; for it may be used not only to bring about a more equal distribution of income, but also to distribute income according to any desired principle. Tax revenue may be used either to subsidize the provision of educational, medical, or other services which are of importance to the poor, or else to supplement small incomes directly by the payment of old age pensions, unemployment relief, widows' and orphans' pensions, or even of an equal 'social dividend' to all persons.

The solution of unemployment by the measures suggested in Part I is the first essential step in a policy of redistributing incomes more equally through taxation. We have already argued in Part I, Chapter V, pp. 48–9, that during a slump tax receipts will fall off because the incomes liable to taxation are reduced, while some items of government expenditure (e.g. interest on the national debt) will remain constant and other items (e.g. unemployment relief) will rise. If the total money demand for commodities were stimulated by the measures suggested in Part I, tax revenue would rise as money incomes rose and government expenditure would not automatically rise as quickly. Without any increase in the rates of taxation on the higher incomes there would therefore be an increased excess of revenue over expenditure, which could be used to diminish inequalities of income by reducing rates of taxation on the lower incomes or by increasing those items of government expenditure which directly or indirectly raise the incomes of the poor.

It has been explained that the reduction of unemployment by the means suggested in Part I involves some immediate fall in the real wage-rate. In fact the whole object of the measures proposed in that Part was to raise the money price offered for commodities without a similar rise in money wage-rates, so that employers would have an incentive to employ more men in order to produce more goods. It is exceedingly improbable that this policy would in itself actually diminish the aggregate real income of the workers. The fall in the real wage-rate would be counterbalanced by the fact that more workers were employed; and if a relatively small fall in the real wage-rate earned by each man was associated with a considerable rise in the total number of men employed, the real income of the workers would be increased. In a depressed state of trade, when a large part of producers' capital equipment is idle, a relatively small rise in the price offered for their product will cause employers to increase their production by a relatively large amount, so that a considerable increase in employment will be associated with only a small fall in the real wage-rate. We argued in Part I, Chapter VII (pp. 74–6) that experience justifies this conclusion.

This cure of unemployment will, however, increase the real income derived from profits as well as the real income of wage-earners; and it may well increase profits more than wages, so that in itself the cure of unemployment may cause income to be less equally distributed. But if rates of taxation on the higher incomes are not reduced, some considerable part of the increased profits will be paid to the Federal and State governments and may be spent in such a way as to diminish inequalities of income. Moreover, as profits increase, the rates of taxation on the higher incomes may be raised. The cure of unemployment means an increase in the total output of goods, or, in other words, an increase in the total real income of the community. It is always possible to arrange the tax policy of the state so that, while all classes gain as unemployment is reduced, the real incomes of the poor increase much and the real incomes of the rich increase little.

For these reasons unemployment should first be cured by the means suggested in Part I before the incomes of the rich are actually reduced by taxation. For it would be absurd to tax the rich to give greater income to the poor as long as there was not full employment, for in this case the real incomes of the poor could be increased without any fall in the real incomes of the rich. But the cure of unemployment is only a first step. Large inequalities of income would still exist even if taxes were so adjusted that the poor received the major part of any increase in real income due to the reduction in unemployment. We have then to discuss the possibility of raising considerably higher rates of taxation on the rich in order to increase the incomes of the poor.

The first step is to discover what types of taxation are appropriate for this purpose, and what are the economic effects of each type. We may divide the important taxes in a modern community into three types: taxes on commodities, taxes on income, and taxes on property. Each of these taxes may have effects upon different aspects of economic activity.

(i) A tax will affect the distribution of income; and it is our immediate object to see which of the three types of taxation is most effective for the promotion of equality.

(ii) A tax may affect the volume of employment; and we must be certain that the taxes which we choose do not react unfavorably on the policies suggested in Part I.

(iii) A tax may affect the distribution of economic resources among different occupations; and we must know that the taxes which we choose do not nullify the policy suggested in Part II.

(iv) A tax may affect the total supply of the factors of production.

In Part IV we shall argue that there is an 'optimum' amount of work which should be done, and an 'optimum' proportion of income which should be saved for capital development in any community in which there is full employment of the factors of production. We must be sure that we do not choose taxes for the redistribution of income which make the achievement of these 'optimum' amounts of the factors impossible. The rest of this chapter will be devoted to a discussion of these four aspects of the three main types of taxes.

Taxes on commodities are open to serious criticism on two grounds. If they are to be used for the redistribution of income they must be levied on commodities bought by the rich and not by the poor.[1] While this can be done to some extent by taxing luxury commodities, it is difficult to do so to any large extent. The commodities which both rich and poor consume such as bread, coffee, sugar, houses, etc., are the main staple commodities, which are produced in large quantities. These are also the commodities which people are least likely to do without when their price goes up in consequence of a tax imposed upon them. From the point of view of raising revenue, they are the obvious commodities to tax. It is administratively easier to tax a few important staple commodities; and the consumption of these commodities, and therefore the revenue obtained from them, is likely to fall off least when the taxes on them are raised. A high tax on a luxury commodity, on the other hand, will cause people to purchase other commodities instead, since they can do without a particular form of luxury and buy others which have not risen in price. If a heavy tax is put on gramophones, people may buy wireless sets instead. In order, therefore, that the tax may bring in considerable revenue, wireless sets must be taxed as well as gramophones; but in that case people may go to the theatre instead, in which case a tax must also be put on expensive seats in the theatre. But again a large part of the revenue may be lost

1. General taxes on commodities, like the 'sales taxes' levied by numerous States during the recent depression, are completely inappropriate for our purpose, although they do not happen to be subject to the two objections mentioned below. For, being levied on all (or almost all) expenditure, they have the effect of a regressive income tax, which takes a larger proportion of a poor man's income than of a rich man's. All income expended is taxed at the same rate, and the poor man spends a larger proportion of his income. Sales taxes also constitute a tax upon employment. It is, indeed, difficult to think of any principle on which they may be defended.

because people now give up the gramophone, radio, and theatre and instead purchase a more expensive car. So in turn cars must be taxed. For this reason, in order to raise revenue by taxing the commodities which the rich consume and the poor do not, practically all the commodities which the rich consume may have to be taxed. This will lead to innumerable small taxes to achieve an object which would be achieved more simply by taxing the income of the rich instead of the commodities they buy.

The second criticism of a tax on commodities is equally important. We have argued in Chapter II of Part II that in order that the available economic resources should be used in the best way to satisfy consumers' needs, commodities should be put on the market at prices which are in proportion to their marginal costs of production. If some commodities are taxed, their price will be raised above their marginal cost, while untaxed commodities continue to sell at prices equal to their marginal costs. Factors of production will therefore be diverted in an uneconomic way from the production of the taxed commodities, so that the first fundamental advantage of competition will be lost. Commodity taxes are therefore impractical as a means of redistributing income, and also have undesirable effects upon the distribution of factors of production among different occupations. We may therefore dismiss them without considering their effect either upon employment or upon the 'optimum' supply of labor and capital.

An income tax will have neither of these disadvantages of a commodity tax. The income tax can be graduated by allowing a certain amount of income to go untaxed and by raising high rates of tax on the higher incomes, so that those with small incomes go untaxed, those with medium incomes pay a moderate proportion of their income in taxation, and those with large incomes a high proportion. Moreover, by granting allowances in the income tax for dependents or for any other reasons considered desirable the income tax can be made a most flexible instrument for aiding any desirable principle of distribution of income. It has, therefore, many advantages as a means of raising revenue for the redistribution of income. Moreover, as a general income tax does not differentiate between different sources of income, it will not disturb the proper distribution of the factors of production among different occupations. Since the tax levied on the income earned by any factor of production will not depend upon the particular industry or occupation in which that income is earned, each factor will still move into that occupation in which the value of its marginal product is greatest; and consumers can freely express their preferences for different commodities through the prices which they offer for each commodity.

In order to discuss the effects of an income tax upon employment and upon the supply of the factors of production, it is important to distinguish between a proportionate and a progressive income tax. A tax is proportionate if the same rate of tax is levied on every income, whatever size it may be; and a tax is progressive if the rate of tax levied on each individual income is raised as the taxable income becomes larger. Tables VII and VIII give examples of proportionate and progressive income taxes. In Table VII we assume that whatever the gross income in column A may

TABLE VII

A Proportionate Income Tax

A Gross income	B Rate of tax	C Amount of tax	D Net income	E Increase in net income
$	%	$	$	$
2,000	30	600	1,400	..
3,000	30	900	2,100	700
4,000	30	1,200	2,800	700
5,000	30	1,500	3,500	700
6,000	30	1,800	4,200	700

be, the same proportion of it—namely 30 per cent, as shown in column B—will be deducted in taxation. In Table VIII, as the gross income in column A rises, there is an increase in the proportion of income deducted in taxation, as shown in column B. In both tables column C shows the amount which will be paid in taxation from different incomes under these two tax systems, and column D shows the net income that will remain to the taxpayer after the deduction of tax. Column E, which is the important column for our purposes, shows by how much a man will increase his net income after deduction of taxation if by some means or another he adds $1,000 to his gross taxable income. Thus in Table VIII when the gross income is $4,000, a net income of $2,800 remains after the deduction of tax; but when the gross income is $5,000 a net income of $3,000 is left after deduction of tax, so that if a man adds $1,000 to a gross income of $4,000, he will add only $200 to his net income after payment of tax.

Table VIII

A Progressive Income Tax

A Gross income	B Rate of tax	C Amount of tax	D Net income	E Increase in net income
$	%	$	$	$
2,000	10	200	1,800	..
3,000	20	600	2,400	600
4,000	30	1,200	2,800	400
5,000	40	2,000	3,000	200
6,000	50	3,000	3,000	Nil

In discussing the effect of taxation upon the volume of employment and the supply of the factors of production an important consideration is the amount which a man can add to his net income by adding a certain sum to his gross income. If, as in Table VII, the income tax is a proportionate tax of 30 per cent, then by earning another $1,000 a man will always add $700 to his net income. If, however, the tax is progressive, as in Table VIII, then a man will add less to his net income by earning an extra $1,000 than would have been the case if the absolute height of the tax were the same but the tax were not progressive.

In both tables an income of $4,000 is taxed at 30 per cent; but in Table VII by earning $4,000 instead of $3,000 a man adds $700 to his net income, while in Table VIII by earning $4,000 instead of $3,000 he adds only $400 to his net income. We may conclude, therefore, that the higher and the more progressive the income tax, the less will a man add to his net income by earning an extra $1,000. In Table VIII the income tax becomes so progressive that although an income of $6,000 is only taxed 50 per cent, a man can add nothing to his net income by earning $6,000 instead of $5,000. Obviously to reduce inequalities of income to a minimum we require as progressive a tax as possible in order to raise the revenue from the rich; but in discussing the effects of income tax on employment and on the supply of the factors of production we have to remember that every increase in the progressiveness of the tax will reduce the addition to net income that can be achieved by earning a greater gross income.

We are now in a position to discuss the effect of income tax upon employment. In Part I, Chapter I, p. 13, it was shown that the volume of employment could be increased either by an increase in the amount of money borrowed and spent on capital development or, with a given volume of expenditure on capital development, by a decrease in the proportion of income which people save and refrain from spending on consumption goods. We must therefore discuss the effect of income tax upon expenditure on capital development and upon the proportion of income saved. An income tax, and especially a highly progressive one, is likely to cause some diminution in expenditure on capital development. In Part I, Chapter II, we argued that the incentive to spend money on capital development depended upon the relation between the rate of profit which producers expected to earn on any new capital development and the rate of interest at which money could be borrowed. If, for example, a producer by installing a machine costing $10,000 expects to add $500 a year to his profits, he expects to earn a rate of profit on this machine of 5 per cent per annum. If he can borrow the $10,000 at 4 per cent, then for an annual payment of interest of $400 a year he will add $500 a year to his profits and will so increase his own income by $100 a year. In these circumstances he will find it worth his while undertaking this item of capital development. But if there is a high and also a progressive income tax, he may by adding this $100 to his gross annual income add very considerably less than $100 to his net income, and the incentive to undertake the trouble and risk of embarking on this capital development will be so much the smaller. A high and progressive income tax will there- fore in itself reduce the incentive to spend money on capital de- velopment at any given rate of interest.

This does not, however, mean that the imposition of a heavy and progressive income tax will necessarily cause total money expenditure to fall and unemployment to increase; and this is so for two reasons. In the first place, the banks may offset the im- mediate effect of the tax on expenditure on capital development by reducing the rate of interest through the measures suggested in Chapter III of Part I. If, in the example of the last paragraph, the banks cause the rate of interest to fall from 4 to 3 per cent when the income tax is imposed, the producer by borrowing $10,000 at 3 per cent to install the machine can add $500 to his profit for the payment of $300 a year in interest. In these circum- stances, therefore, he will add $200 instead of $100 to his gross income. If the income tax removes 50 per cent of this additional $200 he will still be able as before to add $100 to his net income if he undertakes the capital development.

Secondly, a heavy and highly progressive income tax will cause a diminution in the proportion of income saved. Richer people are more able to save than poorer people, and in fact we find that richer people save not only a larger amount but also a larger proportion of income. It follows that the more equally a given income is divided among a number of individuals, the smaller will be the amount saved out of that income. Suppose for instance that a man with $9,000 saves 33⅓ per cent or $3,000, a man with $5,000 saves 15 per cent or $750, and a man with $1,000 saves 5 per cent or $50. Then the total income of these men will be $15,000, out of which $3,800 will be saved. If the $15,000 were divided equally between the three men, each would have $5,000 and each would therefore save 15 per cent or $750. The total savings of the three men would therefore fall from $3,800 to $2,250.

There is a further reason why a steeply progressive income tax is likely to cause a fall in the proportion of income saved. People save, in part at least, in order to increase their future incomes by the interest on their additional property. If there is a steeply progressive income tax, an amount of saving which would add $100 to their gross income in the future might add only $40 to their net income in the future; and an amount of saving which would be worth while if it added $100 to annual income in the future might be considered no longer worth while if it added only $40.[1] Indeed in the extreme case in which the tax is so progressive that nothing can be added to net income by increasing gross income, this important motive for saving would be entirely removed.

A diminution in inequality of income brought about by a heavy and highly progressive income tax will therefore reduce the proportion of income saved; and for this reason it will help to reduce unemployment. For, as we have argued in Chapter II of Part I, this additional expenditure on consumption goods will cause a direct increase in the output of consumption goods, will raise the incomes of those producing these goods, and will thus cause still further increases in expenditure. Such increases will, moreover, make industry more profitable, and will therefore increase the incentive to borrow money for expenditure on capital development, since a higher rate of profit may be earned on new machinery installed for the production of consumption goods. If, there-

1. This argument is not conclusive. A person who is attempting to accumulate a capital sum which would yield a certain fixed income in the future, for example, would try to save more if the rate of net income from the capital saved were diminished. Probably on balance neither of these effects would be great; the important consideration is the reduction in the *ability* to save resulting from the redistribution of income.

fore, the banks prevent any rise in the rate of interest, the diminution in the proportion of income saved will in itself stimulate the expenditure of money on capital development, and will help to offset the tendency of a progressive income tax to diminish expenditure on capital development. We may conclude, therefore, that a progressive income tax will almost certainly increase the volume of employment if the rate of interest is not allowed to rise; for it will directly stimulate expenditure on consumption and so indirectly the expenditure on capital development. And if the income tax caused unemployment by reducing the incentive to spend money on capital development more than it stimulated expenditure on consumption goods, this could be offset by a lowering of interest rates by the banks.

We have now to discuss the effect of income tax upon the supply of the factors of production. In Part IV, Chapter II, pp. 276–8, we shall argue that there is an 'optimum' amount of work which should be done by each member of the community; and we shall conclude that for this 'optimum' amount of work to be provided by each person the real wage-rate offered to each worker for an hour's work must be equal to the marginal product of his work, so that by working a little more each individual will add to his real income an amount equal to the difference in the real output of the community. Any tax on earned income will mean that the real wage-rate of labor is lower than the marginal product of labor, since no worker will be offered more than his marginal product and part of this offer will not reach the worker but will be removed by the income tax. Moreover, the more progressive the income tax, the smaller the proportion of his gross wage-rate which any worker adds to his net income by working more; and thus the discrepancy between a worker's marginal product and the increase in his net income, due to his doing more work, is increased by every increase in the progressiveness of taxation. A heavy or highly progressive income tax on earned incomes will therefore disturb the 'optimum' amount of work to be done by each individual.

We shall also argue in Chapter III of Part IV that there is an 'optimum' supply of savings. *On the assumption that there is full employment provided by the policies suggested in Part I*, it is impossible for the community to produce and consume more consumption goods without transferring resources from the production of new capital equipment; and in these circumstances a reduction in the proportion of income saved must mean that less capital development is undertaken. It is possible to provide full employment when a large proportion of income is saved if the rate of interest is lowered to stimulate a sufficient volume of expenditure on capital development. Alternatively, when a small proportion of income is saved, full employment may be provided with a smaller volume of expenditure on capital development and, therefore, with a higher rate of interest. We shall argue in Chapter III of Part IV that there is an 'optimum' proportion of income which should be saved on the assumption of full employment, because a certain proportion of the fully employed resources should be applied to the production of new capital equipment. A heavy and highly progressive income tax by diminishing the proportion of income which is saved may reduce this proportion below the 'optimum.'

It is, however, easy for the state or Federal government itself to save part of the tax revenue, if such taxation threatens to reduce the supply of savings below the optimum. Suppose that $1 billion are raised in taxation of the rich to increase the incomes of the poor. The rich must reduce either their expenditure on consumption or their savings to pay the $1 billion. Suppose that they reduce their expenditure on consumption by $600 millions and their savings by $400 millions. If the whole billion were spent by the poor on consumption goods, the net effect would be a diminution of savings by $400 millions. If the state wished to prevent this, it might raise the $1 billion in taxation, pay $600 millions of this to the poor to increase their expenditure on consumption goods, and itself save $400 millions to replace the diminished savings of the rich. This $400 millions could be used by the state to reduce its outstanding debt or to invest in any other forms of property which it was suitable for the state to hold.

We have next to consider taxes on property as a means of raising revenue to redistribute income and also to consider their effects upon the distribution of the factors of production among different occupations, upon the volume of employment, and upon the optimum supply of the factors of production. We shall consider, as the typical form of property tax, inheritance and estate duties on property passing at death. These may be proportionate or progressive. They are proportionate if the same percentage is levied in duty regardless of the size of the total property, or of the individual bequest, which is left at death. They are progressive if either of two principles of graduation is adopted. With the first principle of progression (which is adopted in the Federal estate duty), the proportion of the property taken in duty increases with the size of the total property left at death. With the second principle of progression, the total property left at death would, for purposes of the duty, be divided into its component legacies and each legacy would be taxed at a rate dependent upon its size. If out of a total property of $100,000 one man is left $80,000, another $10,000, and two others $5,000 each, the $80,000 bequest would be taxed at a higher rate than the $10,000 bequest, which in turn would be taxed at a higher rate than either of the $5,000 bequests.

For the purpose of redistributing income more equally, progressive estate duties have less advantages than a progressive income tax. In as far as inequalities of income are due to the unequal ownership of income-bearing property such duties are as effective as an income tax. Progressive estate and inheritance duties—especially those which are graduated on the second of the two principles mentioned in the previous paragraph—will take large amounts of property from those who inherit large properties and so obtain large incomes from property; and the revenue may be used to increase directly or indirectly the incomes of the poor. But while the income tax will also diminish inequalities of income from work, estate duties will not directly have this effect, since they cannot be levied on incomes from work. But indirectly they will diminish inequalities of earned income. For, as we have shown in Chapter II of this Part, inequalities of income from work are partly due to inequalities of opportunity to train for the higher paid occupations, so that an equalization of incomes from property would indirectly diminish inequalities of income from work. In a community in which the main inequalities are due to the unequal distribution of property, and in which many of the inequalities of income from work are due to inequalities of opportunity, progressive estate duties will be almost as effective as a progressive income tax in reducing inequalities. And if, as will be shown in what follows, estate duties have other marked advantages over an income tax, they are to be preferred as the main instrument for promoting equality.

Estate duties, if they are levied impartially on all forms of property at death, will, equally with an income tax, have no adverse effects upon the distribution of economic resources among different occupations. Consumers will be free, through the prices offered for different commodities, to express their marginal preferences for different commodities; and since capital will be subjected to estate duties in every form of occupation, the factors of production including capital will still flow into those industries in which their marginal products are of the greatest value to the consumers.

In their effect upon employment progressive estate duties are to be preferred to a progressive income tax. We have argued that the effect of taxation upon employment will depend first upon its effect on the incentive to spend money on capital development at the current rate of interest, and secondly, upon its effect on the proportion of income which will be saved. It was shown that a highly progressive income tax would reduce the incentive to spend money on capital development. People will borrow money for this purpose only if they expect to earn on the new capital goods installed a profit somewhat in excess of the interest to be paid on the borrowed funds, and this margin of profit may be seriously reduced by a progressive income tax. In the case of estate duties, where the borrower is a corporation this margin will not be reduced at all, for corporations do not die. Where the borrower is an individual, there may be some detrimental effect on the inducement to invest, but probably not as much as in the case of the income tax. To the extent that he is investing to increase his own income during his lifetime there will be no detrimental effect whatever. Certainly, on balance, the incentive to spend money on capital development at the current rate of interest will therefore be less affected by estate duties than by an income tax.

This result may appear paradoxical. But it should be clear if it is realized that the incentives to spend money on capital development are quite different from the incentives to accumulate property. A man can accumulate property by spending less than his income; but, having accumulated property, he must make the independent decision whether to hold money, securities, or a machine. A man can decide to accumulate wealth without deciding to build a new machine; for he may decide simply to hold more money or securities. A man can decide to build a new machine without deciding to accumulate more property; for he can use some of his holding of money, or can sell securities for money, or borrow, in order to purchase the new machine, without himself spending less than his income. The incentive to spend money on capital development at any given rate of interest should, as we have argued, be little affected by estate duties.

But progressive estate duties, just as a progressive income tax, will almost certainly cause a diminution in the proportion of the national income saved, if the proceeds of these taxes are used to increase the incomes of the poor. This will be so for two reasons. First, this policy will diminish inequalities of income; and we have already argued that a transference of income from rich to

poor causes a fall in the savings made out of that income, because
the poor save a smaller proportion of their income than the rich.
Secondly, if the estate duties are progressive, any one who is saving will know that the larger the property which he accumulates,
the greater will be the proportion taken at his death by the state
and the smaller, therefore, the proportion which he can leave to
his heirs. This may reduce the incentive to accumulate property
for the benefit of his heirs.[1]

It is, however, sometimes maintained that estate duties will
reduce the proportion of the national income which is saved to
a greater extent than an equivalent income tax, because estate
duties are a tax on capital and the income tax is a tax on income.
There is no basis for this belief. Suppose that a man is determined
to leave a fixed amount of property for the benefit of his heirs.
If he has to pay income tax during his life he must restrict his
expenditure on consumption in order to accumulate as much
as before to leave to his heirs. If a duty will be levied on his property at death, then he must equally restrict his consumption
during his life in order to accumulate a larger property than before, of which only a part will pass to his heirs. An income tax,
the revenue from which is used by the poor for expenditure on
consumption, will reduce the proportion of the national income
which is saved, in so far as the taxpayers in order to meet the
tax do not reduce their expenditure on consumption but save
less. An estate duty, the revenue from which is spent on consumption, will reduce the proportion of the national income
which is saved only in so far as those whose property will be
taxed at death fail to restrict their consumption during life sufficiently to offset the effect of the duty on their heirs' inheritance.
There is, therefore, no *a priori* reason why estate duties should
diminish the proportion of income saved more than an income
tax, although equally there is no reason why they should diminish
it less. Since estate duties will diminish the incentive to spend
money on capital development less than an income tax, and will

1. But compare the footnote on page 255.

diminish the proportion of income saved as much as an income tax, we may conclude that estate duties will have a greater effect in reducing unemployment than an income tax.

Finally, we must discuss the effect of estate duties upon the optimum amount of work and upon the optimum proportion of income which should be saved when there is full employment. As we argued on p. 256, an income tax, and especially a progressive income tax, may have disadvantageous effects upon the amount of work done by each person, because a progressive tax on earned incomes will cause a discrepancy between the real reward of work and its marginal product. Estate duties will not have this effect; for they do not prevent a man who by working more adds something to his income from keeping the whole of this additional income. In this respect estate duties have great advantages over an income tax.[1]

Estate duties will reduce the proportion of the national income which is saved at least as much as an equivalent income tax. There is therefore the same possibility that, if full employment has been achieved by the measures suggested in Part I, progressive estate duties may reduce the proportion of the national income which is saved below the optimum, as defined in Part IV. But for this there is the same simple remedy as in the case of the income tax. The state may use only part of its revenue from such duties to increase the incomes of the poor, and may itself save the remainder, using these sums to redeem its debt or to purchase any other appropriate forms of property. By such means the state can prevent any undesired reduction in the proportion of the national income which is saved.

All the arguments employed in this discussion [2] of estate duties are equally valid in the case of any taxes levied on property or on

1. This argument applies to the extent that people work to increase their own incomes during their lifetimes. To the extent that they work to leave property for their dependents estate duties will, in effect, prevent them from keeping the whole of additional sums they earn, and thus interfere with the proper balance between work and leisure.
2. An exception should perhaps be made of the argument that an estate duty will have less effect on the incentive to invest than an income tax. A tax

income from property as opposed to income from work. Such taxes include a progressive income tax from which earned income is exempted, and taxes levied annually on the value of the property owned by each individual like the general property tax on which State and local governments have relied largely for their revenue. We may therefore summarize the arguments of this chapter in this way: incomes may be redistributed by taxing the rich and using the revenue to increase the incomes of the poor. For this purpose commodity taxes may be ruled out, both because they are inappropriate taxes for the raising of revenue from the rich and because they cause an undesirable redistribution of factors of production among different occupations. A highly progressive income tax is the best instrument for the purpose of redistributing incomes, and further it has no disadvantageous effects upon the distribution of factors of production among different occupations. It will probably help to cure unemployment. Although it may somewhat reduce the incentive to spend money on capital goods at any given rate of interest, it will certainly reduce the proportion of income which is saved and will so stimulate activity. The great disadvantage of a general income tax is that it may upset the proper balance between work and leisure. If the income tax reduces the proportion of income saved to an undesirably low level in conditions of full employment, this may be remedied by the state itself saving part of the tax revenue. Estate duties or any taxes on property or on income from property alone will be slightly less efficient than an income tax in redistributing incomes, since they cannot directly affect inequalities of income from work. But they have two distinct advantages over the income tax. First, they will not diminish so much the incentive to spend money on capital development. Secondly, they will probably have less disturbing effects on the proper balance between work and leisure. In their other effects they are similar to an income tax. From this we may conclude

on property, or on income from property, would have precisely the same effect on the incentive to invest as an income tax of equal severity.

that redistribution of income through progressive estate duties or other taxes on unearned income can have no serious economic disadvantages provided that, if necessary, the state is itself prepared to save part of its tax revenue for the purchase of property of one form or another.

V

REDISTRIBUTION OR PUBLIC OWNERSHIP OF PROPERTY

In order to remove the most important cause of inequalities of income, namely the unequal ownership of property, measures might be taken to insure that property was owned in more equal amounts by all members of the community and not concentrated in the hands of a few persons. The ideal at which this solution would aim is the attractive 'distributist' state [1] in which all men are free, equal, and independent, because all men own a modicum of property without any glaring inequalities in such ownership.

This 'distributist' state could be brought about by means of steeply progressive estate duties, which would take all, or nearly all, property above a certain figure away from the rich to give it to the men who had less property. No single redistribution of property would suffice, unless some provision were made for the redistribution of property at death. Otherwise inequalities would soon appear again, and would perpetuate and accentuate themselves; for once one family obtained a measurable advantage in income over others it would be easier for it to accumulate still more property and easier for its members to train for the best paid occupations. Alternatively, the 'distributist' state might be attained by fundamental changes in the laws of inheritance, whereby a man who died was not allowed to leave more than a certain amount to any single individual, or—better still—whereby no man was allowed to inherit an amount of property so great that together with the property which

1. Here, as elsewhere in the book, the term 'state' is used in a general sense to refer to any political division. See the footnote on p. 54 for an explanation of the usage of the words 'state' and 'State.'

he already owned he would possess more than a certain total estate.

Such a policy would have the same advantages and disadvantages as progressive estate duties, which were discussed at the end of the last chapter. It would help to cure unemployment, since it would have little effect on the incentive to borrow money to spend on capital development at any given rate of interest, and since it would cause a reduction in the proportion of income which was saved. It would in no way prevent factors of production from flowing into those occupations in which the value of their marginal products was highest. It would not interfere with the proper balance between work and leisure, since it would not prevent any man from earning for his work a reward equal to the value of his marginal product. On the other hand, it might seriously reduce the supply of savings below their optimum level in circumstances of full employment. If all rich men knew that they could not leave more than a moderate sum to their own dependents, the main incentive for a very large part of the community's savings would be entirely removed. For this reason the state might be obliged to fill this gap by raising revenue to devote to the purchase of property of one form or another.

We have concluded that in redistributing income, either by progressive taxes used to increase the incomes of the poor or by a direct redistribution of property, the state will probably be obliged itself to accumulate property as soon as full employment is achieved. Such action will gradually lead to public ownership of a considerable amount of property. We must therefore discuss how governments should use the income from their own property to promote equality.

If the Federal government owns a considerable amount of income-bearing property, it will be in a position to control directly the proportion of the national income which is saved. In Part IV, Chapters III and IV, we discuss the principles upon which this decision should theoretically rest. That part of its income from property which the state decided to save would either be handed over to those in charge of nationalized industries for expenditure on capital development, or would be used to purchase securities and other forms of property in the market, or would be lent at interest to privately controlled concerns. By this means the government could insure that the savings flowed into those uses in which the real yield on capital was highest. It could use part of its income from property to finance its ordinary expenditure on justice, defense, etc., without raising money by commodity taxes or by an income tax. This is a further advantage of public ownership of property, since taxes on particular commodities will disturb the best distribution of the community's resources between different occupations, and an income tax is likely to upset the best balance between work and leisure. The remainder of governmental income from property could be used to promote equality. It could either be spent on education, health services, pensions for old age or for widows, or family allowances, or could be distributed as an equal 'social dividend' to all members of the community.

To achieve substantial equality of income by this means does not necessarily imply that all property should be publicly owned. If the state owns sufficient property to insure that the optimum amount of the national income is saved, to achieve a considerable degree of equality in incomes, and to finance its ordinary expenditure without resort to commodity or income taxes, the rest of the community's property might well be left in private ownership. In order to prevent such private ownership from causing the regrowth of great inequalities, private estates over a certain size could be subjected to heavy estate duties, designed in such a way as to prevent any man from leaving an estate over a certain moderate size to any one individual. As we have already argued in Part II, Chapter VIII, p. 204, a clear distinction must be drawn between public ownership and public control of property. It is quite possible for the government to own land and to let it out at a fixed rent to private individuals to manage and to farm. It is equally possible for the government to leave the land in private ownership and itself to hire it at a fixed rent in order that agriculture may be publicly managed. In Chapter VIII of Part II we concluded that, in order to achieve the best use of the community's resources, property in monopolistic industries should be publicly managed. In this chapter we conclude that to obtain equality of income a certain amount of property should be socially owned. It may be that the state should own more property than it manages or should manage more property than it owns. This depends simply upon the amount of property which must be socially owned to achieve equality and the amount which must be socially managed to offset the effects of monopoly. The important point to realize is that state ownership and state management are not the same thing, that they are desirable for quite different reasons, and that they do not necessarily go together.[1]

By public ownership of property complete equality of income from property could be achieved. At first sight it appears that by this means all inequalities of income from work might also be offset. For the state could use part of the income which it received from its property in order to pay allowances to individuals who earned little from work, so as to equalize their total incomes with the incomes of those whose earnings from work are high. In particular industries, which were socially owned and controlled, the state could deliberately pay wage-rates greater than the marginal product of labor, if this was necessary to promote equality of incomes from work. But such policies would be open to two serious objections, because a man's total income would no longer depend upon the value of the marginal product of his work. First, no man would have any incentive to move from

1. It should be emphasized that this distinction between ownership and control is an *economic* one. The economic advantages to be gained from each are distinct and different. It is not meant to deny that there are grave practical and political difficulties in the way of control without ownership or of ownership without control. The former is likely to be thwarted by the influence of the private owners, as much regulation of public utilities by States has been. The latter would involve the government in the assumption of risk without responsibility.

occupations in which his marginal product was low to occupations in which it was high, so that labor would no longer tend to distribute itself automatically among different occupations in such a way that consumers' needs were best satisfied. Secondly, the correct balance between work and leisure would be upset. If each individual knows that his total income will not vary even if his income from work varies, he will no longer have any incentive to choose the best balance between work and leisure. He would presumably work as little as possible, so that the state would have to set minimum hours of work. But the state is unlikely to impose the proper balance between work and leisure, the judgment of which is best left to individuals, or small groups of individuals in similar circumstances.[1]

We are here up against a fundamental dilemma in any attempt to distribute income equally. It may be desirable from the point of view of the distribution of income to get rid of inequalities of income from work, but to do so will cause considerable difficulty in achieving the best use of the available labor and the best balance between work and leisure. For by whatever means equality of earned income is achieved, it is bound to mean that people's net incomes will not vary with the value of the marginal product of their work. In the choice of a tax policy or of a policy of paying allowances to supplement low incomes, the advantage of greater equality of earned incomes must be balanced against these disadvantages. But if complete equality of income from property is obtained by the social ownership of property, and if complete equality of opportunity for training for the best jobs is insured by means of an educational policy based on the principles outlined above in Chapter II of this Part, inequalities of income will be greatly diminished, even if the remaining causes of inequalities of income from work were left untouched.

If we accept this method of achieving equality, there remains for discussion the problem of the transition from private to public ownership of property. The Federal or state governments must

1. See Part IV, Chapter II, pp. 276-80.

first raise surplus revenue by taxation and use the proceeds to buy up privately owned property. Clearly the first block of such property to be bought up would be the public debt. As the capital sum of the public debt was redeemed, the amount which had to be paid in interest on the debt would be diminished so that taxes on the poor could gradually be remitted, or expenditure designed to promote equality could be increased. After the debt had been redeemed, the surplus revenue could be invested in the purchase of other forms of privately owned capital. A government would naturally choose in the first place to redeem the privately owned debt of any industries which had been nationalized, and would for example buy up the stock of the Federal Reserve Banks or of similar public concerns. After this it might invest in the debt of local governments. Finally, it might purchase the bonds of private industries or invest in the purchase of land. Each stage would either diminish the state's expenditure on interest on debt or would increase the state's income from interest or rent. It would thus gradually be in a position to develop fully its policy for the redistribution of income.

We have already discussed in the last chapter the principles upon which the revenue for the nationalization of property might be raised. We concluded there that progressive estate duties might be imposed, part of the revenue from which could be used by the state to purchase property if the imposition of these duties threatened to reduce the community's savings to too low a level. The transition towards state ownership of property can always be speeded up by imposing heavier duties on privately owned property. The payment of these duties will in itself increase the proportion of income saved in as far as the taxpayers reduce their expenditure to meet the duties, and will reduce the proportion of income saved in as far as the taxpayers reduce their savings or sell part of their property to meet the heavier levies. By using a larger part of the revenue to promote expenditure by the poor the state can prevent such a policy from causing so large an increase in savings that unemployment results, and by using a larger part of the revenue to buy up privately owned property the state can prevent the proportion of income saved from falling below the optimum in conditions of full employment.[1]

---

1. In this discussion we have ignored the possibility that owners of property may attempt to escape the levy by removing themselves and their capital to other countries. In Part V, Chapter III, we shall discuss the effects of an increase in foreign lending, and shall suggest measures by means of which the government can, if necessary, prevent an export of capital.

Part IV

THE SUPPLY OF THE PRIMARY FACTORS OF PRODUCTION

I

LAND, LABOR, AND CAPITAL

WE are still left with one fundamental economic problem, which it is the object of this Part to discuss. Since the amount of the primary factors of production is not rigidly fixed, we have to decide how these factors can be made available to the community in the best or 'optimum' amounts.

It is usually held that there are three primary factors of production—land, labor, and capital—from the use of which all the real income of the community is obtained. This view is correct so long as the nature of these three factors is properly interpreted. By land we must mean all the natural resources of the community which are useful for the production of commodities or for the immediate satisfaction of human needs. Land, therefore, must be interpreted to include not only the surface of the earth, but also the fertility of the soil, the natural supply of minerals, the water supply available for power and for other purposes, and all the resources whose presence is not due to human activity. Labor must be interpreted to mean the whole of man's current activity in producing goods and services. It must include, besides ordinary manual labor, the work of technicians, of those directing business concerns, and of doctors and others who provide direct personal service. Capital is the whole stock of man-made instruments of production in existence at any one time which are useful for the production of real income. Capital must include the stock of machines, buildings, and raw materials, the existing improvements in the land which are due to human labor, and even such immaterial things as the existing stock of human knowledge and capability which is due to the expenditure of past human effort on the education and training of men.

If we accept these interpretations of the three primary factors of production we can see that the production of any finished commodity or service is wholly due to the use of these three factors in one form or another. In Part I, Chapter I, p. 5, it was argued that the costs of any firm could be reduced to six items:

(i) the wages of labor employed by the firm;

(ii) the interest to be paid on the capital borrowed by the manufacturer;

(iii) the rent or royalties to be paid for the use of land or other natural resources by the manufacturer;

(iv) the cost to the manufacturer of purchasing the necessary raw materials to make the finished product;

(v) the payment to be made for the repair and replacement of machinery and plant which wears out as the finished commodity is produced;

(vi) a profit to the manufacturer sufficient to make him willing to carry on with the production of the commodity.

All these items of cost can be reduced to payments for the use of the three primary factors of production: land, labor, and capital. Item (i) is clearly a payment for labor, item (ii) a payment for land, and item (iii) a payment for capital. Items (iv) and (v) can, as we argued in Chapter I of Part I, be reduced to the wages, rent, interest, and profit earned in the industries producing raw materials and machines, so that they are made up of payments for labor, land, and capital together with a certain profit of management. But this profit of management together with item (vi), the profit received directly by the producers of the final commodity, represents either a payment to the manufacturers for their own labor of management or else interest on capital, in so far as the manufacturers themselves own the capital which they use.

All the factors of production used in the production of any

commodity can be reduced to land, labor, and capital; but it is not possible, as has sometimes been supposed, to reduce capital itself to land and labor. It is true that the physical capital goods, such as machinery, must have been produced in the past by the use of natural resources and of human labor. But in spite of this, capital is a factor of production independent of labor and land. We can see this best by taking a simple illustration. Let us suppose that the production of a certain amount of shoes requires the employment of 50 men and a unit of land in the shoe manufacturing firm, and of 50 men and a unit of land in industries producing raw materials and machines, in order to replace the shoe manufacturers' stock of capital goods as they are used up or worn out. Then the production of these shoes requires 100 units of labor and 2 units of land; but it *also* requires the existence of a stock of machines in use and of raw materials in process. If there were no such stock of capital the 100 units of labor and the 2 units of land could be used directly without any equipment in an attempt to produce shoes; but clearly a smaller number of shoes would in these circumstances be produced. If a certain amount of capital equipment is used, only part of the labor and land will be used directly to produce shoes, and the other part will be used to maintain the stock of capital goods and equipment as it is used up by the production of shoes. In the one case, few shoes would be produced with a given amount of labor and land but no capital; in the other case more shoes would be produced with the same amount of labor and land and with a certain constant stock of capital. Thus three primary and independent factors of production exist:

(i) the current use of an existing stock of capital, i.e. of instruments of production and of raw materials;

(ii) the current expenditure of a certain amount of human effort, part being used directly to produce the finished commodity and part to maintain the stock of capital goods intact; and

(iii) the current use of a certain amount of natural resources, part again being used directly to produce finished commodities and part to maintain the existing stock of capital goods intact.

In deciding how the primary factors of production may be supplied in the 'optimum' amounts, it is clear that as far as natural resources are concerned there can be no problem. For these are things which man cannot vary in amount, but which are supplied in certain quantities by nature. But in the case of labor and capital, man can decide how much of these primary factors shall be supplied; for it is possible to vary the amount of work done and also the size of the stock of capital goods in existence. Chapter II of this Part will deal with the principles which should govern the total supply of labor on the assumption that there is a constant stock of capital in existence; Chapter III will deal with the principles which should govern variations in the total stock of capital on the assumption that there is a constant supply of labor. In Chapter IV we shall discuss briefly the principles upon which the supply of labor and of capital should be varied simultaneously if at the start neither is supplied in the optimum amount.

II

THE OPTIMUM SUPPLY OF LABOR

THE total amount of labor may be varied by a change in the amount of work done by each member of the community or by a change in the size of the population. When both these variables are at their optimum point, we have the optimum supply of labor. A discussion of these two optima, on the assumption that there is a constant stock of capital, forms the subject of this chapter.

Different ways in which the amount of work done by each person can be varied have already been mentioned in Part III, Chapter III, pp. 239–41. An increase in the work done per member of the community may be obtained by an increase in the number of hours worked per day or in the number of days worked per year, by lowering the age at which people start work or raising the age at which they retire from work, or by an increase in the number of members of each family who seek work—e.g. a wife may decide to go out to work instead of staying at home. It may appear unreal to suppose that the average worker has any control over his daily hours of work. In occupations in which a man is his own master, he may be free to decide whether he will work more or less. But if a man is employed in a factory in which the hours of work are fixed he must either work the fixed number of hours a week or not at all. But even so the number of hours of work done per person can be varied considerably. The workers, either directly or through their trade unions, in settling the terms of work with their employers, can bargain for a reduction or for an increase of hours of work at the current hourly wage-rate; and hours of work have, in fact, been considerably changed by this means in the course of the last century.

Our first task then is to decide how to achieve the optimum

balance between work and leisure. This optimum balance may be defined in either of two ways:

(i) We may say that the optimum balance has been achieved for any individual when it is impossible for that individual by working more or less to improve his own position without diminishing the economic welfare of any other individual, and we shall call this the *individual* optimum. It is easy to see that—with certain reservations to be made later—it is this *individual* optimum balance which will be achieved if people are paid rewards equal to the value of their marginal products and are then left free to decide how much work they will do.[1] For the individual optimum will be achieved so long as people work up to the point at which the marginal disutility of work, i.e. the amount of satisfaction which they would lose by doing another hour's work, is just equal to the marginal utility of the marginal product of work, i.e. the additional satisfaction which is to be obtained from the consumption of the extra product due to doing one more hour's work. If the marginal disutility of work is less than the marginal utility of the marginal product of work, people would be better satisfied if they worked more. By working an extra hour they would diminish their satisfaction, through the loss of leisure and the unpleasantness of the extra work, by less than the addition to their satisfaction from the extra product produced. It follows that, if people are paid for their work a wage-rate equal to the value of the marginal product of work, and if they

---

1. This decision may be made either by each individual acting alone or through collective action by trade unions or other similar organizations. Since individuals have different desires for real income and for leisure according (e.g.) to their tastes and the size of their dependent family, it is often argued that collective action is useless for the purpose of obtaining the best balance between work and leisure. This is, however, an exaggeration. Often for technical reasons every one in a factory must work the same number of hours, so that every individual cannot obtain the best balance between work and leisure. But collectively the workers can bargain for a change in the number of hours worked at a given hourly wage-rate to obtain that number of hours which represents the 'center of gravity' of the wishes of the different individuals. For this reason collective action may have a useful function in achieving the best balance between work and leisure.

are left free to decide how much work they will do, there will be a tendency for the *individual* optimum amount of work to be done per head of the population. Workers will then bargain for those hours of work and for those holidays at the current marginal product of work, which represent the *individual* optimum balance between work and leisure. The wife will go out to work only if the utility of the additional product due to her work is greater than the disutility of the work. The worker will retire when the utility of the additional product due to his staying in work is less than the disutility of his work.

The only important modification of this method of securing the *individual* optimum amount of work per head is in the age at which persons start work. As we have argued in Part III, Chapter II, pp. 230–3, the investment of a certain sum of money in a longer education—which sum must include the actual cost of the education plus the amount which the child might have earned during the years of education—may considerably increase the earning power of the child and may represent a capital investment which from the purely economic point of view has a high yield. But either because parents underestimate the actual increase in earning power which education can bring, or because from sheer impatience they wish to launch the child at once into an occupation in which he can earn, or because poor parents are unable to provide sufficient security to borrow money for education at the current rate of interest, much desirable expenditure on education, and the consequent rise in the age at which work begins, may not take place unless the state interferes. Further, if there is no state interference, it is the parents who must make the investment in education and the sacrifice which it involves, while it is in the main the children who will gain through the increased ability to earn. For any or all of these reasons children may be set to work earlier than is desirable even from the strictly economic point of view.

(ii) But there is a second and more complete way in which the optimum balance between work and leisure may be defined. Let us suppose that the *individual* optimum has been achieved in every case, so that no individual by working more or less can be better off without making some one else worse off; even so, it is possible that an individual by working more could add more to some one else's satisfaction than he lost in satisfaction himself if part or all of the extra product which he produced were paid to some one who was in greater need than himself. We may say that the *social* optimum balance between work and leisure is achieved only when it is impossible for any man by working more or less to increase the total satisfaction of the community; i.e. to increase any one else's satisfaction by more than he would diminish his own.

This *social* optimum balance between work and leisure will be achieved (a) if, being free to choose how much he will work, each individual is paid a wage equal to the value of his marginal product, and (b) if at the same time the marginal utility of income is the same to every individual. We have seen that if the former condition is satisfied each individual will tend to do that amount of work which makes it impossible for his position to be bettered without worsening the position of some one else; and if the second condition is also satisfied it will be impossible for any one by working harder to produce an additional output which would satisfy any one else more than it could satisfy him. In fact, however, as we saw in Part III, the payment of each individual in accordance with his marginal product means that incomes will almost certainly be unequal, and where incomes are unequal there is a strong presumption that the marginal utilities of income to different people are also unequal; that, in other words, a little additional income will have less significance for a rich man than for a poor one. In order that both the conditions necessary for the *social* optimum should be simultaneously satisfied, it would be necessary (a) to insure that each worker was paid his full marginal product for each *additional* hour's labor, and (b) to levy on the rich taxes of a fixed sum and to pay to the poor subsidies of a fixed sum, which would not vary with the amount of work done, in such amounts that the marginal utility of income was the same to all persons.

Such a programme would be quite obviously impractical, and it is necessary to resign ourselves to some sort of compromise which will secure as nearly as possible the *social* optimum balance between work and leisure. In general, any policy which insures that workers will be paid rewards more nearly equal to their marginal products without causing greater inequalities of income, or any policy which secures greater equality of income without causing a further divergence between rewards and marginal products, is bound to help towards the achievement of the *social* optimum.

In several of the decisions which we have already reached in the previous Parts of this book we have referred to the necessity of considering the effect upon the best balance between work and leisure of the policy adopted. Here we may discuss these points briefly in the light of the foregoing argument.

(i) Of the various taxes which we found to be desirable on other grounds for the purpose of redistributing wealth and income (cf. Part III, Chapter IV), the property tax is clearly superior from the point of view of securing the optimum supply of work. For it makes incomes more equal without in any way affecting the equivalence of marginal product and a worker's earnings. A progressive income tax is less desirable, for while it makes net incomes, and thus the marginal utilities of income to different people, more equal, it results in people receiving less than their marginal product for additional hours of work. It follows that an income tax is less than ideal, but not that it should not be levied, for on balance the income tax could not be positively harmful unless it caused individuals to work less than they would if the income tax had not been levied, and this is not necessarily the case. It would be more likely to be the case the more progressive was the income tax. Since property taxes would probably not yield sufficient revenue, and since a progressive income tax is highly desirable on other grounds, it would probably be necessary to include it in the tax system. Taxes levied per unit of labor employed, or per unit of wages, as in the case of contributions under the Federal social security schemes, have unfavorable repercussions on the distribution of income, and also result in workers being paid less than their marginal product (cf. Part I, Chapter IX).

(ii) Subsidizing wages in competitive industries in an attempt to increase employment without reducing the real wage-rate will have repercussions on the distribution of income and will result in labor receiving more than its marginal product. The net effect on the amount of work done may be unfavorable (cf. Part I, Chapter IX).

(iii) There is a strong presumption against legal restrictions of hours of work and compulsory retirement from industry at a given age in order to reduce unemployment (cf. Part I, Chapter IX). Men, acting individually or through their organizations, should be permitted, as well as enabled, to make such choices for themselves.

(iv) In Part II we have shown that in monopolistic conditions labor, being one of the hired factors of production, will be offered a reward lower than the value of its marginal product. This involves two evils: (a) the maldistribution of labor among different occupations, and (b) the possible disturbance of the proper balance between work and leisure. To cure the former evil it is only necessary to insure that the value of the marginal product of labor is the same in every industry, but to cure the second it is necessary to insure: (i) that labor is paid its marginal product in every occupation; and (ii) that the earnings of labor are as nearly as possible equal to the average income of the community. On both these counts it is preferable to remove the wastes of competition by measures which make the reward of labor equal to the value of its marginal product—e.g. by fixing maximum commodity prices and minimum wage-rates or by placing monopolistic industries under public corporations—rather than by measures which merely insure that the value of the marginal product of industry is the same in every industry—e.g. by a system of taxes and subsidies on employment in different occupations (cf. Part II, Chapter VII).

(v) The payment of state allowances to equalize earned incomes or the raising of the wage-rate paid in publicly-controlled industries above the marginal product of labor may cause the proper balance between work and leisure to be upset. In so far as earnings are being equated to the average income of the community the effect on this balance will be favorable, but the resulting inequality between marginal product and wage-rate will have an unfavorable effect (cf. Part III, Chapter V).

We must now turn to changes in the total supply of labor due to variations in the size of the population. We have here to answer the following questions: What do we mean by an optimum population? Is there any reason to believe that the population automatically tends to grow to this optimum size? If not, how can we judge whether the population is too large or too small? Finally, how can we control the size of the population and cause it to tend to the optimum size?

We may mean by an optimum population either that population which will produce the greatest total amount of satisfaction, or that population which will produce the greatest satisfaction per head. Suppose that real income per head would be high if there were only a small population, and would be lower, but not very much lower, if there were a considerable increase in the population. In such circumstances satisfaction per head would be greatest with a small population, whereas with a larger population the total amount of satisfaction would be greater, since there would be a much larger number of persons each enjoying a slightly lower amount of satisfaction. We have therefore to determine whether—from the purely economic point of view [1]—we

1. Other considerations may be important besides economic satisfaction. For example, an increase in the number of human souls may itself be thought of value. In the text we are concerned only with the maximization of economic welfare, and our conclusions may need modification if the maximization of some other good requires a different policy.

desire that number of persons which will raise the individual standard of living as high as possible, or that number which will insure the greatest aggregate sum of human satisfaction. In my opinion the proper definition of the optimum population is that which maximizes satisfaction per head, which is, of course, the same as the population which provides the greatest real income of commodities and services per head. In what follows the optimum population will be defined in this sense, and it is left to any reader who chooses the alternative definition to modify the argument appropriately.

If the growth of population is not consciously controlled, it will be an accident if the population happens to be of the optimum size, as we have defined that term. The motives which cause people to have larger or smaller families are obscure and are not primarily economic, so that there is little probability that people will adjust the size of their families in such a way that the population is of the optimum size. If—as was at one time held to be true—workers always increased the size of their families so long as their income was above the subsistence level, the population would always grow beyond the optimum. If, as is probably nearer the truth, people restrict the size of their families with the object of insuring that their children will be in a position to enjoy a higher standard than they enjoyed, there is still no reason to believe that the population will automatically approach the optimum. If the population is below the optimum, the standard of living would be raised by an increase of population; but people may still restrict the size of their families in an attempt to obtain a better start in life for each child.

How then can we judge whether the population is greater or less than the optimum size? In this chapter we shall assume that there is a certain stock of natural resources and of capital to be used by the working population; and we shall inquire how we can decide whether real income per head would be increased by an increase or by a diminution in the numbers of the working population, without any change in the amount of capital with which it is to co-operate. If in these circumstances the population [1] were very small, real income per head could be increased by a growth in the population. After a certain increase, real income per head would reach a maximum, and any further growth in the population would cause it to fall.

There are two opposing forces at work. If the population is very small there will be little opportunity for the specialization of work among different workers, i.e. for 'the division of labor.' If there were only one man in the community, he might have to spend one-third of his time making bread, one-third of his time making clothes, and one-third of his time building and repairing his house. If, however, there were three persons, one of whom spent all his time making bread, one making clothes, and one building houses, the community's supply of bread, clothes, and houses would be more than three times as great. For each man, by concentrating on one job, would save time, would obtain a greater skill, and would choose that job for which he was naturally most suited. In the production of each commodity there are a large number of slightly different processes and jobs, and there are also a large number of different commodities to be produced. In order, therefore, that there may be the fullest division of labor, the population must grow to a considerable size.

There is a further reason why, up to a point, a growth in the population to be employed with a given amount of land and capital will cause real income per head to increase. In Part II it was pointed out that in every industry the capital equipment must for technical reasons be of a certain minimum size, however small an output is produced, so that the output could be increased up to a point without a proportionate increase in equipment. To print one copy of a book or newspaper requires a minimum capital equipment of type and machinery, and similarly to produce a few motor cars requires a minimum plant. To run

---

[1]. We shall talk about the population instead of the working population, making the assumption that the working population is a constant proportion of the total.

two instead of one train a day requires no larger equipment of tunnels, stations, embankments, lines, etc. If, therefore, the population is very small, an increase would raise real income per head; for the increased population could be set to work to use the capital more fully, and there would be little or no increase in the work necessary to maintain and repair the existing stock of capital. If there is not a full utilization of capital equipment, which for technical reasons can only be fully utilized if there is a fairly large total demand for the products of industry, a growth in the population, by causing an increase in the total aggregate demand for commodities, will cause the capital to be more fully utilized and will so lower real costs of production per unit of output; and this means that the growth of population may cause a rise in real income per head.

But there is a second and opposing tendency at work. Before the population has benefited fully from the division and specialization of labor and from the full utilization of the capital equipment, a further growth in the population will cause a fall in real income per head. For if there is a given amount of natural resources and a given stock of capital equipment, a growth in the population must mean that each worker is equipped with less capital and natural resources, and this in itself will tend to cause output per head to fall. As the population grows, a point will be reached when the fact that each laborer would have a smaller equipment of natural resources and of capital outweighs the advantages to be gained from the greater specialization of labor and the fuller use of certain types of capital equipment. The larger the population, the less important will the advantages of large-scale production become, and the more important will be the fact that there is little capital and land to use with each worker, so that at some point output per head would be reduced by a further growth of numbers.

If it is agreed that, with a given equipment of land and capital, real output per head will grow up to a maximum point and then fall as the population increases, we can discover a method of determining whether the population is less or greater than the optimum. This point can be explained by means of the arithmetical illustration given in Table IX.

In this Table the figures in column A represent the total population, the figures in column B show the output of commodities per head of population, the figures in column C show the total output for each population and are obtained by multiplying the figure in column A by the corresponding figure in column B. The figures in column D show the marginal product of labor, or the amount by which the total output in column C is increased by increasing the population by one unit; these figures are obtained by subtracting from the corresponding figure in column C the previous figure in column C. When the population grows from 8 to 9, the total output increases from 768 to 891 and the difference between these figures—namely 123—is shown in column D as the marginal product of the 9th worker. The figures in this Table have been chosen so that output per head rises as the population increases up to 10 or 11 and then falls, so that the

TABLE IX

The Optimum Population

A	B	C	D
Population	Output per head	Total output	Marginal product
5	75	375	. .
6	84	504	129
7	91	637	133
8	96	768	131
9	99	891	123
10	100	1,000	109
11	100	1,100	100
12	99	1,188	88
13	96	1,248	60
14	91	1,274	26

optimum population is 10 or 11. It is to be observed that so long as the marginal product of labor is greater than the existing output per head, an increase in the population would raise the output per head. Suppose that the population is 7 and the existing output per head is therefore 91. Table IX shows that the marginal product of an extra or 8th man is 131, which is greater than the existing output per head, so that to have an 8th worker would raise output per head from 91 to 96. This is a natural and necessary fact. If an increase in population by one unit would increase the total output by more than the existing output per head, then an increase in the population will raise output per head, just as a pitcher will raise his earned run average by pitching an additional game and permitting more earned runs than his previous average (cf. p. 111 above). From Table IX it can also be seen that as soon as the marginal product of labor has fallen below the existing output per head, an increase in the population would cause output per head to fall; for if the employment of one more man adds less to the total output than the existing output per head, output per head must be reduced by his employment.

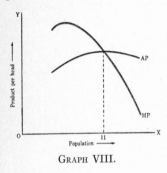

GRAPH VIII.

[These conditions of an optimum population can be represented on a very simple graph. If we measure population on the horizontal axis and product on the vertical, we can plot two curves AP and MP showing the population's average and marginal product respectively. This is done on Graph VIII. Where the average product is a maximum and the population is therefore at the optimum (11 on the graph) the two curves intersect. For any population greater than the optimum it is clear that marginal product per head is less than average, and for any population less than the optimum, marginal product is greater than the average.]

We now have a method of judging whether with a given amount of land and capital the population is greater or less than the optimum. If the marginal product of labor is less than the average output per head, the population is greater than the optimum, and a fall in the population would raise output per head. If the marginal product of labor is greater than the average output per head, the population is below the optimum and an increase in the population would raise output per head. The test, therefore, is simply this: if the payment of wages to labor, equal to the marginal product of labor, would not absorb as much as the total output of the community, because output per head is greater than the marginal product of labor, the population is greater than the optimum. If, however, output per head is less than the marginal product of labor, so that there would not be a sufficient output to pay labor a wage-rate as great as its marginal product, the population is too small.

This principle does not imply that there is too great a population if in a *laisser-faire* economy the whole of the product does not go to labor. If the population is of the optimum size, a small increase in the population will cause no rise or fall in output per head; for until this point is reached, an increase in population would cause a rise in output per head, and after this point an increase in population would cause a fall in output per head, so that at this point an increase in population would cause no change in output per head. In other words, at the optimum population a 1 per cent increase in the supply of labor would cause a 1 per cent increase in the total output. In this case a 1 per cent increase in the supply of capital and land as well as of labor would cause output to increase by more than 1 per cent, since a 1 per cent increase in labor alone is sufficient to cause a 1 per cent increase in total output. In other words, in these circumstances there must still be some economies to be derived simply from producing on a larger scale; for in the absence of any such economies a 1 per cent increase in every factor of production would cause total output to rise by no more than 1 per cent. But there can be economies of large-scale production only if there are still economies to be derived from the further division and specialization of labor, or from the further utilization of certain forms of capital equipment. If this is so, there are bound to be monopolistic conditions. For these economies can exist only if the total demand for a product is not sufficient to allow the fullest utilization of *one* single form of capital equipment, such as a railway line, or if the total demand for a product is not sufficient to allow the fullest division of labor among different tasks, even if there is only *one* single worker undertaking each specialized task. In these circumstances there cannot be perfect competition; there must in some industries be only one, or at the most a few, independent units of capital equipment, or independent firms in which labor is specialized on different tasks. But as we have seen in Part II, Chapters IV and V, in a *laisser-faire* economy labor will be paid less than the value of its marginal product if monopolistic conditions exist. It follows that in a *laisser-faire* economy labor will not receive the whole product if the population is of the optimum size, because at this point it would receive less than its marginal product.

If, however, all monopolistic industries are socially controlled and managed on the principles suggested above in Part II, Chapter VIII, pp. 204–19, and an attempt is made everywhere to pay labor a wage equal to the value of its marginal product, it is possible immediately to say that the population is at the optimum if this absorbs the whole product; that it is greater than the optimum if this absorbs less than the whole product; and that it is less than the optimum if such payment of labor is impossible because it would absorb more than the whole product of industry. This does not mean that if the population is at the optimum the wage paid in each separate industry should just absorb the total product of that industry. For in some industries, in which the economies of large-scale production are not important, the marginal product of labor may be less than the output per head and these industries will pay to labor less than the total output of the industry. But in others in which the economies of large-scale production are very important, the marginal product of labor may still be considerably in excess of output per head, and these industries will be operated by the public bodies controlling them in such a way that their wage-bill is greater than their total receipts. Their losses must therefore be financed by the profits earned in the first class of industry, in which labor's wage does not absorb the whole of the product. If

the population is at the optimum, the payment to labor throughout the whole of industry of wages equal to the value of its
marginal product will just absorb the whole income of the community. It follows that if the population is near the optimum and
if labor is paid a wage equal to the value of its marginal product
in all industries, it will be necessary for the state to own *all* property, since the income derived from property in industries which
still make profits will be required by the state to subsidize those
industries in which losses are made.

In these circumstances the state must revert to taxation to
raise funds for its ordinary expenditure or to provide funds for
savings; for there would be no net income from state-owned
property to be used for these purposes. Estate and inheritance
taxes would be inadequate, since no significant amount of property would remain in private ownership. Commodity taxes
would be open to the objection that they divert factors of production to the wrong occupations (cf. p. 249). The choice would
have to be made between poll taxes [1] and income taxes. The
former would have the advantage that they would enable a man
to be remunerated for extra hours of work according to his marginal productivity, which is an advantage from the point of
view of securing the *individual* optimum balance between work
and leisure. The latter would have the advantage that they could
be made proportionate or as progressive as seemed desirable
from the point of view of the proper distribution of income. Even
from the point of view of securing the best balance between work
and leisure the superiority of the poll tax over a moderately progressive income tax is not obvious; for, as we have seen on
p. 279 above, the equality in incomes which the income tax
would promote is itself a factor conducive to securing the *social*
optimum balance between work and leisure, and this must be
set off against its unfavorable effect in making rates of remu-
neration less than marginal products.

1. I.e. taxes which levy the same fixed sum from each individual regardless
of the size of his income.

By the methods discussed in this chapter it can be decided whether the population is too great or too small, but it is impossible to take any practical steps to remedy the situation until we have learned why the population is the size it is, and the nature of the forces which cause it to increase and decrease. Apart from immigration and emigration, the increase of a population is equal to the excess of births over deaths in the community. But the excess of the birth-rate over the death-rate is a very misleading measure of the fundamental trend of a population. In this country at the present time it happens that an abnormally large proportion of the population is between the ages of 20 and 50. This means that an abnormally large proportion of the population is made up of women of child-bearing age, while an abnormally small proportion of the population is of the age—either very young or very old—at which people are most liable to die. In consequence at present births exceed deaths, although the number of children being born is probably not quite sufficient to replace their parents, so that there is a fundamental tendency for the population to decline. In a few years' time, when the present abnormally large number of women of child-bearing age grow old, births will decline and deaths will rise, and the population will begin to fall.

The most satisfactory measure of the trend of the population

TABLE X

The Net Reproduction Rate

A Age-group	B Number of female babies born to 1,000 women in each age-group	C Number of survivors out of 1,000 female babies	D Number of female babies reproduced by 1,000 female babies
20–25	200	900	180
25–30	250	800	200
30–35	250	700	175
35–40	200	600	120
Total	900	. .	675

is to be found in the 'net reproduction rate'; the calculation of this rate is illustrated in Table X, the figures in which are chosen arbitrarily for the purposes of simple illustration. If we start with 1,000 female babies and then estimate how many female babies these 1,000 will leave behind them as they grow up and pass through the child-bearing age, we can tell whether, at present fertility and mortality rates, there is a fundamental tendency for the population to reproduce itself or not. If 1,000 female babies will leave only 750 female babies behind them, then the population is reproducing only $\frac{3}{4}$ of itself in each generation and the net reproduction rate is said to be 0.75. If they will leave more than 1,000 behind them, then the net reproduction rate is greater than 1, and there is a fundamental tendency for the population to grow.

For the purposes of simplification we suppose in Table X that the child-bearing age is from 20 to 40; and column A shows these child-bearing years divided into four groups. The figures in column B show the number of female children that are born at present fertility rates to each 1,000 women as they pass through the different child-bearing ages of column A. Thus we suppose that 1,000 women bear 250 children as they pass through the ages 30 to 35, and 200 children as they pass through the ages 35 to 40. If we sum up the figures in column B, we find the number of female babies which will be left behind by 1,000 female infants, as they pass through life, *provided that none of these 1,000 infants dies before the end of the child-bearing age.* In Table X this total is 900; and in consequence the *gross* reproduction rate is said to be 0.9, which means that in the absence of any death before the end of the child-bearing period the population will at present fertility rates reproduce $\frac{9}{10}$ of itself in each generation. But we must next allow for the fact that some female infants will never reach child-bearing age, while others will not complete their child-bearing period. The figures in column C show what proportion of female infants will, with the existing expectation of life, survive to each of the child-bearing ages. Thus we suppose that out of 1,000 female infants, 900 will survive to the ages 20 to 25, while only 700 will survive to the ages 30 to 35. The figures in column D show how many female babies will be left behind by 1,000 female babies, as these 1,000 babies grow up and, allowing for death on the way, pass through the child-bearing age. The figures in column D are obtained from those in columns B and C in the following way. Column C tells us that out of 1,000 female infants only 900 will survive to the ages 20 to 25; and since column B tells us that 1,000 women passing through this age-group would bear 200 female infants, we may reckon that

900 passing through this age-group will bear $\dfrac{900}{1,000} \times 200$ or 180

female babies, which figure is shown in column D. The sum of the figures in column D shows the number of female infants which will be left behind by 1,000 female babies, as these 1,000 babies grow up and pass through the child-bearing age, some dying and others marrying and bearing children. In Table X 1,000 female babies would leave only 675 female babies behind them, which means that at the assumed fertility and mortality rates each generation of mothers is reproducing only $67\frac{1}{2}$ per cent of itself. In this case the net reproduction rate is said to be 0.675.

We can see now how unsatisfactory a comparison of the birth-rate and death-rate may be as a measure of the trend of population. In this country the net reproduction rate, as nearly as it can be calculated from inadequate statistics, is just less than 1, which means that each generation is not quite reproducing itself, although there is still a considerable excess of births over deaths owing to the fact that an abnormally large proportion of the population is of the child-bearing age. This means that if rates of fertility and mortality continue at their present level an approximately stationary population will inevitably result. And that if the fertility rate continues to fall as it has for the last few decades the population will start on a rapid and continuous decline.

This discussion may be applied to the choice of a population policy. It is the net reproduction rate and not the balance between the birth-rate and the death-rate which shows the real tendency of the population to rise or to fall; and this, together with the test of over- and under-population outlined above, will show whether the population already has a tendency to move towards or away from the optimum size. If the net reproduction rate shows a tendency for the population to move away from the optimum, immediate steps are necessary to counteract this population trend. If, however, the net reproduction rate shows that the trend of population is already in the direction of the optimum size, no immediate steps are necessary to exaggerate this trend. Indeed, it must always be remembered that the population will continue to grow or to fall without limit so long as the net reproduction rate is above or below one. Suppose, for example, that the population was above the optimum, but that the net reproduction rate was below one. The population would already show a tendency to fall towards the optimum, but this fall might be continued far beyond the optimum unless measures were taken to raise the net reproduction rate, so that it would have risen to one by the time that the optimum population was reached. In such circumstances it would be appropriate to encourage an increase rather than a decrease in the size of the family, since the desired fall in numbers towards the optimum will occur in any case and may proceed too far unless appropriate measures are taken.[1]

The question still remains what steps might appropriately be taken to alter the net reproduction rate. Direct state control of the numbers of the population is not only difficult, but to many will appear repugnant for reasons that are not economic. Yet if this test of the optimum size of the population were recog-

[1]. This is the sort of situation in which the United States probably finds itself at the moment, with its population greater than the optimum (with the existing quantities of capital), and increasing, but with a net reproduction rate less than unity and decreasing. The initial fall in population will be in the direction of the optimum, and should therefore raise the potential standard of life, but it will be continued far beyond the optimum point unless steps are taken in time to raise the net reproduction rate back to one by the time the optimum is reached.

nized, there would, at least, be a scientific basis for informing individuals whether the general standard of living would be raised by an increase or by a decrease in the size of the family. The state might go farther, and encourage large families by paying substantial allowances for each child in the family. In any case there might, of course, be a direct conflict between the best distribution of the national income and the prosecution of a policy designed to promote an optimum population. For example, in order to reduce the numbers of a population which was above the optimum, it might be desirable to tax large families in order to pay allowances to the childless, although such action would distribute the national income in an uneconomic fashion. But at present, with the country threatened by a severe and unlimited decline in population, and therefore, sooner or later, by underpopulation, family allowances are desirable from every point of view.

There is one final point which will be important for our argument in the next chapter. The fact that, if the population is of the optimum size and labor is paid a wage equal to its marginal product, there will be no income left over to go in interest on capital or rent of land, does not mean that the marginal products of capital and land are zero. The population is of the optimum size when the economies of large-scale production are just offset by the fact that, with a given amount of land and capital, an increase in the population would cause each unit of labor to be equipped with less land and capital. But if this is so, it must still be of importance to have a greater supply of land and capital —or of one of them at least—so that an increase in their supply would cause some increase in the total output.

THE OPTIMUM SUPPLY OF CAPITAL

In this chapter we shall discuss what determines the optimum size of the stock of capital, on the assumption that there is a given supply of labor. To do this we must show, first, how the amount of capital may be varied without any variation in the amount of land or labor, and, secondly, how the marginal product of capital may be measured. Suppose that there are 3 units of land and 300 units of labor to be employed. If this land and labor were all used directly to produce wheat, there would be no capital in existence and the output of wheat would be small.[1] Suppose, however, that 1 unit of land and 100 units of labor were used to produce plows and the remaining 2 units of land and 200 units of labor were employed with the plows to produce wheat. There would now be a constant capital stock of plows in existence and the 1 unit of land and 100 units of labor would be employed in constructing just sufficient plows to replace the existing stock of plows as they wore out. The output of wheat would almost certainly be greater if the 3 units of land and 300 units of labor were employed in this way than if they were all employed directly to produce wheat without any stock of plows. If now 2 units of land and 200 units of labor were set aside to produce agricultural machinery and only 1 unit of land and 100 units of labor were left to produce wheat directly with this machinery, there would be the same amount of land and labor used directly or indirectly to produce wheat, but there would be a larger capital stock of machinery to be employed with this labor and land. The output of wheat might be further increased

1. Strictly speaking no wheat could be produced with no capital. Some 'circulating capital' in the form of stores of grain would be necessary to support the laborers from one harvest to another.

by adding to the capital stock in this way, although a point will be reached at which the use of more labor and land to maintain a larger stock of capital equipment will leave so little labor and land to use that equipment that the final output would be reduced.

By setting a larger proportion of a given supply of labor and land to produce machinery and other capital goods a larger stock of capital can be maintained, and up to a point this increase in the stock of capital goods will increase the total output of the community. In these circumstances, *as soon as* the capital stock has been increased, a larger output of finished goods will be produced by the given amount of labor and land, but *while* the stock of capital goods is being built up, the output of consumption goods will be smaller than before. Only by going without consumption goods which could otherwise have been produced, can a greater stock of capital goods be produced, in order that the output of consumption goods may be permanently increased in the future.[1]

Thus if 1 unit of land and 100 units of labor are used to maintain a stock of plows by means of which 2 units of land and 200 units of labor produce wheat, the output of wheat will be permanently greater than the output which would be produced if all the 3 units of land and the 300 units of labor were permanently employed to produce wheat directly. But in order to move from the second position to the first, the consumption of wheat must be temporarily reduced. For when 1 unit of land and 100 units of labor are set to produce the first plows, the remaining 2 units of land and 200 units of labor must produce wheat directly without the aid of plows, until the first plows have been constructed. During the time in which the stock of capital is being built up, consumption of finished goods must be cut down to allow some of the factors of production to produce the additional capital goods.

1. We are, of course, assuming throughout this Part that full employment of the available resources has been achieved by the policies suggested in Part I.

We can now show how the marginal product of capital goods should be measured. Let us suppose that one more plow is to be added to the stock. If the *same* amount of labor and land were to be used directly with one more plow in the production of wheat this would add something—let us say 20 units of wheat—to the annual output of wheat. We may call this the gross marginal product of a plow. But as one more plow has been added to the stock of plows, more labor and land will have to be used to produce plows to maintain this greater stock. Let us suppose that 1 more unit of land and 2 more units of labor must in future be regularly employed in the production of plows for this purpose. The net addition to the output of wheat will therefore be 20 units minus a reduction in output due to the fact that 1 less unit of land and 2 less units of labor are available to produce wheat directly with the increased stock of plows. This reduction in the output of wheat is equal to the marginal product of a unit of land used directly in producing it, since 1 less unit of land can be used for this purpose, plus twice the marginal product of labor used in the direct production of wheat, since 2 units of labor have had to move from its direct production. If the marginal product of land used directly for the production of wheat is 5 units of wheat a year and the marginal product of labor used in this way is also 5 units of wheat a year, then the net or true marginal product of a plow is 5 units of wheat a year. Its use would add 20 units to the annual output if it were used with the same amount of land and labor, but its maintenance requires the withdrawal of a certain amount of labor and land from the direct production of wheat and so a consequent reduction in the annual output of wheat by 15 units. The value of the net marginal product of a plow can be easily calculated if labor and land in all industries are paid rewards equal to the value of their marginal products. If the farmer who intends to add one plow to his stock decides how much he would add to his output of wheat by using one more plow with the *same* amount of labor and land, and multiplies this by the current price of wheat, he will thereby calculate the value of the gross marginal product of the plow. If he subtracts from this sum the amount which he must set aside for the repair and maintenance of the extra plow, then—on the assumption that the factors of production are paid rewards equal to the value of their marginal products—the result will give the value of the net marginal product of the plow. He will have subtracted from the value of the gross marginal product of the plow an amount equal to the value of the productivity in wheat production of the extra factors required to maintain an additional plow in the capital stock. If, therefore, all products are sold at prices corresponding to their marginal costs, so that the cost of maintaining an extra plow represents the value of the product which the factors so employed might have produced in any other occupation, the marginal product of a capital instrument may be measured by the value of its gross marginal product minus the cost of its upkeep and maintenance.

The marginal product of capital may best be measured as a percentage rate of profit in order that the value of the marginal products of different forms of capital instruments may be compared. Suppose that there are two forms of capital instrument—a mechanical plow and a mechanical reaper—both costing $1,000. If all commodities are sold at prices corresponding to their marginal costs, this means that it costs the community the same amount of factors to produce another plow as it does to produce another reaper. If the marginal product of the mechanical plow is $50 a year, reckoned by subtracting from its gross marginal product the annual cost of its upkeep, while the marginal product of the mechanical reaper is $30 a year, reckoned in the same way, the community would be better off if it used its factors to produce another plow costing $1,000 rather than to produce another reaper costing the same amount. Since the investment of $1,000 in a plow adds a net annual amount to the community's output valued at $50, we may say that the marginal product of capital invested in a plow is 5 per cent per annum; and similarly the marginal product of capital invested in a reaper is only 3 per cent per annum. It is to the community's interest that capital should be invested in those occupations in which the marginal product of capital reckoned in this manner is highest.

From this discussion of the nature of capital we may conclude that the community should continue to add to its capital equipment until the capital stock is so large that its net marginal product has fallen to zero. If, for example, the marginal product of capital is still 5 per cent, this means that by spending $100 on the construction of an additional capital instrument—i.e. by one single sacrifice of consumption goods valued at $100 enabling the factors of production to be released to produce the capital instrument—the community can add *for ever* a net amount to its annual real output valued at $5. At the end of 20 years the community will have received an additional income equal in value to the sacrifice of consumption goods necessary for the investment, but the increase in annual income will continue, since we have allowed for the cost of permanent upkeep of the capital before reckoning its net marginal product.

Granted then that the stock of capital goods should be increased by saving until the marginal product of capital is zero, we have still to decide how much should be saved this year and how much of the necessary savings should be postponed until later years. It is possible to work out an answer to this problem in terms of the marginal utility of present and potential future incomes, and of the increases in productivity which would result from successive acts of saving. Since the last of these can be estimated only very approximately, and the others not at all, the evolution of the formula is of purely academic importance.

There are, however, two reasons why it seems improbable that individuals, left to their own devices, will save at the proper rate.

In the first place, individuals will not always give up a present satisfaction simply because a greater satisfaction can thereby be obtained in the future. They are impatient—if for no other reason—because they are mortal, and do not consider the needs of their descendants as important as their own. On the other hand, the state does not die, and can consciously attempt to save more so long as the future gain is greater than the present loss.

There is a second reason why individuals may not save the optimum amount. As we have seen in the last chapter, if the population is near the optimum the whole of the national income will be required to pay labor a reward equal to its marginal product. For this purpose it will be necessary for the state to own most of the community's capital and land in order to subsidize the payment of wages in those monopolistic industries in which the payment of wages absorbs more than the total output from those competitive or less monopolistic industries in which the payment of wages absorbs less than the total output. In such circumstances, even if new saving could be left to the initiative of individuals, no interest could be offered on capital, so that the incentive to save would be very largely removed. And yet it may be proper for the state to save in these circumstances, since as we saw at the end of the last chapter the marginal product of capital may still be positive, even though the payment of a reward to labor as great as its marginal product absorbs the whole national income. In these circumstances the state would have to raise the funds for its saving by means of taxation, and this point was discussed in the last chapter (p. 290).

Although no income will remain over to pay as rent or interest if the population is near the optimum and labor is paid a reward equal to its marginal product, it is important not to neglect the marginal products of land and capital. First, in order that the available amount of land and capital should be used in those occupations in which they are most useful, those in control of the publicly-controlled industries must estimate their marginal products. The state must allot the available amount of land and capital between different industries by comparing the estimates of their marginal products in different industries and the rate of interest and rent which is offered for their use in any competitive occupations remaining in private control. Secondly, the state must know whether the marginal product of capital is positive, in order to know whether more capital should be accumulated.

We may conclude that the community should save something as long as the marginal product of capital is positive, but that the state must decide in a rather arbitrary manner how much income should be saved each year.

IV

SIMULTANEOUS VARIATIONS IN THE SUPPLY OF LABOR AND CAPITAL

In Chapter II of this Part we examined how the supply of labor should be varied on the assumption of a given stock of capital; and in Chapter III we examined how the stock of capital should be varied on the assumption of a given supply of labor. In this chapter we must see whether the conclusions of those two chapters need modification if both labor and capital are varied at the same time.

In Chapter III we defined the optimum supply of capital as that amount which would be sufficient to reduce its marginal product to zero, so that no permanent increase in income could be obtained by a further accumulation of capital. Variations in the total supply of labor will, however, alter the size of this optimum stock of capital. For if the population is small, it will require a relatively small stock of capital to satisfy all the possible ways in which capital can be used in co-operation with labor to increase the output of commodities; whereas if the population is large, it will require a larger amount of capital before all the possible productive uses of capital have been used up.

In a similar way the optimum size of the population may alter if there is an alteration in the total stock of capital. In Chapter II it was argued that the optimum size of the population depended upon the importance of economies of large-scale production. For the greater the advantages to be obtained simply from producing on a large scale, the more important is it to have a large population in order to maximize output per head. It is probable—though not certain—that an increase in the total stock of capital makes economies of large-scale production more important. It is probably less important to be able to produce on a large scale in a community in which hand work is important, because the absence of a large amount of capital necessitates working with a small amount of machinery per head. If this is so, an increase in the supply of capital will itself cause the optimum size of the population to increase.

For these reasons the conclusions of the last two chapters need modification. Suppose that at the moment the population is greater than the optimum, i.e. that the marginal product of labor is less than the output per head, and that the stock of capital is below the optimum, i.e. that the marginal product of capital is still positive. According to the conclusions of the last two chapters the population should be diminished and the stock of capital increased. But one of these two things *may* in fact be unnecessary. For if the population is diminished, this, as we have just seen, will diminish the optimum size of the capital stock; and it is possible that when the population has been diminished, the existing stock of capital will become so great relatively to the reduced amount of labor that its marginal product is reduced to zero, so that no addition to the capital stock is required. On the other hand, if the stock of capital were increased by saving because at the moment its marginal product is positive, this might, as we have seen, increase the optimum size of the population; and it is possible that the existing population, which at the moment is above the optimum, will itself become the optimum, when the capital stock has been increased sufficiently to reduce its marginal product to zero.

If the population could be varied in amount instantaneously, the conclusions of the last two chapters would be correct without modification. In this case the population should be adjusted at every moment of time to the existing stock of capital in such a way that the population was of the optimum size relative to that stock of capital, i.e. so that the marginal product of labor was at every point of time equal to the output per head of population; and the capital stock should be increased so long as the marginal product of capital was positive. But even if there were the fullest possible state control over the growth of the population, the working population could not be instantaneously adjusted so as to be of the optimum size with every different stock of capital goods. The birth-rate cannot be immediately raised or lowered without limit, and the working population is not affected by a change in the birth-rate until the new infants become of working age. It would clearly be absurd, for example, to start a decline in the population now simply because the population was above the present optimum, if the growth in the stock of capital would within ten years cause the present population to be of the optimum size.

There is a certain size of the population and a certain size of the capital stock which together would cause the population and the capital stock to be simultaneously of the optimum sizes, so that, at the same time, the marginal product of labor equalled the output per head and also the marginal product of capital was zero. We may call these the absolute optima of population and capital; and these are the supplies of labor and capital which in the end are desirable in the community. If we could judge the size of these two absolute optima, we could say for certain that the population should be diminished if the existing population were greater than the absolute optimum, and that the capital stock should be increased if it were below the absolute optimum. But there is in fact no way by which the size of the absolute optima of labor and capital can be judged. By the means suggested in the last two chapters we can say whether income per head could be increased, either if the population diminished with the given capital stock or if the capital stock increased with the given population. We cannot possibly judge how great the population ought to be if the capital stock were very much greater than it is now, or how great the capital stock should be if the population were much smaller than it is now.

As the best working rule for practice, we must adopt the conclusions of the last two chapters—namely, that the population should be increased or diminished according as the marginal product of labor is greater than or less than output per head, and that the stock of capital goods should be increased so long as the marginal product of capital is greater than zero. For if this is done the absolute optima of population and capital will eventually be reached, since the supplies of labor and capital will continue to be adjusted until both are simultaneously of the optimum size. The only disadvantage of such a policy is that it may not avoid the wastes (e.g.) of increasing the stock of capital goods now beyond the point which may in the future be necessary when the population has diminished, or of diminishing the population now, although some increase may be found to be necessary when the stock of capital has been increased.[1] The conclusions of the last two chapters may, therefore, provide a working criterion of the direction in which the population or the stock of capital should be changed at any time; but the rates at which the state—in as far as it can control them—should cause the population and the stock of capital goods to change must be determined arbitrarily.

1. A difficulty similar in many respects to that discussed in this chapter is caused by technical progress. A population which is optimum, or a supply of capital which is optimum, in a given state of technical knowledge, may no longer be so after a series of technical inventions. In the past most inventions have had the effect of opening up new uses for capital, and if this should continue to be the case in the future there is no reason why the optimum amount of capital should ever be accumulated. It would be approached continuously by a progressive community, but would as continuously recede as the result of fresh technical advances. The best working rule for practice, in this case as in the other, is to foster that trend in population and capital accumulation which is indicated assuming other circumstances—which here mean the state of technical knowledge—to remain unaltered.

Part V

INTERNATIONAL PROBLEMS

I

THE BALANCE OF PAYMENTS

IN the four preceding Parts we have examined the four fundamental economic questions which must be answered if the standard of living in any economic society is to be as high as possible.
But we have discussed these problems on the assumption that
the economic system with which we have been dealing was a self-
contained system with no economic relations with other systems.
In this Part we shall see how the arguments of Parts I to IV are
affected by making allowance for economic contacts with other
states.

All important economic contacts between one country and
other countries involve a money payment between the nationals
or the government of the one country and the nationals or government of the other countries. Thus, if goods are imported into
America or if Americans lend to foreigners, Americans must pay
money to people in other countries. We may, therefore, introduce
a study of international economic problems by examining America's Balance of Payments, which is simply a statement of all the
payments which Americans have made to foreigners and which
foreigners have made to Americans over a certain period of time.
Table XI gives a list of the reasons which may give rise to payments between America and other countries. All the items on the
left-hand side of Table XI represent payments made by foreigners to Americans. Thus, if a foreigner buys American goods or
gold, uses American ships, comes to America to spend money,
makes a gift of money to an American, pays interest on money
borrowed from an American, pays tribute to the American government, lends money to Americans, or repays a debt to Americans, the foreigner must make a money payment to an American.

Conversely, all the elements on the right-hand side of the account represent payments made by Americans to foreigners.

If all the items in the Balance of Payments are properly and completely recorded, the total of all the items on the receipts side valued in dollars must be equal to the total of all the items

TABLE XI

The Items in America's Balance of Payments

American receipts	American payments
(a) Value of American commodity exports.	(a) Value of American commodity imports.
(b) Value of American gold exports.	(b) Value of American gold imports.
(c) Value of American services (shipping, financial, etc.) sold to foreigners.	(c) Value of foreign services (shipping, financial, etc.) used by Americans.
(d) Expenditure in America by foreign tourists.	(d) Expenditure by American tourists abroad.
(e) Gifts made by foreigners to Americans.	(e) Gifts made by Americans to foreigners, including remittances by immigrants to their families abroad.
(f) Interest received by Americans on capital invested by them in foreign countries.	(f) Interest paid by Americans on capital invested by foreigners in America.
(g) Interest, capital repayments, tribute, reparations, indemnities received by the American government from foreigners.	(g) Interest, capital repayments, tribute, reparations, indemnities paid by the American government to foreigners.
(h) Amount borrowed by Americans from foreigners (i) on long-term and (ii) on short-term.	(h) Amount lent by Americans to foreigners (i) on long-term and (ii) on short-term.
(i) Repayment by foreigners of sums previously lent by Americans.	(i) Repayment by Americans of sums previously borrowed from foreigners.

on the payments side valued in dollars; the Balance of Payments must balance. This is in reality an obvious but none the less important fact. All the items on the receipts side of the American Balance of Payments represent the purchase of American money, i.e. of dollars, with foreign money, i.e. with pounds, francs, marks, etc. For if a foreigner possessing foreign money has to make a payment to an American, either the foreigner must purchase American money in order to pay the American, or the

American will purchase American money with the foreign money that is paid to him. In either case a payment of money by (e.g.) an Englishman to an American involves the purchase of dollars with pounds. Similarly, a payment by an American to an Englishman involves a purchase of pounds with dollars. But every time a dollar is bought with foreign money, some one must be selling that dollar to purchase foreign money. Every time, therefore, that a dollar is paid to an American by a foreigner, some American must be selling a dollar to make a payment of that value to a foreigner, so that the sum of all the receipts items must be equal to the sum of all the payments items in the Balance of Payments over the same period of time, just as sales are necessarily equal to purchases. In this chapter we shall take it for granted that the Balance of Payments balances—as indeed it clearly must do. In the next two chapters we shall see by what mechanisms the amount of a foreign currency which people wish to buy is equated to the amount which holders of it wish to sell.

We must next distinguish between the Balance of Trade, the Balance of Payments on Current Account, and the Balance of Payments. A country's Balance of Trade means properly the value of a country's commodity exports minus the value of its commodity imports over a certain period of time (e.g. a year). Its Balance of Trade is said to be positive or 'favorable,' if the value of its exports is greater than the value of its imports, and negative or 'unfavorable,' if the value of its imports exceeds the value of its exports. Thus, if in any year America exports goods worth $2,000 millions and imports goods worth $2,400 millions, she has an unfavorable or negative Balance of Trade of $400 millions in the course of the year. A country's Balance of Trade need not balance. If, for example, America is importing $400 millions more goods than she is exporting but is receiving interest payments from foreigners of $400 millions in the year, her Balance of Payments will balance, although she has a negative or unfavorable Balance of Trade. By a country's Balance of

Payments on Current Account is meant the value of all the payments made to the country for all current purposes such as the purchase of that country's goods, the payment of interest to it, the use of its shipping services, etc.—i.e. all the receipts items in Table XI except items (h) and (i)—minus all the payments made to foreigners for current purposes, which include all the payment items in Table XI except items (h) and (i). Thus, a country's Balance of Payments on Current Account measures the total amount which is available for that country to lend abroad or to use to reduce its indebtedness to foreigners, and is said to be favorable or positive if the country in question is on balance lending money abroad or reducing its existing indebtedness to foreigners, and is unfavorable or negative if on balance it is borrowing from abroad.

These distinctions can be made clear if we take a simple example. It will be clear from Table XI that all the items in the Balance of Payments are not equally important. We will suppose for illustration that between America and other countries there are no payments except for trade in commodities, for shipping and financial services, for interest payments, and for lending or the repayment of past borrowing. Then we can draw up a simplified Balance of Payments, as in Table XII, in which we have given money values to the different items for the purposes of illustration.

In Table XII the Balance of Payments balances at $2,700 millions. But America has exported goods to the value of only $2,000 millions and has imported $2,400 millions worth of goods, so that her Balance of Trade is negative or unfavorable to the amount of $400 millions. Against this America has received $560 millions for other current purposes (i.e. $60 millions in payment for shipping and financial services and $500 millions in interest from foreigners). On the other hand, she has $120 millions to pay to foreigners for other current purposes (i.e. $50 millions for the use of foreign services and $70 millions in interest to foreigners). In other words, America has an unfavorable Balance of Trade of $400 millions but from other current payments has received a net amount of $440 millions; therefore, she has a favorable Balance of Payments on Current Account of $40 millions, which represents the net amount of money which America has available to add to her foreign investments in the

TABLE XII

Illustration of Main Items in Balance of Payments

American receipts	$ millions	American payments	$ millions
1. Commodity exports .	2,000	6. Commodity imports .	2,400
2. Shipping and financial services sold to foreigners . . .	60	7. Foreign shipping and financial services bought by Americans . . .	50
3. Interest paid by foreigners to Americans .	500	8. Interest paid by Americans to foreigners .	70
4. Amount borrowed from abroad . . .	40	9. Amount lent by Americans to foreigners .	160
5. Repayment by foreigners of sums previously lent to them . .	100	10. Repayment by Americans of money previously borrowed from foreigners .	20
	$2,700		$2,700

course of the year. From items 9 and 10 in Table XII we see that she has lent $160 millions abroad and has repaid $20 millions of money which she has in the past borrowed from foreigners, but from items 4 and 5 we see that she has borrowed $40 millions from foreigners and that foreigners have repaid $100 millions of past borrowings, so that the figure of $40 millions (i.e. 160+20−40−100) represents the net amount of America's foreign lending in the year. To sum up, America's Balance of Payments balances at $2,700 millions, she has an unfavorable Balance of Trade of $400 millions, but she has a favorable Balance of Payments on Current Account of $40 millions, which represents the net amount which she is enabled to lend abroad in the course of the year.

The figures of Table XII are represented in a simpler manner in Table XIII. If we compare items 1 and 6 of Table XII, we see that America spent $2,400 millions on imports and received $2,000 millions for her exports, so that her trade in commodities left a net balance of payments to be made for imported goods of $400 millions; and in Table XIII this net figure is shown in item 3. If next we compare items 2 and 7 of Table XII we see

Table XIII

Alternative Method of Illustrating the Balance of Payments

American receipts	$ millions	American payments	$ millions
1. Net receipts from shipping and financial services .	10	3. Net excess of imports over exports, or unfavorable Balance of Trade .	400
2. Net receipts of interest from abroad . . .	330	4. Net amount lent abroad in the course of the year	40
	$440		$440

that America spent $50 millions on foreign services but received $60 millions from foreigners for her services, so that she had a net figure of $10 millions to receive from foreigners for services. This net figure is shown in item 1 of Table XIII. Similarly, by comparing items 3 and 8 of Table XII we see that America received a net balance of interest from foreigners of $330 millions, which is shown in item 2 of Table XIII. And by comparing items 4 and 5 with items 9 and 10 of Table XII we see that America lent abroad a net amount of $40 millions in the course of the year, which is shown in item 4 of Table XIII. Table XIII expresses the same facts as Table XII, but shows only the net balance of receipts or payments under each head of commodity trade, services, interest, and lending.

In order to discuss in the next two chapters the mechanism which insures that a country's Balance of Payments is in equilibrium, we must outline the factors which determine the size of the different items in a country's Balance of Payments. In Table XIII there are four different items to be discussed:

(a) the total value of the excess of a country's imports over her exports;

(b) the total value of the excess of a country's receipts from shipping and other services over payments to foreigners for such services;

(c) the net amount of interest payments received by a country from foreign countries; and

(d) the net amount lent by one country to others.

(a) Let us first consider the factors determining the value of America's exports. A fall in the price in dollars of American exportable goods will in itself almost certainly increase the total value of American exports. If the price of American machines falls, foreigners will certainly buy more American machines, both because they will want more machines when their price falls, and also because they will buy American machines instead of machines made in other countries in which the price has not fallen. It is not quite certain, however, that the total value of American exports of machines will rise. Suppose that America is exporting 100 machines at $100 each, and that the price of the machines then falls to $80. If in consequence America exports 150 instead of 100 machines, the value of her machine exports will rise from $10,000 ($= 100 \times \$100$) to $12,000 ($= 150 \times \$80$). But if American exports rose only to 120 machines, then the value of her machine exports would fall from $10,000 ($= 100 \times \$100$) to $9,600 ($= 120 \times \$80$). But since the exports of any one country will probably compete with similar goods produced in many other countries, it is probable that when the price of a single country's exports falls there will be a relatively large increase in the amount sold, because the lowered price will enable them to compete better in many markets. For this reason the total value of American exports is likely to rise in consequence of a fall in the price of her exportable goods. We may take this as the normal result of a fall in the home price of any country's exportable goods.

The price of American exports in foreign markets may, however, fall, not because the price of the American goods expressed in dollars falls, but because the value of the dollar itself depreciates in terms of other foreign currencies. When the rate of exchange between the dollar and the pound is $5 to £1 an Englishman must give £100 to purchase an American machine costing $500. If, for one reason or another, the dollar depreciates in value in terms of pounds, and the exchange rate becomes, say, $6 to £1, the Englishman will have to pay only £83⅓ for the same machine. A depreciation in the value of the dollar in terms of the pound itself lowers the price of American exports in terms of English prices and will, therefore, if other conditions are unchanged, cause the English to buy more American machines. In these circumstances, since the price in dollars of American machines has not changed, the value of American exports measured in dollars will certainly be increased.

A rise in the foreign price of foreign goods which compete with American export goods will cause a rise in the value of American exports. A rise in the price in pounds of English machines will cause Englishmen to buy more American machines, if the price of American machines has not risen and if the rate of exchange between the pound and the dollar has not changed, because it will become cheaper to buy in America rather than in England.

A rise in money incomes in foreign countries will in itself cause a rise in the value of American exports. If Englishmen for one reason or another have larger pound incomes to spend, they will spend more on all commodities and will probably, therefore, purchase more American goods as well as more English goods.

Finally, the value of American exports depends upon the tariffs, quotas, prohibitions, or other restrictions placed in foreign countries on the import of American goods. A reduction in tariffs, or a diminution in other legal restrictions, imposed on the import of American goods into England will increase the value of American exports, if other conditions do not alter at the same time.

The value of American imports is determined by the same factors as the value of her exports, if we substitute 'foreign' for 'American' and 'American' for 'foreign' throughout our discussion of the factors determining the value of American exports. Thus the value of American imports will be increased (i) by a fall in the foreign price of foreign exportable goods, (ii) by an appreciation in the value of dollars in terms of foreign money, since a rise in the amount of shillings obtainable for a dollar will cause a fall in the American price of English goods, (iii) by a rise in the price of American goods, (iv) by a rise in American money incomes, and (v) by a reduction of the legal restrictions placed on the import of goods into America. We may therefore conclude that the value of the excess of a country's imports over her exports will be increased (i) by a rise in her prices compared with foreign prices, (ii) by an appreciation in the value of her money in terms of foreign money, (iii) by a rise in her money income compared with foreign money incomes, and (iv) by a reduction in her tariffs compared with foreign tariffs.

(b) A country's net receipts from shipping and other services will depend upon similar considerations. A fall in the American price of such services (e.g. in the shipping freights and charges made by American shipping firms), or a rise in the foreign price of such services, will increase foreign expenditure on American services, and diminish American expenditure on foreign services. Both Americans and foreigners will use the American services which have become cheaper rather than similar foreign services which have become dearer. A depreciation of the value of the dollar in terms of foreign money will increase the price in America of foreign services, since more dollars have to be paid to obtain a given amount of foreign money, and will decrease the price of American services in foreign countries, since more dollars can be obtained for a given amount of foreign money. A depreciation of the value of the dollar in terms of foreign money will therefore increase the value of American services sold abroad and will diminish American expenditure on foreign services. A fall in

American incomes, which will diminish American expenditure on all goods, will among other things diminish the American demand for foreign services; and a rise in foreign incomes, which will increase the foreign demand for all goods and services, will increase the foreign demand for American services among other things. The net value of a country's receipts from shipping and other services will therefore be increased, (i) by a fall in her prices compared with foreign prices for the services, (ii) by a depreciation in the value of her currency in terms of foreign currencies, and (iii) by a fall in her money incomes compared with foreign money incomes.

(c) The net amount of interest payment received by a country will depend upon the following conditions: (i) the amount of capital which the country in question has lent abroad in the past and the rate of interest at which it was lent, (ii) whether this money has been lent at fixed interest or whether the payment of interest on it depends upon the profits earned by the concern in which the money is invested, and (iii) whether any fixed interest which is to be paid on past loans is fixed in terms of the money of the country receiving interest or in terms of the money of the country paying interest.

It is clear that the net amount of interest which a country receives from abroad will depend mainly upon the amount lent abroad in the past and the rate of interest at which it was lent. But to some extent its receipts of interest from abroad will depend upon present conditions at home and in foreign countries.

If Americans have lent money to English industries or municipalities at fixed rates of interest, the prosperity of English business will have no effect upon the amount of interest received by Americans on these loans, except in so far as a depression in English business may drive English industries or municipalities into bankruptcy. But if the Americans have invested the funds in English business in common stocks, then a rise in English money incomes, and therefore in the profits earned by English industry, will increase the amount of interest received by Americans from England.

A depreciation of the value of the dollar in terms of foreign money will increase the amount of dollars received by Americans in interest on past foreign investment if these past investments take the form of loans to foreigners yielding interest or profit fixed in terms of foreign money. For if the dollar depreciates from $5 to £1 to $6 to £1, the payment of £1 in interest or profit to Americans will mean the receipt of $6 instead of $5. But if Americans have lent money to foreigners at interest fixed in terms of dollars, a change in the value of the dollar in terms of foreign money will have no effect upon the amount of dollars received by Americans.

To sum up, the net amount of interest received by a country will depend in the main upon the amount which it has lent abroad or borrowed from abroad in the past, and the rates of interest at which it has borrowed or lent. But a rise in money profits at home may increase a country's payment of profit to foreigners and so may reduce its net receipt of interest from abroad. A rise in foreign money profits will increase its net receipt of interest from abroad in so far as the country in question has in the past invested in foreign common stocks. A depreciation of a country's money in terms of foreign money will raise its net receipt of interest from abroad in terms of its own currency in so far as it receives interest or profit fixed in terms of foreign money, but will reduce its net receipt of interest from abroad in so far as it owes to foreigners interest fixed in terms of foreign money.

(d) Finally, we must consider the factors which determine the net amount which a country lends abroad. The net amount lent abroad by America is equal to the gross amount lent by Americans to foreigners, plus the repayment by Americans of their indebtedness to foreigners, minus the gross amount borrowed by Americans from foreigners, minus the repayment by foreigners of their indebtedness to Americans. The gross amount lent abroad by Americans must include all the dollars with which

Americans purchase foreign money for the purpose of increasing their holding of capital in foreign countries. This figure includes the amount lent on long-term to foreign governments, municipalities, or businesses, whether the foreign securities bought are newly issued securities or existing securities. It includes the amount spent by Americans on the purchase of land or buildings in foreign countries, on the purchase of short-term foreign securities, and on the purchase of foreign money to deposit in foreign banks or to hold as a capital asset in the form of notes or coins. The amount of capital which Americans repay to foreigners must include all purchases by Americans of debts of Americans to foreigners, and includes, therefore, the amount of existing American securities and money which are owned by foreigners and bought from them to be held by Americans, as well as the actual amount of any money debt repaid by an American to a foreigner. Conversely, the amount of foreign lending to America must include all the purchase of dollars by foreigners for the purpose of increasing their holding of capital in any form—securities, land, buildings, bank deposits, or cash—in America; and the amount of capital repaid by foreigners must include the total amount of foreign property—securities, land, or money—which is in the ownership of Americans and which is bought back from them by foreigners.

A fall in interest rates in America and a rise in interest rates abroad will increase America's net lending abroad, because it becomes more profitable to lend money abroad rather than in America.

The net amount lent abroad is also increased by an expectation that the profitability of American industry will in the future fall or that the profitability of foreign industry will rise. For people will wish to sell American common stocks, the dividends on which and the capital value of which are expected to fall as profits fall, in order to purchase foreign assets, the profits from which and the capital value of which are expected to rise.

An expectation that the value of the dollar will depreciate in terms of foreign money will cause the net amount lent abroad by Americans to increase. If the dollar depreciates in terms of foreign money, the yield in terms of dollars on a foreign asset bought before the depreciation takes place will be greater than the yield on the foreign assets reckoned in terms of foreign money. For example, suppose that the rate of interest both in England and America is 5 per cent, and that the dollar is expected to depreciate from $5 to £1 to $6 to £1. If $500 is invested in America, $25 per annum can be obtained in interest. But the $500 might be used to purchase £100, which invested at 5 per cent in England would bring in £5 per annum. If subsequently, as is expected, the dollar depreciates to $6 to £1, these £5 will purchase $30. In other words, though the rate of interest both in England and in America is 5 per cent, the investment of $500 in America will yield 5 per cent, whereas the immediate investment of this sum in England together with the subsequent depreciation in the dollar will bring in a yield of 6 per cent on the $500. The expectation of high yields from long-term foreign lending due to the expectation that the dollar will depreciate in terms of foreign money is important only if the dollar is expected not merely to depreciate but also to remain for a long time at the depreciated value. For if the dollar depreciates in value from $5 to $6 to the pound for a short time and then rises again in value to $5, the yield from foreign investment will not be raised in any significant way. For as soon as the dollar appreciated in value again to $5 to £1, the interest of £5 on the foreign investment will again yield only $25 or 5 per cent on the foreign investment of $500.

But short-term foreign investment will be increased by the expectation that the dollar will depreciate even if the depreciation is expected to be only temporary. An American can purchase £100 by the investment of $500 in English money if the rate of exchange is $5 to £1; if subsequently the rate of exchange moves to $6 to £1, this £100 will be sufficient to purchase $600. Even, therefore, if little or no interest is gained on the money in England, because it is held in English cash or on deposit at an English bank, the American, by purchasing $500 worth of pounds at $5 to £1 and by waiting to repurchase dollars at $6 to £1, can make a profit of 20 per cent on his original $500. And if he purchases pounds, just before the dollar depreciates, and then sells pounds for dollars, he may make this 20 per cent in a very short time.

Finally, the net amount lent abroad depends on the size of money incomes at home and abroad. If Americans have larger money incomes from which they can save, they will probably lend more in America and more abroad. Conversely, a fall in foreign incomes will decrease the amount which foreigners have to lend, and they will probably lend somewhat less to America. Consequently, the net amount lent abroad by America will be increased by a rise in American incomes and a fall in foreign incomes.

To summarize, the net amount lent abroad by any one country will be increased,

(i) by a rise in the rate of interest abroad or by a fall in the rate of interest at home;

(ii) by an expectation that foreign profits will rise or home profits fall;

(iii) by an expectation that the value of the home money will depreciate in terms of foreign money; and

(iv) by a rise in home incomes or a fall in foreign incomes, from which savings can be made.

II

THE GOLD STANDARD

In the last chapter we showed that the Balance of Payments must always balance in the sense that the total amount in dollars used to purchase foreign money must always be equal to the total amount in dollars bought by foreigners with foreign money; in this and the following chapter we shall show by what monetary mechanism it is insured that people *wish* to buy and sell exactly the same number of dollars.

There are two distinct methods of adjustment of the Balance of Payments, the first of which operates when the countries in question are all on a common monetary standard, and the second when the countries are on independent monetary standards. The most important common monetary standard is the gold standard, which we shall discuss to illustrate the operation of an international standard. The reader can himself apply the argument to any other international monetary standard (e.g. a silver standard), since the principles of operation do not depend on the metal.

A number of countries are on an effective gold standard only if the value of the currency of each country is fixed, within narrow limits, in terms of the currency of any other country on the gold standard. For this to be so two conditions must be fulfilled. First, the price of gold in terms of the money of each country must be fixed within narrow limits. Secondly, there must be freedom of movement of gold between the different countries on the gold standard. We will discuss these two conditions in turn, and will start by describing the three possible devices by which the price of gold may be fixed in terms of a country's money.

(i) The price of gold in terms of a country's money will be fixed if the legal money of that country consists of gold coins of a certain weight. In this case the government office which is responsible for the coining of gold must always be willing to coin a fixed weight of gold into a certain number of gold coins of a fixed value in terms of the country's money; and at the same time individuals must be free to melt these gold coins or to export them for the purpose of melting them. Thus, until the Banking Act of 1933 gold coins—the eagle, double eagle, and dollar—were legal money in the United States. The government mints and assay offices were under an obligation to buy gold and coin it at the fixed rate of $20.67 per ounce. By this means the value of an ounce of gold was prevented from moving appreciably above or below $20.67. It could not fall appreciably below $20.67 (though it might fall fractionally below since certain mint charges were levied to cover costs) since that price could always be obtained for it from the government. Nor could it rise appreciably above $20.67 since if it did it would pay individuals to melt down gold coins and offer them on the market until the price fell to that level. When the price of gold is fixed in terms of a country's money by these means, the country is said to be on a Gold Specie Standard.

(ii) But the price of gold in terms of a country's money may be fixed without the use of gold coins. Since 1934 the price of gold in terms of dollars has been fixed, although there have been no gold coins in circulation. The Treasury has been ready to buy gold from any one who wished to sell it at a fixed price of $35 per ounce, and to sell it to any one wishing to export it to a gold standard country at the same price. The price of gold therefore, even if private dealings in the metal had been allowed, could not have risen above $35 per ounce, since it could be obtained from the Treasury at that rate; nor could it have fallen below $35, since people could sell gold to the Treasury for $35. When the price of gold in terms of a country's money is fixed by these means the country is said to be on a Gold Bullion Standard; for the price of gold bullion (i.e. of gold in an uncoined form) is fixed in terms of the country's money.

(iii) There is a third way in which the price of gold may be fixed. If the Central Bank of a country is under an obligation to buy and sell the notes of some second country which is on a gold specie or gold bullion standard at a price fixed in terms of its own notes, then the price of gold is indirectly fixed in terms of the money of the first country. Suppose that England is on a gold bullion standard, so that the pound note is always worth a fixed amount of gold. If the German Central Bank is under an obligation to buy and sell English pound notes at a fixed price for mark notes, the price of pound notes will be fixed in terms of marks. Indirectly, therefore, the price of gold will be fixed in terms of marks. Even if there were no gold in any form in Germany, the German Central Bank by holding a reserve of pound notes—or of deposits in England which give it a claim to pound notes— could fix the price of gold in terms of marks by this means. When a country fixes the price of gold in terms of its own money in this way, it is said to be on the Gold Exchange Standard. It has fixed the value of its own money in terms of gold by fixing the rate of exchange between its own and some other money, which in turn has a fixed value in terms of gold.

If, by operating gold specie, gold bullion, or gold exchange standards, both of two countries fix the price of gold in terms of their own money, and if there is freedom of export and import of gold in both countries, the rate of exchange between the moneys of the two countries will be fixed within narrow limits. Suppose, for example, that both England and America are on the gold standard and that the price of a certain amount of gold is fixed in England at £1, and that the price of the same amount of gold is fixed in America at $5. Then the par rate of exchange between the pound and the dollar is said to be £1 to $5.[1] If the pound appreciates in value in terms of dollars considerably above the par

1. As a matter of fact the par rate of exchange between the pound and the dollar both before 1914 and between 1925 and 1931, when both countries were on the gold standard, was £1 to $4.866. In other words the amount of gold which in England was bought and sold by the Bank of England for £1 was bought and sold by the Federal Reserve Banks in America at the fixed price of $4.866. The par rate of exchange of £1 to $5 is chosen in the text in order to simplify the illustration.

rate of exchange—if, for example, the pound becomes worth $5½ instead of $5—Englishmen will find it profitable to purchase dollar notes with pound notes, in order to buy gold in America at the fixed price in dollars and to ship it to England to sell at the fixed price in pounds. For with £1 in notes they can buy notes worth $5½, and with $5 of these notes purchase a certain amount of gold in America which they can sell to the Bank of England for £1. Thus on each such transaction they make a profit of $½. On the other hand, no Americans with dollar notes would be willing to purchase pound notes at $5½ for £1; for they could obtain pounds more cheaply by buying $5 worth of gold in America and selling it in England for £1. For these reasons if the rate of exchange was £1 for $5½, Englishmen would want to buy dollar notes with pound notes in order to ship gold from America to England, while no Americans would be willing to purchase pound notes with dollar notes, but would make their payments in England by shipping gold. The demand for dollar notes with pound notes would be great and there would be no demand for pound notes with dollar notes, so that the amount of dollar notes which could be obtained for a pound note would necessarily fall from $5½ towards $5, and the rate of exchange between the pound and dollar would approach the par rate again.

Conversely, if for any reason the value of the pound were to depreciate in terms of the dollar from the par rate of £1 for $5 to £1 for $4½, it would pay people to send gold from England to America. Englishmen with payments to make in America would purchase gold from the Bank of England for £1 and would sell this gold to the American banks at the fixed price of $5, rather than give a £1 note directly in exchange for only $4½ in notes. At the same time Americans with $4½ in notes would purchase a £1 note and with that would buy gold from the Bank of England, export it to America, and sell it at the fixed price of $5, making a profit of $½ on each such transaction. The demand for pound notes with dollar notes would be great, while no one with pound notes would purchase dollar notes directly at this rate. In consequence, more dollar notes would have to be given to obtain a pound note, and the rate of exchange between the pound note and the dollar note would move from $4½ for £1 towards the par rate of $5 for £1.

If there were no cost involved in shipping gold between England and America and if the price of gold were rigidly fixed in terms of English money and American money, the rate of exchange between the pound and the dollar could not alter at all from the par rate of £1 to $5. For no one with dollars would ever offer more than $5 for £1, since they could obtain £1 by shipping $5 worth of gold to England; and no one with pounds would accept less than $5 per £1, since they can obtain $5 by shipping £1 worth of gold to America. But the shipment of gold between America and England involves a certain cost, and because of this cost the actual rate of exchange between the dollar and pound can fluctuate within limits set by the cost of moving gold, even if both countries are on the gold standard. The cost of shipping gold consists of the freight charged by the shipping company, the insurance of the gold against loss at sea, and the interest which is lost by using money to ship gold. It takes time to move gold from London to New York, and if a man therefore buys £100 worth of gold to ship to New York, he loses the interest which he could have obtained on the £100 if he had invested this money for the time in an interest-bearing security. Suppose that it costs 2 cents to ship between England and America that amount of gold which sells in England at the fixed price of £1 and in America at the fixed price of $5. In these circumstances it will not pay to ship gold from England to America until the pound has depreciated to £1 for $4.98 or less. For an Englishman would be willing to accept anything above $4.98 in direct exchange for a £1 note rather than bear the cost of shipping £1 in gold to America to obtain $5. Similarly, it will not pay to ship gold from America to England until the pound has appreciated to £1 for $5.02 or more. At this point the rate of exchange between the pound and dollar is said to have reached the English gold import point or the American gold export point. As soon as the rate of exchange is £1 for anything less than $4.98 it is said to have reached the English gold export point or the American gold import point, since at this point it becomes profitable to ship gold from England to America.

We can now show how it is insured that the Balance of Payments balances when all countries are on the gold standard. If the total amount of payments which Americans wish to make to foreigners is equal to the total amount of payments which foreigners want to make to Americans, there is no difficulty in arranging for these payments. There are a number of technical methods of making them; but the principle involved is the same. We may assume that there are a number of foreign exchange dealers, who are individuals or bankers holding a certain amount of pounds on deposit with American banks and a certain amount of foreign currencies on deposit with foreign banks. If an Englishman with pounds wishes to make a payment to an American, the exchange dealers will give the Englishman some of their dollars deposited in American banks in exchange for deposits in an English bank paid to them by the Englishman. But at the same time Americans who wish to make payments to English people will be giving the exchange dealers dollar deposits in exchange for some of the exchange dealers' holding of pounds on deposit in English banks. If, at the current rate of exchange, the amount of pounds which Americans wish to purchase from exchange dealers is equal to the number of pounds which English people want to exchange into dollars, the total amount of pounds held by exchange dealers on deposit with English banks and the total amount of dollars held by them on deposit in American banks will not alter.

But suppose now that Americans for some reason or another —e.g. because their desire for English goods increases—wish to pay $50 millions more a week to Englishmen than Englishmen wish to pay to Americans. At the current rate of exchange between the pound and the dollar of £1 to $5 the exchange dealers are receiving $50 millions more a week from Americans than they are selling to Englishmen, and are paying out £10 millions a week more to Americans than they are receiving from Englishmen. The dollar deposits of the exchange dealers in American banks are therefore rising by $50 millions a week and their pound deposits with English banks are falling by £10 millions a week. As long as this continues the exchange dealers themselves are exchanging their capital from English money to American money, which represents a capital movement or loan of $50 millions a week from England to America. The Balance of Payments still balances; American commodity imports have gone up by $50 millions a week, but against this there is a capital transfer of $50 millions a week from English money to American.

If Americans continue to spend $50 millions a week more on imports, the exchange dealers would soon have no more pound deposits to pay out and would hold all their balances in the form of dollars deposited with American banks. In order to stop people buying so many pounds with dollars they will reduce the number of pounds which they will give for a given number of dollars. In other words the dollar will depreciate in value in terms of the pound. The exchange dealers will, for example, offer £19.9 instead of £20 for $100. But if both countries are on the gold standard, a small depreciation of the dollar will make it cheaper for Americans, who have payments to make in England, to ship gold to England rather than to continue to buy pounds directly from exchange dealers with dollars. As soon as the dollar has depreciated sufficiently to make Americans purchase $50 millions a week of gold from the Treasury to make their payments in England, the exchange dealers' receipts and payments of pounds and their receipts and payments of dollars will balance again, so that their balances held in pounds will cease to diminish. There will now appear a new item in the Balance of Payments, namely an export of $50 millions worth of gold a week from America, which is being sold in England for pounds. The Balance of Payments will still balance. Against the additional commodity imports of $50 millions a week is now an export of gold of $50 millions a week, which takes the place of the capital transfer of $50 millions a week from English to American money.

But this state of affairs is also only temporary. For as long as it continues America must be exporting $50 millions of gold a week, which is being purchased by Americans from the Treasury. If, however, America is to stay on the gold standard, this drain of gold must be stopped. The Treasury cannot for ever pay out gold at a fixed price for dollars, since its gold reserves must sooner or later be used up. We have already seen in Part I, Chapter III (p. 29), that, if people cash part of their deposits with the ordinary commercial banks, the cash reserve ratio of these banks will be reduced, and that in order to prevent this fall in their cash reserve ratio the banks will be obliged to sell securities and raise interest rates in order to diminish their deposit liabilities. An export of gold from America will have the same effect. If Americans find it profitable to purchase gold from the Treasury, this must normally cause the cash reserves of the Federal Reserve and the legal reserves of the commercial banks to fall. For the Treasury will use the money which it receives to retire an equal amount of the gold certificates which comprise the reserves of the Federal Reserve Banks, while the deposits of the commercial banks with the Federal Reserve, which comprise their reserves, has been diminished directly by the check on his bank with which the purchaser of the gold has paid the Treasury. The consequence of the gold export is, therefore, that the banks must sell securities and raise interest rates in order to preserve their cash reserve ratio.

This rise in interest rates will, as we have argued in Chapters II and III of Part I, cause money incomes and money prices to fall in America, since Americans will be less willing to borrow money to spend on capital development at the higher rates of interest. This reduction in American money incomes and prices will cause American imports to fall off and American exports to rise, since people will now prefer the cheaper American goods to foreign goods and since Americans will have smaller incomes to spend on imports. Moreover, the fall in American incomes from which savings can be made together with the rise in the rate of interest in America will cause a reduction in America's net lending abroad. At the same time gold will be imported and sold to the Central Banks of the foreign countries. The reserves of the foreign banks will be increased by the import of gold just as the reserves of American banks are diminished by the export of gold, and the foreign banks will be able to lower their interest rates and purchase securities, in order to increase their deposit liabilities. In consequence the rate of interest will fall in foreign countries as it rises in America, and prices and money incomes will rise in foreign countries as they fall in America. This provides a further reason why American exports should rise and her imports fall, and why the net amount lent abroad by America should fall off.

As the export of gold continues, the rate of interest rises in America and falls in foreign countries, while money incomes and prices fall and foreign money incomes and prices rise. When the consequent rise in American exports, the fall in her imports, and the diminution in her net lending abroad have together become as great as the original increase in her demand for imports which first caused the export of gold, then the normal payments of Americans to foreigners and of foreigners to Americans will balance again. The Balance of Payments will be in a new equilibrium, and the export of gold from America will cease.

We have illustrated the operation of the gold standard by supposing that a country's demand for imports increases, leading to a loss of gold by that country; but from our discussion of the Balance of Payments it follows that any change which increases the payments which it must make to foreigners or reduces the payments which foreigners must make to it, will cause a country to lose gold. The following are therefore the most important reasons why a country may lose gold:

1. A country which is on the gold standard will lose gold if there is a fall in money prices and incomes abroad unaccompanied

by a similar slump in money prices and incomes at home, or if there is a rise in money incomes and prices at home unaccompanied by a similar rise in other countries.

Let us suppose that there is a world-wide slump in money prices and incomes, causing prices everywhere to fall below costs of production and so leading to unemployment in all countries, but that America by adopting the policies suggested in Part I prevents the growth of unemployment through banking action designed to reduce interest rates, through public works expenditure, and through measures designed to stimulate directly the expenditure of money by consumers on consumption goods. The rise in American money incomes and prices relatively to money incomes and prices in foreign countries will, as we have seen, cause American imports to rise and her exports to fall, so that America will lose gold. There are two further reasons why in these circumstances America is likely to lose gold. First, if in America the rate of interest is being deliberately lowered by the banks to prevent unemployment, while the slump in money prices and incomes is continuing abroad unchecked by any similar deliberate reduction in interest rates, it will become more profitable to lend money abroad, since the rate of interest in America has fallen relatively to interest rates in other countries. For this reason America's net lending abroad will rise, which will further increase the payments to be made by America to foreign countries and so intensify the loss of gold. Secondly, as the slump develops in foreign countries America's receipts of dividend and interest from past investments in foreign countries will fall. For industries in foreign countries will become less profitable, and will pay lower dividends. If the slump in money incomes and prices abroad goes far enough, foreign businesses, municipalities, and governments may be driven into bankruptcy and so default on their payments of interest on fixed-interest securities. In as far as Americans have invested in such securities, America's receipt of dividends and interest from abroad will fall, which will increase the flow of gold from America.

2. If there is a rise in foreign tariffs or other legal restrictions placed upon the import of American goods, the value of American exports will fall; and this will cause an export of gold from America.

3. If the productivity of labor and other factors of production increases in other countries more rapidly than in America in the production of commodities which compete with American products either in the American market or in foreign markets, the cost and so the price of such foreign goods will fall more rapidly than the American price of similar goods. This will cause a fall in American exports or a rise in her imports which will lead to a loss of gold by America.

4. If the tastes of consumers in America or in other countries change so that they prefer the type of goods produced in foreign countries, America will lose gold because her imports will rise or her exports fall.

5. The imposition of a tribute, indemnity, or reparations to be paid by America to other countries would cause an increase in the amount of payments to be made by America to other countries, and would so cause America to lose gold.

6. An increase in the desire of Americans to lend money abroad, by causing an increase in the payments of money to be made to other countries, would lead to an export of gold by America. An important new invention abroad or the opening up of an undeveloped territory might cause Americans to expect abnormally large profits on money lent abroad to finance these new developments. Greater political security in other countries and a diminished sense of security in America, by increasing the safety of capital held abroad relatively to capital held in America, would cause a rise in net lending abroad.

Any of these things may cause a country to lose gold. We have already shown that a drain of gold from one country can be stopped only if the country losing gold allows its interest rates to rise and its money prices and incomes to fall, or if the countries importing gold adopt monetary policies designed to lower their rates of interest and raise their money prices and incomes. There is, however, no reason to believe that the monetary policy which a country must adopt in order to operate the gold standard will be the same as the monetary policy which is appropriate on the principles outlined in Part I to preserve a high level of employment. For money prices and incomes may fall in foreign countries, or foreign countries may raise their tariffs, at a time when unemployment is appearing at home. In these circumstances deflation of money prices and incomes is necessary to prevent an export of gold and so to maintain the gold standard, while an inflation of money prices and incomes is appropriate to prevent unemployment.

There is one way in which this conflict between the two appropriate monetary policies might be resolved. We saw in Chapter VII of Part I that it is the relationship between the money wage-rate on the one hand and the level of money incomes and prices on the other which determines the volume of employment. Unemployment can be reduced if money wage-rates are reduced relatively to money prices, since this will reduce the real wage-rate. If there is sufficient flexibility in the money wage-rate, there need be no conflict between the monetary policy designed to maintain full employment and that designed to maintain the gold standard. If, for example, a country lost gold at a time when unemployment was appearing at home, the loss of gold could be stopped by monetary action designed to reduce money incomes and prices; but this deflation would be compatible with simultaneous reduction in unemployment if the money wage-rate was reduced more quickly than the reduction in money incomes and prices. If money wage-rates always fell quickly so long as there was unemployment, the monetary authorities could concentrate on controlling the level of money incomes and prices in such a way that there was no import or export of gold, while the money wage-rate automatically adjusted itself to this level of money prices in such a way as to preserve full employment.

This is a possible solution of the conflict between monetary policies designed to preserve internal and external equilibrium; but it is not necessarily the best solution. For in a country in which there are important blocks of indebtedness fixed in terms of money, an extensive and rapid fall in prices and incomes will greatly increase the real value of these debts. If, in order to stay on the gold standard, a country with a large internal government debt lowers its money incomes, prices, and wage-rates, it will be necessary to raise the rates of taxation to meet the interest on its fixed debt; for as its money incomes fall, the tax revenue raised by the existing rate of taxation will fall, while the fixed amount to be paid by the government in interest on debt will remain unchanged.

However, in fact, money wage-rates in most communities cannot be very rapidly and extensively altered. This is particularly true of a country in which many wage-rates are fixed for long periods of time either by bargaining between employers' and workers' associations or by legislation or official boards. In such circumstances any *rapid* adjustment of money wage-rates must be ruled out as a possible solution of our problem. It will, in these circumstances, be possible to operate a gold standard successfully without causing unemployment only if the necessity for large or rapid adjustments of money prices and money wage-rates can be avoided. For this reason there are six important conditions which must be fulfilled if the gold standard is to be operated successfully in modern conditions.

1. The most essential is that the important countries on the gold standard should adopt internal policies, designed on the lines discussed in Part I, to prevent violent fluctuations in money incomes and prices. If all countries are consciously and successfully adopting internal policies to prevent serious slumps in money prices and incomes, no one of them will be faced with a sudden slump in the demand for its exports due to a fall in incomes and prices in other countries. The main reason for rapid internal deflation to preserve the gold standard will be removed. Agreement among the major countries that they will all lower

interest rates, expand the volume of money, spend more on public works, and stimulate consumers' expenditure when unemployment appears, is therefore an essential condition which must
be fulfilled before any one country can operate a gold standard
successfully without fear of unemployment at home.

By these means the necessity for violent and rapid readjustment of money prices, incomes, and wage-rates by any one
country could be avoided; but some readjustment would still be
necessary from time to time. To take a single example: the
technical efficiency of production might be increasing more rapidly in America than in England in the production of goods
which compete with English exports. In this case English exports
would fall as American prices fell relatively to English prices, and
England would lose gold. In order to remain on the gold standard England would be obliged to let her money prices fall as
American prices fell; and to prevent unemployment in England
money wage-rates would have to fall, as English prices would be
falling more quickly than the productivity of English labor was
rising. But in this case a very rapid adjustment would not be
necessary; for a fall of American costs relative to English costs
due to more rapid technical progress in America would be relatively slow, when compared with a fall of American prices relatively to English prices which was caused by an uncontrolled
slump of all money prices and incomes in America.

2. Since some adjustment of money prices and costs will still
be necessary, the second condition for the effective operation of
the gold standard is that countries losing gold should allow their
money incomes and prices to fall, while countries receiving gold
should allow their money incomes and prices to rise. We have
already argued that an export of gold from a country will cause
a fall in money incomes and prices in that country by restricting
the cash reserves of the banks, and that an import of gold will
cause a rise in internal money prices and incomes. It is, however,
possible for the Treasury or the Central Bank to prevent these
effects of gold movements. If the Central Bank of a country

which is losing gold purchases securities in the open market, this, as we saw in Part I, Chapter III (pp. 26-7), will in itself cause a rise in the cash reserves of the ordinary banks, so that by purchasing securities in the market a Central Bank can prevent an export of gold from causing any reduction in the reserves of the ordinary banks. And similarly, by selling securities in the open market a Central Bank can prevent an import of gold from increasing the ordinary banks' cash reserves.[1] It is essential that the Central Banks should not offset gold movements in this way. If they do so, there will be no fall in prices in the country losing gold and no rise in prices in the countries receiving gold, so that the gold movement will be unchecked and sooner or later the country losing gold will be driven off the gold standard. Indeed, it may be desirable for the Central Banks to adopt the opposite policy and to accentuate the effects of gold movements by selling securities when they lose gold and purchasing securities when they receive gold. It is important that the countries gaining gold should inflate their money incomes and prices; for unless they do so, the whole readjustment must be achieved by a deflation of money incomes and prices in the country losing gold, which deflation must be so much the greater. The gold standard can be expected to work effectively only if a movement of gold from one country to another is met partly by a deliberate inflation in the country gaining gold, and partly by a deliberate deflation in the country losing gold.

3. In order that any deflation of money prices necessary to prevent an export of gold shall not cause unemployment, money wage-rates must be lowered as money prices fall; and in order that any necessary inflation of prices should not lead to an excess of profits, money wage-rates must be raised as prices rise. A coun-

---

1. The same result is achieved if the Treasury buys gold when it is imported and places it in an 'inactive' account; i.e. does not deposit with the Federal Reserve Banks an equivalent amount of the gold certificates which serve as the Reserve Banks' reserves: and sells gold for export from this same inactive account. This is the method which has been used in America since 1936.

try should, therefore, be unwilling to operate the gold standard if there is not sufficient flexibility of money wage-rates to meet all the readjustments that will be necessary.

4. When a country is on the gold standard, the Central Bank of that country must have certain reserves of gold. For it must be able to meet any demand for gold on the part of people who wish to export gold. There are various legal provisions in different countries regulating the minimum gold reserve which the Central Bank must hold. Of these the two most important are the Proportional Reserve system, which is in operation in America and France among other countries, and was discussed in Part I, Chapter III (p. 26), and the Fiduciary Issue system, which is in operation in England. With the Fixed Fiduciary Issue system the Central Bank is only allowed to issue notes equal in value to the gold held by the Bank plus a certain fixed amount of notes backed by other assets. With the Proportional Reserve system the Central Bank must hold a minimum gold reserve equal in value to a certain proportion of its note issue, or of its deposit liabilities and its note issue (e.g. as in the United States, 40 per cent of its note issue and 35 per cent of its deposit liabilities).

In any case the Central Bank must hold a certain minimum gold reserve, which is related in some way to its note issue or to the total value of its liabilities in the form of notes and deposits. The Central Bank must be able to meet all possible demands for gold for export; and the amount of gold which it must hold for this purpose depends upon the total volume of monetary transactions undertaken. For the larger the volume of monetary transactions undertaken, the greater is the possible fluctuation in any figure in the Balance of Payments and so the greater the possible demand for gold to meet a disturbance in the Balance of Payments. In order, therefore, that the gold standard should operate successfully, the total supply of gold reserves available for all the Central Banks of the countries on the gold standard must be sufficient to form an adequate backing against that volume of monetary transactions which is necessary to prevent a world-wide slump in money prices and incomes.

Let us suppose that throughout the world capital is being accumulated and the population is growing, so that the output of goods and services is increasing. To obtain full employment of the factors of production it may be necessary for money incomes and expenditure to increase as real output increases, in order to prevent the prices of commodities falling below their costs. In these circumstances the volume of money in all countries, and therefore the note issue and the deposit liabilities of the Central Banks, must be increasing. If on the average an increase of 2 per cent per annum in Central Banks' note issues and deposit liabilities is just sufficient to prevent unemployment on the one hand, or boom conditions on the other, their gold reserves should also be increasing at a rate of 2 per cent per annum. It may so happen that the output of new gold is just sufficient for this purpose. But if the output of gold is less than sufficient, unemployment will not be avoided unless money wage-rates can be reduced appropriately. But if money wage-rates are not very flexible, some means must be found of adjusting the total stock of gold reserves to the requirements necessary to preserve a high level of employment throughout the world.

The Central Banks can to some extent meet this difficulty by alterations in the proportion between their total liabilities and their gold reserves. If the output of gold is too small, the Central Banks of the different countries in co-operation might diminish the proportion of their liabilities which they cover with gold reserves. This will enable them to adopt monetary policies which preserve full employment. It may of course involve an alteration in the legal limits below which their reserves are not allowed to fall. There are, however, limits to the possible reduction in the reserve proportion of any Central Bank. It must not fall below a minimum which is necessary to enable the Central Bank to meet any possible demands upon it for gold.

In the second place the difficulty can be met by an extension of the gold exchange standard. If a Central Bank holds part of its reserves in the form of the money of some foreign country deposited with a foreign bank, this reserve is as useful as gold in meeting any demand for foreign money to make payments abroad, and so economizes in the total amount of gold. Suppose that the rate of exchange between the pound and the dollar is £1 for $5, and that the Bank of England keeps £100 worth of its reserves in the form of $500 deposited in an American bank. If this American bank holds gold reserves of only 10 per cent against its deposit liabilities, then $50 (or £10) worth of actual gold is acting as a gold reserve of £100 for the Bank of England.

There is, however, a danger in the extension of the gold exchange standard. Suppose that a country which is operating the gold exchange standard loses reserves to another country. Then instead of selling gold for export, which would reduce the gold reserves of the first and increase the gold reserves of the second country, the Central Bank of the first country may sell part of its deposit in the second country to those who wish to make larger payments to the second country. This will cause the reserves of the Central Bank of the first country to fall, but will not cause any increase in the reserves of the Central Bank of the second country; for there is no import of gold into that country but simply a change in ownership of some of the deposit liabilities of the ordinary banks of that country. There will therefore be a reduction in the total volume of Central Bank reserves, and the whole of the adjustment must be brought about by a deflation of money incomes and prices in the country operating the gold exchange standard. Conversely, if an increase takes place in the payments made to a country which is on the gold exchange standard, the Central Bank of that country will increase its reserves by holding more money on deposit in the other country, but there will be no export of gold from the country making the payment. In this case the whole adjustment in the Balance of Payments must be brought about by an inflation of money prices and incomes in the country on the gold exchange standard. There is therefore a danger of a general deflation of money prices and incomes when countries on the gold exchange standard lose reserves, and a danger of a general inflation of money prices and incomes when countries on the gold exchange standard gain reserves.

This difficulty could be met if the countries operated a gold exchange standard but kept their reserves in the form of deposits with a single International Bank. Suppose that the Bank of England and the American Federal Reserve Banks deposited all their gold with the Bank for International Settlements in Basle, and counted these deposits of Swiss francs of a fixed gold value as their gold reserves. Then if England lost reserves to America, the deposits of the Bank of England with the Bank for International Settlements would fall, but at the same time there would be a rise in the reserves of the Federal Reserve Banks in the form of extra deposits with the Bank for International Settlements. The necessary readjustment would therefore fall partly on England and partly on America. At the same time the Bank for International Settlements could control the total volume of Central Bank reserves by buying securities from or selling securities to the different Central Banks. Suppose, for example, that in order to prevent a world-wide slump it was necessary to increase the total volume of gold reserves by 10 per cent. The Bank for International Settlements could purchase an amount of securities from the Bank of England equal in value to 10 per cent of the Bank of England's reserves and could pay for these securities by increasing its deposit liability to the Bank of England. By a similar purchase of securities from the Federal Reserve Banks and the Central Banks of the other countries on the gold standard, the total value of Central Bank reserves could be raised by 10 per cent.

This is probably the simplest method of controlling the total volume of gold reserves; but there is a third method, which might be preferred. If there was a shortage of gold reserves, all the Central Banks might agree to raise their fixed buying and selling prices of gold by the same proportion. Suppose that an ounce of gold is bought and sold by the Bank of England at the fixed price of £4 and by the American Federal Reserve Banks for $20. Then the par rate of exchange between the pound and dollar is fixed at £1 for $5. Suppose that the Bank of England raised its fixed buying and selling price of gold by 25 per cent from £4 to £5 an ounce, and that the Federal Reserve Banks at the same time raised their buying and selling price of gold by 25 per cent from $20 to $25 an ounce. The par rate of exchange between the pound and dollar would remain unchanged at £1 for $5, so that the main advantage of the gold standard, namely the fixity of the rates of exchange between the currencies of the countries on the gold standard, would be preserved. But the nominal value of the gold reserves both of England and America would be raised by 25 per cent in terms of pounds and dollars, and this would enable the English and American banking systems to expand the total amount of money in the way required to prevent a world-wide slump in money prices and incomes.

This revaluation of the gold value of the pound and the dollar would provide a money profit to the Central Banks or Treasuries. If, for example, the U.S. Treasury held $5 billions of gold reserves, these reserves would become worth $6¼ billions if the buying and selling price of gold was raised from $20 to $25 an ounce. The government could use this extra sum for extra expenditure not covered by taxation; and the expenditure of this sum would in itself help to prevent the fall in money incomes and prices which it was the object of the revaluation to avoid.

In a similar way, if the total value of Central Bank reserves became too large to prevent a world-wide boom, the Central Banks and Treasuries might reduce their buying and selling prices of gold simultaneously by the same percentage. This would reduce the gold stocks of the banks valued in terms of pounds and dollars, and so would cause the necessary contraction. The loss, which in this case would be caused by the fall in the value of their gold reserves, should in each country be met by the government; and the necessary reduction in expenditure or rise in taxation would itself aid the desired fall in money incomes and prices.

5. If the gold standard is to work successfully, appropriate rates of exchange between the different currencies must be chosen. This consideration is of vital importance when countries are intending to return to the gold standard. For example, suppose that at a rate of exchange of $5 for £1 the American Balance of Payments is in equilibrium. Suppose, however, that America is not on the gold standard, while England is on the gold standard at a buying and selling price of gold of £5 an ounce; if then America returned to the gold standard at a fixed buying and selling price of gold at $20 an ounce, the rate of exchange would be fixed at £1 for $4. Since America's Balance of Payments was in equilibrium at £1 for $5, America would now lose gold; for at the rate of exchange of £1 for $4 American goods and services would be too expensive in England and English goods and services would be too cheap in America. In order to preserve the gold standard at the rate of exchange of £1 for $4, American prices and incomes would have to be reduced relatively to English prices and incomes. If before America's return to the gold standard both countries had that internal level of interest rates, prices, and incomes which just preserved full employment, this would involve deflation and unemployment in America or a profit boom in England. If the English monetary authorities prevented any import of gold into England from leading to a rise in prices and incomes there, the necessary deflation in America would be so much the more severe. Unless wage-rates could be rapidly reduced in America, a prolonged period of unemployment would begin. In returning to the gold standard countries must choose those rates of exchange at which the Balance of Payments between them will be in equilibrium when their internal prices are so adjusted to their money costs of production that there is full employment.

The criterion therefore for the correct rates of exchange is to be found simply in the Balance of Payments. With those interest rates, money prices, and money incomes which give a country internal equilibrium, there will be one rate of exchange between its currency and other currencies which will enable its Balance of Payments to balance without gold movements. A higher value of its currency in terms of foreign currencies will cause a drain on its reserves; a lower value for its currency will cause a drain on other countries' reserves. If a number of countries wish to return to the gold standard at a time when they are not already in internal equilibrium the method of trial and error alone can be used to find the appropriate buying and selling price of gold and so the appropriate rates at which the exchanges should be stabilized. The authorities in consultation must fix upon certain rates of exchange, which they think are appropriate, and must then *temporarily* fix their buying and selling prices of gold at figures which give these chosen rates of exchange. The monetary authorities can then continue with their internal policies which are designed to preserve a high level of employment at home. If there is a steady drain of gold from country A and a steady import of gold into country B, this is a sign that the currency of country A has too high a value in terms of other currencies, while that of country B has too low a value. Country A must raise and country B must lower its buying and selling price of gold by an amount which is judged sufficient to stop the steady flow of gold. By readjustments of the rate of exchange of this kind, a final rate of exchange for each currency could be obtained which would put each country both in internal equilibrium and in equilibrium with the other countries.

6. If a country receives a large amount of interest or of reparations from abroad, its Balance of Payments will be in equilibrium only if it lends more abroad than it borrows from abroad or if it imports from abroad more than it exports. A creditor country, if it is not willing to lend sufficient abroad, must import more than it exports. There is in many people's minds a fallacious belief that a country is better off if it has a 'favorable' balance of trade or an excess of exports over imports than if it has an excess

of imports over exports; but the only real advantage to a nation from interest or other such receipts from abroad is that it can obtain some part of its imports without exporting any goods or services in return for them. If countries work on the hypothesis that an 'unfavorable' balance of trade is always undesirable, creditor countries will raise tariffs, quotas, and prohibitions on imports and will subsidize their exports, so long as their balance of trade is unfavorable. But this must result either in a continual flow of gold from the debtor to the creditor countries, since the debtors are unable to export more than they import by reason of the tariff policy of the creditor countries, or else in a repudiation of their indebtedness by the debtor countries. If international debts are not to be repudiated, the creditor countries must adopt a tariff policy which allows an excess of imports over exports in order to receive payment of that part of their interest which they do not wish to lend abroad again. This is true whether the countries are on the gold standard or not; but the gold standard will certainly break down if the tariff policy of the creditor countries causes a continued loss of gold reserves by the debtor countries to meet the interest on their indebtedness. This argument does not prove that there must be a complete absence of tariffs for the gold standard to work, but simply that the tariffs of the creditor countries must not be so raised as to make it impossible for the debtor countries to export more than they import. The pros and cons of tariffs on other grounds will be argued in Chapter V of this Part.

III

FREE EXCHANGE RATES

If any of the six conditions discussed in the last chapter are not fulfilled, the gold standard cannot be successfully operated; and in these circumstances a country should retain an independent monetary standard. We must therefore consider the way in which the Balance of Payments is adjusted in the case of countries which are not on an international monetary standard. Suppose that the American legal money is simply the Federal Reserve note, and that neither the Treasury nor the Reserve Banks are under any obligation to buy and sell gold at a fixed price in terms of these notes. In these circumstances the rate of exchange between the dollar and the pound is no longer fixed within any prescribed limits. The only way to obtain dollars for pounds or pounds for dollars is to exchange the dollar notes or deposits directly for pound notes or deposits; and there are no longer any fixed gold import or export points to prevent a wide fluctuation in the rate of exchange between the pound and the dollar.

To show how the Balance of Payments is adjusted in these conditions we may suppose again that all exchange dealings take place through a number of exchange dealers, who hold deposits of pounds in English banks and deposits of dollars in American banks, and who exchange dollar deposits for pound deposits for people who wish to make payments between the two countries. Let us suppose that the rate at which the exchange dealers are exchanging dollars for pounds and pounds for dollars is £1 for $5, and that at this rate of exchange the total amount of pounds which Americans wish to purchase with dollars is just equal to the total amount of pounds which English people wish to sell for dollars. Then the Balance of Payments is in equilibrium; and the balances of dollars and of pounds held by the exchange dealers

344

will remain unchanged, since the exchange of dollars for pounds by Americans will just offset the exchange of pounds for dollars by Englishmen. If Englishmen then decided to spend £10 millions a week more on American goods, the amount of pounds offered to the exchange dealers by Englishmen to obtain dollars would be £10 millions in excess of the amount of pounds bought from exchange dealers by Americans each week. As long as the rate of exchange remained £1 to $5, the exchange dealers' holding of pounds would increase by £10 millions a week, and their holding of dollars would diminish by $50 millions a week. The Balance of Payments still balances; English imports have risen by £10 millions a week, but the amount lent to England has also risen by £10 millions a week, since the exchange dealers themselves are moving £10 millions worth of their capital from dollars to pounds each week.

As long as this continues, the exchange dealers' holding of pounds will continue to increase and their holding of dollars to diminish, and they must take steps to prevent their dollar balances from dwindling to nothing. They will offer less dollars per pound, in order to stop part of the English demand for dollars, and the rate of exchange will move from £1 for $5 to—let us say—£1 for $4. As the value of the pound depreciates in terms of dollars, American goods will become more expensive in England, since less dollars can be obtained for a pound, and English goods will become cheaper in America, since a pound can be obtained with less dollars. In consequence English imports will diminish and English exports will increase. The value of the pound will continue to depreciate so long as the demand for dollars with pounds is in excess of the demand for pounds with dollars; for so long as this is so, the exchange dealers will be increasing their holdings of pounds and will be running short of dollar balances. But there will come a point in the depreciation of the exchange value of the pound at which English imports have diminished and English exports have increased just sufficiently to equate the total amount of pounds bought by Americans to the total amount of pounds sold by Englishmen. At this point the Balance of Payments will again be in equilibrium. This readjustment can come about without any change in money incomes and prices or in interest rates in England or in America; the depreciation of the exchange value of the pound is itself sufficient to adjust the Balance of Payments.

A country which is not on the gold standard will therefore be free to concentrate upon its internal monetary policy in order to preserve a high level of employment, and can leave the exchange rate with other countries to find that level at which the payments and receipts in its Balance of Payments are equal. While this should be the essential principle of policy for any country which is not on the gold standard, some control over its Balance of Payments would still be desirable.

If a country's exchange rate with other countries is not fixed, some control should be exercised over the movement of short-term funds between it and other countries. The reason for this can be shown by an illustration. Suppose that the existing rate of exchange between the pound and dollar is £1 for $5, but that people expect the dollar to depreciate from $5 to $6 to £1; due, let us say, to the fact that a slump was developing in England, while it was known to be the policy in America to prevent any fall in money prices and incomes. So long as people expect this depreciation in the value of the dollar, there is a profit to be made by exchanging dollars for pounds at £1 for $5 in order to purchase dollars with pounds in the near future at £1 for $6. But this purchase of pounds with dollars in order to move short-term funds abroad will in itself cause the dollar to depreciate in value, and this will have two undesirable effects. In the first place, because speculators are attempting to anticipate future events, it will cause the dollar to depreciate *before* the fall in prices and incomes in England has made the exchange depreciation necessary to adjust the other items in the Balance of Payments. And secondly, it may cause the dollar to depreciate much more than is really necessary to adjust the other items in the Balance of

Payments. While a depreciation of the dollar from $5 to $5½ to £1 may be all that is necessary to preserve equilibrium in America's Balance of Payments, the speculative movement of funds into pounds may cause the dollar to depreciate to $6 to £1, because people overestimate the extent to which English prices and incomes will fall or the extent to which the dollar must depreciate to maintain equilibrium in face of a given fall in English prices. The exchange depreciation should be controlled in such a way that it is neither more rapid nor more extensive than is necessary to adjust the normal item in the Balance of Payments to the changed conditions. For any unnecessary depreciation in the exchange value of a country's money will raise unnecessarily the price of imported goods, and so will reduce the real wage-rate and the standard of living below what is necessary to preserve full employment. If the price of foreign goods is falling, a depreciation in the exchange value of a country's currency which is just sufficient to offset the fall in foreign prices will not lower the standard of living at home; the fact that fewer pounds can be obtained for a given number of dollars will be offset by the fact that the pound will buy more English goods. But if there is a rapid depreciation in the exchange value of the dollar caused by the speculative movement of short-term funds from dollars to pounds, the exchange value of the dollar will depreciate before pound prices fall, and the amount of English goods which can be purchased with a dollar will fall.

A second reason for avoiding a speculative movement of funds abroad is that it will intensify unnecessarily the slump in prices and incomes in other countries. If an internal monetary policy is being adopted in America to preserve full employment, a depreciation of the exchange value of the dollar sufficient to offset any fall in English prices and incomes is necessary to allow this policy to be successfully carried out. But if there is a large movement of short-term funds from America to England the exchange value of the pound must depreciate more than this; the price of American goods in England will fall more quickly than the price of English goods, and the price of English goods in America will rise. In consequence American goods will compete more strongly with English goods both in English and American markets. The consequent increase in American exports and fall in her imports is necessary in order to finance the movement of short-term funds to England; but it is unnecessary in order to preserve full employment in America, since full employment is being preserved by the American internal monetary policy. In England, however, the slump will be intensified, because English producers will lose part of their markets to American producers. If, however, the speculative movement of short-term funds to England were avoided, American goods would not compete any more strongly with English goods, and the slump in England would not be intensified.

When one country alone is successfully adopting an internal monetary policy designed to preserve a high level of employment, there is a strong case for the control by it of the amount of capital lent abroad on long-term as well as of the movement of short-term funds. Suppose that the long-term rate of interest in America and in England is 5 per cent and that a slump starts in both countries. If America by her monetary policy reduces the rate to 3 per cent to avoid the slump, while England does not reduce the rate from 5 per cent and suffers a slump in consequence, there will be an increase in the purchase of pounds with dollars due to the sale of American securities with a 3 per cent yield in order to purchase English securities with a 5 per cent yield.[1] This increase in long-term foreign lending will have the

---

1. This is true in the case of individuals who buy and hold securities as an *investment* on the basis of their yield. Those who buy securities as a *speculation* in order to realize a gain or avoid a loss in their capital value would tend, in this case, to sell English securities and buy American. For the capital value of many English securities—all except 'gilt-edge'—would fall as a result of the depression; whereas the capital value of American securities would tend to rise because of the fall in the rate of interest. This speculative movement of capital to the more prosperous country might be of greater magnitude than the movement of capital seeking investment where rates of interest are higher. But a net movement in either direction which is unjustified by the underlying long-run factors has the disadvantages which have been pointed out on the two preceding pages.

same effects as the increase in short-term foreign lending, which we have just examined. To finance the increased lending abroad American exports must rise and her imports fall, and to bring this about the pound will depreciate to an extent more than sufficient to offset the fall in English prices and incomes. This will cause an unnecessary fall in the American real wage-rate, and by enabling American goods to compete on better terms with English goods will intensify the slump in England. We shall argue in Chapter VI of this Part that from the international point of view capital should always be allowed to flow from a country in which its real yield is low to one in which its real yield is high. But the free movement of capital from a country in which the real yield on capital is low to a country in which monetary policy has failed to lower the rate of interest in conformity with the true yield on new capital development, will merely lower standards of living by raising the price of imports in the first and by intensifying the slump in the second country.

The principles upon which any control of capital movements should be exercised are clear. All movements of short-term funds which are taking place simply to profit from expected alterations in the rate of exchange should be prevented. It will be the duty of the monetary authority which is exercising the control to judge what movements of short-term funds fall into this category. In the case of long-term capital movements the criterion is somewhat more difficult. The object should be to prevent any flow of capital which is not justified by differences in the long-term interest rates which would rule if all countries were following the policy of avoiding unemployment by the methods outlined in Part I. Movements of long-term capital caused either by the prospect of speculative profits from increases in the capital values of securities, or by temporary differences in interest rates due to one country attempting to prevent unemployment which would otherwise occur during a world slump, or by panic, should be prevented. In practice the decision must be somewhat arbitrary.

The net amount lent abroad by any country, and thereby, in the absence of the gold standard, the exchange value of its currency, can be controlled by means of an Exchange Stabilization Fund. Such a Fund, in order to function successfully, must have in its possession a considerable quantity of both the domestic and foreign currencies; or assets, such as gold, which can be converted into either. When there is an international capital movement which it desires to offset, the Fund simply initiates an equal and opposite movement, and thus prevents the exchange value of its currency from being affected. Thus, if there was a speculative movement of capital to America, an American Fund could use its dollars to buy foreign currencies. If the movement were out of America into foreign currencies, the Fund could use its francs and pounds, say, to buy dollars.

The American Exchange Stabilization Fund, which initially consisted of $2 billions, was financed from the profits resulting from the revaluation of the gold stocks held by the Treasury in 1934. The Fund is in a somewhat anomalous position in a country on the gold bullion standard, since the value of the dollar on the foreign exchanges in terms of other gold standard currencies is fixed; but it can be used in the event of an unwelcome flow of capital between America and some other country with an inconvertible currency, for the value of the dollar in terms of this currency would be affected by capital movements. The Exchange Stabilization Fund was not intended to prevent an appreciation or depreciation of the dollar which was due to fundamental changes in the Balance of Payments; it was intended simply to prevent speculative short-term movement of funds from causing unnecessary movements in the exchange rates.

This method of control is subject to two criticisms. In the first place the government risks losing considerable sums on the exchange operations involved. Suppose that to offset a movement of funds to America the Fund bought pounds at $6 for £1, when the equilibrium rate of exchange was near this figure. If subsequently prices and incomes rise in England so that the equilibrium rate of exchange moves to \$5 for £1 and the Fund then has to sell pounds for dollars to offset a movement of funds from America, the Fund will lose. The Fund will make a profit if it has to buy pounds when they are cheap and to sell them when they are expensive in terms of dollars. But if speculators are intelligent in their expectations of the way in which the equilibrium rate of exchange is likely to change, the Fund is bound to make a loss: for speculators will move funds from a currency that will depreciate to one that will appreciate, and in order to prevent an alteration in the rate of exchange before it is necessary, the Fund must purchase the currency that is about to depreciate in value.

A more serious criticism of this method of control is that it cannot be effective if there is a very considerable movement of short-term funds. If the Fund is holding only \$1 billion worth of foreign money and gold at a time when people wish to move more than \$1 billion of short-term funds abroad, the Fund cannot prevent this movement of short-term funds from having some effect upon the rate of exchange. For when it has sold all its foreign money and gold it can exercise no further control. If it is certain that America by her internal policy will prevent her prices and money incomes from falling, and if a considerable slump has started abroad, it will be certain that the dollar will sooner or later depreciate considerably. In these circumstances the amount of funds moved abroad might be very large, and the Fund might not hold sufficient foreign money to prevent the dollar from depreciating more quickly than was necessary to preserve equilibrium in the normal items in the Balance of Payments.

The only certain method of controlling the volume of foreign lending is by the monopolization of exchange dealings in a country's currency—both at home and in foreign markets—in the hands of some central monetary authority, such as the Central Bank. If this method were adopted in America, the Federal Reserve Banks would hold a reserve of foreign money or of gold which could be sold for foreign money, and would then fix a rate of exchange between the dollar and foreign money which it con-

sidered would put the American Balance of Payments in equilibrium if there were no speculative movements of short-term funds.
At this rate of exchange it would allow the purchase and sale of
foreign money in unrestricted amounts for the purposes of import and export of goods and services, for the payment of interest
on debt, tourist expenditure, and all other current items in the
Balance of Payments. But it could disallow any purchase or sale
of foreign money for the movement of short-term funds or for
'abnormal' movements of long-term capital. If it had in fact
chosen the correct rate of exchange, it would then find that the
amount of dollars which it received from customers desiring to
purchase foreign money for approved purposes was just equal to
the amount of dollars which it paid out to foreigners wishing to
purchase dollars for approved purposes. Its holding of foreign
money would therefore be unchanged. If, however, it had fixed
the exchange value of the dollar at too high a figure, its customers
would purchase fewer dollars from it for foreign money than they
sold to it for foreign money, and its balances of foreign money
would fall. In these circumstances it would revise the fixed rate
of exchange and would offer less foreign money per dollar. The
Central Bank would concentrate on its internal policy, would
allow all purchases and sales of foreign money for approved purposes, and by a process of trial and error would adjust the rate of
exchange with other currencies to the rate which kept the Balance of approved Payments in equilibrium.

To make the control of capital movements complete, further
powers would be necessary besides the monopolization of foreign
exchange dealings in the hands of a single authority; for there are
certain ways in which people can move funds abroad without
purchasing foreign currencies. An American who obtains his income in foreign money can lend money abroad by refraining from
purchasing dollars with this money. American exporters or American owners of foreign securities can lend money abroad by refraining from purchasing dollars with the foreign money obtained
from the sale of their goods or received as interest on their capital.

In order to control the volume of foreign lending the central monetary authority must have the legal power to force such persons to sell this foreign money to it for dollars at the current rate of exchange. Information about the income received from foreign sources should not be impossible to obtain. For the customs authorities can inform the relevant authority of the value of all goods exported. And the income tax authorities for the purpose of taxing income derived from foreign investments already collect information about the foreign securities owned by Americans.

If a country which is not on the gold standard has to face an unemployment problem at home, it can raise its money incomes and prices by the means discussed in Part I. If other countries are not at the same time adopting a similar policy of internal expansion, this will cause some increase in its imports from abroad and some fall in its exports, unless the exchange value of its currency depreciates sufficiently to offset the rise in its prices and incomes. We have argued that countries which are not on the gold standard should attempt to cure unemployment at home by these means, and should allow the exchange value of their currencies to depreciate by an amount just sufficient to keep their Balance of Payments in equilibrium. Such a policy will have no adverse effects upon the trade of other countries; for if America, for example, allows the exchange value of the dollar to depreciate as American prices and money incomes rise, this will not restrict the markets of other countries. The exchange depreciation of the dollar will only prevent an increase in American imports and a fall in her exports which would otherwise have occurred because of the rise in her internal prices and incomes.

But a country which was not on the gold standard might attempt to cure unemployment by depreciating the exchange value of its currency by more than was necessary to offset any rise in its internal prices and incomes, in order thereby to increase its exports and to restrict its imports so that it obtained markets at the expense of foreign countries. Suppose that the American Balance of Payments is in equilibrium, but that America depreciates the exchange value of the dollar without at the same time raising her prices and incomes at home by internal monetary expansion. The money demand for American goods will increase, because foreigners will buy more American exports and because Americans will buy less foreign and more home-produced goods. This increase in expenditure on American goods will cause their price to rise and employment will increase in America both in the exporting industries and in the industries which produce goods previously imported. Such a depreciation in America's exchange rate might be brought about in a number of ways. The Exchange Stabilization Fund might purchase foreign currencies with dollars, although there was no movement of short-term funds to offset. This is equivalent to a movement of short-term funds abroad manipulated by the American government in order to depreciate the exchange value of the dollar. Or if America were on the gold standard, by raising the buying and selling price of gold in terms of dollars at a time when her Balance of Payments is already in equilibrium she could depreciate the exchange value of the dollar in such a way that her favorable Balance of Trade increased.[1] The expansion in American exports and contraction in her imports would in this case be financed by an import of gold. This flow of gold must in the end be stopped by a rise in American money prices and incomes and by a fall in money prices and incomes in other countries; and in this case America will have achieved an expansion of her own internal purchasing power at the expense of a similar fall of purchasing power in other countries.

It is not to be denied that such action can ameliorate unemployment in America, if other countries do not retaliate. But there are three reasons why this method of curing unemployment should be avoided. First, it will almost certainly be made ineffec-

---

1. This is the method which America employed during the latter part of 1933 when the buying price of gold was progressively raised by presidential proclamations. It did not prove immediately and fully effective in depreciating the value of the dollar on the foreign exchanges because the Treasury was under no obligation to buy all gold offered at the official price.

tive by foreign retaliation. If America begins by such methods to depreciate its exchange rate and thus floods the world markets with its exports and restricts its market for imports, other countries will almost certainly retaliate by devaluing their currencies (i.e. by raising their buying and selling prices of gold), or by setting up Exchange Stabilization Funds to depreciate their currencies as quickly as, or more quickly than, America, or by imposing special tariffs on American goods. In this case there will be no net extension of the markets for American goods. Secondly, if retaliation does not take place and America does succeed in diminishing unemployment by this means, there will be an unnecessarily large fall in the American real wage-rate. For the method consists in raising the price of imported goods by depreciating the exchange value of the dollar without any primary rise in its own money incomes to offset the rise in the price of imports. Thirdly, if the method is successful, it will cure unemployment in America at the expense of creating unemployment in other countries. For the increase in American exports and fall in her imports will take place at the expense of the markets for foreign products. For these reasons each country should meet its unemployment problem by internal monetary expansion and by allowing only that depreciation in the exchange value of its currency which is necessary to preserve equilibrium in its Balance of Payments, rather than by measures designed to manipulate an increase in its favorable Balance of Trade, which may enable it to expand at the expense of other countries.

INTERNATIONAL TRADE

WE have now to examine the theory of international trade in order to see how such trade should be regulated. The theory of trade between nations differs from the theory of trade within a nation for a number of reasons, the most important being that in the case of internal trade the factors of production may be expected sooner or later to move to those districts and occupations in which the rewards are highest, whereas the movement of the factors of production between nations is not free. The movement of labor between nations is hindered not only by the cost of such movement, but also by language barriers and ties of sentiment. The movement of capital between nations is less restricted; but it is to some extent because of ignorance on the part of investors and because the ownership of capital in a foreign land involves greater risks.

In Part II it was argued that the best distribution of resources among different occupations in a single community was that which would make the value of the marginal product of each factor the same in every occupation. If there were free movement of factors between nations, there would be nothing more to add. Factors of production should move from those nations in which the value of their marginal products was low to those nations in which it was high. But if the factors of production cannot move freely while their products can be imported and exported we have to decide how the factors of production can be distributed among different occupations within a nation in order to achieve the greatest advantage from international trade in commodities.

In discussing the way in which the maximum advantage can be obtained from international trade we must distinguish between the 'national' optimum and the 'international' optimum.

The 'national' optimum will be achieved when any country is adopting that trade policy which maximizes its income, regardless of the effects on other countries. The 'international' optimum is achieved only when each country is adopting that policy which maximizes the income to be obtained from international trade, regardless of the distribution of this income between the different nations. It is not suggested that there is always necessarily a conflict between the policy which will achieve the national and that which will achieve the international optimum; but one of the main problems of this and the following chapter will be to see in which conditions these two optima conflict.

Let us start then by discussing how any one country can obtain the national optimum advantage from international trade. Suppose that in America the marginal cost of producing a yard of cloth is 10 cents and the marginal cost of producing a pint of wine is 40 cents. This means that America by producing 1 less pint of wine can release factors valued at 40 cents, and can therefore produce 4 more yards of cloth. Suppose that in France a yard of cloth is sold for 4 francs and a pint of wine is also sold for 4 francs; this means that by selling 1 more yard of cloth in France enough money can be obtained to purchase 1 pint of wine. *And let us suppose at first that these prices in France will be unaffected by any trading policy which America may adopt.* We shall modify this assumption below (pp. 361 and 368ff.). It follows then that if America gives up the production of 1 pint of wine in order to produce 4 yards of cloth, she can sell these 4 yards of cloth in France and obtain thereby sufficient French money to purchase 4 pints of wine. By this means America can obtain 3 extra pints of wine. In such circumstances she should concentrate on the production of cloth and obtain her wine by import from France; for she can obtain more wine by this means than by using some of her factors at home to produce wine instead of cloth.

This does not necessarily mean that America should abandon the production of wine entirely. For as she produces more cloth and less wine the marginal cost of producing cloth is likely to rise

and that of producing wine is likely to fall. If the marginal cost
of producing cloth has risen to 25c. and of producing wine has
fallen to 25c., and if the price in France of cloth and wine has remained 4 francs, she can only obtain 1 pint of wine for each yard
of cloth exported. In these circumstances there is no gain to be
derived from any further movement of the factors from producing wine to producing cloth. It can be seen from this that—always assuming relative prices abroad to be unaffected by her
policy—America will obtain the maximum advantage from international trade if the factors of production in America are distributed among the production of the different importable and
exportable commodities in such a way that the ratio between
the marginal costs of these commodities in America is the same
as the ratio between the prices of these commodities in foreign
markets.

If there is perfect competition in America and if America
adopts a free-trade policy, this condition will be fulfilled. In conditions of perfect competition commodities will sell at prices
which are equal to their marginal costs of production, as we have
shown in Chapter I of Part II. Therefore, if the marginal cost of
wine were four times as great as the marginal cost of cloth in
America, while the price of French wine was the same as the
price of French cloth, cloth would be exported from America to
obtain wine from France. An American merchant could sell a
yard of cloth in France for the price of a pint of wine, and could
then sell this pint of wine in America for the price of 4 yards of
cloth. Such trade would be continued until the ratio between
the prices of cloth and wine in America—and so also the ratio
between their respective marginal costs in America—was the
same as the ratio between the prices of cloth and wine in France.
Whether the two countries are on the gold standard or on independent monetary standards, it will pay Americans to export
cloth and import wine as long as the ratio between the cost of
cloth and the cost of wine in America is higher than the ratio
between the price of wine and the price of cloth in France.

This fundamental advantage from international trade can be obtained by America even if there is not perfect competition in the American economy. The essential thing is that different commodities be sold in America at prices which are proportional to their marginal costs of production; and this can be achieved, as we saw in Chapters VII and VIII of Part II, in the absence of perfect competition by some form of public control of industry. So long as commodities are selling in America at prices which are proportional to their marginal costs, America can obtain the full advantages of international trade by exporting commodities so long as the foreign price is higher than the American marginal cost of producing them, and by allowing the free import of commodities so long as the foreign price is lower than the American marginal cost of producing them.

It is important in this connection to make perfectly clear what a 'free-trade' policy involves. If steps have been taken to secure perfect competition within the country, free trade will result from an international trade policy of *laisser-faire*. But 'free trade,' in our sense, is equally possible where marginal costs have been equated to prices by placing industries under the control of public corporations, as outlined in Chapter VIII of Part II. The free-trade principle applied to nationalized industries involves:

(1) allowing consumers to purchase freely from abroad;
(2) the sale by nationalized industries of their products at the same prices at home and in foreign markets; i.e. at prices equal to marginal costs; and
(3) the purchase by nationalized industries of their raw materials from home or abroad according as the home or foreign price is the lower.

The final requirement of a free-trade policy, whether perfect competition rules internally or industries have been placed under monopolistic public corporations, is that the adjustment of the money exchange rate with other countries, or the raising or lowering of all money prices and wage-rates at home, be done in accordance with the principles discussed in the last two chapters, until with the free import and export of commodities the Balance of Payments is in equilibrium.

If all these things are done, there will only be equilibrium when the factors of production in America have moved to the production of those commodities from which consumers' needs can be best satisfied whether by internal or international trade.

This is the fundamental argument in favor of free trade. If the ratio between the marginal costs of two importable and exportable commodities in America is different from the ratio between their prices in foreign markets, America can obtain more of the one commodity without having less of the other by importing the commodity whose marginal cost in America is relatively high and by financing these imports through the export of the commodity whose marginal cost in America is relatively low. It is to be observed that this argument for a free-trade policy does not depend upon the assumption of a free-trade policy in other countries. If the price at which American merchants can sell cloth in France is 4 francs, this may be due to the fact that the marginal cost and so the price of cloth is 4 francs in France, and that France is adopting a free-trade policy. But it may equally well be due to the fact that the marginal cost and price of cloth in France is 6 francs, and that France imposes an import duty of 2 francs on each yard of cloth, so that the American exporter obtains only 4 francs for each yard while the French consumer pays 6. From our point of view the cause of the price ratios in France is immaterial; whether they are due to free-trade or protectionist policies America can gain by importing wine and exporting cloth so long as the prices at which an American merchant can sell cloth and buy wine in France are both 4 francs while in America the marginal cost of wine is greater than the marginal cost of cloth.

Thus we see that the argument for free trade rests upon purely national considerations *on the assumption which we made above* (*p. 357*) *that the trade policy adopted by the particular country concerned does not affect the prices of commodities in other countries.* In many cases, of course, this assumption is untrue. Since America, for example, is a large and important producer of cloth and consumer of wine, a restriction of the amount of wine which she will take from France may itself depress the price of wine in France, and a restriction of the amount of cloth which she will sell to France may raise the price of cloth in France. In such a case America by imposing restrictions on trade will obtain an advantage in international trade by being able both to sell her cloth at a higher price and to purchase her wine at a cheaper price. The 'national' advantage to be obtained in this way is discussed at length in the next chapter (pp. 368–74).

But even though there may be a 'national' advantage to be obtained in this way from a restrictive trade policy, the 'international' optimum advantage from international trade can be obtained only if every country adopts a policy of free trade. We can show this by means of an example. Suppose that in France the marginal cost of producing a pint of wine and of producing a yard of cloth is 4 francs, while in America the marginal cost of producing a yard of cloth is 10 cents and of producing a pint of wine 40 cents. These figures are shown in columns A and C of Table XIV. Since the marginal cost of a yard of cloth is the same as the marginal cost of a pint of wine in France, by producing 1 less yard of cloth France can produce 1 more pint of wine. In America, however, the marginal cost of a pint of wine is 4 times as great as the marginal cost of a yard of cloth, so that by producing 1 less pint of wine America can produce 4 more yards of cloth. It follows, therefore, as is shown in columns B and D of Table XIV, that if France produces 1 more pint of wine and America 1 less pint of wine, the total output of cloth may be increased by 3 yards, since France will have to produce only 1 less and America can produce 4 more. If both cloth and wine can be imported and

TABLE XIV

The Ratio between the Marginal Costs of Two Commodities
Differs in Two Countries

	A Marginal cost in France	B Change in output in France	C Marginal cost in America	D Change in output in America
Yard of cloth	4 francs	−1	10 cents	+4
Pint of wine	4 "	+1	40 "	−1

exported, both countries could have the same amount of wine
and $1\frac{1}{2}$ more yards of cloth. This result would be achieved if
France produced 1 less yard of cloth in order to produce 1 more
pint of wine to export to America, and if America produced 1
less pint of wine in order to produce 4 more yards of cloth and
exported $2\frac{1}{2}$ of them to France in exchange for the imported pint
of wine.

But if the ratio between the marginal costs of cloth and wine
is the same in both countries, no gain can be obtained from international trade. Such a situation is illustrated in Table XV,
where in France the marginal cost of wine is 6 francs and of cloth
is 3 francs, while in America the marginal cost of wine is 30 cents
and of cloth 15 cents. In both countries now the marginal cost of
wine is twice as great as the marginal cost of cloth. In these circumstances no increase in the total output of cloth is possible
without a diminution in the total output of wine. If 1 more pint
of wine is produced in France, 2 less yards of cloth must be produced there; while the production of 1 less pint of wine in America releases factors which can produce no more than 2 additional
yards in that country.

In order therefore that the total world output of exportable
and importable commodities should be maximized, in the sense
that it shall be impossible for any country to have more of one
of these commodities without any other country having less of
any other commodity, the factors of production in each country
must be concentrated on the production of those exportable and

TABLE XV

The Ratio between the Marginal Costs of Two Commodities Is the Same in Two Countries

	A Marginal cost in France	B Change in output in France	C Marginal cost in America	D Change in output in America
Yard of cloth	3 francs	−2	15 cents	+2
Pint of wine	6 "	+1	30 "	−1

importable commodities for which the marginal costs of production are relatively lowest. This result will automatically be brought about if in all countries all commodities are sold at prices equal to their marginal costs and if there is free trade between them. For as long as the ratio between the marginal cost of wine and that of cloth were higher in America than in France, merchants would purchase the relatively cheap cloth in America, would sell it in France to purchase wine, and would sell this wine in America for a price greater than that which they had paid in the first place for the American cloth.

It has so far been implicitly assumed that costs of transport in international trade are negligible. This is not usually the case, of course, and where they are material these costs must be included, for the purpose of computing the gain from international trade, as part of the marginal cost of production. It will not pay America to export cloth to France for wine in the example in Table XIV if the cost of transporting a yard of cloth to France is 10 cents and the cost of transporting a pint of wine to America is 20 cents. For in this case America, by producing 1 less pint of wine, would release factors worth only 40 cents. If 10 cents worth of these were put to work making cloth for export, and 30 cents worth put to work transporting cloth and wine in international trade, only 1 additional yard of cloth could be produced, transported to France, exchanged for 1 pint of wine, and transported back to America; which would leave total consumption just what it was before. In the case of some commodities, such as houses and fresh milk, the cost of transport is so high that they are not commonly classed as 'exportable' or 'importable' at all.

The argument for free trade implies nothing about the absolute efficiency of the factors of production at home and abroad.[1] In the example which we gave above (see Table XIV), the marginal costs of wine and cloth were the same in France, while in America the marginal cost of wine was four times as great. Nothing was said, and nothing need have been said, about the absolute height of 'real costs' in the two countries. It might be that in France 8 more units of labor, land, and capital would be needed to produce another yard of cloth or another pint of wine, whereas in America only 1 more unit of labor, land, and capital would be needed to produce another yard of cloth and only 4 more units of labor, land, and capital would be needed to produce another pint of wine. It would still be true that the marginal costs of cloth and wine were the same in France, and that the marginal cost of wine was four times the marginal cost of cloth in America. Both countries could still gain if France produced wine instead of cloth and America produced cloth instead of wine. America would be importing from France a commodity which she could make twice as cheaply as France, and exporting a commodity she could make eight times as cheaply as France. If the factors of production could move from France to America, the result would be quite different. French factors of production would migrate to America to produce both wine and cloth, since the marginal product and so the reward of the factors is greater in America in both occupations. For this reason internal trade—where the factors of production will move to the occupation in which their real reward

---

1. It does, however, depend upon the Balance of Trade being in or nearly in equilibrium. For if one country, e.g. had arbitrarily depreciated its currency by the measures suggested in the last chapter, the money costs of all commodities in that country might be less, at the current rate of exchange, than the money costs of all commodities in other countries. In this case, whatever the relative costs of commodities in the two countries, all would tend to be exported from the country with the unduly depreciated currency. Since no country can permanently undervalue her currency this proviso is relevant only in the short run.

is highest—is said to depend upon differences in absolute costs, while international trade—where the factors of production cannot move—is said to depend upon differences in comparative costs, i.e. upon differences in the ratio between the costs of commodities in different countries.

We have shown that if the ratio between the marginal costs of producing two commodities is different in two countries a gain can be obtained if each concentrates on the production of that commodity in which its marginal cost is relatively low. But we have not yet shown which country will obtain the greater part of this advantage. The distribution of the gain from trade between two countries, e.g. America and France, can be measured by the 'terms of trade' between them; i.e. by the amount of imported goods which America obtains from France for each unit of her exports to France. In Table XIV it is assumed that before trade takes place 1 pint of wine costs 1 yard of cloth in France, whereas 1 pint of wine costs 4 yards of cloth in America. When America exports cloth and imports wine, there will be a net gain so long as she has to pay less than 4 yards of cloth for each pint of imported wine; and France, similarly, will gain so long as she obtains more than 1 yard of cloth for 1 pint of wine. The terms of trade which permit both countries to gain lie between 1 yard for 1 pint and 4 yards for 1 pint. If 1 pint of wine is exchanged for $1\frac{1}{2}$ yards of cloth, America will obtain much and France little of the gain; whereas if the terms of trade are $3\frac{1}{2}$ yards of cloth for 1 pint of wine, France will gain much and America little.

When trade starts, America will sell cloth to France and France will sell wine to America. The price of wine will fall in America as Americans have more of it, and the price of cloth will fall in France as Frenchmen have more cloth. The terms of trade will tend to be favorable to America if, as Frenchmen have more cloth, they offer only a slightly lower price for cloth, and if, as Americans have more wine, they offer a much lower price for wine. For if the price of cloth falls only slowly in France but the price of wine falls quickly in America, America will be able to obtain a large amount of wine for each yard of cloth exported to France.

The terms of trade will normally become more favorable to a particular country,

(a) if tastes change so that its nationals spend less on imports or so that the demand of foreigners for its exports increases;
(b) if the country in question receives more interest or tribute from abroad or pays less to foreign countries; and
(c) if the country in question borrows more from abroad or lends less abroad.

If, for example, tastes change in America so that there is a fall in the American demand for imported goods, the American demand for foreign money will fall below the foreign demand for American money, since American people will be purchasing less foreign money to buy foreign goods. If America is on the gold standard, gold will flow to America from other countries; and equilibrium in America's Balance of Payments will be restored only when American prices have so risen and foreign prices have so fallen that the consequent rise in American imports and fall in her exports has made the American demand for foreign money equal again to the foreign demand for dollars at the fixed rate of exchange. But in this new position America will be obtaining her imports at a cheaper price and will be selling her exports at a higher price; for it is only because of the rise in price of American goods relatively to the price of foreign goods that America is importing more again and exporting less. In other words, America will be obtaining more imports per unit of exports, and the terms of trade will have moved in her favor. An increase in the foreign demand for American goods, the receipt by America of more interest or tribute from abroad or the payment by America of less money on these accounts, the borrowing of more money from abroad or the lending of less money abroad by America—any of these changes will either increase the foreign demand for dollars or reduce the American demand for foreign money, and will therefore cause a flow of gold to America. This flow of gold can only be stopped by a rise in American prices and a fall in foreign prices, i.e. by a movement of the terms of trade in America's favor.

These same changes will also cause the terms of trade to become more favorable to America if America is not on the gold standard. A reduction in the American demand for foreign goods, for example, will as before cause the American demand for foreign money to fall below the foreign demand for dollars. In this case the Balance of Payments will be brought into equilibrium by an appreciation of the exchange value of the dollar, which will make the price of foreign goods lower in America and the price of American goods higher in foreign countries. The appreciation of the exchange value of the dollar will continue until American exports are so restricted by the rise in their price in foreign countries and American imports are so increased by the fall in their price in America, that the Balance of Payments is again in equilibrium. The terms of trade will have moved in America's favor. The price in dollars of America's goods has remained unchanged, while the price in dollars of foreign goods has fallen, so that America is obtaining more imports per unit of exports. And similarly, an increase in America's net receipts of interest or tribute from abroad, or a diminution in her net lending abroad, will also cause the exchange value of the dollar to appreciate, so that the terms of trade move in America's favor.

V

FREE TRADE AND PROTECTION

In this chapter we shall see to what extent the fundamental argument for free trade, presented in the last chapter, must be modified by the arguments which can be brought forward in favor of a policy of protection. There are seven such arguments which we shall examine:

(1) that by imposing a tariff a country can move the terms of trade in its favor;

(2) that by means of a tariff a country can tax the foreigner;

(3) that a tariff is useful to protect infant industries;

(4) that by protecting its industries a country can diminish unemployment at home;

(5) that a country should protect its industries against the competition of cheap foreign labor;

(6) that a tariff may improve the distribution of income within the country concerned; and

(7) that a tariff may increase economic security, even though at the cost of some immediate reduction in real income.

1. We stated in the last chapter (p. 361) that the argument for free trade was a purely national one on the assumption that the particular country concerned could not affect the price of its imports or exports in foreign markets by restricting the volume of its trade with foreign countries. We have now to examine the factors determining the 'national' optimum advantage from international trade on the assumption that the trade policy adopted by any one country may affect the terms of trade between it and other countries.

We assumed in the first part of the last chapter that the price

368

at which America could sell cloth and purchase wine in France would remain 4 francs, however much or little America traded with France; or in other words that the terms of trade were fixed at 1 pint of wine for 1 yard of cloth. But the imposition of a tariff on imports may move the terms of trade in America's favor, if other countries do not retaliate by raising tariffs. If America puts a tariff on commodities imported from France, the immediate effect is to raise the price of French products to American consumers without raising the price which France obtains for her exports. The difference between these two prices is caused by the import duty, and provides a revenue for the American government. America's demand for French commodities will fall in consequence of the rise in their price to American consumers; and a smaller total amount will be paid to Frenchmen for their exports to America. If America and France are both on the gold standard, gold will flow to America, American prices will rise, and French prices will fall; or if America is not on the gold standard, the dollar will appreciate in value in terms of the franc, so that the price of American exports rises in France and French products are offered by Frenchmen at a lower price in dollars in America.

In either case America receives more French commodities per unit of her exports to France. This does not, of course, mean that the price of French products will be lower to American consumers than before the imposition of the tariff; for the duty itself will raise the price of French products in America. But the price in dollars which Frenchmen receive for their products will be lower; and the difference between this price and the price of French products to American consumers will go to the American government as an extra revenue. In so far, therefore, as the imposition of the American tariff enables America to obtain more French products per unit of her exports, Americans do gain by the tariff. For although American consumers are paying a higher price than before for French products, the Frenchman is receiving a lower price in dollars for these goods and the difference accrues to Americans in the form of a reduction of other taxes or in the form of increased expenditure by the American government.

But we cannot conclude that America will necessarily gain by the imposition of the tariff. It is true that for every unit of French products still imported, America is exporting less than before. But it is also true that the total volume of American imports and exports will be smaller than before. America is importing less because of the duty on these imports, and is exporting less, because the American Balance of Payments has only been adjusted by means of a rise in the price of American goods in France which causes France to purchase less from America. On every unit of her goods exported in return for French products America is making a larger gain than before; but she is exporting less of her goods. *She is therefore making a larger gain per unit of trade on a smaller volume of trade.* If the increased gain per unit of trade (i.e. the movement in the terms of trade) is small, but the diminution in the volume of trade is large, America will lose by the imposition of the tariff. If the gain per unit of trade is large and the diminution in the volume of trade small, she will gain by the imposition of the tariff.

America will therefore lose by the imposition of a tariff if a slight rise in the price of American goods in France causes French people to reduce their purchases of American goods considerably, and if a slight fall in the price offered by America causes a large diminution in the amount of goods which Frenchmen will offer for sale in America. For in these circumstances there will be a considerable reduction in the volume of trade with only a small movement of the terms of trade in America's favor. If France can obtain from other countries or by her own manufacture the goods which she is importing from America, and if France can sell in other markets the goods which she is exporting to America or can easily turn her factors of production from the production of exports for America to the production of something else for other countries or for her own use, the price of American goods in

France will not rise much and the price at which France offers goods to America will not fall much.

If America is a small country and France is a large country—which bears some resemblance to the truth if France stands in our example for the rest of the world with which America is trading—these conditions are likely to be fulfilled. For there will be other sources of supply open to the rest of the world for goods which were being bought from America. And if America is small in relation to the rest of the world, any diminution in America's demand for foreign goods due to the imposition of the tariff would cause only a relatively small fall in the total world demand for those goods, so that what was now no longer sold to America could easily be absorbed at slightly lower prices in the rest of the world market. America could move the terms of trade considerably in her favor by means of a tariff only if she exported goods which other countries must have but could not easily make for themselves, and if she bought a large proportion of the world output of the goods which she imported, so that those countries which supplied America could not readily sell their products in other markets without causing a large fall in the price. We may conclude that if America can move the terms of trade in her favor by imposing a tariff, she will gain something by the imposition of a tariff, provided that the tariff is not so high that the gain in the terms of trade is outweighed by the loss in the volume of trade. The more easily America can cause the terms of trade to move in her favor without losing a considerable volume of trade, the higher is the tariff which will bring her the maximum advantage. But only a low tariff is justified by this argument if a large loss of trade would be caused by a small movement in the terms of trade in America's favor.

This argument holds good only if other countries do not retaliate when America raises her tariff. Just as America can cause the terms of trade to move in her favor by imposing a tariff on foreign goods, so foreign countries can cause the terms of trade to move in their favor by imposing a tariff on American goods.

If America raises a tariff on imports from France, which reduces the American demand for French products, France by imposing a tariff on American goods can reduce the French demand for American goods. If the French tariff just offsets the American tariff, there will be no flow of gold between the two countries and no change in the rate of exchange between their currencies; and the terms of trade will remain unchanged.

In this case it is certain that both America and France will be worse off after the imposition of the tariffs. For suppose that there is an American tariff on wine imported from France and a French tariff on cloth imported from America, and that the terms of trade between America and France are 3 yards of American cloth for 1 pint of French wine. In this case the price which France obtains from America for a yard of cloth is 3 times as high as the price which America obtains from France for a yard of cloth. Since there is a tariff in America on the import of wine, the price of a pint of wine to American consumers will be more than 3 times—say it is $3\frac{1}{2}$ times—the price of a yard of cloth, which means that American consumers are still willing to give up as much as $3\frac{1}{2}$ yards of cloth for another pint of wine. And since there is a tariff in France on the import of cloth, the price of a pint of wine in France will be less than 3 times—say it is twice— the price of a yard of cloth to French consumers. This means that French consumers are still willing to give up a pint of wine if they can get as much as 2 yards of cloth for it. If both countries reduced their tariffs, so that they undertook more trade in cloth and wine at the same terms of trade of 3 yards of cloth for a pint of wine, consumers in both countries would gain from the additional trade. For American consumers would get more wine at a price of 3 yards of cloth for each additional pint, though they are willing to give $3\frac{1}{2}$ yards for each extra pint; and the French consumers would get 3 yards more cloth for each additional pint of wine exported, though they are willing to give up a pint of wine for 2 yards of cloth.

Agreements among nations to reduce their tariffs on each

other's goods will invariably benefit each individual country if the tariff reductions made by each country are such that the extra demand for each country's goods is the same. In this case the tariff reductions will cause no flow of gold and no change in the rate of exchange between the currencies of the different countries, so that there will be no change in the terms of trade between them. Moreover, it is almost certain that *any* agreement among nations to reduce their tariffs simultaneously will benefit each individual nation. For each nation will gain from the increased volume of trade, and the change in the terms of trade is unlikely to be large if they all reduce their tariffs at the same time.

We have seen that one country may gain by imposing a tariff if it can thereby change the terms of trade considerably in its favor and if other countries do not retaliate by the imposition of tariffs. But even in this case a net loss will be inflicted on all countries taken together. If a single country gains by imposing a tariff, other countries will lose more than the single country gains. Suppose that there is an American tariff on the import of French wine, while France allows the free import of American cloth, and that the terms of trade are 3 yards of American cloth for 1 pint of French wine. Then in France a pint of wine will be 3 times as expensive as a yard of cloth, which means that French consumers would be willing to give up 1 pint of wine for 3 yards of cloth. In America, since there is a tariff on the import of wine, a pint of wine will be more than 3 times as expensive to consumers as a yard of cloth. If it were $3\frac{1}{2}$ times as expensive, American consumers would be willing to give up $3\frac{1}{2}$ yards of cloth for an extra pint of wine.

A reduction in the American tariff would cause an increase in the volume of trade, but would move the terms of trade against America. Suppose that it would move the terms of trade from 3 yards of American cloth for 1 pint of French wine to $3\frac{1}{4}$ yards of cloth for 1 pint of wine. In these circumstances both American and French consumers would gain on all the *additional* trade. For America pays only $3\frac{1}{4}$ yards of cloth for each additional pint of wine imported, although American consumers would give $3\frac{1}{2}$ yards for an extra pint of wine; and France gets $3\frac{1}{4}$ yards of cloth for each extra pint of wine exported, although French consumers would give a pint of wine for only 3 yards of cloth.

But America may lose by reducing her tariff, because the gain she gets by importing more pints of wine at $3\frac{1}{4}$ yards per pint may be more than offset by the fact that she will have to give $3\frac{1}{4}$ instead of 3 yards for each pint of wine which she is *already* importing. France on the other hand, besides gaining on all the additional trade in wine, will also gain on all the pints of wine which she is already exporting, for which she will now get $3\frac{1}{4}$ instead of 3 yards of cloth. By the lowering of the American tariff both America and France will gain on the additional trade, while America will lose and France will gain on the existing trade. But the loss of America on the existing trade is exactly equal to the gain of France on the existing trade. America is giving $3\frac{1}{4}$ instead of 3 yards of cloth per pint of wine; France is getting $3\frac{1}{4}$ instead of 3 yards per pint. It follows that the gain to America and France on the *additional* trade, caused by the tariff reduction, is a net gain from the international point of view. We have already shown in the last chapter (pp. 362 to 365) that the world output of importable and exportable commodities will be maximized, only if all commodities are sold in all countries at prices equal to their marginal costs and if there is free trade in these commodities between the nations. To maximize the economic well-being of the world free trade is therefore essential.

2. The second argument for protection is that a country by raising taxes on its imports can force the foreigner to contribute to its budget revenue. If America imposes a tariff on imports from France, either the price of these commodities must rise to American consumers by the amount of the tax, in which case the American consumers bear the burden of the tax, or else the price obtained by the Frenchman for these commodities must fall, in which case the Frenchman is contributing to America's tax revenue. As we have shown, the price of French products will be sig-

nificantly reduced by the imposition of the American duty only if Frenchmen cannot easily sell these commodities in other markets, cannot easily shift the factors to produce other products, and cannot easily find alternative sources of supply for the goods which are being bought from America. In other words, whether or not America is in a position to tax the foreigner depends upon whether or not America is in a position to turn the terms of trade in her favor by imposing a tariff. This second argument for protection is, therefore, merely another way of stating the first argument for protection, which we have already discussed at length.

3. It is argued that a tariff can properly be imposed to encourage an infant industry. We have shown in Part II that there are certain industries in which economies of large-scale production are important. In these industries the cost of production would be high if only a small output were produced, but could be lowered if the output were considerably increased. It may well happen, for historical reasons, that America is not producing a particular product which is being produced on a large scale in France. If this product is one in which the economies of large-scale production are important, it will not be profitable for American producers to embark on its production on a small scale. But if America were producing this commodity on a large scale, its marginal cost in America might be so reduced that it would really be advantageous to produce it in America. For this reason, it is argued, the production of this commodity should be protected until the industry had been organized on so large a scale behind the tariff that the product, when sold at a price equal to its marginal cost, would compete economically with the imports from France.

This argument is perfectly sound. If, however, by the means suggested in Part II, Chapters VII and VIII, steps are taken to insure that every product is sold at a price equal to its marginal cost, the protection of an infant industry need only be temporary. For if, when the commodity is being produced on a large scale in America, its marginal cost were not reduced below the price of imports from France, the industry should not have been pro-

tected. The protection of an industry by means of a tariff is justified on this principle only if it is genuinely considered that when
the industry has once grown it will be able to compete with foreign products by selling at a price equal to its marginal cost. It
must, however, be remembered that, as we argued in Part II,
Chapter VII (pp. 195 to 197), the marginal cost of a commodity
will remain below its average cost when the total market demand for it is less than the output of a single firm of optimum
size. In such cases it is proper permanently to sell the commodity
at a price lower than its average cost by means of a permanent
subsidy or by nationalizing the industry and selling its product
at a loss. Both in internal and in international trade it is the
marginal and not the average cost which should determine how
much of each commodity should be produced.

4. The fourth argument in favor of protection is that it will
diminish unemployment. In Part I it was argued that unemployment could be cured if a rise in money prices and incomes were
brought about by monetary expansion without a similar rise in
money wage-rates. If this policy is adopted, the rise in internal
prices and money incomes will in itself cause the demand for
foreign goods to rise and the foreign demand for the country's
goods to fall. To maintain equilibrium in the Balance of Payments the exchange value of the country's currency may be depreciated, as we argued in Chapter III of this Part (pp. 344 to 347).
But this exchange depreciation is not necessary. The imposition
of a tariff on imports will also reduce the country's demand for
foreign goods and so restore equilibrium to its Balance of Payments, provided that the tariff is high enough and provided that
other countries do not retaliate. The tariff has no peculiar advantages for that purpose; there is nothing that a tariff will do
in these circumstances that cannot be done equally well by allowing a depreciation of the exchange value of the country's
currency. A 10 per cent tariff on a country's imports and a 10
per cent rise in the amount of the country's money which must
be given to obtain a given amount of foreign money will both

raise the price of foreign goods by 10 per cent, and will both, therefore, restrict the import of foreign goods by the same amount. The imposition of a tariff will allow a country to adopt an internal policy of expansion without a depreciation in the exchange value of its currency, and will therefore enable it to reduce unemployment by these means without going off the gold standard. But unemployment could equally well be reduced without the imposition of a tariff either by a general reduction in money wage-rates accompanied by a monetary policy designed to prevent a similar fall in internal prices and incomes, or by a monetary policy designed to raise internal prices and incomes accompanied by a depreciation of the exchange value of the country's currency. Since these other means are compatible with the maintenance of free trade, they are to be preferred if the arguments in favor of free trade are accepted.

The imposition of a tariff on imports to preserve equilibrium in the Balance of Payments, at a time when a country is expanding its money incomes and prices at home, will not intensify unemployment in other countries. The imposition of the tariff does not restrict the total markets for foreign goods but only prevents the internal expansion from causing an increase in the demand for the products of other countries. But a tariff imposed at a time when the country's Balance of Payments is already in equilibrium and unaccompanied by a monetary expansion at home, may diminish unemployment at home at the cost of intensifying it elsewhere, just as a manipulated depreciation of the exchange value of a country's currency which is not necessary to offset a rise of incomes and prices in that country will intensify unemployment in other countries, as we argued in Chapter III of this Part (p. 355).

The imposition of a tariff in a single country without a rise in its prices and money incomes, and without an appreciation in the exchange value of its currency, will cause imports to fall off without any immediate fall in exports. This will diminish unemployment at home at the expense of employment in other countries by increasing the demand for home-produced goods at the expense of the demand for foreign goods. The country imposing the tariff may prevent the fall in its demand for foreign goods from causing an appreciation in the exchange value of its currency in either of two ways. It may remain on the gold standard, in which case the increase in its favorable Balance of Trade will be financed by an import of gold. In this case sooner or later the gold flow will be stopped by a rise in its own prices and incomes and by a fall in foreign prices and incomes, until its Balance of Payments is in equilibrium again. But it will have raised its own money prices and incomes at the expense of a fall in the money prices and incomes of other countries. If, on the other hand, it is not on the gold standard, it may prevent an appreciation in the exchange value of its currency by the use of an Exchange Stabilization Fund, which can purchase foreign currencies to move short-term balances abroad as the purchase of foreign currencies for the purpose of financing imports falls off. In this case the country can maintain the increase in its favorable Balance of Trade so long as the Exchange Stabilization Fund continues to operate in this way.

If the fall in a country's demand for imports is met neither by an inflow of gold nor by an increase in its lending abroad, the exchange value of its currency must appreciate until this has caused a sufficient rise in imports and fall in exports for the Balance of Payments to be in equilibrium again. If this happens, the unemployment position in other countries will not be worsened. For the appreciation in the exchange value of the country's currency will cause it to increase its demand for foreign goods again and will cause foreigners also to spend less on its goods and more on their own. This rise in the demand for foreign goods will offset the fall in the demand for foreign goods which was caused in the first place by the imposition of the tariff.

To sum up: the best policy for a country to adopt to cure unemployment is to raise its prices and money incomes by monetary expansion and to allow the exchange value of its currency to depreciate just sufficiently to keep its Balance of Payments in equilibrium. This combines the advantages of full employment with the advantages of free trade. If, however, a country wishes to cure unemployment by internal monetary expansion but does not wish to allow the exchange value of its currency to depreciate, it should raise tariffs just sufficiently to keep its Balance of Payments in equilibrium as its prices and incomes rise. If, however, it should wish for some reason or another to impose a tariff without any accompanying internal monetary expansion, then, if it is not to intensify unemployment in other countries, it should allow the exchange value of its currency to appreciate sufficiently to keep the normal items in its Balance of Payments in equilibrium, and should not prevent this exchange appreciation by lending more on short-term abroad or by allowing a drain of gold from other countries. But in this case it would find that it had made no net reduction in its unemployment by the imposition of the tariff.

5. It is sometimes argued that, while the case for free trade is in general acceptable, a country should protect the standard of living of its inhabitants if a particular industry is undercut by the products of another country in which the standard of living of the workers is very low. To take an example, it may be argued that the New England cotton industry should be protected against the competition of Japanese cotton goods because of the very low wages of Japanese cotton operatives. A reduction in the price of Japanese cotton goods—whether it be due to low wages in Japan or to great efficiency of labor in Japan—will increase the sale of such Japanese goods in Japan, in America, and in other markets in which America was previously selling her cotton goods. American exports will fall and her imports will rise. In order to preserve equilibrium in the American Balance of Payments together with full employment in America, American money wage-rates may be reduced until America has obtained sufficient foreign markets—either in the sale of cotton goods again or in the sale of other American goods which have become

cheaper by the fall in American wage-rates—to replace the loss of markets to the Japanese. Or, alternatively, the dollar may be allowed to depreciate in terms of the Japanese yen and of the currencies of other countries, until, at the level of American prices which will give full employment at home, the price of Japanese cotton goods and of other foreign goods in America has so risen and the price of American cotton goods and other products in Japan and other countries has so fallen that American imports and exports balance again.

By either of these means America can in part meet the Japanese competition in cotton goods and in part expand the markets for her other products, and can therefore preserve full employment in face of the Japanese competition. But in either case there may be a fall in the American standard of living; for the fall in American money wage-rates which is necessary if America is to stay on the gold standard, or the rise in the price of imported goods caused by the depreciation in the exchange value of the dollar, may be much more serious than the fall in the price at which Japanese cotton goods are offered to the American consumers. It is not to be denied, therefore, that a reduction in the cost of Japanese cotton goods may reduce standards of living in America. But could America prevent this by imposing a tariff on such goods instead of reducing her money wage-rates or depreciating the exchange value of the dollar?

The imposition of a tariff on Japanese cotton goods will prevent an increase in American imports by keeping up the price of cotton goods to American consumers, and will thus enable America to preserve full employment at home with a smaller fall in American money wage-rates or with a smaller depreciation in the exchange value of the dollar than would otherwise have been necessary. But from the point of view of preserving full employment a tariff has this disadvantage: it can only protect the American internal market, whereas a reduction in American money wage-rates or a depreciation in the exchange value of the dollar will enable American goods to compete on better terms with

Japanese goods both in America's internal market and in her export markets. Since, therefore, a tariff is a less effective method of preserving full employment, it should be used only if America can thereby turn the terms of trade considerably in her favor, or can thereby prevent the terms of trade from moving considerably against her, when the Japanese competition becomes more keen. We have already examined at the beginning of this chapter the conditions in which this will be possible. If America is in a position to turn the terms of trade considerably in her favor by means of a tariff, this may be the best means from America's point of view to meet the Japanese competition. But if America can gain in this way after the intensification of the Japanese competition, she was probably in a position to do so before, and should, therefore, have already imposed the tariff.

There is, therefore, no special argument in favor of a tariff to meet competition due to cheap foreign labor. For the effect on America of a reduction in the price of foreign goods is the same, whether this reduction in price is due to cheap foreign labor, to great efficiency of labor in foreign countries, to the subsidization by foreigners of their exports, or to favorable natural conditions in foreign countries. And since America can always preserve full employment by means of a reduction in her money wage-rates or by a depreciation in the exchange value of the dollar, she can gain by a tariff only if she can thereby turn the terms of trade considerably in her favor. But this argument for a tariff exists whether wages are high or low in other countries.

6. It is sometimes argued that the adoption of a protectionist policy will improve the distribution of income within the country concerned. In certain conditions this is perfectly true. The imposition of a tariff on imports to America will divert demand from the products of American export industries to those of the industries competing with imports. If the proportion of labor to other factors employed in American export industries is lower than in the industries competing with imports, this diversion of demand from commodities in producing which labor is relatively

unimportant to those in producing which it is relatively important, will increase the demand for labor relatively to other factors
of production and will therefore raise the reward of labor relatively to the reward of the other factors. In fact in America the
supply of capital and natural resources is plentiful compared
with the supply of labor, and for this reason the ratio between
the reward of capital and natural resources on the one hand and
of labor on the other is lower than in other countries. This means
that in America goods produced with much capital and land and
little labor will be cheap relatively to goods produced with little
capital and much labor, so that America is likely to export the
former and import the latter type. It is therefore probable that
America's protectionist policy does increase labor's relative share
of the national income; and conceivable that it might increase
labor's absolute share.

But though this reasoning is sound, it does not constitute a
very convincing argument for tariffs. A better solution would be
to adopt that foreign-trade policy which made the nation's income a maximum, and then, to the extent to which it seemed
desirable, to redistribute that income by the methods outlined in
Part III above.

7. In some countries a free-trade policy would lead to the concentration of a very large proportion of the factors of production
of that country on one single commodity or on one type of commodity. Thus Brazil concentrates very largely on the production
of coffee, and would not find it profitable to produce industrial
products for herself unless her industries were protected. But to
put all one's eggs in one basket in this way may be economically
dangerous for a country as for an individual. When the demand
for Brazilian coffee in other countries falls violently for some
reason unforeseen by Brazilian producers, e.g. because new
sources of supply are developed or because a substitute beverage
is produced, a vast proportion of Brazil's factors of production
will be reduced directly to conditions of penury. If Brazil during
the period of high demand for coffee had sacrificed some of the

income which could have been obtained by specializing solely on this product, and by a system of tariffs had developed other industries, she would be faced with a much less formidable task of finding other uses for her factors if the demand for coffee were to slump. For this reason a moderate system of protection is no doubt justified—as an insurance policy—in those countries in which there would be very little diversification of productive activity in free-trade conditions.

Similarly for reasons of security a country may be justified in levying tariffs which prevent too large a proportion of its factors of production from producing exports for foreign markets. For such a country will be less severely affected by a general depression in other countries, and will therefore be able more easily to preserve full employment by the means suggested in Part I if the other countries do not adopt similar policies to maintain their demand for goods in general. This particular argument would, of course, have no validity if all countries were successfully to adopt the measures suggested in Part I for the prevention of general depression, or if the country considering the tariff had not adopted them.

VI

INTERNATIONAL MOVEMENTS OF LABOR
AND CAPITAL

IT has been pointed out in Chapter IV of this Part (p. 356) that the theory of international trade is based upon the assumption that the factors of production cannot move from one country to another; and it was shown that this assumption is to a large extent true. But movement of the factors of production between nations is not always impossible, and we must therefore decide on what principles such movements should be encouraged or prevented.

In the case of land we have no problem to discuss; for land by definition includes all the natural resources in a particular country, over which man has no power, and which cannot, therefore, be transferred from one country to another. There remain for discussion the principles upon which the movement of labor and capital between nations should be regulated.

Let us suppose that in America and France—whether because there is perfect competition in both countries or because monopolistic conditions are controlled in both countries on the principles suggested in Chapters VII and VIII of Part II—all commodities are bought and sold freely at prices equal to their marginal costs, and that each factor is paid a reward equal to the value of its marginal product. If in these circumstances labor obtains a higher real wage in America than in France, it would be *possible* by transferring labor from France to America to increase the welfare of the laborer so transferred without diminishing the welfare of any one else. For the reduction in the output in France due to the loss of the single worker is of less real value to that worker than the increase in output due to his employment in America. On this principle labor should be allowed to move freely from France to America until the real wage, represented by labor's marginal product in each country, was the same in each country. This principle must, of course, be modified, on the principle discussed in Part II, Chapter II (pp. 118 and 119), if it costs something to move labor between the countries. Labor should move from France to America only if the excess of the real wage in America over the real wage in France is more than sufficient to compensate for the cost of movement. Apart from legal restrictions on the international migration of labor, which on the present principle should be abolished, the movement of labor will be hindered by the difficulty of obtaining capital to finance the cost of movement, by ignorance of opportunities for employment in different occupations in different countries, and by language difficulties. The principle of free international migration of labor suggests that these hindrances should be lessened by measures of the type suggested in Part II, Chapter VII (p. 185) in the case of movement within one country.

The free movement of labor from France to America in search of the highest real wage-rate might, however, be to the detriment of labor already employed in America. Unless the population in America is below the optimum, the marginal product and so the real wage-rate of labor will fall in America as the supply of labor increases; and unless the population in France is below the optimum, the marginal product and so the real wage-rate will rise in France as the supply of labor decreases. But although there will be these effects on the distribution of income between laborers in America and France, and similar effects on the distribution of income between the laborers and other factors in each country, there is clearly a net gain from the international point of view if labor moves from France to America in search of higher wages. For the marginal product which is secured in America is greater than the marginal product which is sacrificed in France. From the international point of view there is a further gain from this transfer of labor. Not only will the transfer of labor increase the total income of the world, because labor moves to a country in which its marginal product is greater; but the consequent fall in the standard of living in America and rise in the standard of living in France will cause the total income of the world to be more equally divided. And for the reasons discussed in Chapter I of Part III a rise in incomes in a country in which the citizens are poor is likely to cause a greater increase in satisfaction than an equal fall in incomes in another country in which the citizens are rich.

We conclude, therefore, that, from the international point of view, free migration of labor is generally desirable, whereas, from the national point of view, free immigration is desirable only if the national population is below the optimum. But there is one condition in which the free migration of labor will be undesirable from the international point of view as well. Let us suppose that the marginal product and so the wage of labor is higher in country B than in country A, but that in country A the population always increases as long as the standard of living is above the subsistence level. As labor moves from country A to country B, the marginal product and so the real wage of labor will rise in country A and fall in country B. But if the rise in the standard of living in country A simply causes the population to increase in that country, the marginal product and so the wage of labor in country A will fall again as more labor seeks employment there. In consequence, more labor will move from country A, in which the marginal product of labor has fallen, to country B in which there has been no further growth in population. This further transference of labor will again raise the marginal product of labor in country A and will lower the marginal product of labor in country B. The rise in the standard of living in country A will cause the population to increase, will cause a fall in the marginal product of labor in that country, will necessitate a further transference of labor to country B and so will cause a further fall in the marginal product of labor and in the standard of living in country B. There will be no end to this process until there has been so great a growth of population in country A and so great a transference of this population to country B that the standard of living in both countries has been reduced to the same subsistence level, which allows no further increase in the population of country A. Even from the strictly international point of view, therefore, free migration of labor should be allowed only if a rise in standards in the country from which labor is emigrating will not cause an excessive and uncontrolled growth of population in that country.

We have next to deal with the principles upon which the movement of capital from one country to another should be controlled. Suppose that in both America and France the rate of interest offered for capital measures the marginal product of capital in each industry, and that there is free trade in commodities between America and France. If the investment of $100 worth of machinery in France will bring in a net annual return of commodities priced at $5, while the investment of $100 in America will bring in a net annual return priced only at $3, then—from the international point of view at least—the $100 should be invested in France rather than in America. The use of $100 more machinery in France will add to the output of the two countries something which is more valued by French and American consumers than the additional output due to the investment of $100 more machinery in America. For this reason if the yield on capital is higher in France than in America, it is *possible*, by the investment of capital in France rather than in America, to raise standards of living in both countries. On this principle the free movement of capital from country to country in search of the highest yield should be allowed. If in any country the government controls the supply of new savings, it should lend abroad rather than at home if the yield on capital abroad is higher. The free movement of capital between countries may be hindered not only by legal restrictions, which on this principle should be removed, but also by ignorance on the part of investors of the yields to be obtained in different countries. Such ignorance might be minimized by an international body performing the functions which we suggested in Part II, Chapter VII (p. 186), might be performed at home by a special body designed to give authoritative judgment of the probable yields of investment in different forms of capital.

But freedom to lend abroad will not always be to the advantage of the people of the country in which the yield on capital is relatively low. The lending of capital to foreign countries may turn the terms of trade against the country, so that its citizens lose more by the movement in the terms of trade than they gain by the higher yield on their capital. If Americans lend more to France, America must increase her exports or diminish her imports until her favorable balance of trade has increased by an amount sufficient to finance the loan to France. If the French borrowers spend the money on capital goods produced in America, American exports will automatically increase by an amount sufficient to finance the loan to France, and there will be no movement in the terms of trade against America. But if the money is spent on French capital goods, then the loan of money from America to France will not automatically increase the demand for American goods. If both countries are on the gold standard, gold will move from America to France, the price of American goods will fall and of French goods will rise, until American imports fall off and American exports rise sufficiently to finance the loan. If the two countries are on independent standards, the exchange value of the dollar will depreciate in terms of francs, and this will raise the price of French products in America and lower the price of American products in France, until the American favorable balance of trade has been increased sufficiently to finance the loan. In either case America will obtain less French imports per unit of her own exports while the loan is being made.

Later, however, when the interest payment on the loan must be made by France to America, the terms of trade will turn in America's favor. For now American imports must increase or her exports must diminish until America has an unfavorable balance of trade sufficiently great to allow France to finance the interest payments to America. But since the capital sum of the loan will be large relatively to the annual interest to be paid on it, America will have to develop a relatively large favorable balance of trade in the year in which the loan is being made. In subsequent years in which the interest payments are being made, America will have to develop only a relatively small unfavorable balance of trade. In consequence it is probable that the movement of the terms of trade against America will be large while the loan is being made, and that the movement of the terms of trade in America's favor will be small in the subsequent years when America is receiving the interest. On the other hand the movement in the terms of trade against America will last only as long as the capital sum of the loan is being transferred, whereas the movement in her favor will last as long as the interest is being paid on the loan or the capital repaid. America may therefore gain or lose in real terms as a result of these changes in the terms of trade.

But from the international point of view there is always an advantage in a movement of capital abroad in search of the highest yield. For if the yield on capital is 5 per cent in France and only 3 per cent in America, this means (cf. pp. 296 to 300) that, for every 100 units of consumption goods given up, 5 units more will be available in every subsequent year if the capital development takes place in France, whereas only 3 units more will be available if the capital is invested in America. If the change in the terms of trade affects one country adversely, it will confer an exactly equal advantage on the other; so that there is a net gain to the two countries taken together equal to the greater productivity of capital in the borrowing country.

There are two ways in which we must modify the principle that, from the international point of view, capital should be free to move in search of the highest yield. These modifications have already been mentioned in Chapter III of this Part. In the first place, suppose that America adopts a policy designed to prevent unemployment and for this reason reduces the rate of interest by her monetary policy from 5 per cent to 3 per cent, which prevents the development of a slump, but that in France the appropriate internal monetary policy has not been adopted, so that the rate of interest remains at 5 per cent although unemployment is developing. In these circumstances there is no real scarcity of capital in France, in which greater capital development could be induced simply by a change in internal banking policy on the lines suggested in Chapter III of Part I. There is, therefore, no real advantage from the international point of view in a movement of capital from America to France. Only if all countries reduce their interest rates by banking policy so as to prevent unemployment is the free flow of capital to the countries with the highest yields clearly desirable from the international point of view.

In the second place, short-term funds may move from one country to another not because the rate of interest is higher in the second than in the first country, but because the exchange value of the first country's currency is expected to depreciate. The rate of interest both in France and in America may be 3 per cent, and this rate of interest may correspond to the real productivity of new capital investment in both countries, but at the same time the exchange value of the dollar in terms of francs may be expected to fall. This will provide an incentive for a short-term movement of capital from America to France, in order that the funds may in the future be exchanged back into dollars when the dollar has depreciated; but there is no fundamental justification for such a movement of capital, since the real productivity of capital is as high in America as in France, and, as we have already seen (pp. 347-9), such a movement is undesirable on other grounds.

Except in these two cases the free movement of capital between nations in the search of the highest rate of interest should be allowed; and we have already discussed in Chapter III of this Part how the movement of capital may be controlled in these two exceptional cases.

VII

INTERNATIONAL ECONOMIC CO–OPERATION

In this Part we have discussed international economic problems mainly from the point of view of the economic policy of a particular country. It is useful to apply the conclusions of the foregoing chapters to decide how countries should co-operate in order that each may obtain the maximum economic advantage. Let us suppose, therefore, that another World Economic Conference is to be summoned. What principles should be adopted in the formation of international economic conventions at this conference? In what follows we shall outline five possible main agreements in order of their importance.

1. **An International Agreement to Provide Employment by Internal Monetary Policy.** We have argued that one country alone can diminish unemployment by internal monetary expansion carried out on the principles discussed in Part I, if it will allow the exchange value of its currency to depreciate sufficiently to keep its Balance of Payments in equilibrium. But such action will be much more effective if other countries are adopting similar policies. Suppose that a world-wide slump in prices starts, and that America by reducing interest rates through banking policy and by other measures causes her prices to rise, while other countries take no such action. There will be a strain on the American exchange rate with other countries, because Americans will attempt to lend more abroad where interest rates have not been reduced, and because foreigners will tend to spend less on imports as their incomes fall. If interest rates were reduced abroad *pari passu* with American interest rates, there would be no abnormal increase in America's foreign lending. If prices and incomes were maintained abroad *pari passu* with American prices and incomes, the demand for American exports would also be

maintained. Internal expansion in any one country raises the demand in that country both for home-produced goods and for imports; if, therefore, there is expansion in all countries at the same time, there will be a rise in international trade as well as a rise in internal trade in each country.

This principle does not involve much technical international co-operation. The necessary action is, in the main, internal, involving the control of internal banking policy, the stimulation of public works expenditure, and of expenditure on consumption goods. But besides a general agreement among the nations to concentrate on such internal expansion to cure unemployment, two specific international agreements are appropriate.

First, the Central Banks can co-operate directly in lowering interest rates. It might, for example, be agreed that the governors of the Central Banks of each country should meet at the Bank for International Settlements at stated intervals to discuss the desirability of lowering or raising interest rates simultaneously in all countries. Secondly, there are many forms of capital development the execution of which depends upon direct co-operation between nations. For example, the development of railways, roads, or air lines, which cross the frontiers of many states, needs the co-operation of many independent national authorities. These International Public Works might be planned ahead by an appropriate International Commission, in such a way that expenditure on them can be speeded up or postponed simultaneously in all countries, in order to increase such expenditure during a world slump.

An international agreement of this character is of the utmost importance. Not only would it directly diminish the world-wide problem of unemployment, but it would make it much easier to reach the two international agreements which we shall discuss next—namely, agreements to minimize fluctuations in the exchange rates between different currencies and to reduce tariffs and other barriers to international trade. Uncontrolled fluctuations in money incomes and prices in one country are the most important cause of large fluctuations in the rate of exchange between two currencies. If each country is preventing any considerable internal fluctuations of prices, the need for changes in the rate of exchange between different countries would be reduced to a minimum. In the modern world the most important cause of tariff barriers is the desire of each country to diminish unemployment at home by preserving the home market to home producers; and this cause will be removed if unemployment is cured by simultaneous monetary expansion within each country.

2. An International Agreement to Minimize Fluctuations in Exchange Rates. When the main cause of exchange fluctuations has been removed by the conclusion of the agreement which we have just discussed, it will be proper for nations to consider the return to an international gold standard, which will stabilize completely the rates of exchange between their currencies. Such an international standard diminishes the uncertainty with which importers and exporters will otherwise have to trade. If the rate of exchange between the dollar and the franc is fixed, the American exporter knows how much he will obtain in dollars for goods which he can sell at a certain price in francs, and the American importer knows how much he will have to pay in dollars for goods bought at a certain price in francs. And if there is a reliable international monetary standard, undesirable speculative movements of short-term funds from currency to currency will be greatly reduced. Americans will lend on short term to France only if the rate of interest in France is higher than the rate of interest in America; they will no longer buy francs for a short period because they expect the franc price of dollars to fall in the future.

But in spite of these advantages of the gold standard it may be better for many countries still to preserve some freedom in their exchange rates with other countries. For even if the international agreement to prevent unemployment by internal monetary policy is fully successful, some readjustment in the Balance of Payments between different countries will still be necessary—caused (e.g.) by a loss of export markets by one country due to more rapid technical progress in the production of similar goods by a competing country. Such readjustments can be brought about without causing unemployment, either if the country whose receipts of foreign money have fallen can reduce its money wage-rates as quickly as its prices must fall, or if it allows its exchange rate to depreciate without any fall in its internal price-level. Countries should therefore return to a rigid gold standard only if money wage-rates are sufficiently flexible. This will be the case, either if there is perfect competition in the labor market without any bargains between employers and employed fixing wage-rates for long periods, in which case wage-rates will fall as soon as there is any unemployment, or if there is a completely nationalized economic system which enables the government to lower all money wage-rates by fiat.

But there are countries, such as England, and, to a slightly lesser extent, America, in which sufficient flexibility of money wage-rates does not exist; and these countries should not return to an unmodified gold standard. Between such countries a scheme of co-operation is needed to minimize fluctuations in exchange rates based upon the following principles:

 (i) that each country should be free to depreciate its exchange rate sufficiently to give it complete freedom to adopt an appropriate internal monetary policy without throwing its Balance of Payments out of equilibrium;

(ii) that each country should guarantee that it will not depreciate the exchange value of its currency—e.g. by purchases of foreign money through its Exchange Stabilization Fund when these are not required to offset a speculative movement of short-term funds—by more than is sufficient to preserve equilibrium in its Balance of Payments; and

(iii) that speculative movements of short-term funds should be offset or prevented, so that they do not cause unnecessary fluctuations in exchange rates, without any limitations of the purchase and sale of foreign currencies for other purposes.

There are many schemes of co-operation by which these objectives might be achieved. The following gives in outline one possible form of international agreement for this purpose:

1. All the countries concerned should agree to work a modified form of the gold standard. Each should agree to fix exchange rates by fixing the price, in terms of its own currency, at which its Central Bank would buy and sell gold, and by allowing the free import and export of gold. But these fixed exchange rates would be revised from time to time by periodical alterations in the Central Banks' buying and selling prices of gold.

2. The Governors of the Central Banks of each country should meet regularly at the Bank for International Settlements to revise the buying and selling prices of gold in terms of the currencies of their own countries. The prices should be chosen so as to fix those rates of exchange between the different currencies which would enable each country's Balance of Payments to be in equilibrium in the absence of any movement of gold and of any speculative transfer of short-term funds.

3. To judge these prices correctly the officials of the Bank for International Settlements should study continually all information relating to the Balance of Payments between different countries. In particular, they should attempt to find out figures for the movement of gold reserves and of short-term funds.

4. Two principles should govern the revision of the buying and selling prices of gold in terms of the different currencies. In the first place, any country which was steadily losing gold should be allowed to raise its buying and selling price of gold relatively to the countries which were steadily importing gold. By a process of trial and error, based on the information at the disposal of the Bank for International Settlements, those gold prices could be found which just remove the disequilibrium in the normal items in the Balance of Payments. Secondly, all countries should raise their buying and selling prices of gold simultaneously if an increase in the total of Central Bank reserves was necessary to prevent a world-wide slump, and should lower their buying and

selling prices of gold simultaneously if a decrease in the total of reserves was necessary to prevent a world-wide boom.

5. The money profit or loss caused in any country by raising or lowering the money price of the gold reserves of that country should accrue to the government. The expenditure of such a profit by the government, or the increase in taxation necessary to finance such a loss, would help in the internal expansion or contraction of money demand.

6. Each Central Bank should agree to concentrate on an internal policy designed to preserve a high level of employment at home regardless of its exchange position, which would, if necessary, be adjusted by the appropriate revision of exchange rates.

7. This system will have the desired effect only if the speculative movement of short-term funds were offset or prevented. For only if this is so will a movement of gold between two countries measure properly the degree to which the normal payments between the two countries are out of adjustment. To offset the speculative movement of short-term funds those directing the policy of the Bank for International Settlements should shift the assets of the Bank from one currency to another—e.g. they should sell American securities and with the dollars so obtained should purchase pounds to invest in English securities, in order to offset a movement of short-term funds from England to America. This would provide an International Exchange Stabilization Fund. To finance this Fund each Central Bank should agree to deposit a certain sum with the Bank for International Settlements, and any loss or profit incurred by these exchange transactions should accrue to the different countries in proportion to the sums deposited by the Central Bank of each country.

8. Each country should give up the use of a national Exchange Stabilization Fund, but should aid the Bank for International Settlements in carrying out its policy of offsetting short-term capital movements.

9. Any country should be allowed to monopolize in a single institution all dealings in foreign exchange to prevent short-term

capital movements, provided that it allowed the purchase and sale of foreign exchange for other purposes in unrestricted amounts at the current rates of exchange.

3. An International Agreement to Reduce Barriers to International Trade. After the conclusion of the two monetary agreements, which we have just outlined, it would be practical politics to discuss tariff reductions again. Tariffs would no longer be necessary to provide employment, since this is provided by the first agreement. They would not be required to protect a country's exchange position, since this would be achieved by the second agreement; and countries could no longer hope to expand their markets at the expense of other countries by raising a tariff, since other countries would be permitted by the second agreement to retaliate by the depreciation of the exchange value of their currencies if the tariff restricted their markets and so caused them to lose gold. Tariffs could only be retained either to protect an infant industry, which is perfectly legitimate, or to prevent the terms of trade from moving against the country imposing the tariff. But if all countries reduce their tariffs simultaneously, the demand for the products of each country will rise, so that there will be little or no change in the terms of trade between them; and any small change against any one country would be more than offset by the advantage accruing to that country from the larger volume of international trade.

As an ideal, all countries should simultaneously agree to a policy of complete free trade. In all probability, very many countries would not agree to a complete abolition of their tariffs, and some might be unwilling to agree to any significant tariff reductions. If universal agreement was prevented by the refusal of some states, a multilateral agreement should be formed among those states which were willing to reduce their tariffs.

At this point difficulties might arise from the existence of the 'most-favored-nation' clause in existing commercial agreements. This clause stipulates that either of the parties to the commercial agreement will not levy duties on the goods of the other party higher than the duties levied on similar goods imported from any other country. In most commercial treaties between nations this clause is included. For example, a commercial treaty between America and Germany would probably contain a clause stating that America will not impose tariffs on German goods higher than the American tariff on similar goods imported from any other country, and vice versa. If, therefore, America reduces her tariff on certain imports from France, she is obliged to reduce her tariffs on German goods of the same kind by the same amount. If America and France attempt to form an agreement to lower their tariffs on each other's goods—both countries having signed treaties with Germany including the most-favored-nation clause —America will have to reduce her tariffs on the goods of Germany as well as on the goods of France, and France will have to reduce her tariffs on German goods as well as on the goods of America. America and France might be able to agree to a simultaneous reduction of their tariffs on each other's goods in such a way that the terms of trade between them would not be appreciably changed. But because of the most-favored-nation clause they might be obliged to reduce their tariffs on the goods of many other countries without any simultaneous reduction in the tariffs imposed on their goods by these other countries, so that the terms of trade with the rest of the world might move considerably against them. Both countries might lose so much in the terms of trade with other countries that it was not to their advantage to reduce their tariffs on each other's goods by agreement.

For this reason attempts to reduce tariffs by agreement among a limited number of countries might be unsuccessful. This difficulty can be surmounted if the most-favored-nation clause is modified so as to permit a limited number of countries to reduce their tariffs on each other's goods without reducing their tariffs on the goods of those countries who are unwilling to come into the general agreement for tariff reductions. A group of countries might form a Free Trade or Low Tariff group, by agreeing to impose no prohibitions or quotas or tariffs over 10 per cent on each other's goods. At the same time they might renew their commercial agreements with other countries to include a modified most-favored-nation clause. A member of the Low Tariff group would promise not to impose a tariff on imports from a non-member of a greater height than the tariff imposed on the goods of any other non-member. By these means each member of the Low Tariff group could reduce its tariffs on the goods of each other member without moving the terms of trade against it, but would be free to use its tariffs to bargain with those countries which refused to join the group.

The three agreements which we have discussed are fundamental to a sane world economic policy. It is as possible for a Socialist state to adhere to them as for a state in which a policy of *laisser-faire* is adopted. A Socialist state can agree

(1) to preserve full employment by speeding up its capital development at home or by increasing the expenditure of consumers at home;

(2) to sell its products at prices equal to their marginal costs at home and abroad;

(3) to allow the free purchase of imported consumption goods;

(4) to import raw materials and machinery when their price abroad is lower than their price at home; and

(5) to adjust its Balance of Payments by alterations in its exchange rate, or by raising or lowering all internal prices through a rise or fall in the general level of wages, when its imports and exports as determined on the above principles do not balance with the other normal items in its Balance of Payments.

Such agreements need not be universal to be effective. They might, for example, be restricted to the American continents. Even if only two important countries adopted them, they would be workable and would greatly ease the economic relations between them. England and America, for example, might agree

(1) to fix their buying and selling prices of gold;

(2) to revise these gold prices periodically, raising them to prevent a loss of gold and lowering them to stop an import of gold;

(3) to operate a joint Exchange Stabilization Fund to offset movements of short-term funds between the pound and the dollar;

(4) to concentrate primarily on their internal policies rather than on the extension of their external markets to cure unemployment; and

(5) not to impose quotas or any tariffs above 10 per cent on each other's goods.

Any monetary or commercial agreements of this kind among a limited number of countries should be left open for the adherence on the same terms of any other country; for the larger the number of countries operating the reformed gold standard or becoming members of the Low Tariff group, the greater is the advantage to each individual member.

4. **An Agreement to Allow the Free International Movement of Capital.** We come now to two agreements which are probably of relatively small importance, and which may be more difficult to attain. We have argued that—so long as countries always reduce interest rates to correspond to the true productivity of capital in order to preserve full employment, for which provision is made in the first international agreement—capital should be free to move from country to country in search of the highest yields, subject only to the restriction of short-term lending due to the expectation of variations in exchange rates, which is provided for in the second international agreement. Such international capital movements might be encouraged by the formation of an International Commission, whose task it should be to provide authoritative information about the probable yield and security of investments of different kinds in different countries, and to assure by appropriate guarantees that every country had equally

free access to invest money in undeveloped areas in which the yield on capital was abnormally high. We have seen that a country may be unwilling to allow its citizens to lend freely abroad because such foreign lending may turn the terms of trade against it; and this consideration may hinder the attainment of this agreement.

5. **An Agreement to Diminish the Restrictions on Immigration.** The free immigration of population into a country in which standards of living are high is desirable from the international point of view, provided that the growth of population in the country whose citizens are emigrating is not excessive. But such migration may lower the standard of living in the country to which people are migrating. An international agreement on this subject will therefore have to discriminate against those countries in which the growth of population is uncontrolled, and will have to overcome the natural determination of other countries to allow no threat to their high standards of living. This agreement is therefore the most difficult to reach. But it would probably be of relatively minor importance if the first three agreements discussed in this chapter could be attained; for the countries with low standards would gain greatly from the greater freedom to trade with other countries and from the greater purchasing power in those other countries.

VIII

THE ECONOMIC CAUSES OF WAR

INTERNATIONAL agreements of the kind outlined in the last chapter would be effective not only in raising the standard of living in the countries concerned, but also in removing the economic causes of war between these countries. It is sometimes argued that it is an illusion to suppose that economic advantages can be obtained by any country through the prosecution of a successful war, because political domination over a particular territory does not in any way alter the fundamental economic conditions upon which the successful country relies for its welfare. If there were a universal system of free trade and of *laisser-faire* between all countries, the advantage which one country can gain from economic contacts with a particular territory would not depend upon political ownership of that territory. If, for example, there were free trade and freedom of movement of labor and capital between Germany and France, and between Germany and all African colonies, Germany would not be able to sell her goods more easily, to purchase her imports more cheaply, to invest money more profitably, or to find a more advantageous outlet for her population by the transference of the Saar from French to German political control, or by the transference of an African colony from British to German political control. While this argument is substantially correct in a world system of universal *laisser-faire*, yet even so it is not entirely true; and in a world in which there are innumerable international economic restrictions it loses all its validity.

In order to see what economic causes of war exist, we may enumerate the following possible ways in which one country can gain economically by waging a successful war and so obtaining the political control over other territories:

1. By imposing a tribute the victor may gain economically, provided that it adopts an appropriate policy of internal monetary expansion which enables it to import more than it exports without thereby causing unemployment at home. In this case the receipt of the tribute will finance its excess of imports over exports, and it will be receiving part of its imports free and no longer in return for its own products.

2. Even if there is free trade, 'trade follows the flag' to some extent for reasons of sentiment and for more substantial reasons such as business connections and language difficulties. In a territory politically controlled by Englishmen an English exporter may obtain a better price for an identical commodity than a Japanese exporter, and goods produced in this territory may be made available to the English at a somewhat cheaper price than to the Japanese; for if English is the official language of the territory and if the political administrators are English, it will be more convenient to deal with English than with Japanese firms. For similar reasons, even in the absence of restrictions upon labor migration and capital investment, Englishmen may obtain better information about the possibilities of earning high wages or interest in the territory, and will have a greater sense of security in migrating to the district or in investing capital in it.

3. There are certain backward territories which are prevented from providing markets for other countries' goods, and from producing raw materials needed by other countries, and from furnishing opportunities for capital investment and labor immigration, by the fact that the inhabitants cannot furnish an efficient police to restrain banditry and to give that security which is essential for the economic development of these areas. In these circumstances political control by a more advanced nation would confer real economic advantages upon the advanced nations. If, however, such intervention were limited to the provision of an efficient police, this should not give rise to conflict between advanced nations, since all advanced nations would share in the gain to be obtained. Indeed, in these conditions, each advanced

nation would hope that some other advanced nation would shoulder 'the white man's burden' and the cost of policing involved. Moreover, the inhabitants of the 'backward' nation would also gain economically if intervention were restricted to the suppression of banditry. But nationalist or racial feeling may cause them to resent the intervention, and this, combined with the economic advantage to the advanced nations, may be a cause of conflict between the backward and advanced territories.

4. When we turn our attention to legal restrictions imposed on the international movement of goods or of capital and labor, we discover much more substantial economic causes of conflict between nations. The use of preferential import and export duties, or of discriminatory quotas, to encourage the trade of a particular country provides the most obvious example. The import of Japanese as opposed to British cotton goods into the British West African colonies is restricted by quota; and this means that English cotton manufacturers gain at the expense both of Japanese cotton manufacturers, who are prevented from selling in this market, and also of the West African native, who is forced to purchase expensive English instead of cheap Japanese goods. If a low export duty is levied on the sale of a raw material by a British colony to the English market and a high duty is levied on sales to other markets, Englishmen will gain both at the expense of other countries, who are unable to obtain their raw material supplies so easily, and at the expense of the colonial producers, who are prevented from obtaining the higher price for their products which may be offered in markets other than the English market.

5. Restrictions on international trade, even if they do not discriminate in favor of a particular country, may yet make the political control of certain territories economically important. The transference of the Saar from French to German control is of advantage to Germany if previously she had to sell her goods in the Saar over the French tariff. And if Germany relies upon imports of raw materials or foodstuffs, so that she *must* sell

abroad to finance the import of essential commodities, it will be peculiarly important for her to obtain political control over other countries in order to determine the tariff policy of territories which might provide good markets for her exports.

6. One country may desire to obtain political control over another in order to remove restrictions on labor migration. Freedom of migration for the Japanese to Australia by reducing the numbers seeking work in Japan and by increasing the numbers seeking work in Australia might raise standards of living in Japan at the expense of the Australians and of future emigrants from Great Britain.

7. The restriction of capital movements by political control may enable one country to gain at the expense of others. When peace is restored and order re-established in China, there will probably be very profitable fields of capital investment to develop the latent resources of that country. If Japan is able to limit such investment to the Japanese, she will gain at the expense of other potential investors, who will be unable to share in the abnormally high yields on capital, and at the expense of the Chinese, because this restriction in the amount to be borrowed by them will maintain the rates of interest which they must pay at a higher level than would otherwise be necessary.

8. The existence of natural or artificial monopolies in certain territories may give rise to conflict over their political control. Certain undertakings such as railways, telegraphs, and canals are bound to be monopolistic, because there is room for only one such service in one district. By controlling the price charged for the service of these monopolies the owners can gain abnormally high yields on the capital invested in them. Political pressure may be exercised by the governments of different countries to obtain the necessary concessions for their own investors; for once such a monopoly is started the free flow of capital will not enable late-comers to share in the high yields, since there is room for only one such concern.

The formation of an artificial monopoly in a certain district may give rise to political intervention by another country. There is no reason in the nature of things why the production of rubber should be monopolized; but if all producers of rubber agree to restrict output, they can make abnormally large profits by raising the price of rubber to consumers. The owners of capital invested in the production of rubber happen to be largely English, while Americans consume large quantities of rubber without being able to produce it. A rubber restriction scheme may therefore enable Englishmen to gain more as producers than they lose as consumers, while Americans only lose as consumers, so that the American government may intervene in an attempt to force the English government to break such an artificial monopoly.

We have shown certain reasons which *may* lead to economic conflict between nations. It is, however, sometimes held that the organization of modern economic systems leads inevitably to war. This view is based on the belief that there is an inherent flaw in modern economic systems, causing less purchasing power to be distributed as income to consumers than is sufficient to purchase at cost the current output of goods. It is argued that this deficiency of purchasing power can be supplemented by one nation only if it can extend its sales abroad without itself spending any more of its income on the goods of other countries. But since in this case some other nation must be buying from abroad more than it sells abroad, the degree to which one nation succeeds in curing its internal problem is an exact measure of the degree to which the problem is intensified for some other country. Thus there arises a wild scramble for external markets, which, as we have just seen, can be obtained and preserved to a large extent by political control of other countries based upon the exercise or the threat of force.

We have already dealt with this argument by implication. We have shown in Chapter I of Part I that there is no insuperable flaw in modern economic systems causing purchasing power to be deficient, although at any time a deficiency of purchasing power may lead to unemployment. But this can be met by either of two means. First, the country concerned may expand its markets at the expense of others by exchange depreciation, by tariffs, and by any other measures which are designed to give it an abnormally large favorable Balance of Trade. Secondly, the country can expand its internal markets by the measures discussed in Part I, and so make up for the deficiency of internal purchasing power without any expansion at the expense of others; and indeed—while one country alone can do a great deal on these lines—if all countries adopt such a policy simultaneously, both the internal and the international markets of each country will expand at the same time.

We may admit that the search for foreign markets to cure unemployment is in the modern world a potent economic cause of conflict between nations. Moreover the growth of unemployment in any country during a general depression gives rise to a very dangerous psychological situation. During a depression people of every class find their livelihoods disappearing; and each class, failing to understand the causes of this general impoverishment and to see an end to the period of poverty, may irrationally lay the blame on other classes of persons. They may choose the Jewish financier or the victor in the last war as their scapegoat. In either case the psychological conditions for internal or international conflict are dangerously promoted. For these reasons the first and second international agreements mentioned in the last chapter are of the utmost importance; for they enable each country to provide full employment without any possibility of expansion at each other's expense. The other economic causes of conflict enumerated in this chapter will be greatly diminished by means of the third, fourth, and fifth international agreements mentioned in the last chapter; for these agreements provide for free trade in commodities and for greater freedom of international movements of capital and labor; and we have seen that the most important economic causes of conflict between nations depend upon the effects of international restrictions upon the movement of goods and of factors of production.

The agreements should, however, be supplemented in two ways. First, the 'open-door' policy must be guaranteed in all colonial possessions. The political control of 'backward' peoples will provide a fruitful economic cause of conflict so long as the country exercising that control can impose discriminatory restrictions upon trade with and investment in those territories. The 'open-door' policy, embodying the principle that whatever country administers the colony, the economic opportunities provided by it shall be open on equal terms to all countries, is not only to the advantage of all other countries but also to the advantage of the natives of the colony, who can then borrow on the most favorable terms and purchase in the cheapest and sell in the dearest markets. This principle may be extended by international conventions or by the administration of colonies under Mandates granted by the League of Nations, in which this principle is guaranteed. Secondly, the prices charged for products which are the monopoly of certain territories must be prevented by government control from being raised in excess of their cost through the formation of monopolistic schemes designed to restrict their supply. International conventions should be formed for this purpose and administered with suitable guarantees.

But above all it is necessary that countries should meet the problem of unemployment not by developing a favorable Balance of Trade at the expense of others, but by internal expansion, carried out if possible simultaneously in all countries; for the former method, if universally adopted, must lead to general impoverishment and eventually to war, whereas by the latter method the way is opened to prosperity and peace.

SUGGESTIONS FOR FURTHER READING

This is not the place for a comprehensive bibliography on economic theory and its application to practical problems; but the reader who has no teacher to guide his work may want to know to what books he can most profitably turn next to extend his knowledge of the subjects with which we have dealt. The compilation of a short list of this sort is necessarily highly arbitrary, and probably no two economists would include the same volumes. But the books mentioned below, we think, if not necessarily the best available, could not fail to be of interest and value to the reader who has mastered the preceding arguments.

On the subject of unemployment and the trade cycle, with which we dealt in Part I, the reader will find a more comprehensive analysis in Haberler, *Prosperity and Depression*. On the Federal Reserve System the most valuable single reference is probably Burgess, *The Reserve Banks and the Money Market* (Revised Edition). On the use of public works as a means of combatting unemployment see J.M.Clark, *Economics of Planning Public Works*.

Chamberlin, *Monopolistic Competition*, gives an analysis of competition and monopoly which is more rigorous and more complete than that which we give in Part II. Burns, *The Decline of Competition*, gives an excellent account of the recent history and present forms of monopolistic organization in the United States —a knowledge of which is essential before intelligent control can be exercised.

Part III could advantageously be followed up with the aid of A.G.Buehler, *Public Finance*. The standard general work on the theory of international trade, which we treated very sketchily in Part V, is Taussig, *International Trade*. Gayer, *Monetary Policy and Economic Stabilization*, will serve as a useful introduction to the gold and alternative standards and the foreign exchanges.

APPENDIX ON THE GRAPHS

As has already been explained, the reader who dislikes or fears geometry may simply ignore the graphs and confine his attention to the text and the arithmetic examples. The graphs contain no information which the text and examples do not. They are included for two reasons. The first is that graphs, for the initiated, are in many cases a simpler method of exposition than words and a neater method than arithmetic tables. The second is that graphs are widely used in more advanced works on economics, and it is clearly desirable that those who are using this book as an introduction to analysis should acquire a knowledge of the economist's chief analytical tools.[1]

There are three principal types of quantity which economists wish to illustrate in their diagrams—marginal, average, and total. Any economic magnitude which is measurable at all—costs, receipts, products, factors of production, etc.—may be represented by quantities of all three types; and the relationships between the total, average, and marginal quantities do not depend upon what is being measured.

The meanings of these terms and the relationships between them should be clear to those who have read as far as Part I, Chapter VII of the text. A *total* quantity is self-explanatory; it measures the whole of a given magnitude. An *average* quantity measures the total quantity divided by some other total quantity; thus, the average product of labor is the total product divided by the number of laborers. A *marginal* quantity measures the increase (or decrease) in a given total quantity associated with a

---

1. The account of the use of geometric methods given here is necessarily very brief and elementary. Those who are interested in a more extensive and somewhat more advanced discussion are referred to Joan Robinson, *Economics of Imperfect Competition*, pp.26–46 and *passim*. An excellent general work on the use of mathematics in economics is R.G.D.Allen, *Mathematical Analysis for Economists*.

unit increase in some other quantity; thus, the marginal product of a tenth laborer would be the total product of ten laborers minus the total product of nine. These distinctions between total, average, and marginal quantities have been explained on pp.72–76. The student is particularly advised to master the discussion of the relations between average and marginal quantities on pp.107–112 before reading this Appendix, the purpose of which is to show how these and similar relations may be illustrated geometrically.

We may take as a simple example the figures in Table III on p.72 of the text showing the total output of a particular commodity which can be produced by different amounts of labor:

Number of laborers employed	1	2	3	4	5	6	7	8	9	10
Total product	10	22	36	52	66	78	88	96	102	106

We can immediately deduce, by the means discussed on pp.72–76 of the text, that the average and marginal products of labor are as follows:

Average product	10	11	12	13	13.2	13	12.6	12	11.3	10.6
Marginal product	10	12	14	16	14	12	10	8	6	4

We next plot these figures for average and marginal products on a graph, measuring on the vertical axis the amount of product, and on the horizontal axis the number of laborers employed. We then connect the points plotted in either of two ways:

(a) If it is possible to make changes in the quantities which are very small compared with the total quantities, we may connect the points by continuous curves, as in Graph A.[1] In this

---

1. Strictly speaking, continuous curves should be drawn only when the changes possible are *indefinitely* small. But if they are merely small proportionately to the total quantity the error introduced by making the curves continuous is slight and may be neglected.

The curves will normally be 'smooth,' as well as continuous, like the

particular example sufficiently small changes would not be possible unless it were possible to vary the *hours* of work as well as the number of laborers. For a change in employment of one laborer is a considerable proportion of a total employment no greater than ten, and only by varying hours would it be possible to change employment by a fraction of a laborer. If the horizontal axis measured thousands of laborers instead of individual laborers, as it would if we were considering a large industrial establishment, it would be legitimate to draw continuous curves even though hours of work could not be varied. For a change in employment of one laborer in this case would be a very small proportionate change.

(b) Where it is not possible to make small proportionate changes in the quantities, the relationship between the quantities must be represented by a series of discontinuous horizontal lines, as in Graph B. The ends of the lines may be connected by vertical lines to help the eye to 'follow the graph.' Graph B is included only for purposes of illustration; in what follows, as in the graphs in the text, it is assumed that indefinitely small changes in all the quantities can be made, and all curves are therefore continuous.

The curve AP on Graph A joining the points representing average products we call the average product curve; the curve MP joining the points representing marginal products, the marginal product curve. An inspection of the graph and of the table accompanying will reveal a number of important relationships which exist between any average curve and the corresponding marginal curve.

1. The marginal and average curves begin at the same point on the vertical axis OY, for the total, average, and marginal

curves in Graph A. In particular cases, however, they may contain 'kinks,' as does the average receipts curve AR_2 in Graph VII, p. 198, at the point representing an output of 10.

products of the first unit of labor are of the same magnitude.[1]

2. If the marginal curve starts by rising, as in Graph A, the average curve will also rise, but less steeply. Conversely, if it starts by falling, the average curve will also fall, but less steeply.

3. As long as the marginal curve is higher than the average, the average will be rising; and as long as it is below the average, the average will be falling. The reasons for this relation, and for (2) above, have been explained in the text, pp.111–112.

4. It follows as a corollary of (3) that if the marginal curve is above the average curve, and falling, it will cut the average where the value of the average is a maximum (as in Graph A). And similarly, if it is below the average curve, and rising, it will cut the average curve where the value of the average is a minimum (as does the marginal cost curve MC in Graph J).

5. It also follows from (3) that if the average quantity is constant in value (i.e. is represented by a horizontal straight line on the graph), the corresponding marginal quantity will be equal to the average. In this case both the average and marginal quantities will be represented on a graph by the same horizontal straight line (cf. the average and marginal receipts curves AR and MR in Graph I on p.143 of the text).

6. An average curve can be drawn from a marginal curve, and vice versa, because both stand in a definite relation to the corresponding total quantity, which can be represented by an area obtained from either the marginal or the average curve. To learn the total product corresponding to any point on an average product curve, it is necessary simply to multiply the average product by the number of laborers. Thus, on Graph C the average product of OB laborers is equal to BP_1, and the total product is represented by the rectangle OBP_1A formed by drawing horizontal and vertical lines from the point P_1 on

---

1. Assuming, of course, that the OY axis represents the zero value of the quantity measured on the OX axis—in this case, labor. On all the graphs used in this book this is the case, and the OX axis similarly represents the zero value of whatever is measured on the OY axis.

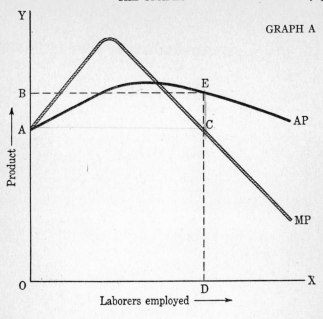

GRAPH A

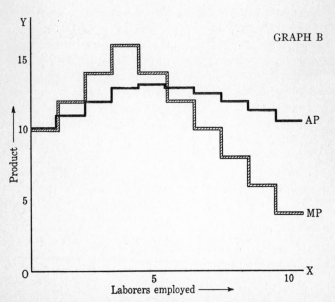

GRAPH B

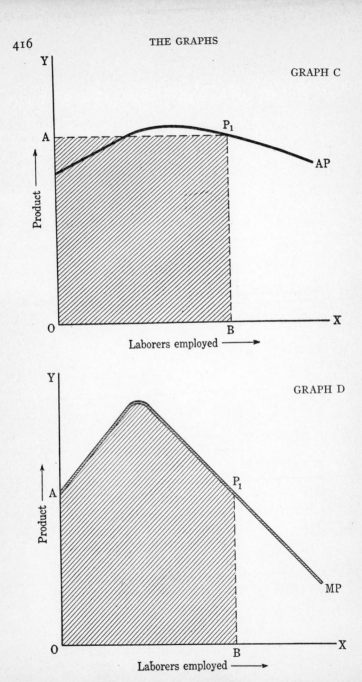

GRAPH C

Y

A

P₁

AP

Product →

0   B   X

Laborers employed →

GRAPH D

Y

A

P₁

MP

Product →

0   B   X

Laborers employed →

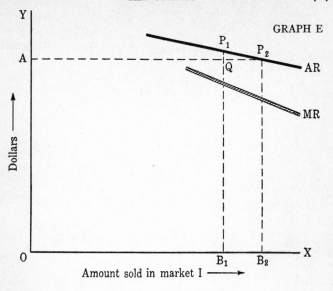

GRAPH E

Amount sold in market I ⟶

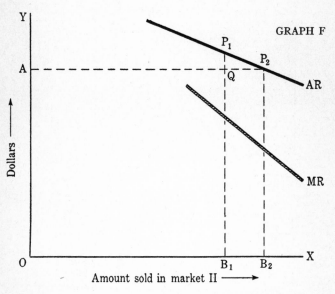

GRAPH F

Amount sold in market II ⟶

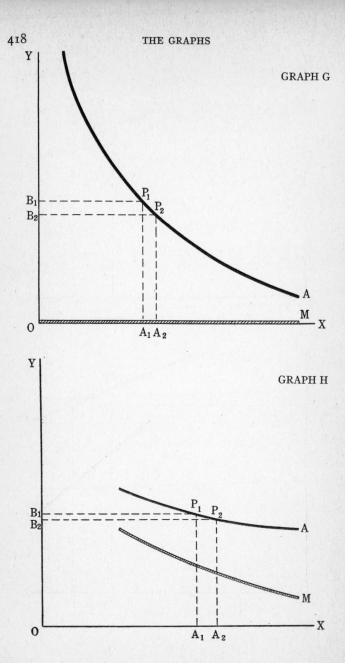

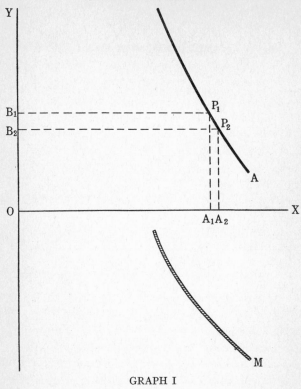

GRAPH I

the average curve to the two axes. If, on the other hand, it is the total product of a given number of laborers which is known, the average product may be computed by dividing the total by the numbers of laborers.

To learn from the marginal product curve the total product of, say, ten laborers, it is necessary to *add* the marginal products of all laborers up to and including the tenth. On Graph D this sum, for OB laborers, is represented by the area AP_1BO beneath the marginal product curve. If, finally, the total product is known, the marginal product of an x'th laborer may be

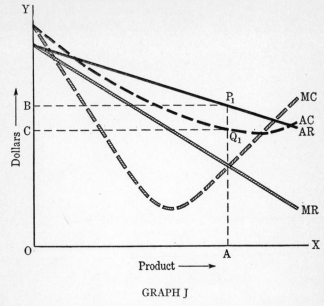

GRAPH J

computed by subtracting the total product of x laborers from the total product of x − 1.

7. It follows as a corollary of (6) that the area of the graph lying beneath the marginal product curve for any given number of laborers is equal to the area of a rectangle drawn from the corresponding point on the average product curve to the two axes. For both these areas represent the total product of that number of laborers. Thus, in Graph A, the area ACDO below the marginal product curve is equal to rectangle EBDO drawn from the average product curve, and both represent the total product of seven laborers.

8. The distance of a marginal curve from its corresponding average curve at any point depends upon the height of the average curve and its 'elasticity' at that point.[1] We can best explain

1. This discussion of elasticity is intended primarily for readers who are using the book as an introduction to further study. It has little relevance to the

what is meant by the elasticity of a curve by an example. Suppose that the following figures represent the sale of a product in two alternative markets:—

Market I

Amount sold	3	4	5	6	7
Total receipts	$16.20	20.80	25.00	28.80	32.20
Average receipts	$ 5.40	5.20	5.00	4.80	4.60
Marginal receipts	$ —	4.60	4.20	3.80	3.40

Market II

Amount sold	3	4	5	6	7
Total receipts	$17.40	21.60	25.00	27.60	29.40
Average receipts	$ 5.80	5.40	5.00	4.60	4.20
Marginal receipts	$ —	4.20	3.40	2.60	1.80

These figures are reproduced in the Graphs E and F.

Suppose that in both markets we start with the sale of the same amount of product OB_1 at the same price B_1P_1, and then sell a *small* additional amount B_1B_2, and so move along the average receipts curve from P_1 to P_2. By the elasticity of this curve is meant the small proportional change in a horizontal direction divided by the small proportional change in a vertical direction; i.e. $\dfrac{P_2Q}{QA} \div \dfrac{P_1Q}{QB_1}$.[1] For example, if a 3 per cent increase in purchases would result from a 2 per cent reduction of price, the elasticity of the demand or average receipts curve—which is known in this particular case as the 'elasticity of demand'—would be equal to $1\frac{1}{2}$ $\left(\text{i.e. } \dfrac{3\%}{2\%}\right)$. This elasticity is greater in Market I, in which the price falls gradually, than in Market II, in which the price falls steeply. By comparing the height of the marginal and average curves in both cases at the same point P_1 we can see that the dif-

text, and it may be omitted even by those readers who are making use of the graphs.

1. A straight horizontal line is therefore said to be 'perfectly elastic,' since the vertical change is nil. A straight vertical line, similarly, is said to be 'completely inelastic,' since, there being no change horizontally, the value of the formula is zero.

ference between the two curves is greater where the elasticity of the average curve is less.

If the average curves had been rising instead of falling, the marginal curves would have been above the average curves; but the difference between them would again be smaller in the case of the more elastic average curve. In general, the less is the elasticity of a falling average curve *at any point*, the farther is the marginal curve beneath it; and the less the elasticity of a rising average curve at any point, the farther is the marginal curve above it.[1]

In measuring the elasticity of any curve we must restrict ourselves to very small proportional changes along the two axes; for the elasticity of a curve may change as we move along it, so that if we deal with large changes we shall obtain only an arbitrary figure dependent upon many elasticities instead of the definite elasticity of the curve at a point, which is what we want.

In the case of a falling average curve the following relationships are interesting and important:

(a) If the elasticity of the falling average curve is just equal to 1, the rectangle below it (OAPB in Graph G) representing the corresponding total quantity, will not change as we move to the right along the curve, since the fall in AP will be just counterbalanced by the increase in BP. Since a marginal quantity represents net additions to the corresponding total quantity, the fact that in this case the total does not change means that the marginal quantity is zero throughout; i.e. that the marginal curve coincides with the OX axis.

(b) If the elasticity of the falling average curve is greater than 1,

1. Expressed algebraically, if A represents the height of the average curve at any point, e its elasticity at that point, and M the height of the marginal curve, $A - M = \frac{A}{e}$; i.e. the distance between the curves measured vertically is equal to the average value divided by the elasticity.

It follows from this formula that if two average curves are tangent to each other at a point, the corresponding marginal curves will be equidistant from the point; i.e. that they will intersect directly beneath or directly above it. For at a point of tangency two curves have the same value and the same elasticity.

as in Graph H, the rectangle OAPB will increase as we move
to the right along the average curve; in this case the marginal
quantities are positive, and the marginal curve therefore lies
above the OX axis.

(c) Finally, if the elasticity of the falling average curve is less
than 1, as in Graph I, the area OAPB will decrease as we
move to the right, so that the marginal quantities are negative, and the marginal curve therefore lies below the OX
axis.[1]

If we wish to compare two or more sets of curves we may, of
course, represent them on the same graph, provided that the
units measured on the two axes are the same. Thus, it is cus-
tomary to show both money costs and money receipts on the
OY axis when units of output are plotted on the OX axis. Let us
assume that a business firm is able to sell its product at the following prices:

Units of product	Average receipts (i.e. price, or receipts per unit of output)	Total receipts	Marginal receipts
1	10	10	10
2	9	18	8
3	8	24	6
4	7	28	4
5	6	30	2

Let us further assume that the costs of production of the firm,
average and marginal, are as follows:

Units of product	Total cost	Average cost	Marginal cost
1	11	11	11
2	17	8.5	6
3	19	6.3	2
4	23	5.8	4
5	30	6	7

All these data may be plotted on a single graph.

1. This last case is illustrated by the figures for the last two units of output in
Table 2b on Chart I at the end of the book.

The manager of the firm, in order to make his profits a maximum, will extend his production to $OA = 4$, where marginal costs are just equal to marginal receipts. For up to this point, by producing an additional unit, he adds more to his receipts than to his costs. And beyond this point, by producing an additional unit, he adds more to his costs than to his receipts.[1] The superiority of the geometric method of exposition is clearly illustrated by an example of this sort; for once the data have been plotted, the result may be 'read off' the graph simply by noting the point of intersection of the relevant curves.

[1]. We can see from the average receipts (or price) curve that he will sell his product at a price equal to AP_1, and at an average cost equal to AQ_1. His total receipts will therefore be equal to the rectangle OAP_1B and his total costs to the rectangle OAQ_1C. His total profits ($=$ total receipts $-$ total cost) are therefore equal to BCP_1Q_1.

INDEX

Advances by banks, 24, 31–3.
Advertisement, 176–8, 183, 186, 190.
Anti-Trust Laws, 181–2.
Apprentices, 102, 229.
Average, *see* Cost, Product, Receipts, Earned run average.

Balance of Payments, 307–20, 321, 326–7, 329, 341–3, 344–7, 351–4, 360, 366–7, 370, 376–9, 393–5, 399.
    Balance of Payments on Current Account, 309–11.
Balance of Trade, 309–12, 342–3, 344n., 354–5, 378, 388–9, 407, 408.
Balance sheet, of commercial banks, 22–5.
    of Federal Reserve Banks, 25–6.
Banking Act of 1933, 322.
    of 1935, 27.
Bank reserves, 23–30, 37, 41, 59, 62, 326–9, 336–40, 396.
Bankruptcy, 65, 79, 316, 330.
Banks, 22–42, 44, 45, 51, 53, 59, 89, 242–3, 254, 256, 326–9; *and see below.*
    Bank for International Settlements, 339, 392, 395–6.
    Bank of England, 324, 339, 340.
    Central Banks, 323, 334–40, 352, 392, 395–6.
    Commercial banks, 22–42, 62–3, 328.
    Federal Reserve Banks, 25–42, 59, 62–3, 204n., 328, 335, 339, 340, 344, 351.
    Member banks, 22–42, 59, 62.
Bills, 25–6, 38–9, 41.
Birth-rate, 240, 294, 305.
Board of Governors of Federal Reserve Banks, 36.
Budget, 46–51, 63, 64–5.
Buyers' preference, 165–7, 170, 174, 176–9, 181–3, 186–7, 190, 205–7.

Capital development, *see* Expenditure on capital goods.
Central Banks, *see* Banks.
Coin, 23, 318, 321–2.
Commercial banks, *see* Banks.
Commodity market, *see* Market.
Commodity taxes, 248–50, 263, 267, 290.
Comparative costs, 365.
Competition, imperfect, 71n., 116, note on Terminology, 132–204; *see also* Monopoly.
    Perfect competition, 71n., 100–32, 289, 358, 384, 394.
    Wastes of competition, 176–8, 183, 186.
Concentration of output, 164–6, 176, 179, 183, 186–7.
Consumers' associations, 183.
Consumers' credits, 54–67.
Cost, average, 107–12, 134, 135, 140, 142, 144, 156–7, 164, 176, 179, 195, 197–9, 208, 376.
    Constituents of cost, 5–14, 273.
    Marginal cost, 107–12, 118, 140–4, 150, 194–6, 198–9, 201, 208, 244–5, 250, 357–65, 375–6, 399.
    Total cost, 110–12, 136–7, 175, 196, 199.
    See also Movement, Transport.
Cross-transport charges, 178, 183, 187, 190.
Currency notes, 25–6, 28, 30, 38, 56, 58, 60, 63, 323–5, 336.

Dairy Association, 161.
Death-rate, 240.
Deflation, 60, 332–3, 335, 341.
Deposits, 23–34, 37, 38, 40, 62–3, 77, 318, 320, 326–8, 338–9, 344.
    Demand and time deposits, 23, 27–8.
Depressed Areas, 217.
Devaluation, 353–5.
Discrimination in prices, 147–50, 161–2.

Distribution of income, 36, 66, 75n., 81, 131, 220–71, 381–2, 385–6.
'Distributist' state, 265.
Disutility of work, 277.
Division of labor, 284–5.
Douglas, Major C.H., 7n.
Dumping, 148–9.

Earned run average, 111–2, 287.
Economic Forecasting Commission, 218–9.
Education, 48, 75, 95, 127, 230–3, 237, 246, 267, 269, 273, 278.
Education of consumers and factors of production, 181–6, 385, 387–8.
Elasticity of demand, 94n., 149–50.
Eligibility of bills, 28, 38.
Employment exchanges, 85, 185, 229.
Estate duties, 66, 258–62, 265–7, 270, 290.
Excess reserves, 24, 27, 28, 40.
Exchange Stabilization Fund, 36, 350–1, 378, 394, 396, 400.
Expenditure on capital goods, 10–20, 42–54, 66, 87–90, 208n., 253–4, 257, 259, 260, 263, 266, 328, 399.
on consumption goods, 5–14, 19–20, 33, 43, 44, 48–9, 54–67, 68, 88–90, 255, 256, 261, 270, 330, 334, 392, 399.
Exports, 308–15, 323, 328–36, 338, 342–3, 345, 348, 352–5, 358–60, 362–7, 369–70, 374, 377–82, 388, 391, 404.

Family allowances, 267, 291.
Federal Reserve Banks, see Banks.
Fiduciary Issue, 336.
Foreign Exchanges, 37, 314–20, 321–55, 364n., 366–7, 369, 372–3, 376–81, 388, 390, 391–7, 399, 407.
Foreign lending, 271n., 308, 310–3, 316–20, 329, 331, 346–53, 366–7, 378–9, 387–90, 391, 393–6, 400–1, 405, 408.
Free trade, 358–61, 363, 368, 374, 377, 379, 382–3, 397, 403, 407.

Gold Bullion Standard, 322–3.
Gold Exchange Standard, 323–38.

Gold export point, 325–6, 344.
Gold import point, 325–6, 344.
Gold reserves, 25–6, 37, 336–40, 396.
Gold Specie Standard, 322–3.
Gold standard, 321–43, 353, 358, 366, 369, 378, 380, 388, 393–6.
Guild socialism, 211.

Hours of work, 91, 95, 100, 240, 241, 276, 277–8.
Hours of Work and Unemployment, 92.
Housing, 15, 18–9, 49, 55, 219.

Imperfect competition, see Competition.
Imperfect market, see Market.
Imports, 149, 307–13, 315, 323, 327–32, 342–3, 345, 353–5, 356–62, 364–7, 370–4, 376–81, 388, 398–9, 404.
Income tax, 48–50, 50n., 248, 250–64, 267, 280, 290.
Indemnities, 308, 331.
Industrial Planning Commission, 207, 211–14, 217–18.
Infant industries, 368, 375–6, 397.
Inflation, 60, 83, 335, 338–9.
Inheritance, 228, 236, 265–6; see also Estate duties.
Insurance schemes, 58–9, 97, 127.
Deposit insurance, 42n.
Interest, 5–7, 24, 79, 113, 209, 254, 260, 273, 301, 352.
Interest on foreign investments, 307, 308, 310–3, 316–7, 330, 342–3, 352, 366, 388–9.
Interest rate, 14–21, 22, 31–4, 36, 44, 45, 47, 52–3, 57, 59, 77, 78, 89, 90, 104, 109, 119, 123, 124n., 208, 208n., 211, 212, 230–1, 242–3, 253–4, 256–7, 266, 318, 320, 328–30, 332, 334, 341–2, 348, 387, 390, 391–3, 400.
International Labour Office, 92.
Inventions, 75–6, 85, 218, 331.

Large-scale production, 110, 134–6, 140, 182, 285, 288–9, 291, 303, 375.
League of Nations Mandates, 408.
Low Tariff group, 398–400.

Management, marginal product of, 166–70, 173–5, 190, 205, 238.
Market:
  Commodity market, 71n., 104, 132, 136.
  Imperfect market, 100n., 136–9, 154.
  Labor market, 71n., 84, 91, 95, 100n., 154, 185n.
  Perfect market, 132, 151.
Marriages, 219, 294.
Mass-production, see Large-scale production.
Migration of labor, 386–7, 401, 405.
Monopoly, 132–203, 205, 229, 268, 281, 289, 301, 384, 405–6.
Most-favored-nation clause, 397–9.
Movement of factors of production, 109, 114–6, 118–24, 184–6, 205, 269, 356, 364–5, 384–90, 400, 401, 404–5.
  Cost of movement, 185, 118–9, 123–4, 183, 185, 205, 216, 226–7, 229, 233, 356–85.

National debt, 50, 51, 246, 258, 262, 270, 333.
National Investment Board, 51–4.
Nationalization, see Public control and ownership.
New Deal, 67n.
Notes, see Currency.
N.R.A., 200.

'Open-door' policy, 408.
Open market committee, 36.
Optimum balance between work and leisure, 263–9, 278–80.
Optimum number of firms, 170.
Optimum population, 282–95, 303–6, 385–6.
Optimum size of firm, 111–2, 117, 124, 159, 164, 183, 190, 195.
Optimum supply of labor, 100, 248, 250, 256, 262, 275, 279–95, 303–6.
Optimum supply of savings, 248, 250, 257, 262, 266–7, 275, 296–306.

Par rate of exchange, 324–5, 340.
Pensions, 95, 97, 246, 267.

Perfect competition, see Competition.
Perfect market, see Market.

Planning, 43–54, 204–19.
Poll tax, 290.
Population, 219, 282–95, 303–6, 385–7.
Price-fixing, 182, 192–203, 229, 236.
Product, average, 72–3, 287.
  Marginal, 72–6, 83, 96, 98, 112–6, 117, 118–24, 131, 145–7, 150, 153–8, 159–64, 166–70, 173–5, 188–94, 198–201, 204–11, 213, 215–8, 228–9, 231–5, 237–42, 256, 259, 269, 277–82, 286–90, 295, 298–302, 303–5, 356, 385–90.
  See also Management.
Professional bodies, 182, 229.
Progressive taxation, 251–3, 257–9, 263, 270, 280, 290.
Property taxes, 248, 258, and see Estate duties.
Proportionate Reserve, 336.
Proportionate taxation, 251–3, 258, 290.
Protection, 360–1, 368–83, 396–400, 404–5, 407.
Public control of banks, 35–42.
  of industry, 51, 53–4, 75n., 192, 204–19, 244, 289–90, 301, 351–3, 359, 395–6.
  Public corporations, 204–11, 238, 281.
  Public ownership, 267–70.
  Public works, 15, 17–8, 43–54.

Quotas, 314, 343, 399, 404.

Rationalization, 181, 186–8.
Rationing of loans, 242–3.
Receipts, marginal, 139, 141–4, 198–9.
  average, 143–4, 198–9.
Rent, 5–9, 107, 208, 242–4, 273.
  of houses, 19.
Reparations, 308, 331.
Reproduction rate, 291–4.
Reserve ratio, 24, 27, 28, 30, 41, 59, 326–8.

Sales tax, 249n.

Satisfaction, 105, 222–6, 279, 300.

Savings, 9–14, 66, 253–6, 260–2, 266–7, 290, 300–6, 320, 329.

Shipping services, 308, 311, 313, 315–6.

Short-term capital movements, 346–54, 378–9, 390, 394, 396–7, 400.

Sinking fund, 50.

Social dividend, 212, 246, 267.

Soldier's Bonus, 64n.

Specialization of product, 178–9, 187, 190.

'Standard' volume of unemployment, 58–65, 84–5, 89.

Standardization, 179–80.

Stocks, 33–43, 270.
    of goods, 44, 87.

Strikes, 84.

Subsidies, 19, 40, 53–4, 97–100, 127, 131, 181, 188–92, 196–7, 199, 209, 215–6, 244–5, 246, 281, 343, 376, 381.

Subsistence level, 283, 387.

Syndicalism, 211.

Tariffs, 149, 314–5, 331–2, 343, 355, 368–83, 392–3, 397–400, 404–5, 407.

Taxation, 47–8, 54, 56, 59, 62, 64–6, 97, 130, 181, 188–92, 246–64, 266, 269–70, 280, 290, 301, 340; see also Commodity, Income, Sales tax, Estate duties, Progressive and Proportionate taxation, and Taxing the foreigner.

Taxing the foreigner, 368, 374–5.

Tennessee Valley Authority, 51n., 204n.

Terms of trade, 365–7, 368–75, 381, 388–9, 397–9, 401.

Tourist expenditure, 308, 352.

Town and regional planning, 45, 216.

Trade Unions, 80, 82, 100n., 182, 200, 229, 241, 276, 277n.

Transport costs, 136–8, 148–50, 165, 182, 363–4.

Tribute, 308, 331, 366, 403.

Unemployment, 3–100, 185n., 202, 212, 217, 233–4, 239, 241, 242, 246–8, 254, 256, 262, 266, 270, 330, 332, 334–5, 337, 341, 349, 353–5, 376–9, 390, 391, 393, 403, 408.

Unemployment Assistance Board, 57–60.

Unemployment benefit, 49, 57–60, 85–6, 97, 246.

Usury, 242.

Utility, marginal, 106–7, 127, 172–3, 205, 280.

Wages, 5–9, 59, 61, 68–81, 82–6, 91–8, 100, 107, 113–5, 147, 153–8, 197–8, 200, 202, 217, 226–35, 238–42, 247, 256, 268, 273, 277, 281–2, 287, 289, 291, 332–7, 341, 349, 379–80, 384–6, 394, 403.

War, 60, 402–8.

Wheat Marketing Board, 150.

'Work or Maintenance,' 86.